MARTHA'S VINEYARD

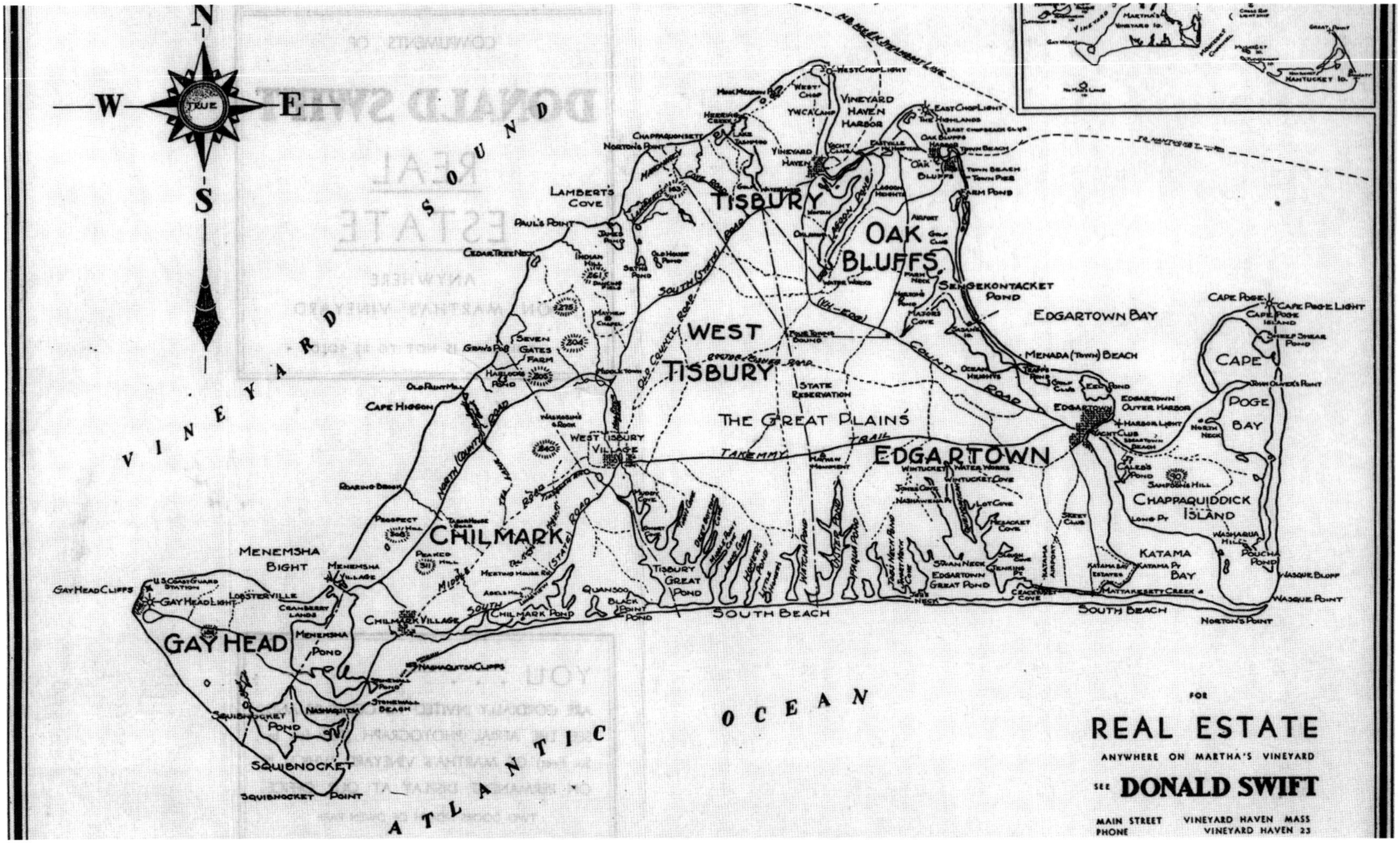

Real estate agent Donald Swift of Vineyard Haven proclaimed Martha's Vineyard "One Hundred Square Miles of Beauty." He distributed this map to his customers and his prospective customers in 1937. At that time, the town that is now called Aquinnah was named Gay Head, for the brilliantly colored cliffs that are its most conspicuous landmark. (Courtesy of the Martha's Vineyard Museum.)

On the Front Cover: Crowds arrived in and departed from the ferry in Oak Bluffs on a typical summer day in the mid-1920s. Some visitors came for spiritual renewal and enlightenment at the Baptist temple or the Methodists' Wesleyan Grove, where camp meetings were held. Others chose to spend carefree vacations at one of the many hotels or guesthouses located across the island. Still others were on their way to seasonal homes or retreats that they returned to year after year. (Courtesy of the Martha's Vineyard Museum.)

On the Back Cover: A group of pleasure boaters returns to a dock in Edgartown Harbor in the early 1900s. The harbor served a busy mix of commercial and recreational boaters at that time. (Courtesy of the Martha's Vineyard Museum.)

MARTHA'S VINEYARD

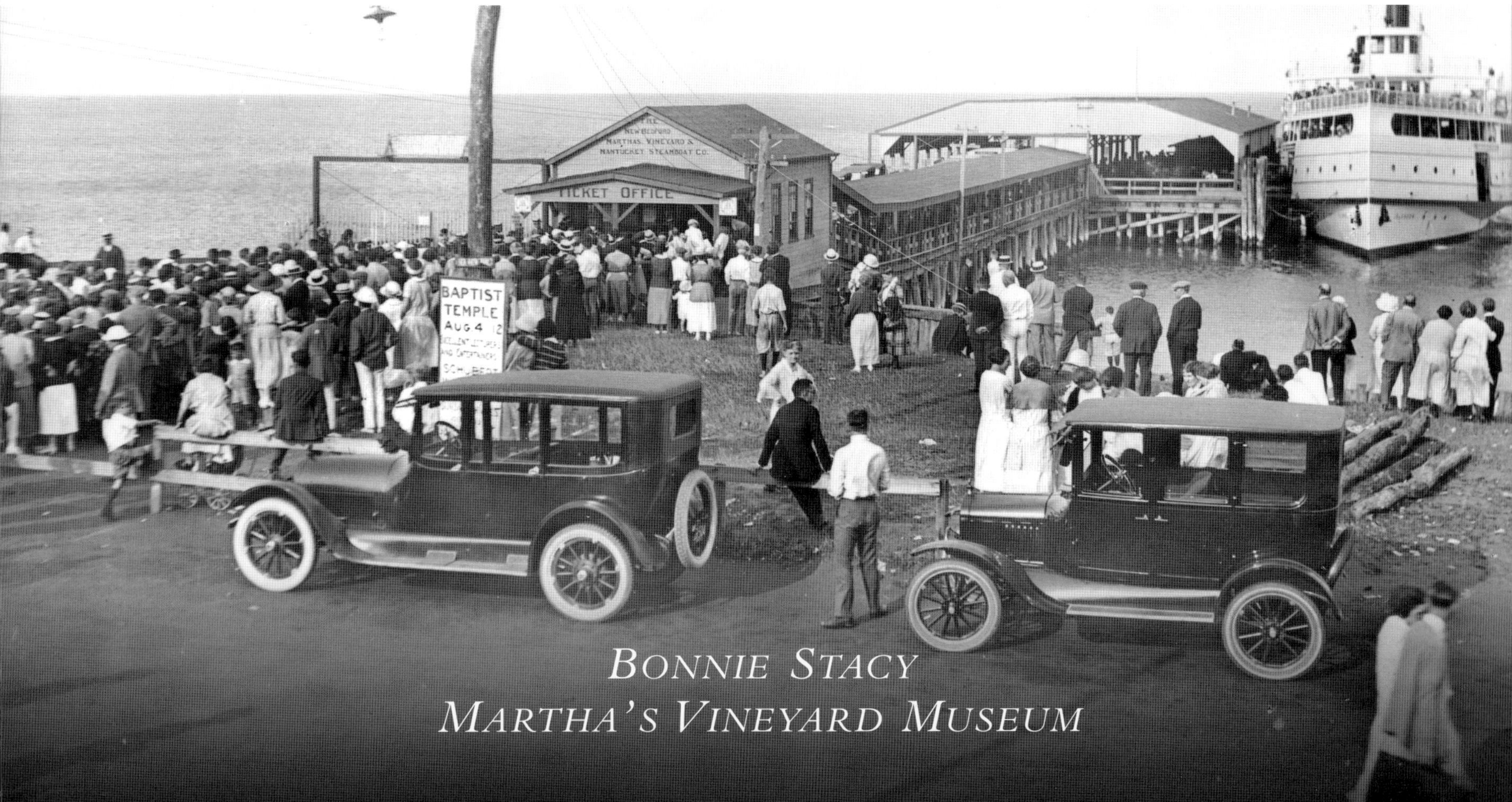

Bonnie Stacy
Martha's Vineyard Museum

ISBN 978-1-4671-2166-8

Published by Arcadia Publishing
Charleston, South Carolina

Printed in the United States of America

Library of Congress Control Number: 2013951890

For all general information, please contact Arcadia Publishing:
Telephone 843-853-2070
Fax 843-853-0044
E-mail sales@arcadiapublishing.com
For customer service and orders:
Toll-Free 1-888-313-2665

Visit us on the Internet at www.arcadiapublishing.com

This book is dedicated to all the Vineyarders.

Contents

Acknowledgments 6

Introduction 7

1. The Sea Supports Us 9

2. Land and Community 45

3. Enchanted Isle 77

4. Nature and Climate 125

ACKNOWLEDGMENTS

This book would not have been possible without the gifts to the Martha's Vineyard Museum from countless donors. It is impossible to name them all here, but I must acknowledge Basil Welch and his daughters Linda M. Voluckas and Laurie C. Clements, who donated a remarkably large and wonderful assortment of photographs and glass-plate negatives accumulated by Basil Welch over a lifetime of collecting; Alison Shaw, who donated and scanned a collection of John N. Chamberlain's glass-plate negatives; John Leavens, whose research materials on catboats and fishing provided many of the wonderful photographs of Menemsha and swordfishing; and Charlotte S. Perry, whose 1923 donation of the glass-plate negatives of her father and brother, Charles and Richard Shute, formed the nucleus of the museum's extraordinary photograph collection.

Also deserving special thanks is Hal Garneau, who made prints from the Shutes' glass plates 35 years ago, thereby bringing their subjects back to life.

As a recent washashore, I have relied upon the knowledge and advice of many Vineyarders, whose experience and understanding of Martha's Vineyard history exceeds mine, to guide me in making this book. The past and present staff members and volunteers at the Martha's Vineyard Museum, either directly or through the good work they left for me to draw upon, were indispensable. I especially thank the museum's executive director, David Nathans, for suggesting and supporting this project. Some, but by no means all, of the museum folks who helped me in one way or another are: Anna Carringer, Nancy Cole, Ann DuCharme, Katy Fuller, Kate Gulick-Tuers, Marian Halperin, Nathaniel Janick, Jessica Johnson, Insley Julier, Linsey Lee, Betsey Mayhew, Kay Mayhew, Barbara Murphy, Chris Murphy, Jim Richardson, Dana Costanza Street, Lara Ullman, Dan Waters, Denys Wortman, and many wonderful interns.

Any errors, omissions, or misunderstandings are entirely my fault.

All photographs, maps, and portraits reproduced in this book are in the collection of the Martha's Vineyard Museum.

INTRODUCTION

Martha's Vineyard belongs to many people. The Wampanoag, the island's first people, are still here. Descendants of English colonists who arrived in the 1600s are here too, as are those of later Portuguese and Azorean immigrants. Farming families still work the land and raise livestock generation after generation. Families return summer after summer. Vacationers spend the same two weeks at the same hotel, guesthouse, or rental every year. But the island's pleasures are perennially rediscovered as well. Thousands of first-time visitors arrive every summer. Couples come here to marry. All have claimed the island in one way or another as home, land, or memory.

The photographs in this book date from the middle of the 1800s to the 1970s. They demolish the idea that the island is an unchanging place. Early photographs show much less tree cover than today, a condition that began long before the invention of photography. The 19th- and early-20th-century farmers whose fields appear here kept the land clear for their crops and livestock. Fences made of large stones are evidence of the heavy work required to make and keep the land usable. The shoreline was, in some places, much more developed than it is now. And the changes are not all manmade. Storms regularly alter the landscape and destroy buildings.

Since the mid-1800s, much of this change has been captured in photographs. All of the images in this book are from the collection of the Martha's Vineyard Museum. Some are familiar, but many have rarely or never been published. As the island's primary repository for its history, the museum has long been the place where Vineyarders trust their heirlooms and memories to be preserved. As a result, there are thousands of photographs in the collection, from famous views to intimate family snapshots. Still, even with all this abundance, the photographs tell an incomplete story, limited by the fact that the museum's collection has gaps and because some events, places, and people escaped the photographer's eye.

Understanding place names on the island can be difficult and confusing. The Wampanoag called the southwest point of the island Aquinnah. Early English maps call it Gay Head, in reference to the spectacularly colored cliffs that face Vineyard Sound. When it was incorporated as a town in its own right, splitting off from Chilmark in 1870, it was called Gay Head. In 1996, the town voted to officially change its name from Gay Head to Aquinnah. The map of Martha's Vineyard shows other Wampanoag place names, including Chappaquiddick, Pohoganut, Sengekontacket, and more.

Layered on top of the Wampanoag geography is that of the English colonists and others who came from away to settle here. From Colonial days until well into the 1800s, there were three towns on Martha's Vineyard. Edgartown and Tisbury were incorporated in 1671, followed by Chilmark in 1694. Now there are six towns. West Tisbury split off from Tisbury in 1884, Oak Bluffs was part of Edgartown until 1880, and Aquinnah (Gay Head) separated from Chilmark in 1870. To make this even more confusing, the first name for Oak Bluffs was Cottage City. But when it was part of Edgartown, part of it was also called Eastville. Many of the earliest references to Tisbury refer simply to the harbor area of Holmes Hole. Now, Tisbury is most often called Vineyard Haven.

Up island refers to the southwest chunk of the Vineyard, the less populous part. Down island refers to Edgartown, Oak Bluffs, and Vineyard Haven.

Each Vineyard town has its own stereotypical character. Edgartown, "the Shiretown," was the first to be settled by the English. Thomas Mayhew Jr. settled the town in 1642. Edgartown is beautiful, charming, and calm—all white clapboards and weathered shingles. In town, houses that whalers built in the mid-1800s and businesses familiar to many from the movie *Jaws* (which was shot there and elsewhere on the island in 1974) lie close together. The Edgartown Light looks over the harbor and Chappaquiddick

Island. Farther out, but still part of Edgartown, are Katama, South Beach, Edgartown Great Pond, and half of Sengekontacket Pond.

Tisbury, more commonly known as Vineyard Haven, is the year-round town. It is the main ferry port and the place where many businesses stay open during the winter for the convenience of the locals. West Chop is part of Tisbury, as is Lake Tashmoo.

Chilmark is rural, with rolling fields, farms, secluded retreats, picturesque stone walls, the fishing village of Menemsha, and the island of Noman's Land, which is owned entirely by the United States Fish and Wildlife Service and is closed to visitors. For much of its history, a significant proportion of Chilmark's small population was deaf, a trait inherited from English ancestors but not considered a disability. Tisbury Great Pond is part of the border between Chilmark and neighboring West Tisbury.

Oak Bluffs is where the religious camp meetings were first held on the Vineyard, and, as a result, it held the germ of the tourist boom. It is where, in the early 1900s, African American vacationers found a welcoming place, which became a community that continues to be vibrant today. It also has the reputation as the Vineyard's party town. It is the home of colorful Victorian houses, expansive parks, and half of Sengekontacket Pond.

West Tisbury is rural and quiet. Working farms sell produce at roadside stands and sheep graze in the open pastures. Every August the Agricultural Fair attracts crowds to the fairgrounds in West Tisbury to admire prize produce, poultry and livestock. Islanders from every town display the fruits of their labor at the fair.

Aquinnah, along with the rest of the island, is the ancestral home of the Wampanoag, who fought for and achieved federal recognition as a tribe in 1987. It is where the Gay Head Light shines above the geologically unique, multicolored cliffs.

As with many stereotypes, the ones regarding Martha's Vineyard have some truth to them, but they do not tell the whole truth. There are farms in Edgartown, year-round businesses in Oak Bluffs, and other characteristics that do not fit the stereotypes all over the island.

This book does not ignore the towns' differences, but it focuses on the island as a single place. It is surrounded, threatened, and supported by the sea; it is nourished by the land; its economy depends on tourism and on the people who return here year after year and who also think of the island as home. These are the things that bind the Vineyard together as a place.

OPPOSITE: Whether for work or pleasure, and despite jokes alluding to a bridge or tunnel, the approximately seven-mile distance between Martha's Vineyard and the mainland has always been negotiated by boat. The relatively recent advent of air travel has expanded the ways people can get to the Vineyard, but the vast majority still arrive by ferry. Scenes like this one of the ferry *Martha's Vineyard* leaving Union Wharf in Vineyard Haven have been commonplace for more than 150 years.

ONE

THE SEA SUPPORTS US

For centuries, the maritime industries of merchant marine, whaling, and fishing provided the primary livelihood for island families. Men went to sea for months or years, traveling great distances all over the world to trade and to hunt whales. Through whaling, Vineyarders had strong ties to San Francisco, Hawaii, the Arctic, and New Zealand, among other distant places. Most traveled to other ports to join their ships. Compared to Nantucket and New Bedford, Martha's Vineyard sent out very few whaleships. But photographs from the 1800s make the importance of maritime industries to Martha's Vineyard abundantly clear.

Busy harbors crowded with ships and boats had their corresponding businesses and services on shore. From 1799 onward, lighthouses warned of coastal dangers. Businessmen like Dr. Daniel Fisher prospered through underwriting trading voyages and establishing businesses that processed whale products, such as his spermaceti candle factory in Edgartown. More modest businesses were important to everyday life—chandleries sold goods needed on shipboard, and blacksmiths made and repaired metal pieces.

Fishermen plied their trade closer to home than whalers and merchants. The abundance of fish in the area was noted as early as Bartholomew Gosnold's 1602 voyage, when he named Cape Cod (as well as Martha's Vineyard—perhaps after his mother-in-law, who financed the voyage). Island fishermen caught fish for their own consumption and also sold them fresh on the island or salted to merchants bound for Boston and beyond.

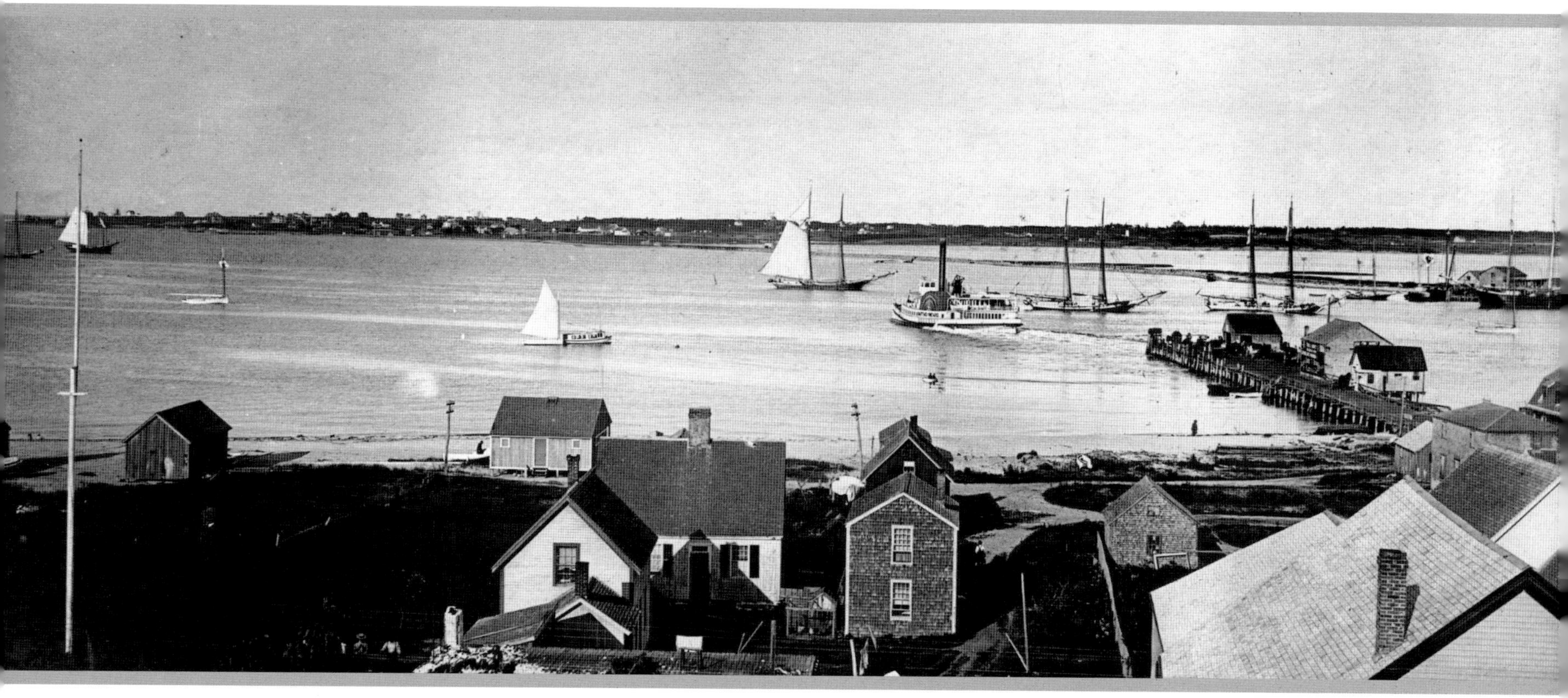

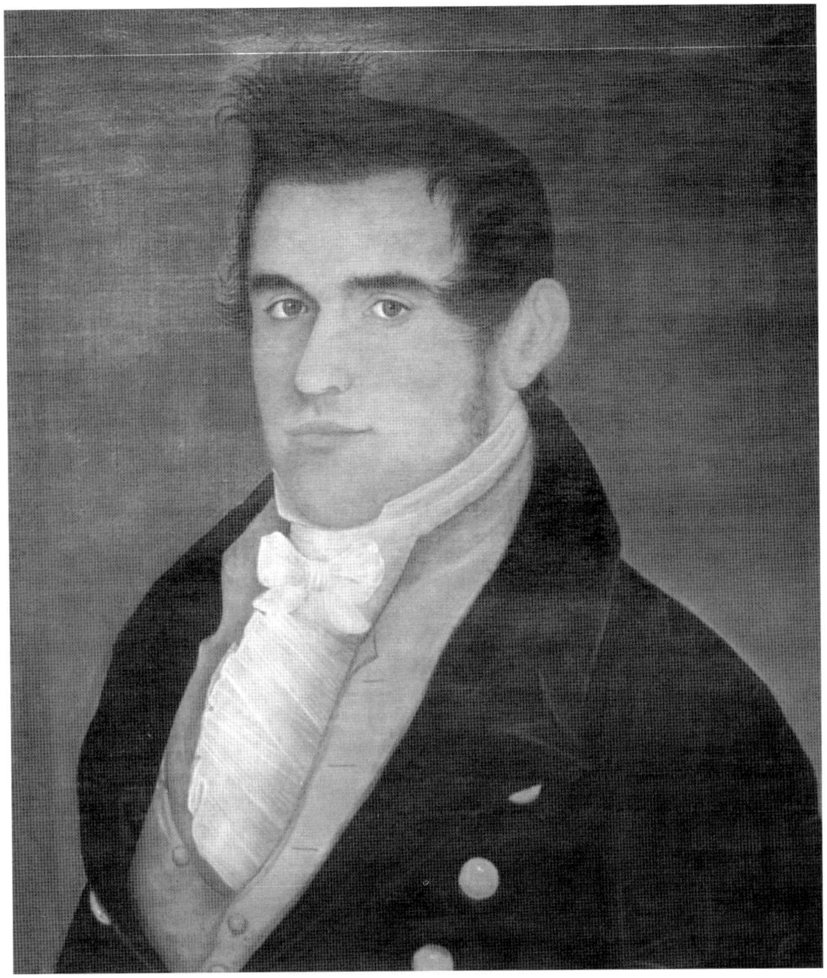

Generations of families from all over Martha's Vineyard worked in the maritime industries. The Worths of Edgartown produced Benjamin Worth (1763–1805, seen here), a successful merchant mariner, and his son, also named Benjamin, a whaling captain. They were just one of many families that sent their sons to sea in the 1700s and 1800s. Others included Mayhew, Hancock, Flanders, Luce, Chase, Beetle, Coffin, Butler, Pease, and many more.

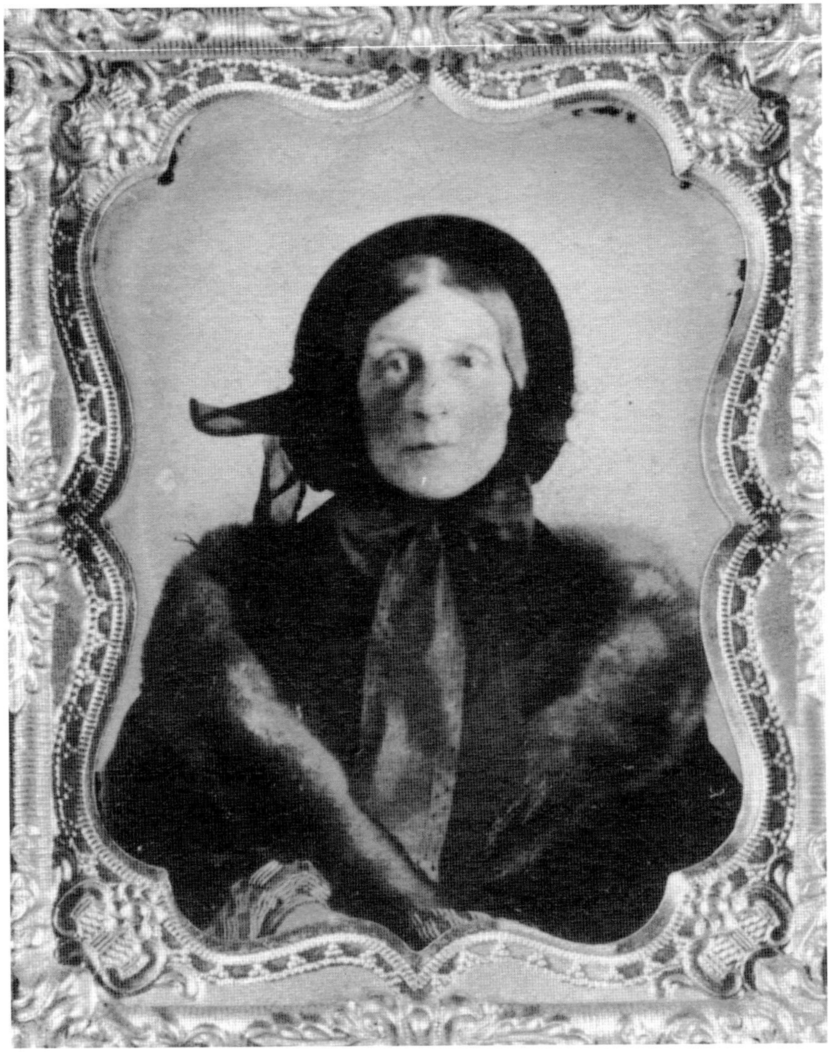

The women of the island did not always remain behind. Some, like Charlotte Hillman Reynolds and Caroline Mayhew (seen here) of Tisbury, traveled with their sea captain husbands. Caroline joined her husband, Capt. William Mayhew, on whaling voyages to New Zealand in the 1830s and 1840s. She was reputed to be a good nurse. Most women, however, stayed home to tend to house, farm, business, and family.

In 1789, Edgartown became a federal port of entry where US customs duties were collected. Thomas Cooke Jr. was the customs collector from 1809 to 1830. There was no official customs house until 1848, so he fulfilled his responsibilities out of his house on Cooke Street, from which he could see ships come into the harbor. This house is now part of the Martha's Vineyard Museum.

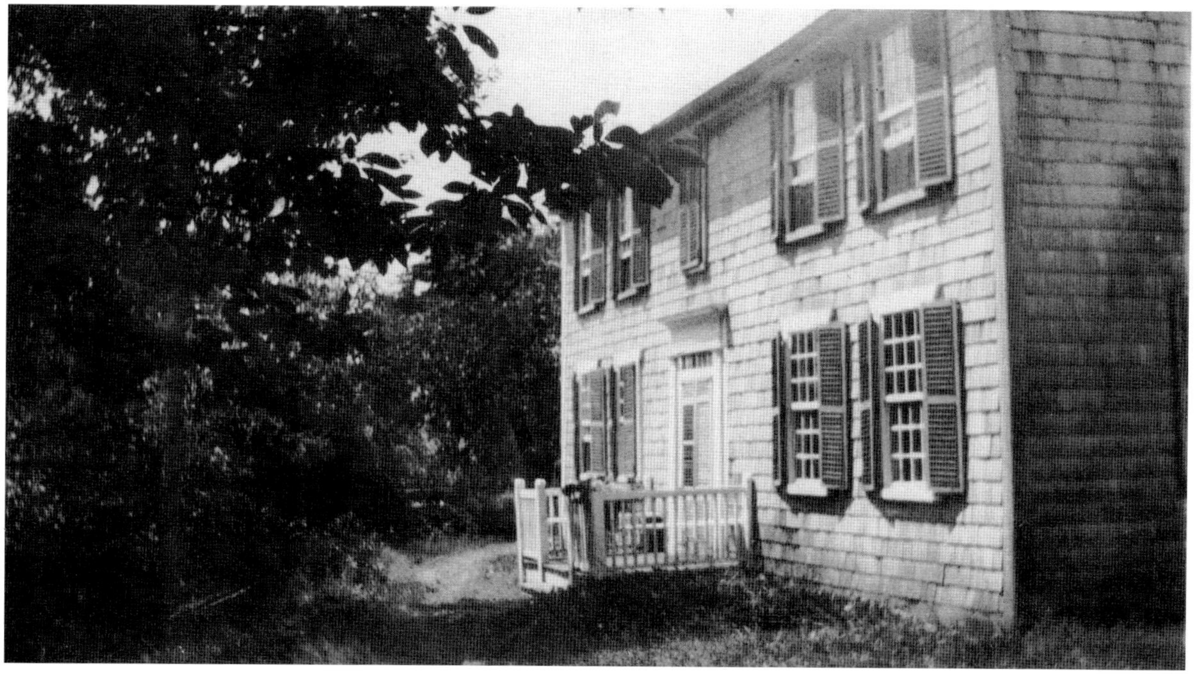

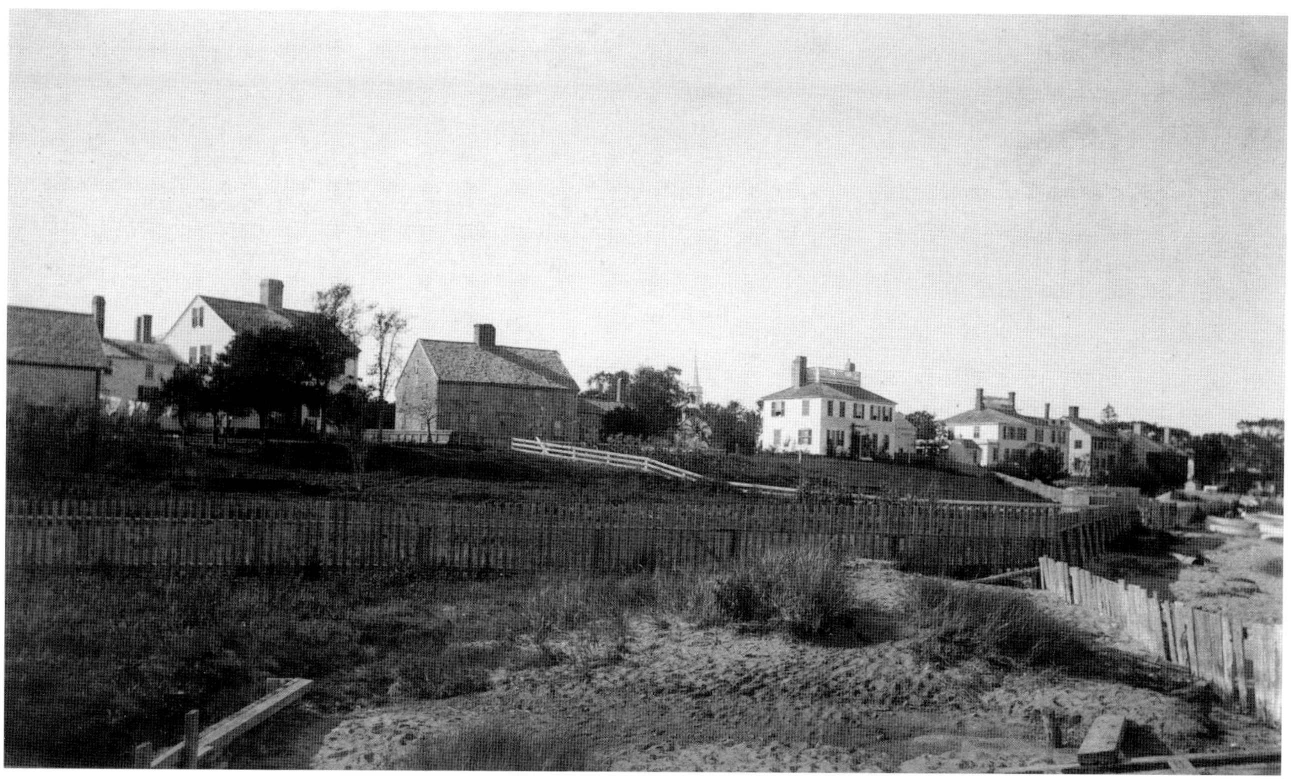

Ships' captains and other affluent mariners built their houses—sometimes grand, sometimes merely comfortable—in all of the towns of Martha's Vineyard. In Edgartown, many of the large houses were constructed along South and North Water Streets, where their occupants could keep an eye out to the harbor. This photograph shows some of the houses that remained around 1950.

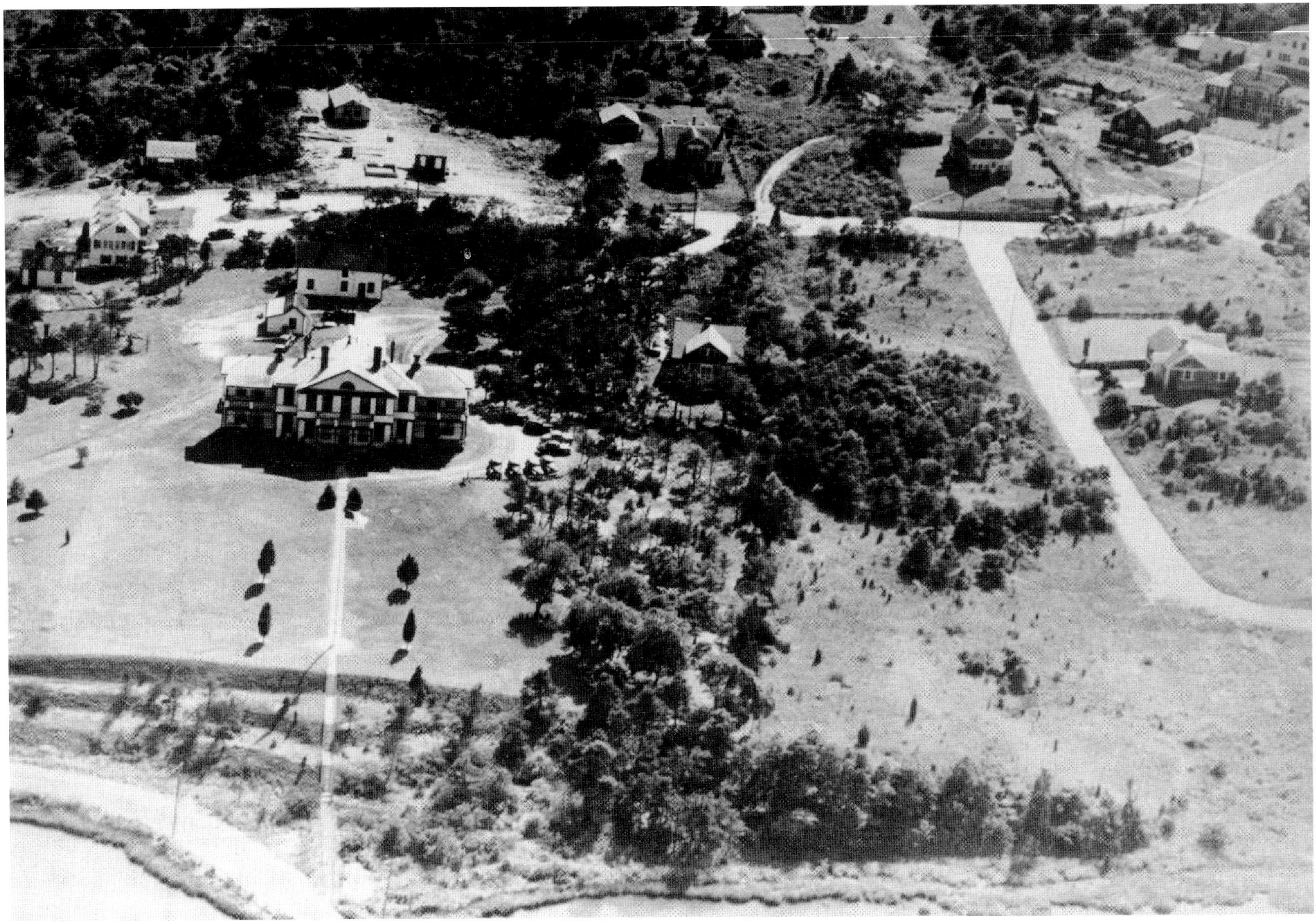

A federal tax levied on seamen's wages in the late 1700s paid for their medical services. At that time, sick mariners were often cared for in private homes. A temporary hospital for seamen was located in the Eastville section of Edgartown, now Oak Bluffs, around 1796. Another was built in 1866 a mile outside of Vineyard Haven. In 1879, an abandoned lighthouse overlooking the Lagoon and Vineyard Haven Harbor was repurposed as the Marine Hospital. Sixteen years later, a large new Marine Hospital opened farther back on the same site. Like its predecessors, it served sailors and members of the military as well as the people of Martha's Vineyard. The US government closed the hospital in 1952. Afterwards, the building became the home of the St. Pierre School of Sport, a sailing camp that operated there from 1969 to 2005.

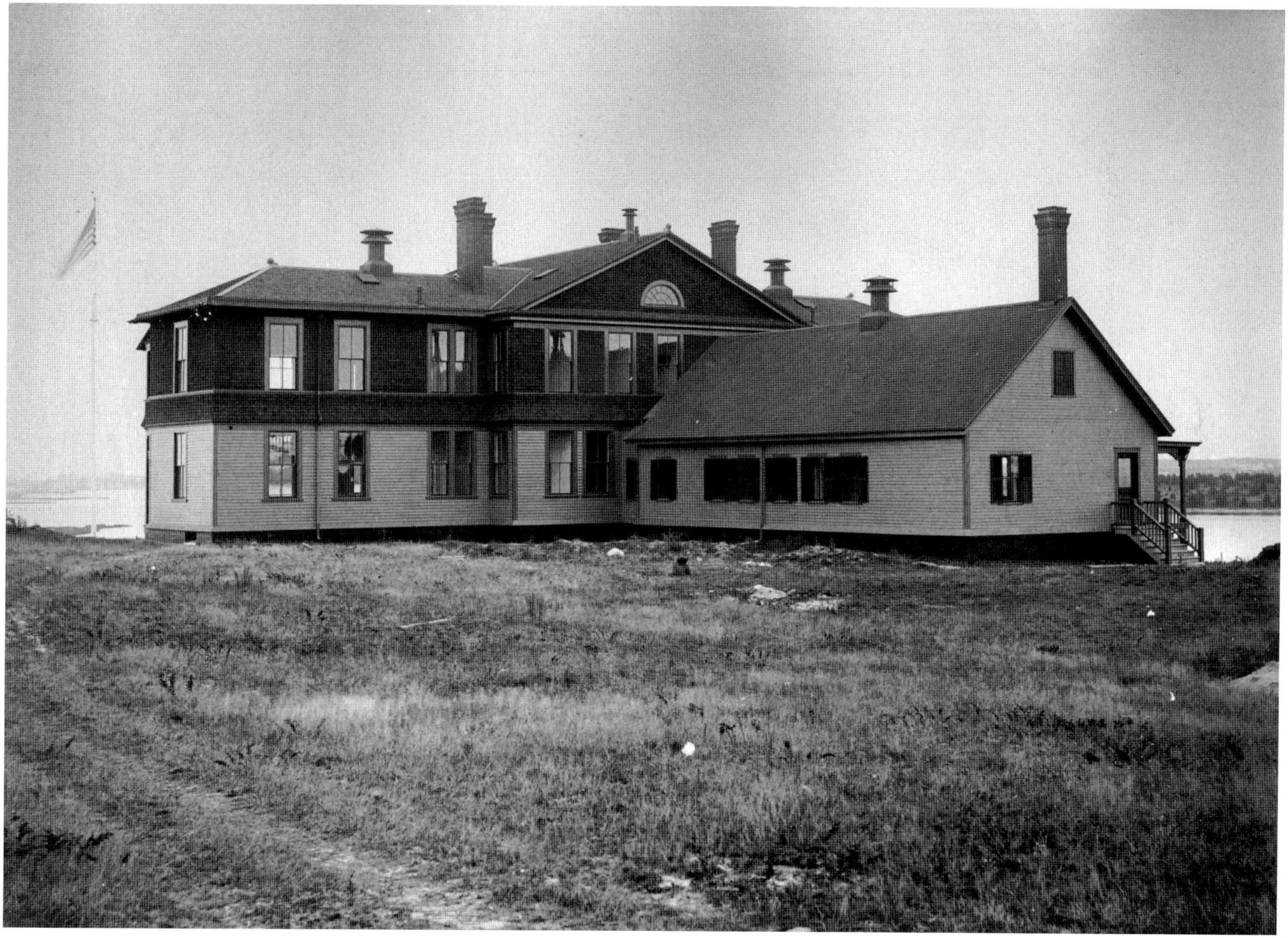

The Marine Hospital, seen here shortly after construction was completed in 1895, incorporated the latest in medical thinking. Large windows allowed light and fresh air to enter the spacious wards, and it had a separate smoking room. A ward that had been added to the old lighthouse buildings at the front of the site just 10 years earlier was moved around and attached to the back of the new structure. It served as the hospital's kitchen until the 1930s.

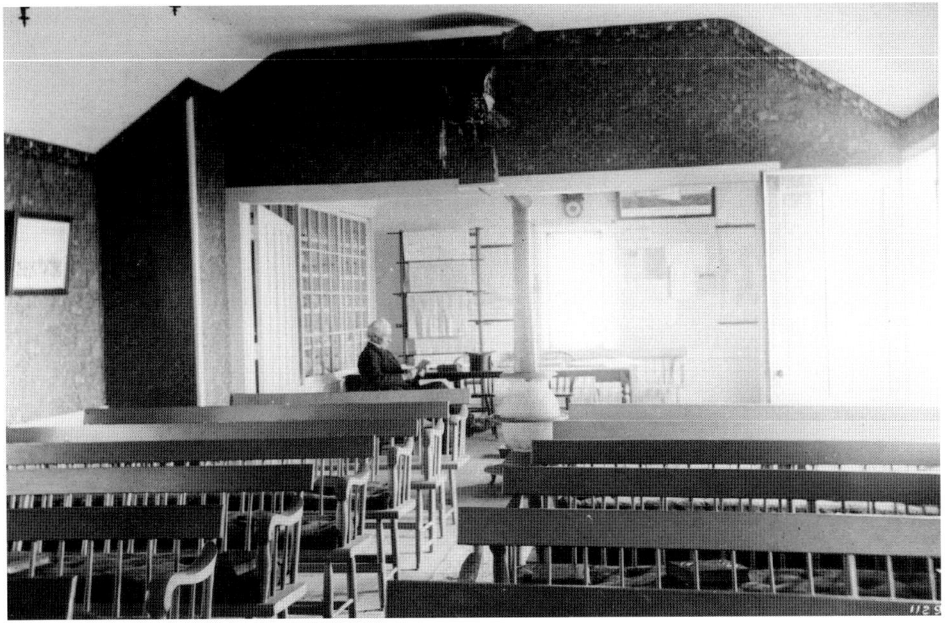

With their medical needs seen to at the Marine Hospital, the spiritual and intellectual needs of sailors were filled by the Seaman's Bethel, a branch of the Boston Seaman's Friend Society. In 1889, it was located over a ship's chandlery, which provided a reading room and worship space (seen here). In 1893, it moved to a building at the foot of Union Wharf in Vineyard Haven. (Photograph by Henry Platt.)

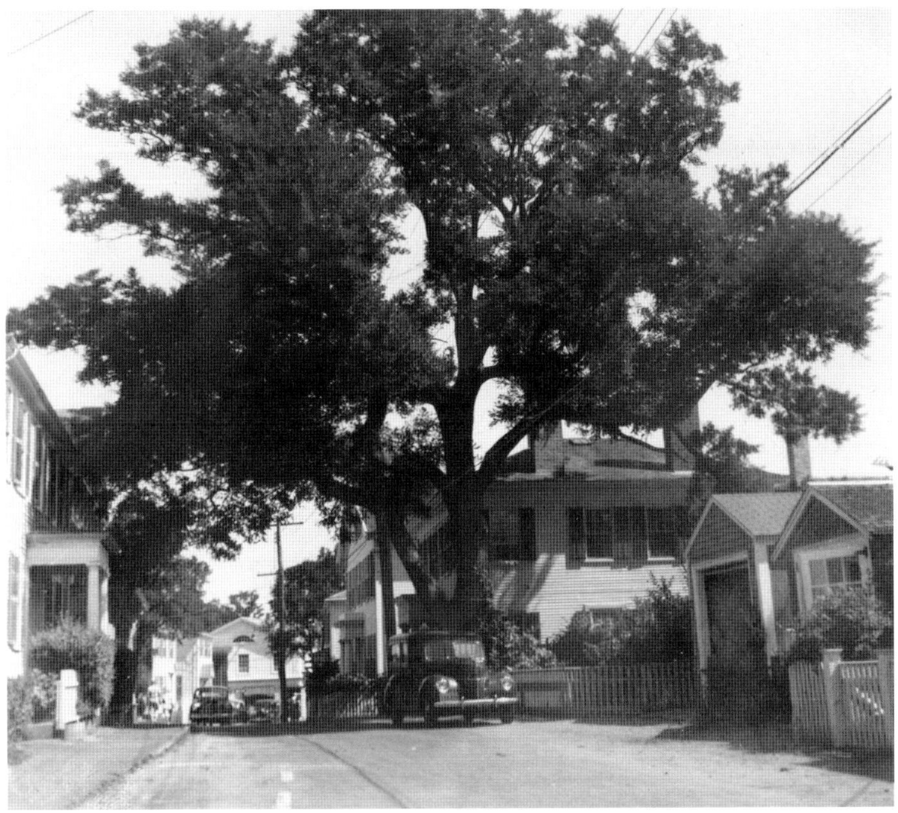

Capt. Thomas Milton brought the now famous Pagoda Tree (*Styphnolobium japonicum*) from China in 1857 and planted it in front of his South Water Street house in Edgartown. In this snapshot, the tree was not quite 100 years old. It is now considered the largest of its kind in America.

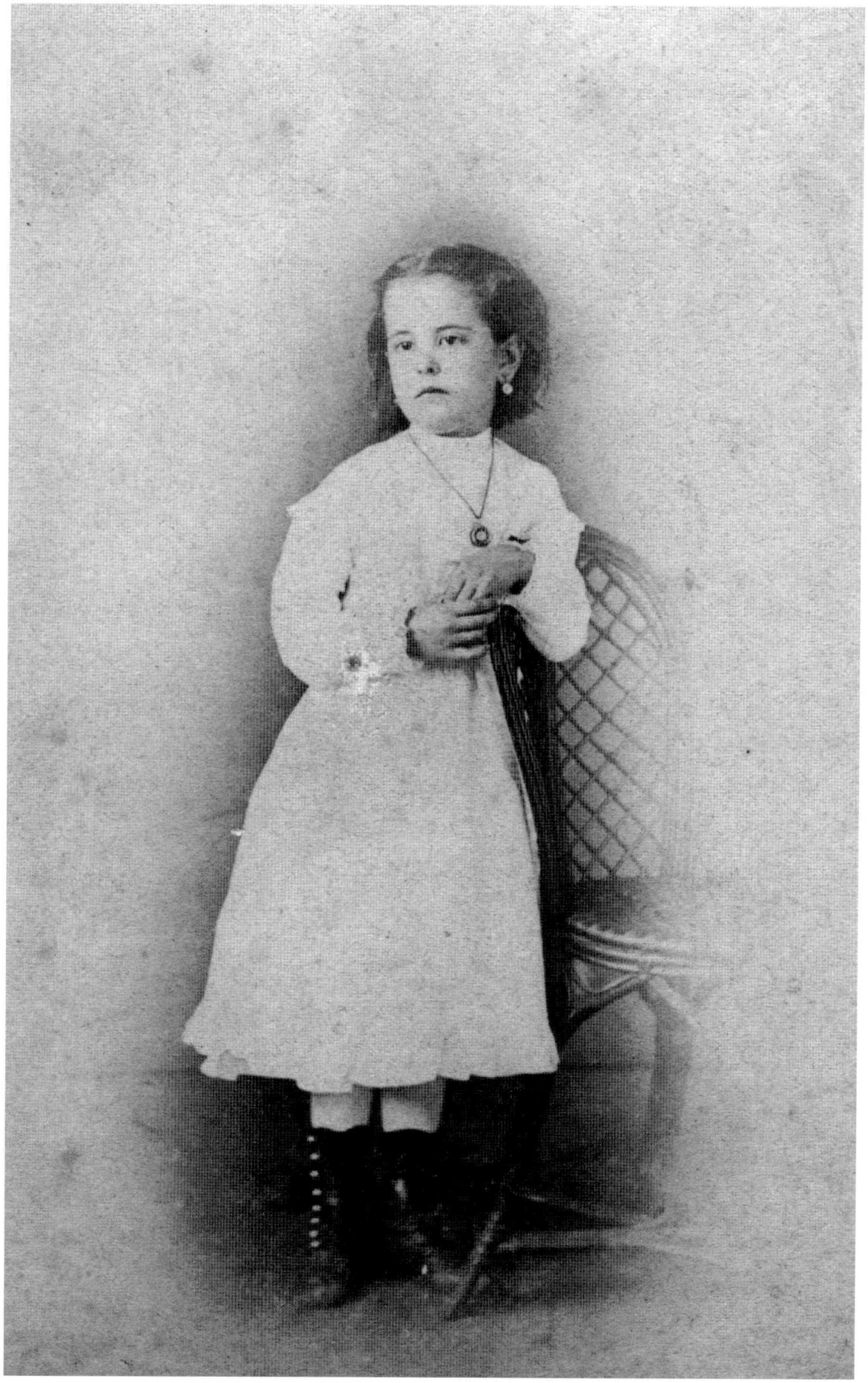

Laura Jernegan's father, Jared, was a whaling captain from Edgartown. He brought his family along with him on the bark *Roman* in 1868. For four years, Laura, her brother Prescott, and her mother sailed the Atlantic and the Pacific. They stayed in Hawaii when Captain Jernegan and his crew went to the Arctic in search of whales. This photograph was taken in Honolulu when Laura was about nine years old. Though families sometimes accompanied captains on their long trips, Laura is perhaps unique in that she kept a journal, beginning at age six, as part of her schooling onboard ship. It still survives, providing an unusual perspective on a whaling voyage. An entry from 1870 reads, "it has blown real hard for two days. Prescott cut his foot last night it bleed. I am in Honolulu. it is a real pretty place. Mama is making a dress for me. Papa is up north wher it is cold. he will come back pretty soon. I have two kittens here and one aboard the ship. good by for today." (Photograph by H.L. Chase.)

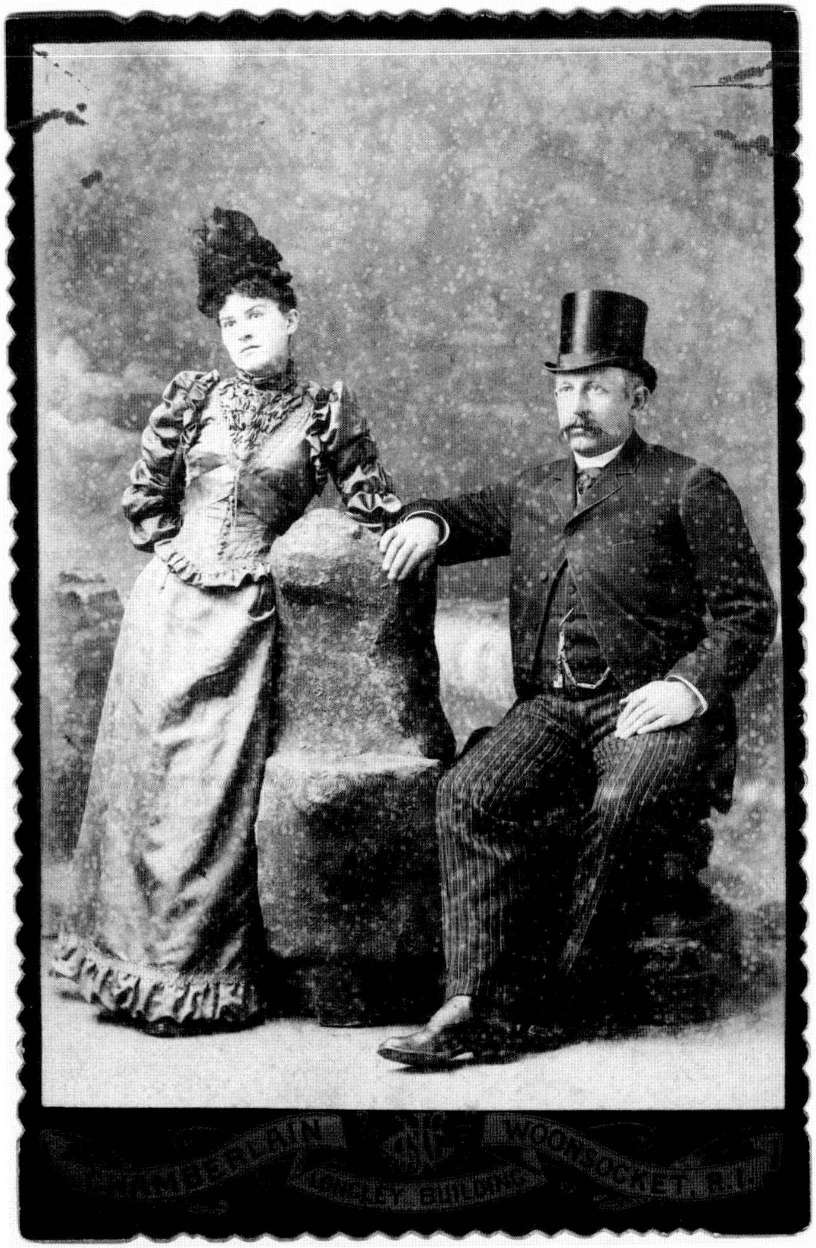

Though Chilmark had the smallest population of the three original towns on the Vineyard, it produced a disproportionately large number of mariners. James A. Tilton (1863–1924) and Grace Mayhew Tilton (born 1853) both came from Chilmark farming families, but James chose to go to sea. He captained 18 whaling voyages in the North Pacific and the Atlantic between 1890 and 1922. (Photograph by John N. Chamberlain.)

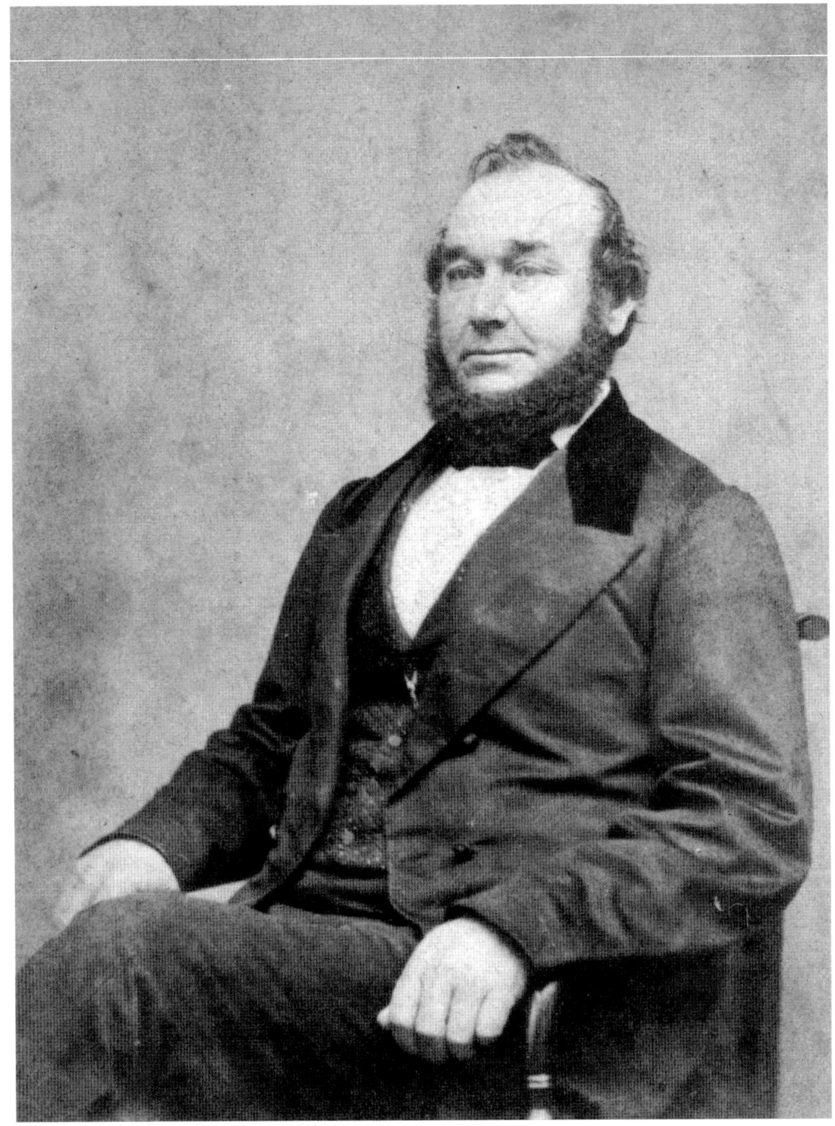

Richard Luce was one of many sea captains from Vineyard Haven. In 1833, he built the first Greek Revival–style house in town on William Street, which became known for its elegant houses. Luce was master on at least 14 whaling voyages that sailed out of New Bedford between 1829 and 1857.

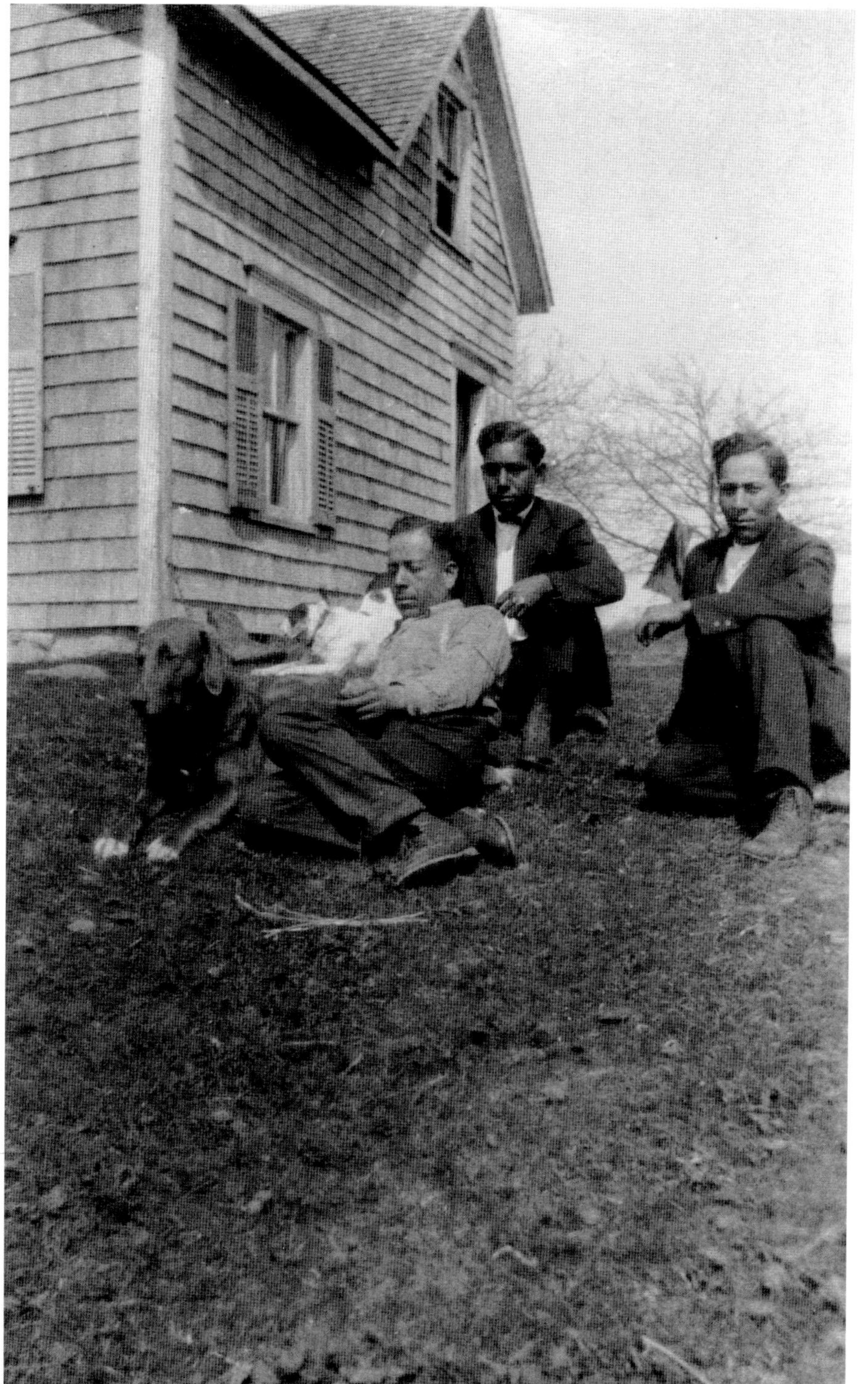

In 1902, Wampanoag whaler Amos Smalley harpooned a 90-foot white whale near the Azores, in the North Atlantic. He later told his story, "I killed 'Moby Dick,'" to *Reader's Digest*. Whether or not the white whale Smalley harpooned really had been the inspiration for Herman Melville's 1851 novel, the fact remains that he was following in a tradition of Wampanoag whalers from Martha's Vineyard that Melville indeed remarked upon in *Moby Dick*. In this snapshot, which appears to have been taken not long after his famous achievement, Smalley (left) lounges on the grass with his brother Norman, a fisherman (center), and Lorenzo Jeffers (right). Jeffers later became a Wampanoag tribal leader and was the second person to serve as supreme sachem of the tribe after the title was revived in 1928.

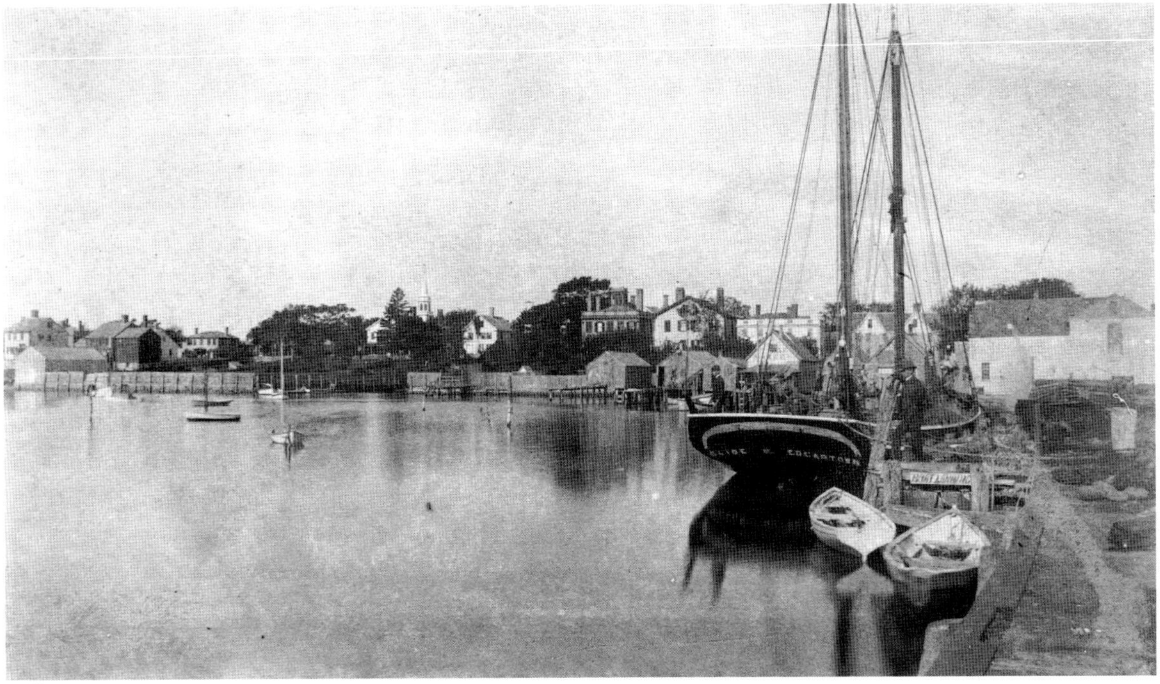

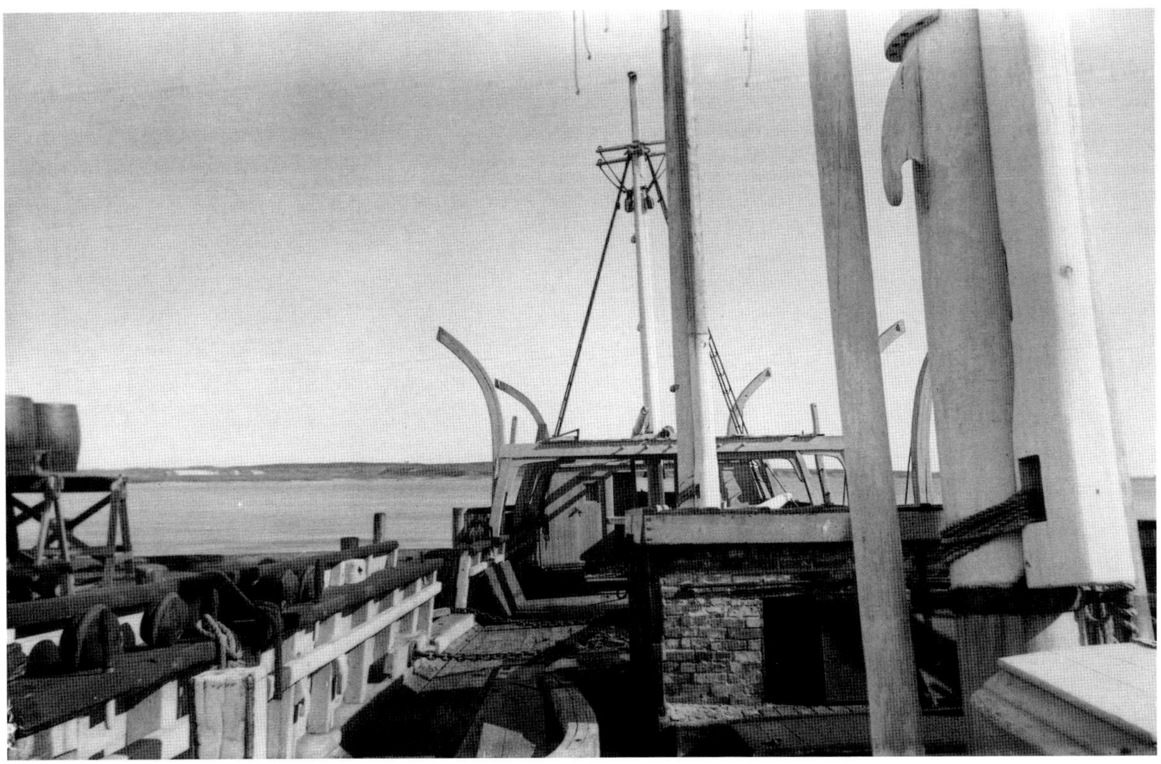

Wealthy Edgartown whaling agent Samuel Osborn Jr. purchased the 50-year-old whaleship *Mattapoisett* in 1886. It was not one of his more successful investments. After a promising voyage out of Edgartown in 1886 under the command of John Reynolds, which returned two years later with 1,140 barrels of sperm oil, *Mattapoisett* spent years tied to Osborn's Wharf. At one point, Richard Shute boarded the *Mattapoisett* to catch some photographs. Though the vessel had long been derelict by then, she is still recognizable as a whaler. The arching supports that extend above the deck would have held whaleboats. Typically, a whaleship carried six whaleboats, which crewmen boarded to pursue the whales. The brick structure in the photograph below is the tryworks. When a whale was killed, it was butchered alongside the ship, and then slabs of blubber were hoisted up where pieces could be cut off and rendered in large try pots. The resulting oil was stored in casks made by the ship's cooper. (Photographs by Richard Shute.)

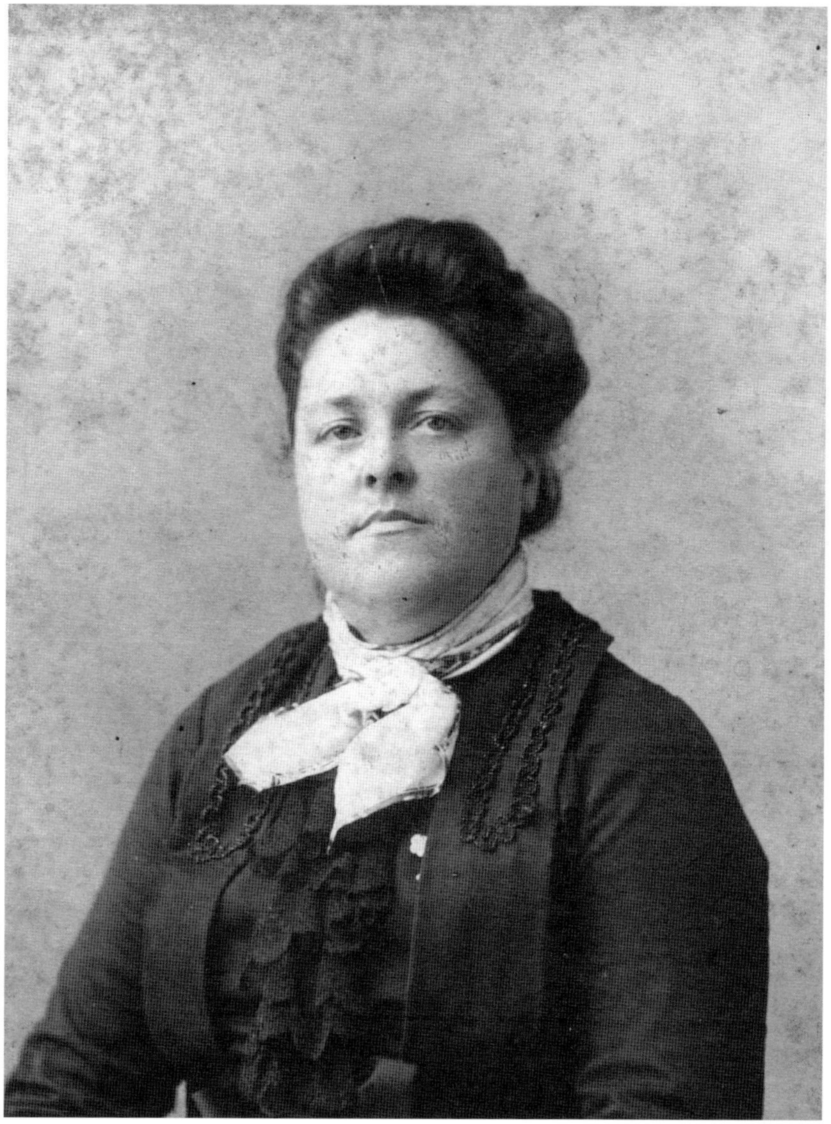

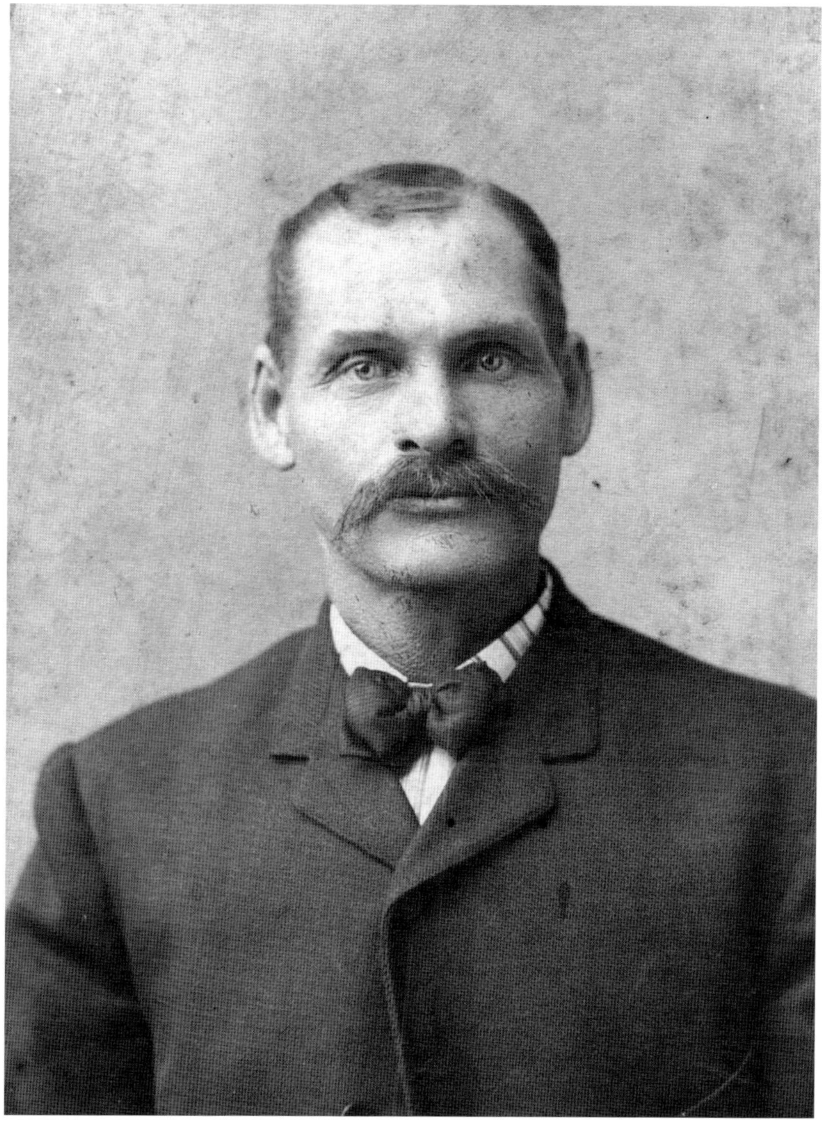

Lyman and Sarah Cottle of Menemsha Creek in Chilmark lived lives similar to those of many Vineyarders of the 19th and early 20th centuries. Lyman is listed in the 1910 census records as a 59-year-old fisherman, but he also went to sea as a mate on the whaleships *Addison* and *Rousseau* when he was a young man in the 1870s. Sarah, 47 in 1910, kept their house and raised two children, Roy and Mary, both teenagers at that time. Roy, like his father, worked as a trap fisherman. Sarah's elderly widowed mother, Sarah Tilton, lived with the family as well.

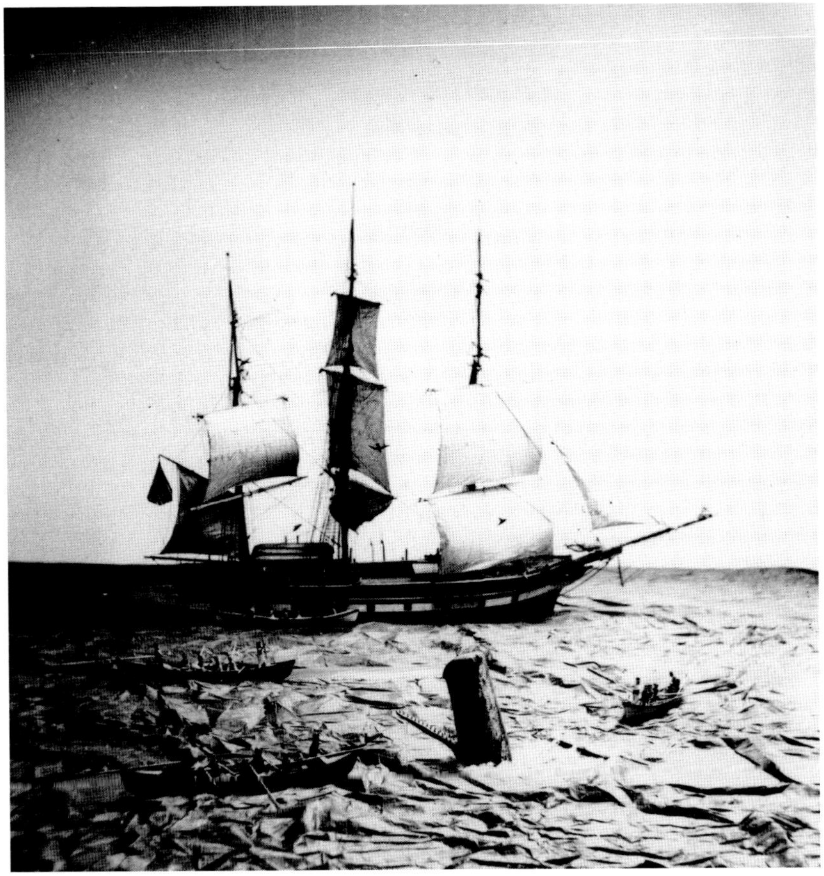

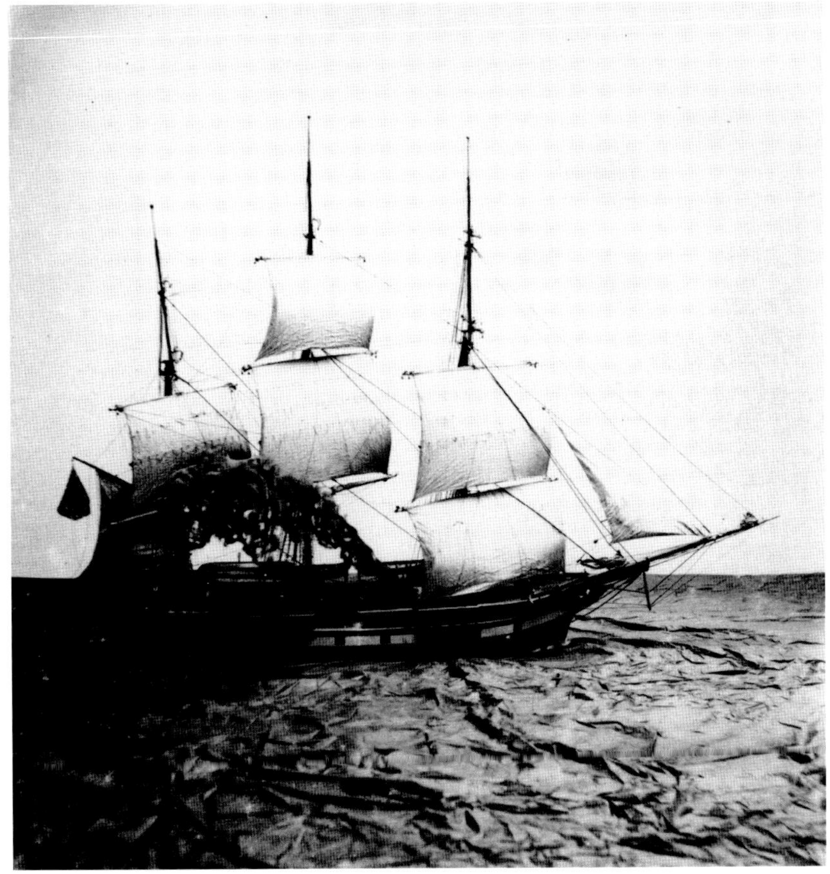

Charles and Richard Shute capitalized on Martha's Vineyard's whaling history when they made a series of stereographs that depicted a whale hunt. The Shutes made realistic dioramas using dark cotton for smoke and crumpled paper for the sea. There were 12 photographs in the series. In 1872, after a fire destroyed the Shutes' studio and all of their negatives, Charles Shute re-created the dioramas and rephotographed the series so they could continue to sell it to tourists, both on the island and by mail order. Both of these photographs are from the second series. The photograph above left shows the whaleship after the manned whaleboats have been launched. They converge on the sperm whale, harpoons ready. Above right, smoke billows from the tryworks on deck, where the whale blubber is rendered into oil. (Photographs by Charles and Richard Shute.)

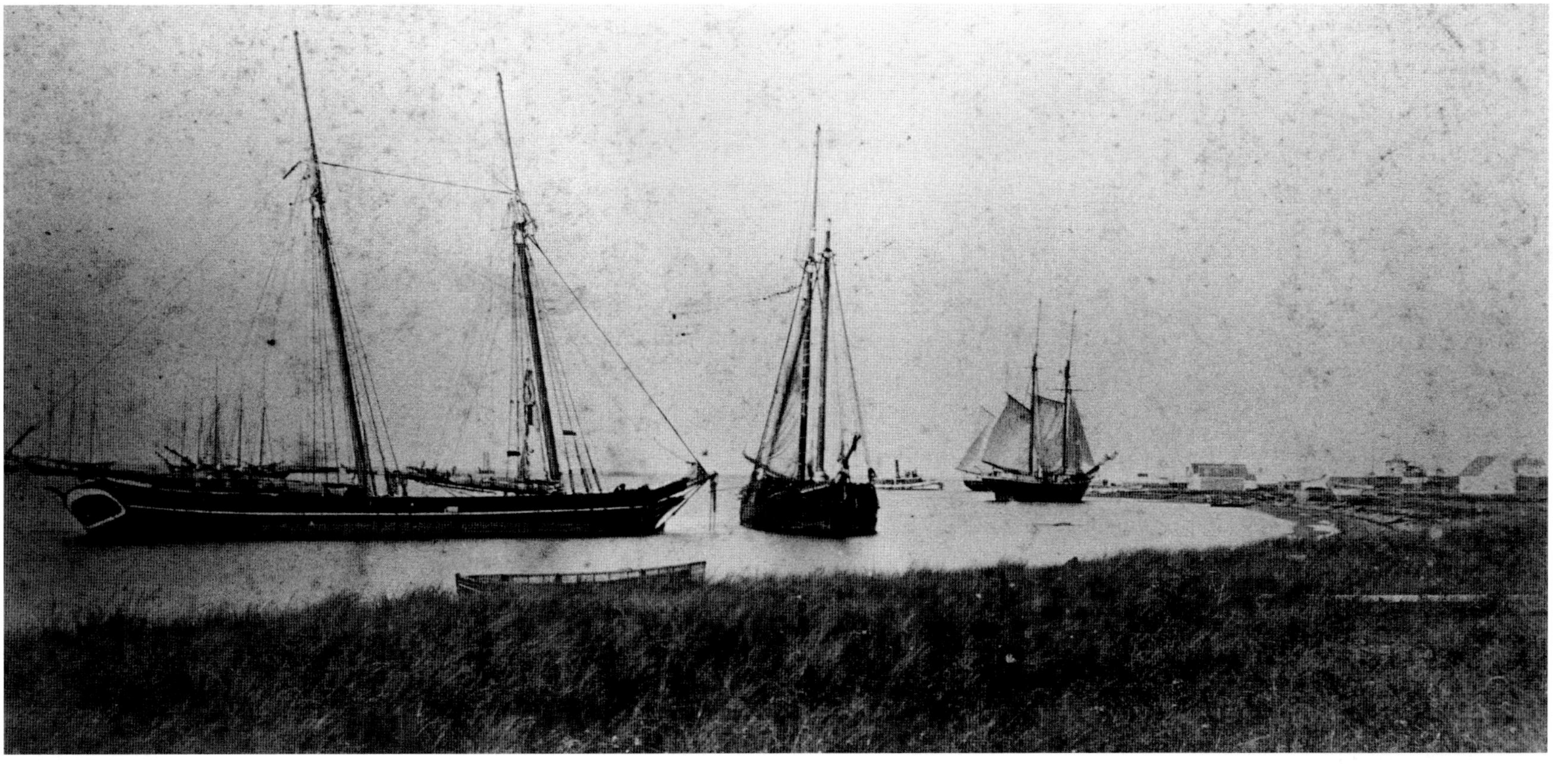

Not all mariners traveled the globe. The coastwise schooners traded up and down the East Coast of the United States, stopping in Vineyard harbors en route. This photograph was taken in Vineyard Haven Harbor around 1898. Before the Cape Cod Canal was dug in 1911, Vineyard Sound was one of the busiest shipping routes in the world. Schooners were sailing vessels, most commonly having two masts but sometimes more.

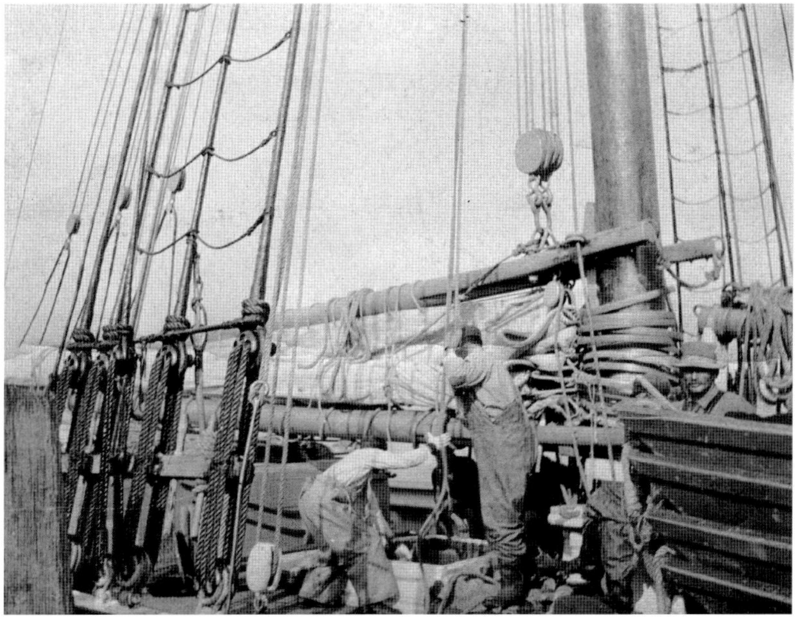

Schooners were quick and could be maneuvered with a small crew. A two-masted schooner typically had a crew of about five sailors. This photograph was taken on the deck of an unidentified schooner that moored in Edgartown Harbor in the early 1900s.

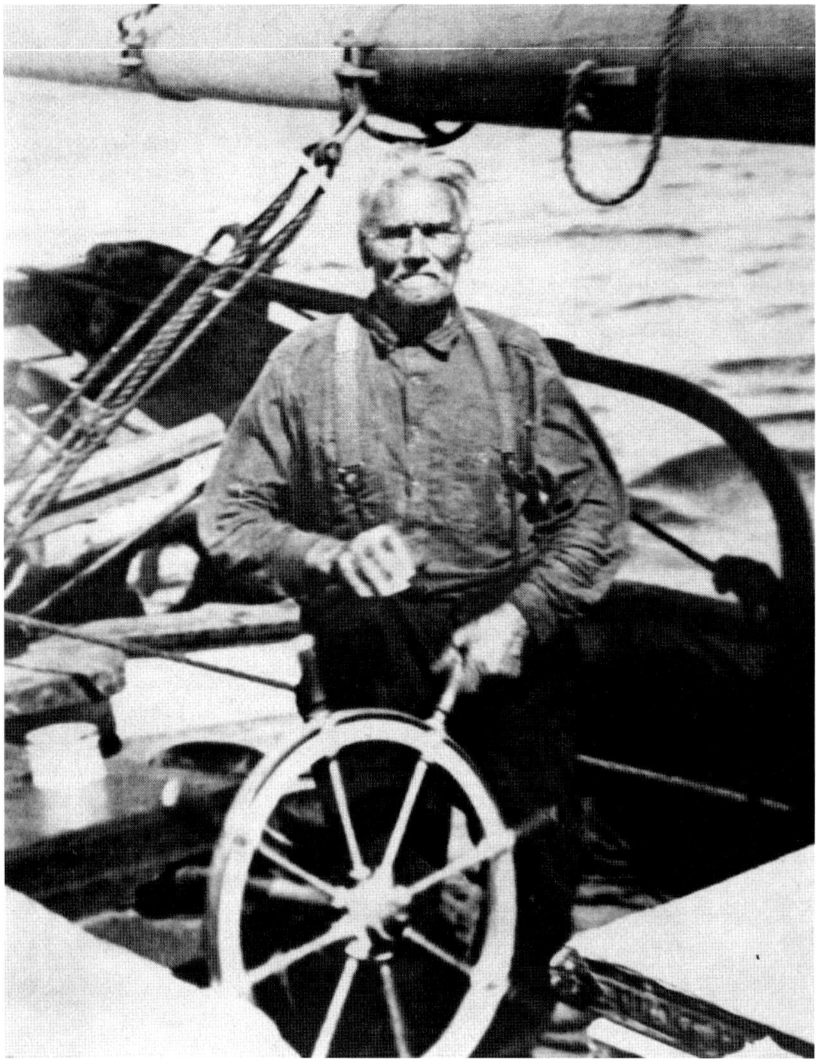

Zeb Tilton (1866–1952) was born in Chilmark. At the age of 15, he went to sea on the schooner *Eliza Jane*, captained by Josiah Cleveland out of Vineyard Haven. For the rest of his life, he sailed schooners, gaining a reputation as a fine seaman and a character. In 1900, Tilton purchased and became the captain of the schooner *Wilfred J. Fuller*. Later, he did the same with the *John B. Norris*.

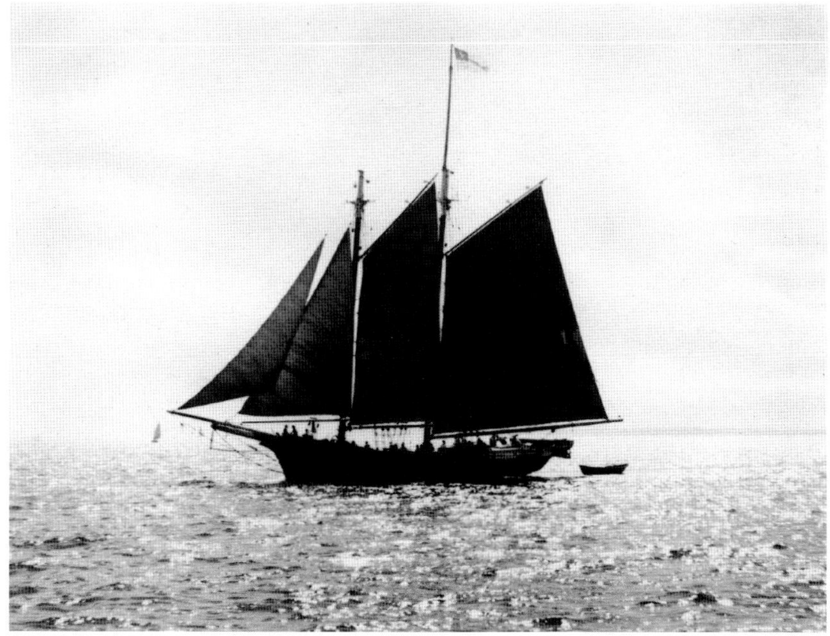

In 1921, at the age of 54, Zeb Tilton bought the *Alice S. Wentworth*, a schooner he had captained briefly years earlier. He sailed her for 18 years, as long as he was physically able to do so. In 1936, debt and poor eyesight forced Tilton to sell the *Alice S. Wentworth*. She was purchased by a group with Vineyard connections; shareholders included Katharine Cornell, James Cagney, and Denys Wortman.

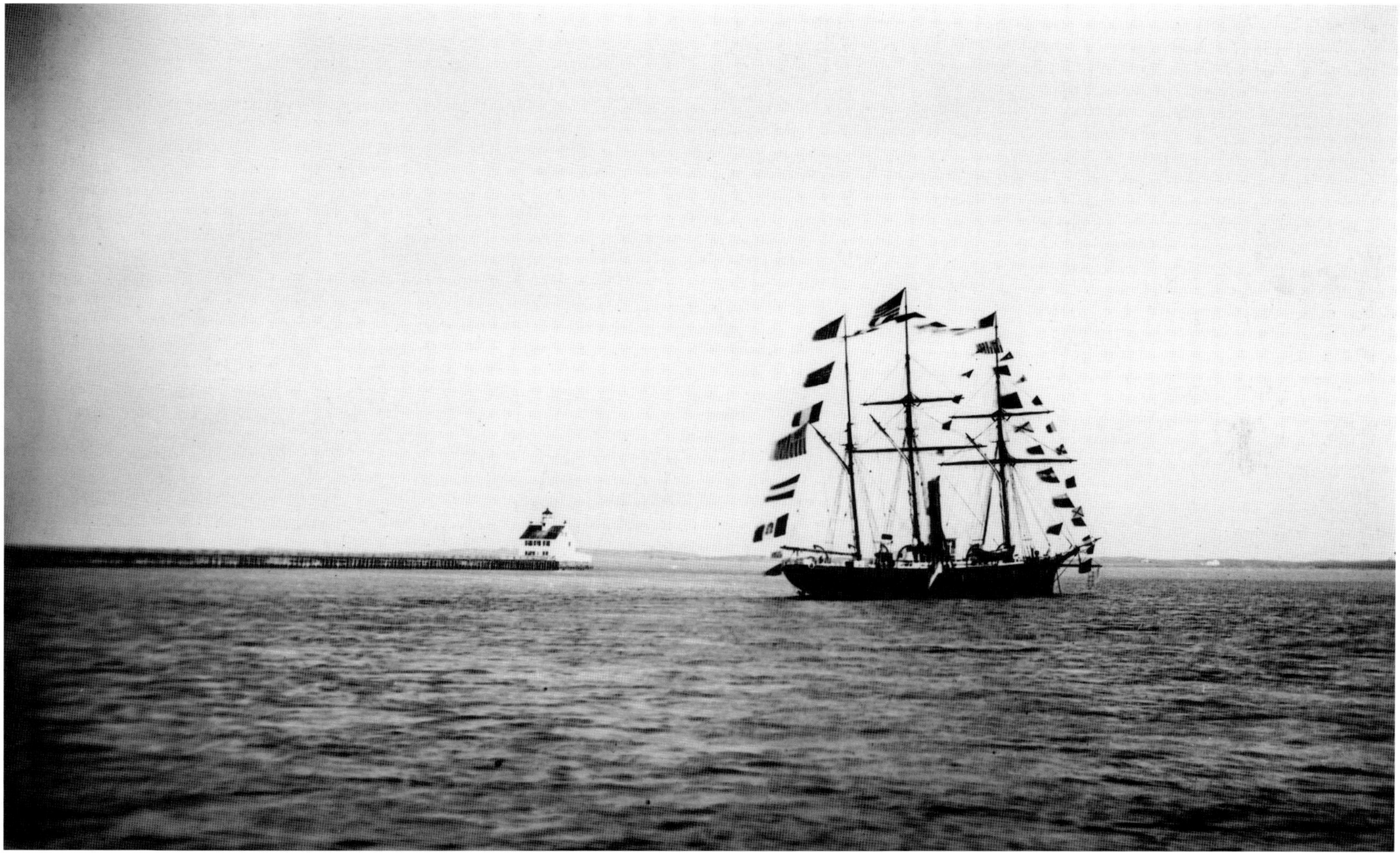

The funnel extending up between the masts of this vessel identifies her as steam powered. This combination of wind and steam was not uncommon in whaleships toward the end of the whaling era in the late 1800s, though it is not clear whether this is a whaleship or not. The occasion for decorating this ship in Edgartown Harbor with the flags of many nations has also been forgotten. The lighthouse in the background is the old Edgartown Light, which was replaced after the hurricane of 1938.

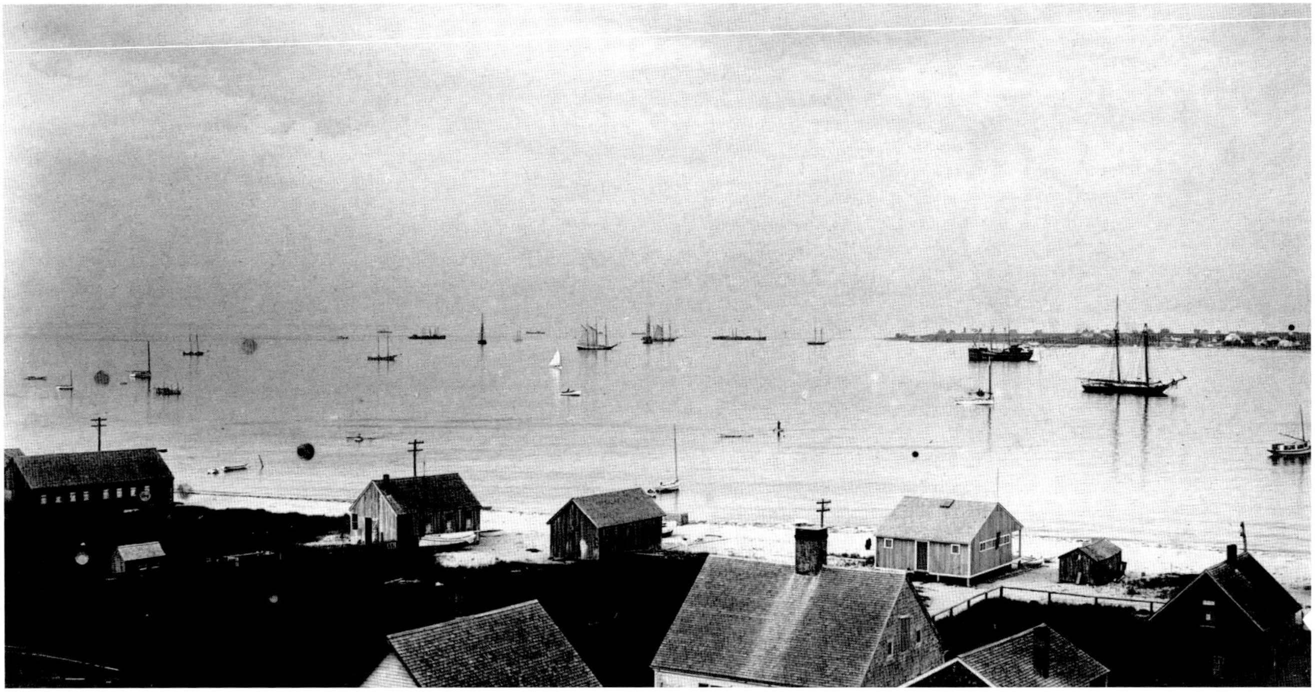

Views like this one of the shore of Vineyard Haven Harbor in the late 1800s or early 1900s, with coastal schooners moored or sailing as far as the eye can see, were once familiar. They serve as reminders of the importance of shipping to the economy of the island.

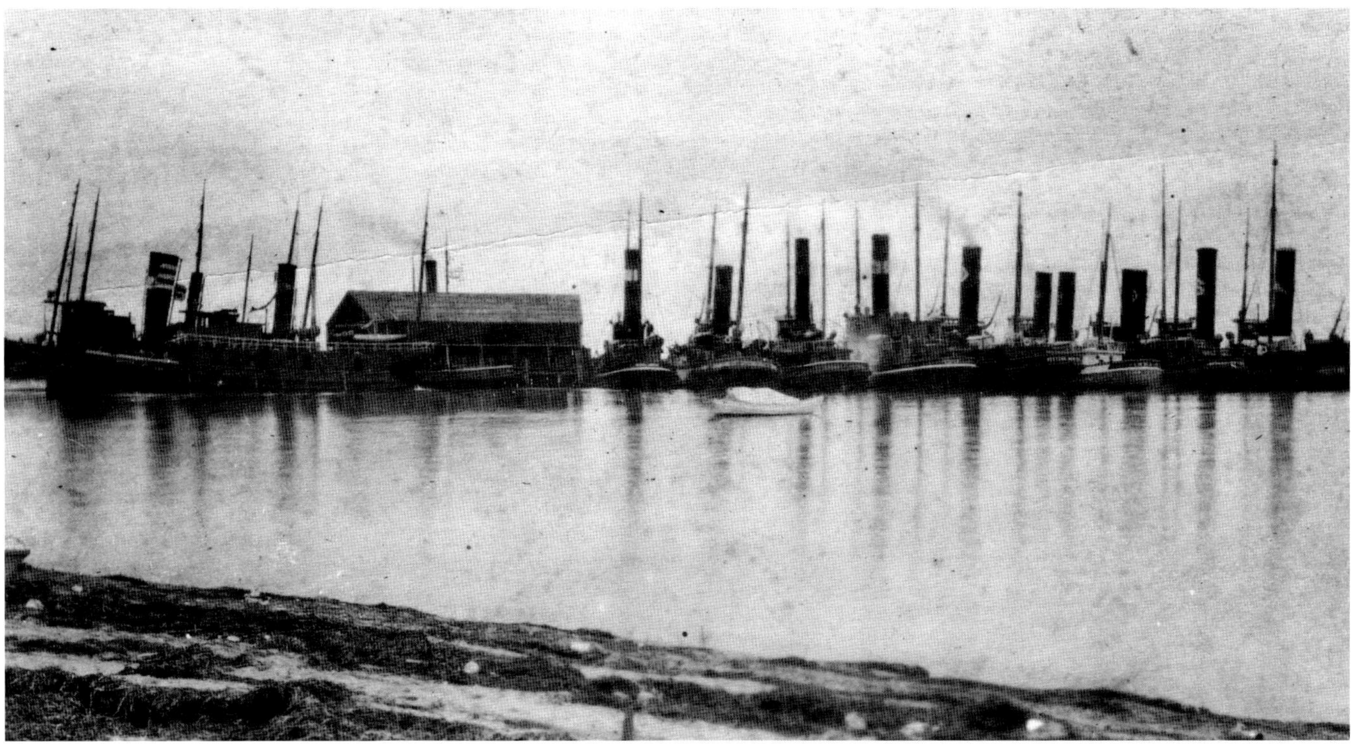

It was common to see tugboats lined up in Vineyard Haven Harbor in the early and mid-1900s. They were necessary to guide large vessels in and out of port.

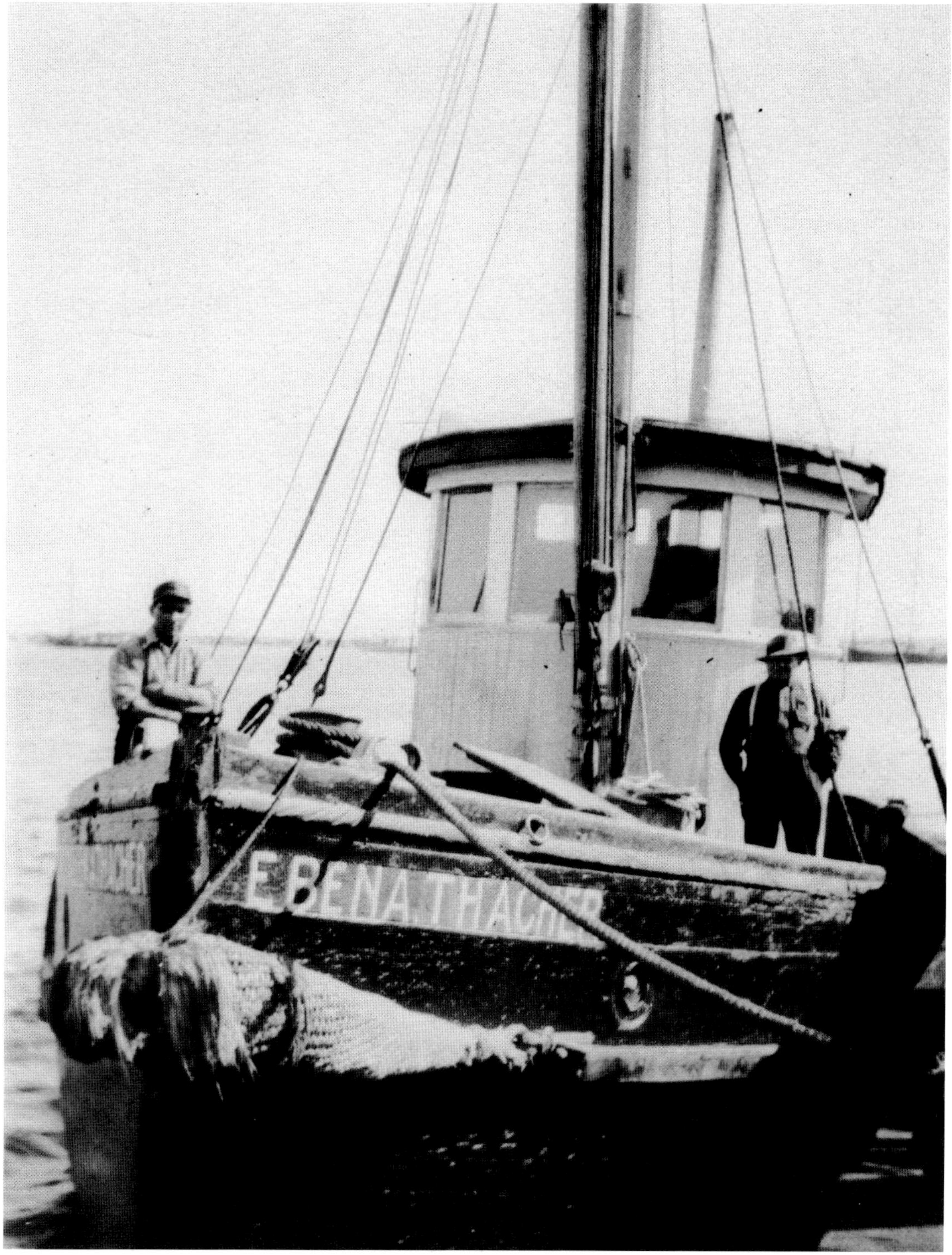

There were two boats called *Eben A. Thacher*, the first built in 1909 in Chelsea, Massachusetts, and the second in 1932 in Fairhaven. This photograph is dated around 1930, indicating that it shows the first *Eben A. Thacher*. Like many good Vineyard boats, the *Thacher* had a number of jobs. During her career, she operated out of Vineyard Haven as a tug, a dragger, and a delivery boat, taking mail and supplies to passing vessels.

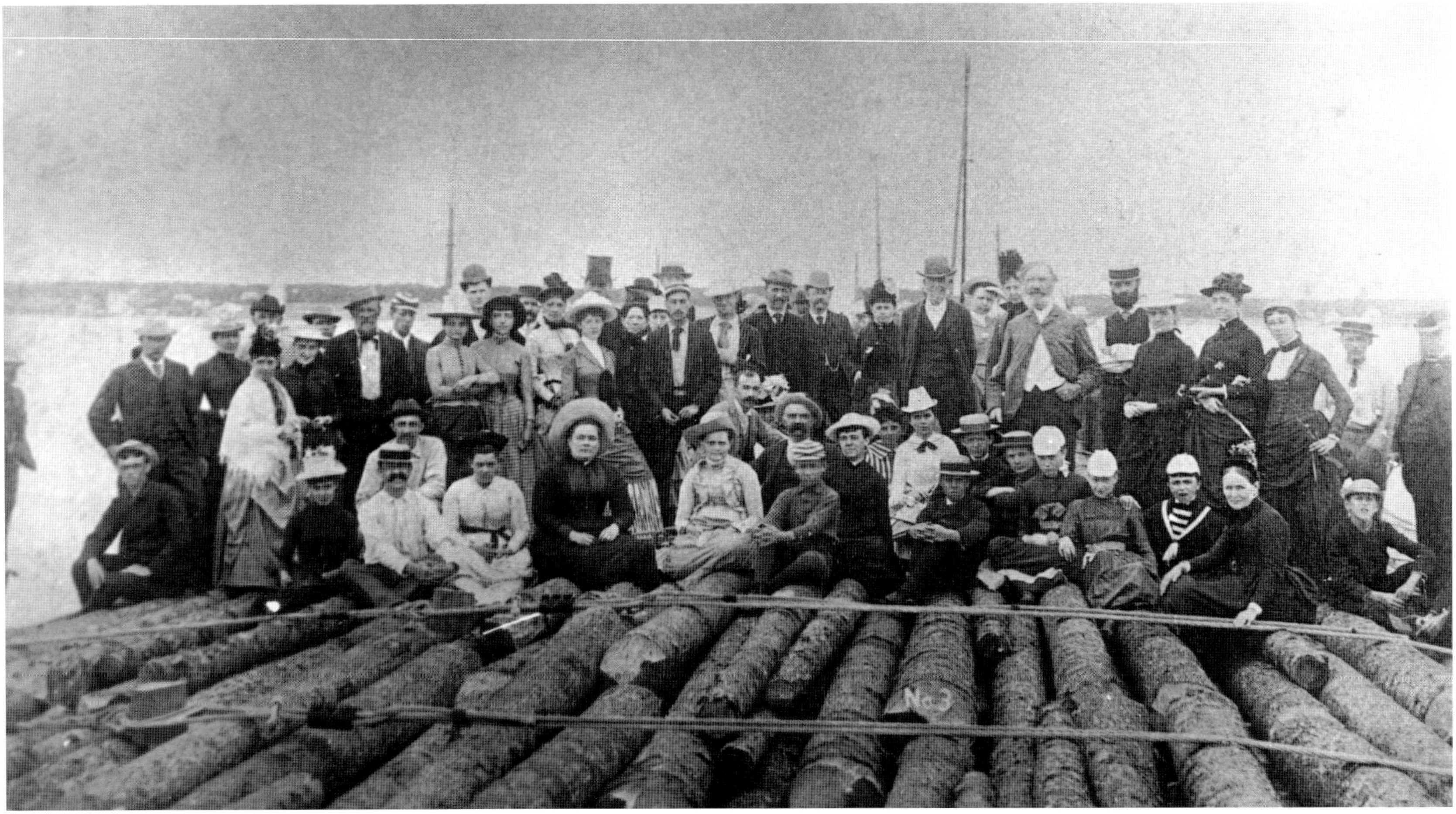

Log rafts were a way to transport timber to market by actually using the product as the vessel. This example was called the Seary Raft. It originated in Nova Scotia and was photographed in Vineyard Haven Harbor in August 1888. It reportedly was 592 feet log, 55 feet wide, had a total depth of 37 feet, and contained 24,000 logs and five million feet of timber. According to a contemporary account, it would have taken nearly 40 schooners to transport that much timber. The steam tugs *Under Writer* and *Ocean King* towed the raft out of the harbor. The photographer, John N. Chamberlain, made a name for himself taking tourist pictures, primarily in Cottage City (later Oak Bluffs) and Nantucket, where he operated studios during the summer months. In the winters, he traveled south to Florida to take pictures of vacationers there. (Photograph by John N. Chamberlain.)

Capt. Josiah Cleveland of the schooner *Eliza Jane* is seen here in his shop on Hatch Road in Vineyard Haven around 1890.

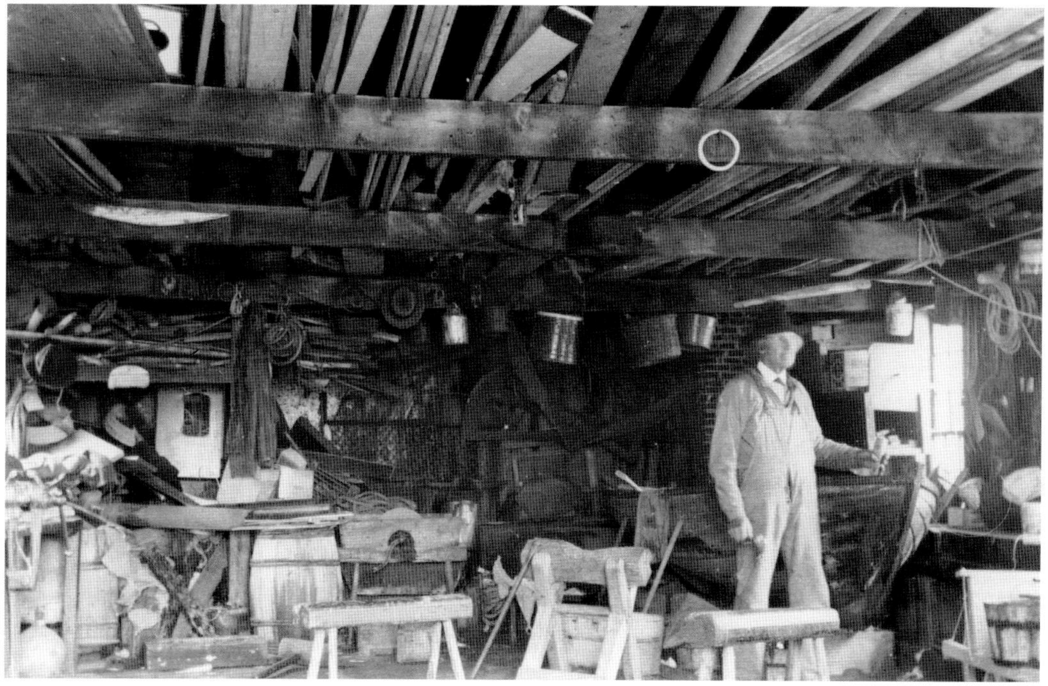

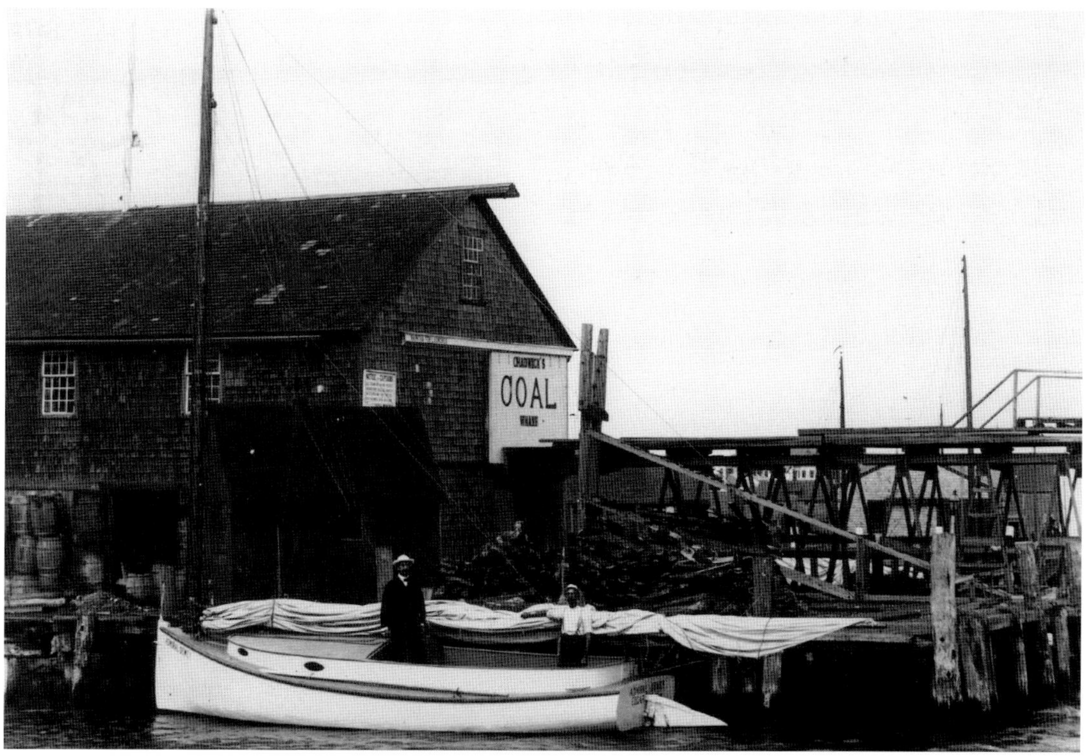

Chadwick's Wharf in Edgartown, the current site of restaurants and gift shops, used to have a business that supplied necessary coal to the steam-powered vessels that came into port. The business also sold naphtha, a fuel source for launches. This photograph was probably taken in the 1920s or 1930s.

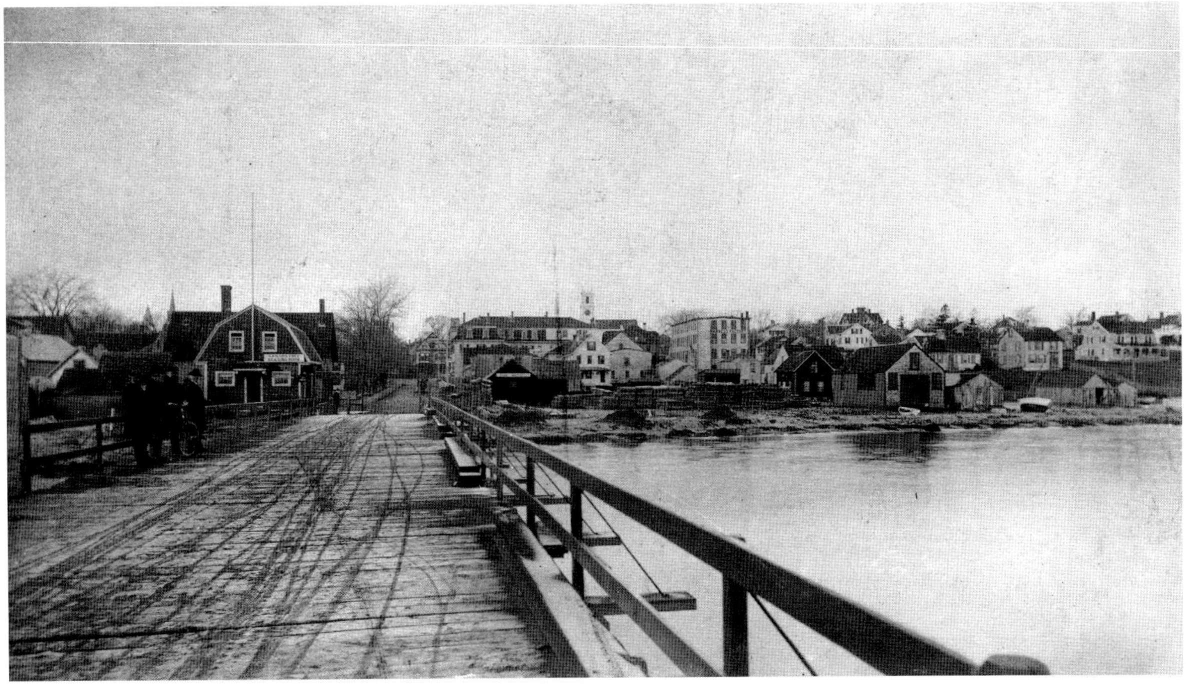

Looking toward town from the end of the wharf in Vineyard Haven, this photograph shows Seamen's Bethel on the left. It is inscribed, "The occasion was just the daily routine, getting the steamboat started for the mainland each morning. The bike was owned by Mr. Golart." From left to right are Dr. Edward Roth, Capt. Gilbert L. Smith, William W. Neifort, and Dr. Winthrop Butler. (Photograph by George C. Golart.)

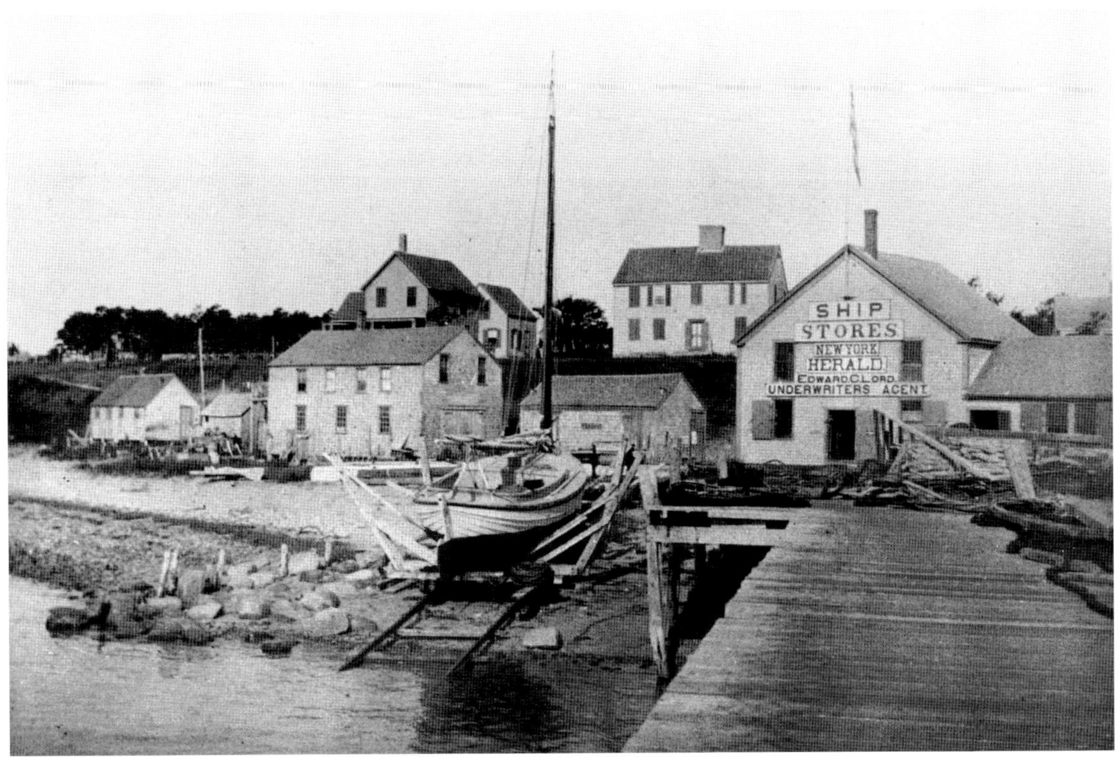

The West Chop ship's chandlery sold supplies for vessels and had a wharf of its own. The arrangement seen in this photograph, with modest working buildings or shacks on the water and imposing houses behind, was typical of 19th-century Martha's Vineyard. Especially in town, the waterfront was less for recreation and more for work.

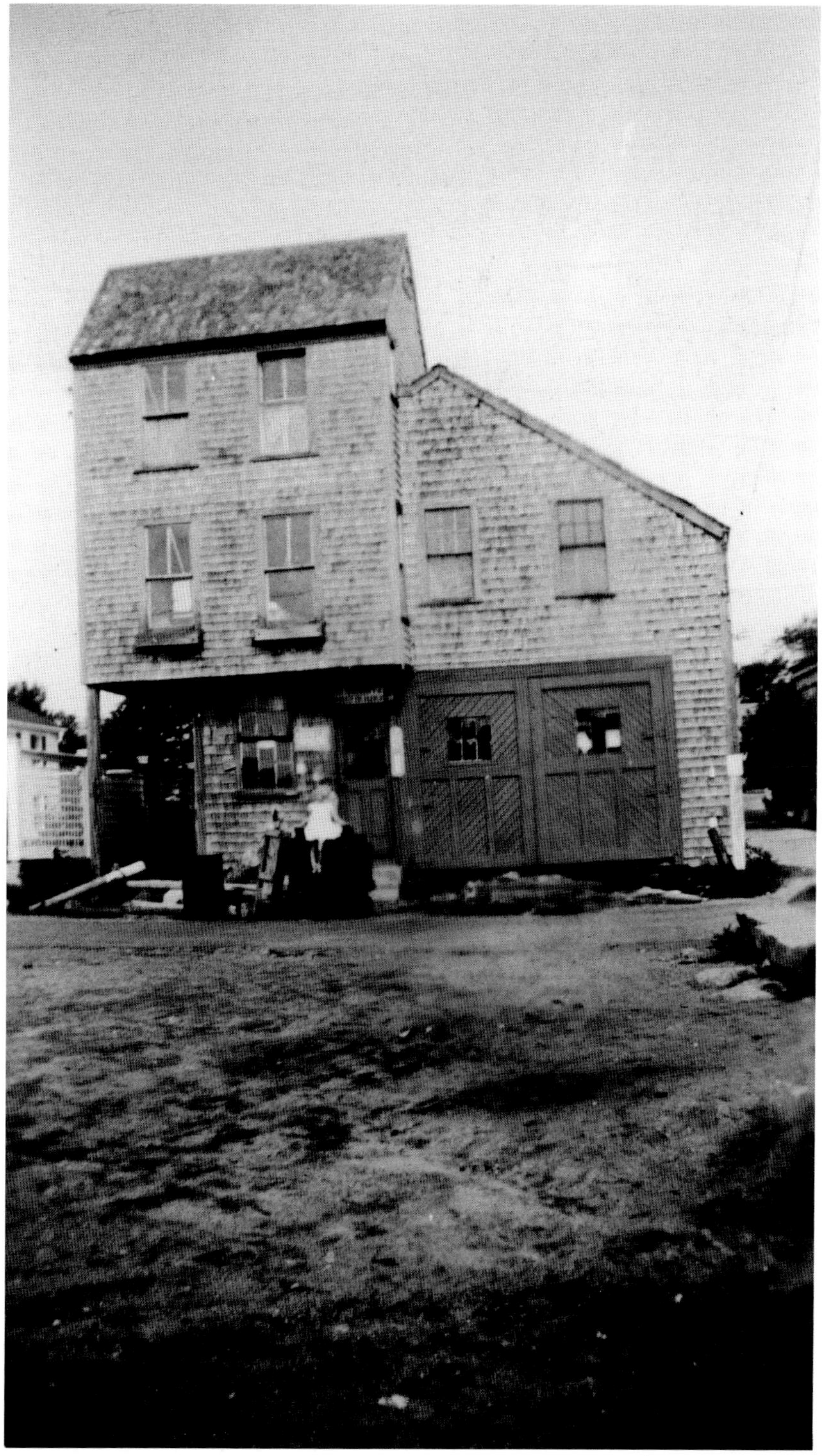

Manuel Swartz Roberts (1881–1963), known as "Old Sculpin," was a renowned Martha's Vineyard boatbuilder who worked out of this Edgartown shop, next to the town wharf, for more than 50 years. Best known for his catboats, he also built beach boats for the Edgartown Yacht Club and built or repaired boats used as Chappaquiddick ferries. The Edgartown side of the Chappy ferry is located just across the street from this building. Before its use as a boat shop, the building was a sail loft, was used for processing whale oil, and was a grain store. The Martha's Vineyard Art Association bought the shop from Roberts in 1954, and it has been the organization's gallery ever since. Well-known artists involved with the art association include William Abbe, Francis Chapin, Mary Coles, Julius Delbos, Loïs Mailou Jones, Ruth Appledoorn Mead, and Vaclav Vytlacil.

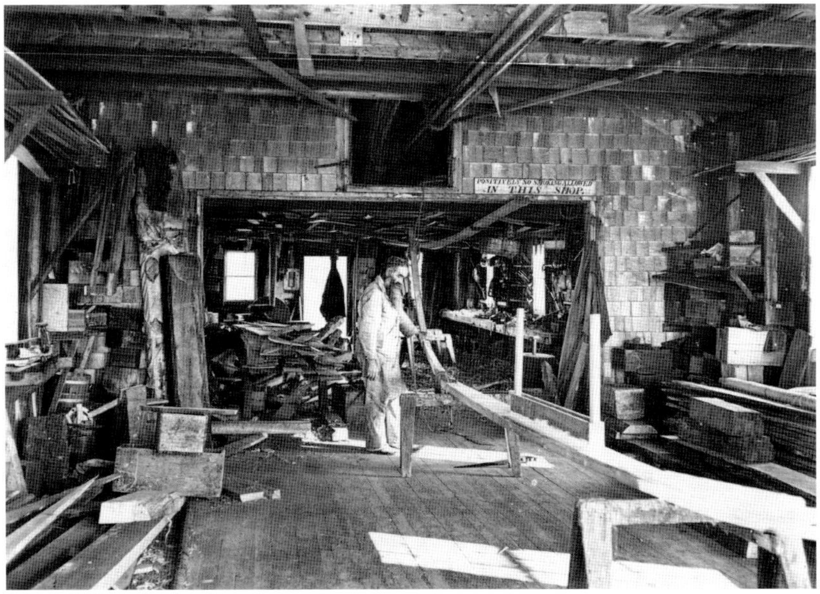

Boatbuilder Charles Gifford is seen here in his Vineyard Haven shop in the 1880s. He has his hand on the keel of a boat that he has just begun to construct, possibly a Noman's Land boat. Named after the island just to the south of the Vineyard, these boats were workaday vessels that could be handled with few men.

The fishing industry was important to Vineyard families, both for providing sustenance and for trade. Even tourists were impressed with the abundance available off the island. The Shutes sold a stereo view showing 360 bluefish taken by one boat on September 7, 1876. (Photograph by C.H. Shute & Son.)

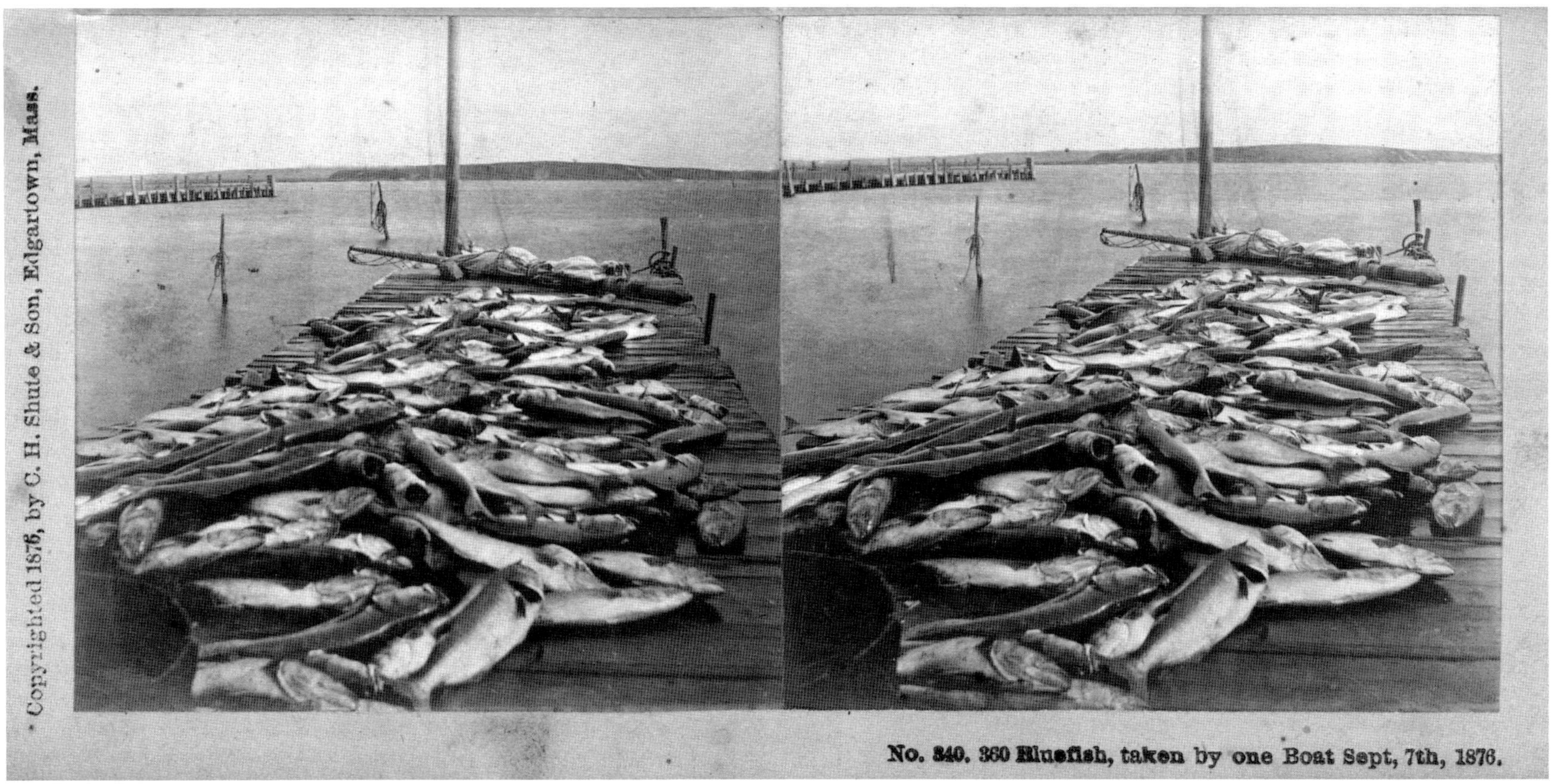

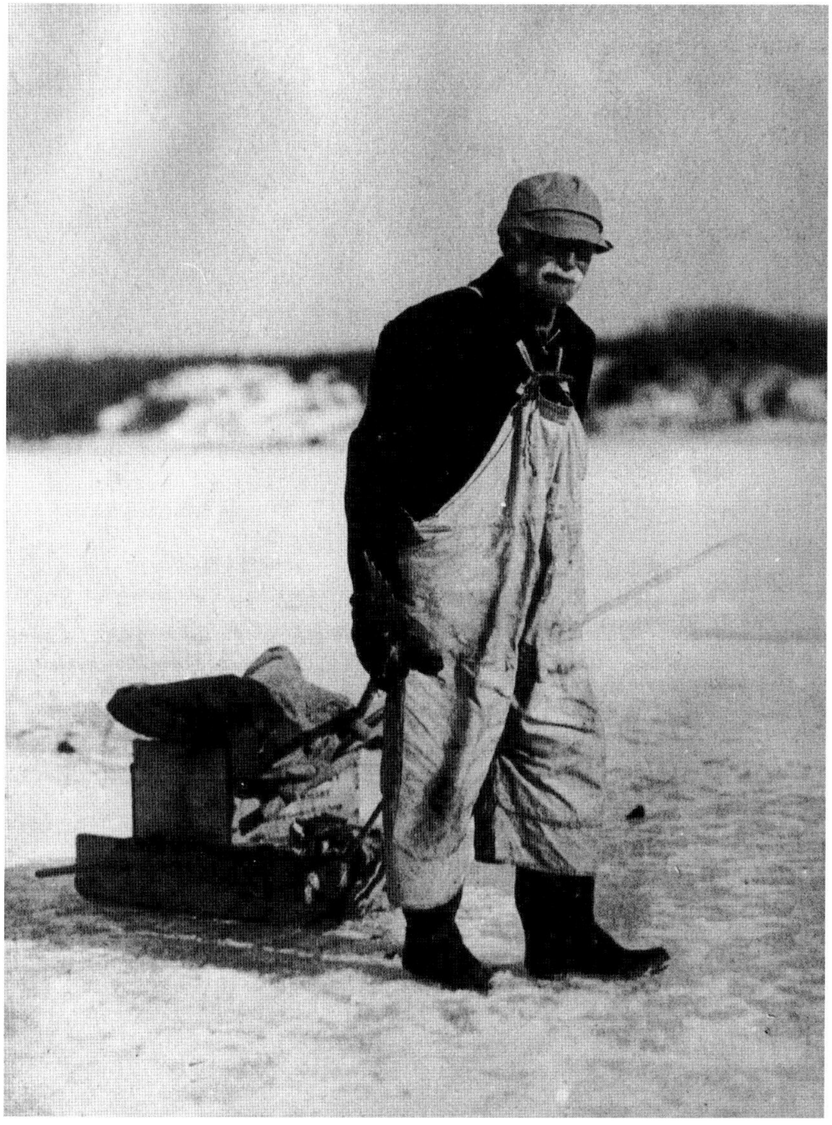

Charles B. Cleveland is pulling his sled with a catch of eels in this undated photograph. Plentiful and relatively easy to trap, eels were one of many fish that formed the diet of Vineyarders. Even as late as the mid-1900s, many year-round residents of the island relied on hunting and fishing to subsist.

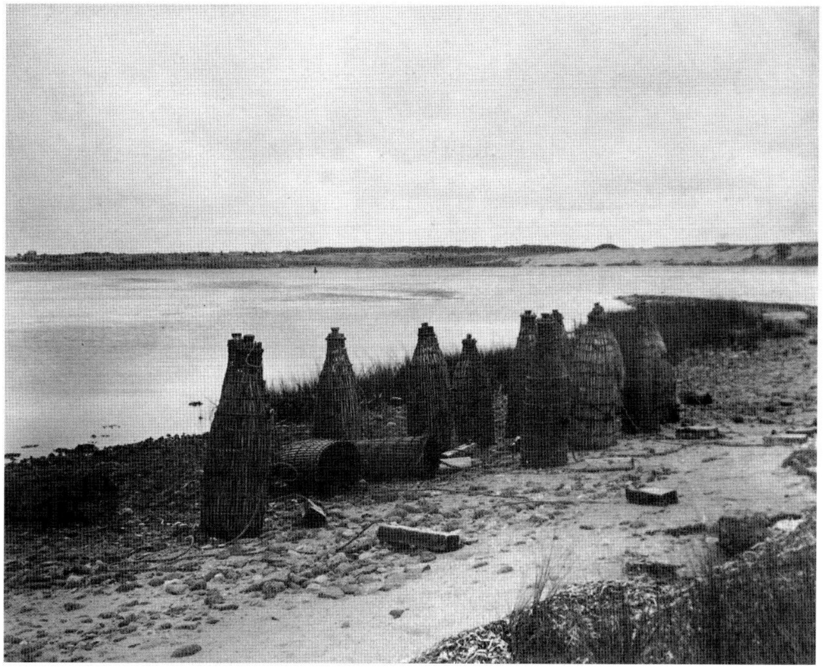

Eel traps were set lying on their sides on the bottom of the ponds. The eel swam into the wide end of the trap through a funnel-like cone made of reeds and remained in the narrow end until collected by the fisherman. The makers of these traps on Martha's Vineyard based their design on Wampanoag examples. (Photograph by C.G. Hine.)

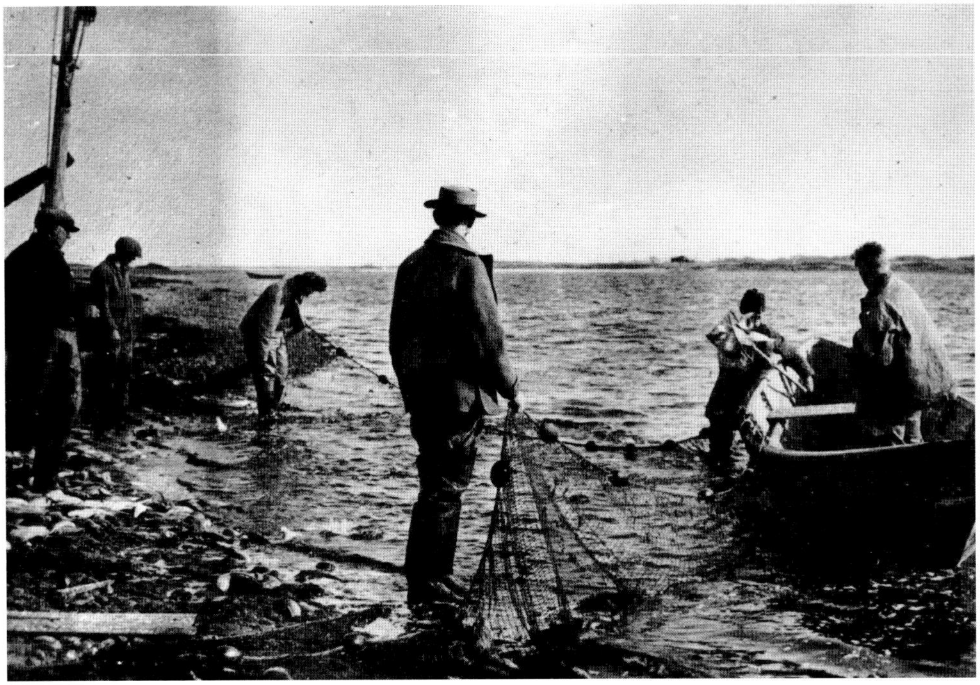

Fish traps were placed in many different island locations. This one is off Edgartown, with Chappaquiddick in the background. After the traps were placed, they were left for a period of time. Fish swam in and could not escape. When the fishermen returned, they scooped the fish out with dip nets. The photograph was taken in the early 1900s, when trap fishing was at its height.

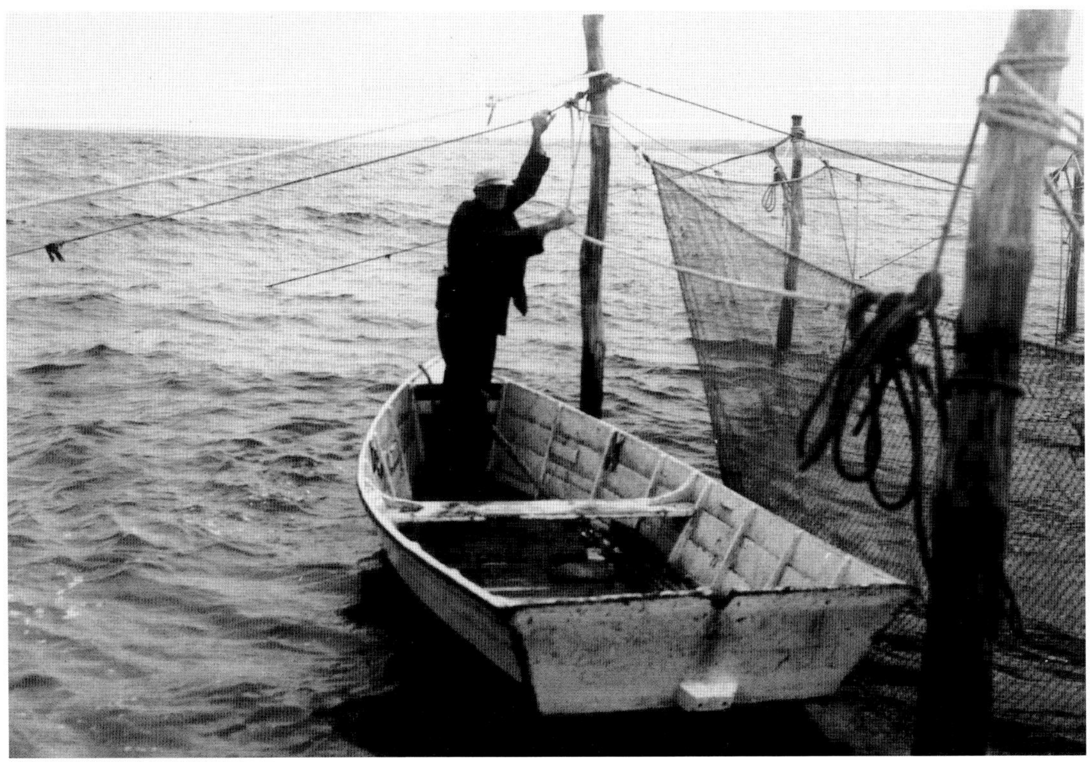

Capt. Norman Benson of Lambert's Cove in West Tisbury was one of the last of the trap fishermen. He is seen here tending his traps "on the north shore" in this undated photograph. Benson had traps as far away as Bourne. He fished until the 1930s.

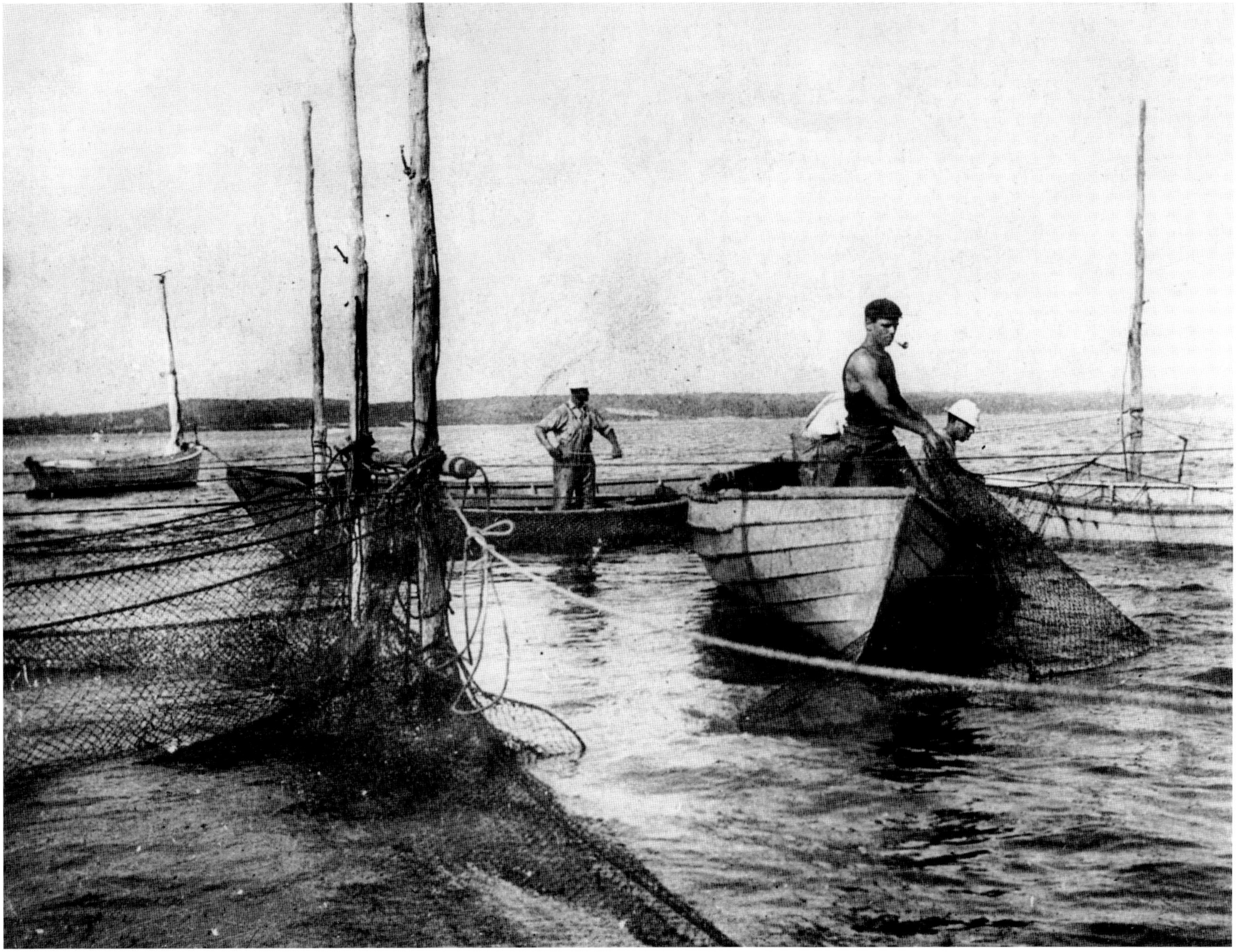

Once a familiar sight off the shores of Martha's Vineyard, trap fishing fell out of common practice by the 1930s. Fish traps required a lot of tending and mending to keep them intact and functioning. In this photograph from around 1915, Charlie Morgan (smoking the pipe) is working with traps off Menemsha, near the old brickyard. The other men have not been identified.

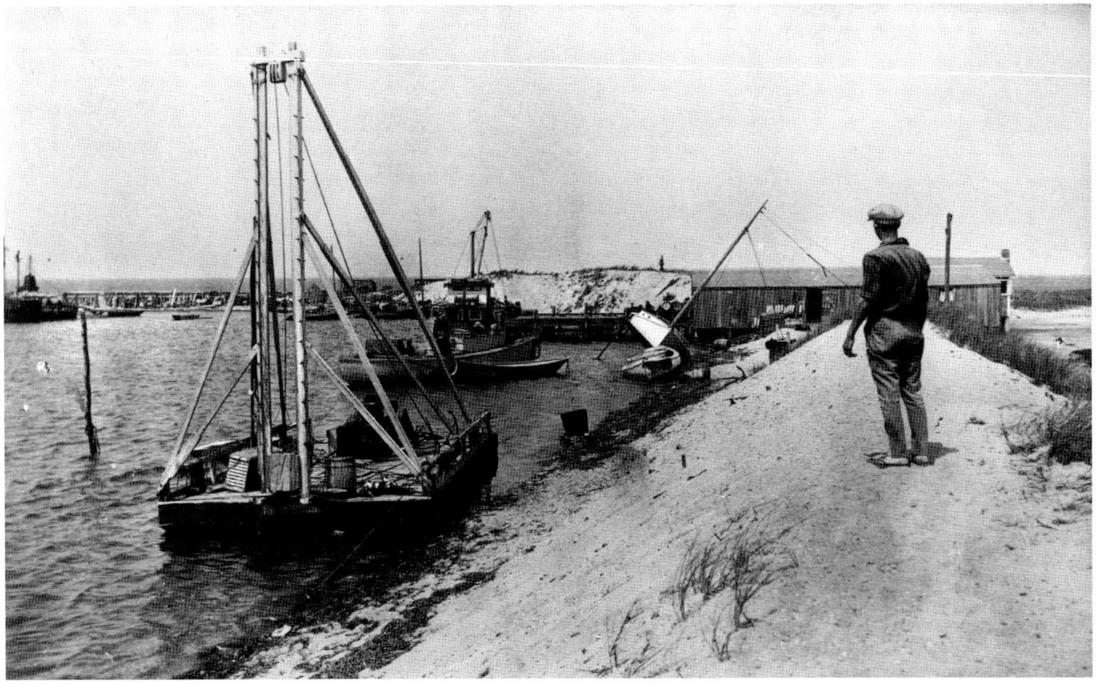

In order to place the traps, long stakes had to be driven into the ground. Nets with floats along the tops were attached to the stakes, creating an area that would catch and hold the fish safely long enough for the fishermen to return for them. This photograph shows one of the scows in the Menemsha Basin used for driving stakes.

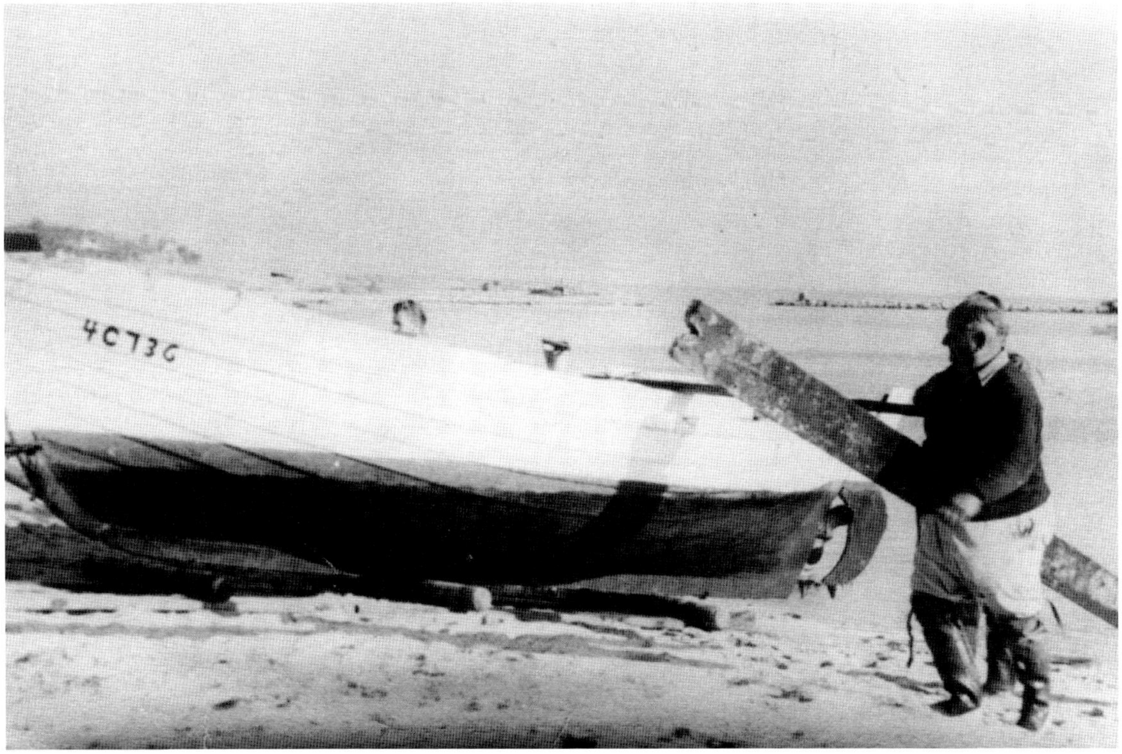

Rodney Cleveland (1893–1966) of Vineyard Haven was a fisherman. The double-end design of his Noman's Land boat allowed it to be pulled up onto the beach with relative ease when necessary. Here, he is hauling it out of the water for the winter. It is up on rollers and attached to a taut line at the bow, which would have been pulled by strong men, oxen, or a tractor.

Fishing shacks, where fishermen kept supplies and were able to sleep near the traps they tended, dotted the waterfront until recently. The simple structures were particularly vulnerable to storms and were never intended to be permanent. These were near Cedar Tree Neck beach in West Tisbury. Stakes for fish traps can be seen extending in lines above the water. (Photograph by Jeannette Ogden Thomas.)

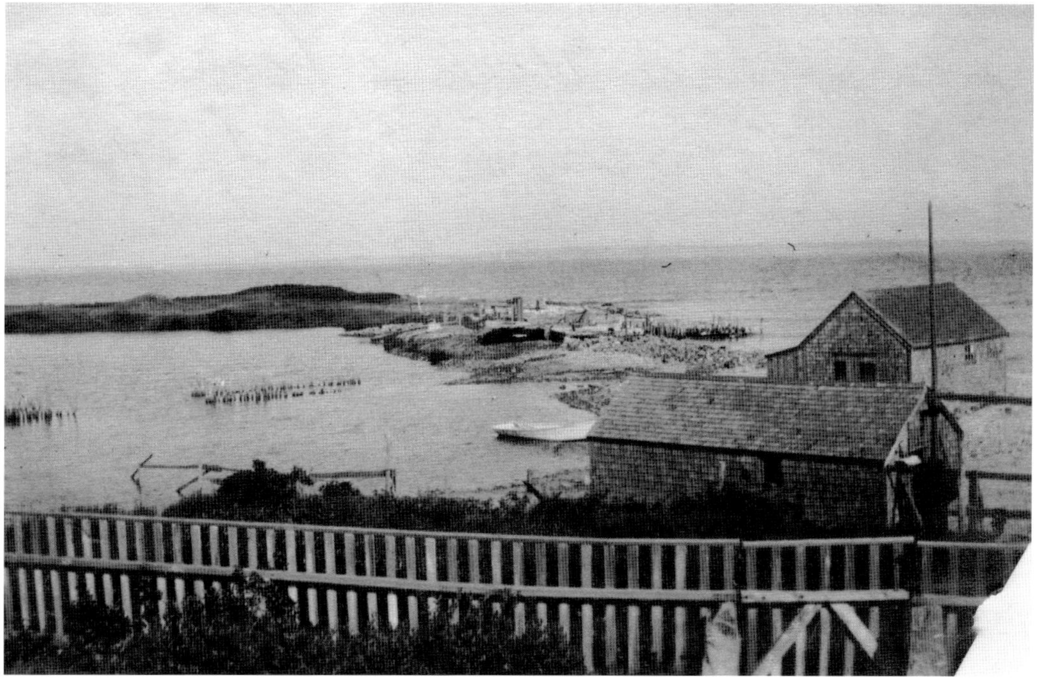

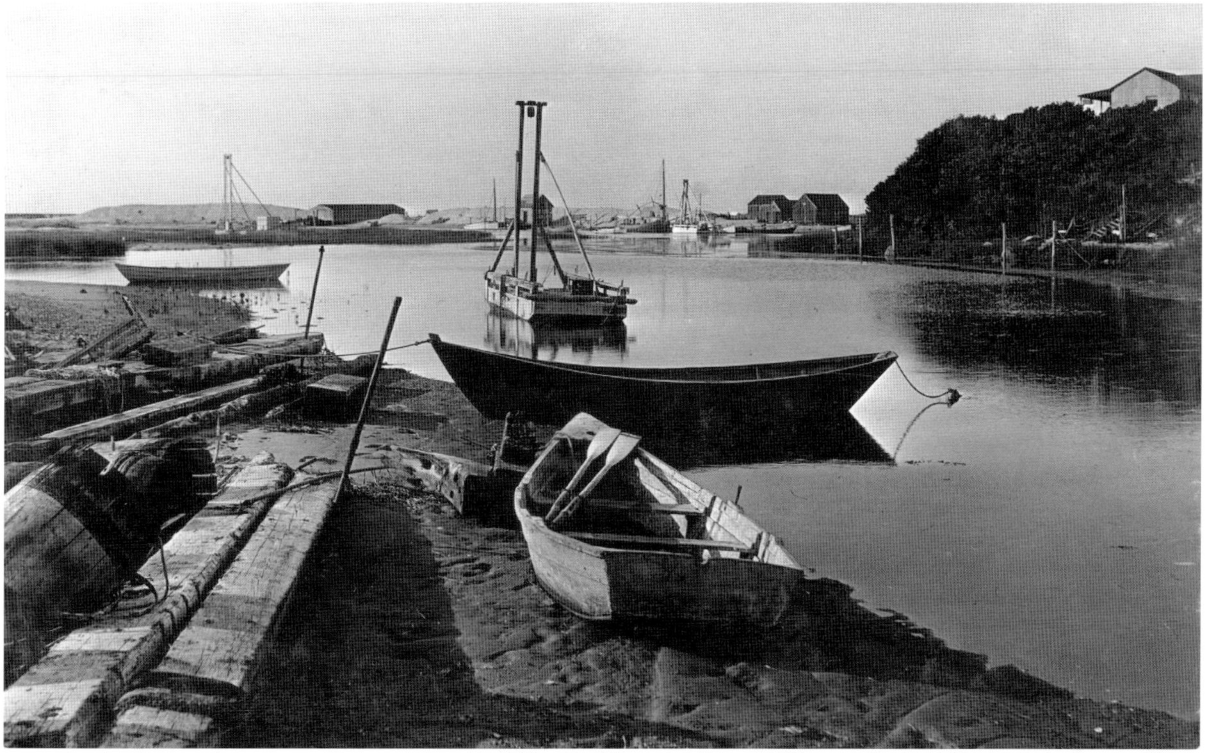

Menemsha Basin was the home port for many of the fishermen on Martha's Vineyard. As the years have passed and the village has changed, fallen on hard times, been destroyed, and then been rebuilt, it has become an emblem of a beautiful New England town where hardworking and tenacious people make a living.

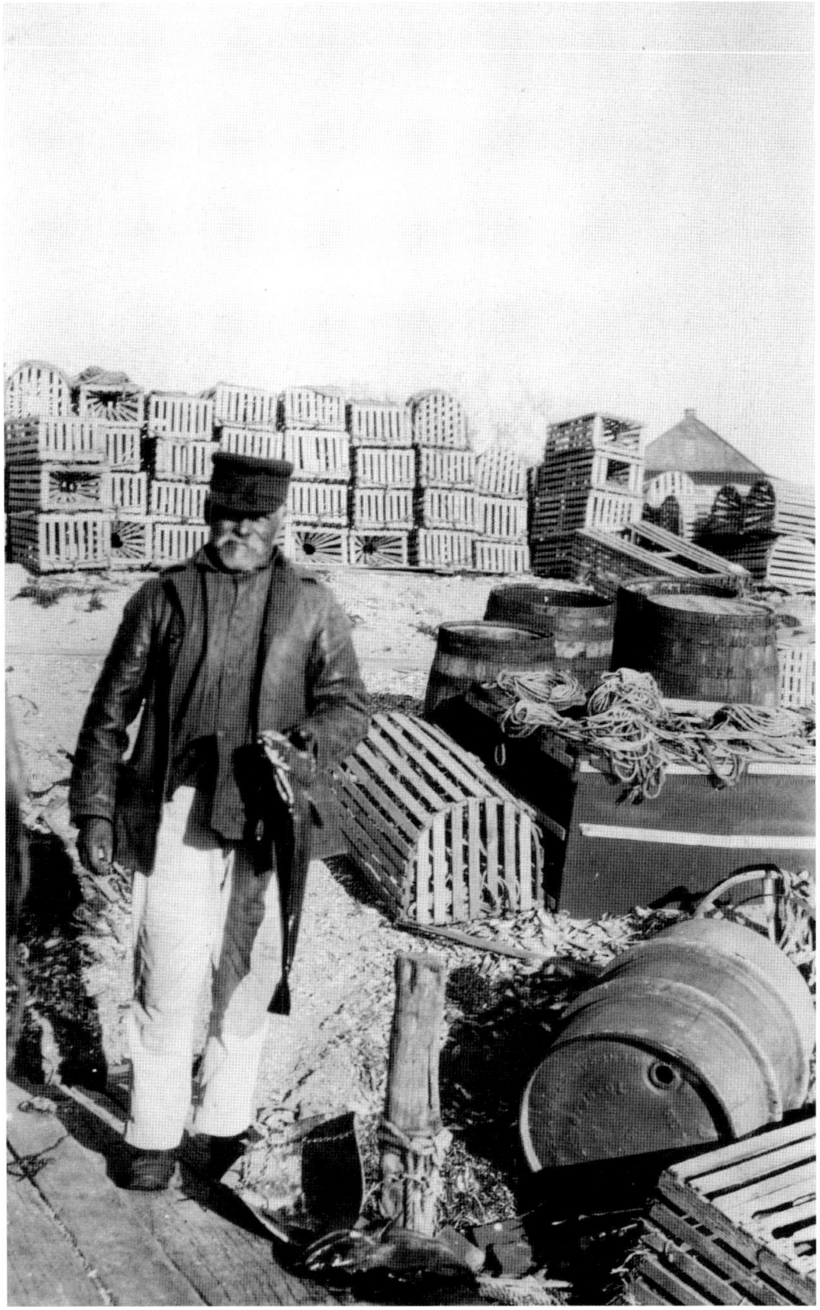

According to the inscription on the reverse of this photograph, "Gay Header John W. Belain (1860–1931) liked a cod now and then." His father was a sailor, but Belain spent a fair amount of time on land. He held public office as pound keeper, constable, and sealer of weights and measures.

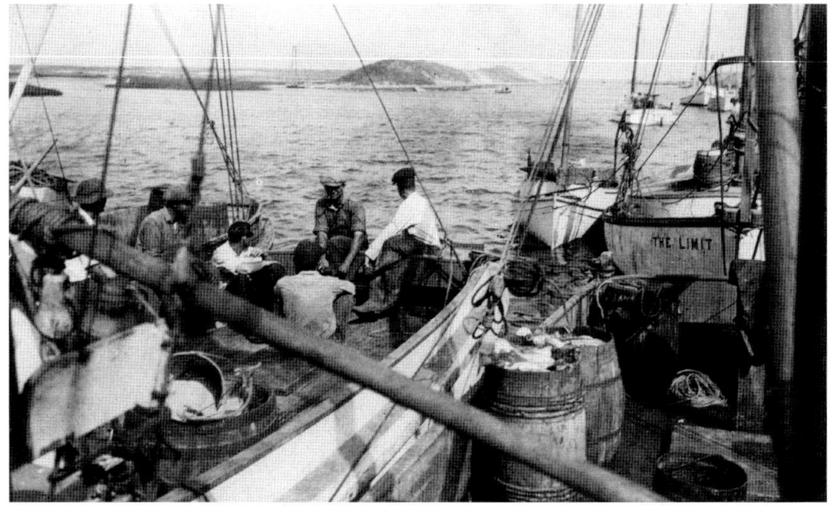

A fishing crew is enjoying a relaxing moment at the stern of their boat, one of many working out of Menemsha in the early 1900s.

The waters around Martha's Vineyard, especially the shallow great ponds, are ideal for scalloping. Fished both commercially and in smaller amounts for personal consumption, these tasty shellfish have long been in demand. In this photograph, Bjarne "John" and Louis Larsen are seen scalloping in Chilmark around 1950.

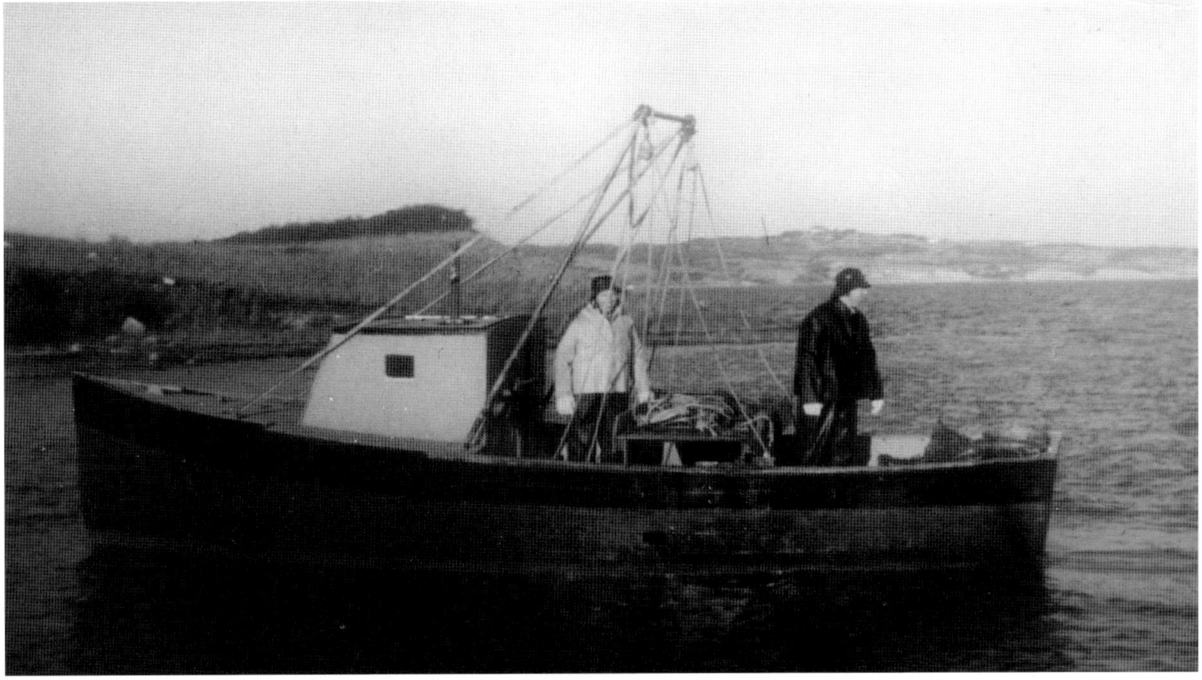

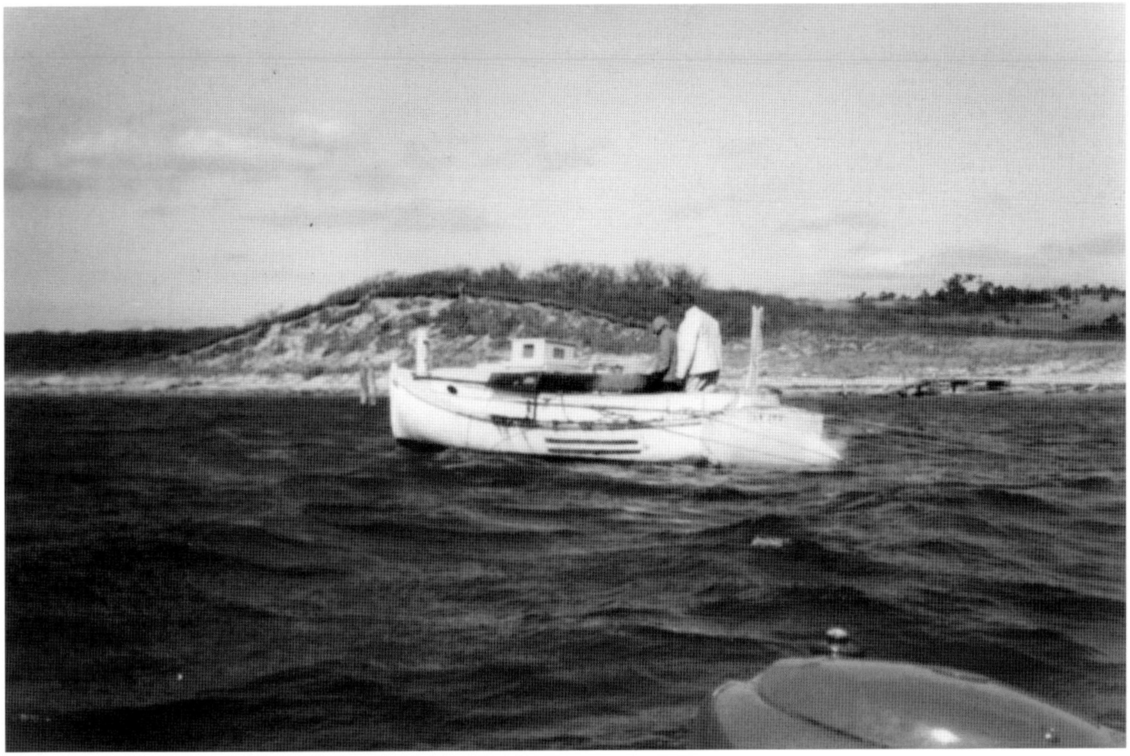

Vanity belonged to Oscar Pease, who fished from her and hired her out as a charter. Built by Manuel Swartz Roberts in 1927, she is considered the last working catboat. Here, Pease is seen scalloping in February 1965. He removed *Vanity*'s mast and, like many fishermen of his era, relied on an engine. *Vanity*, her mast restored, is now a sailing boat in the collection of the Martha's Vineyard Museum.

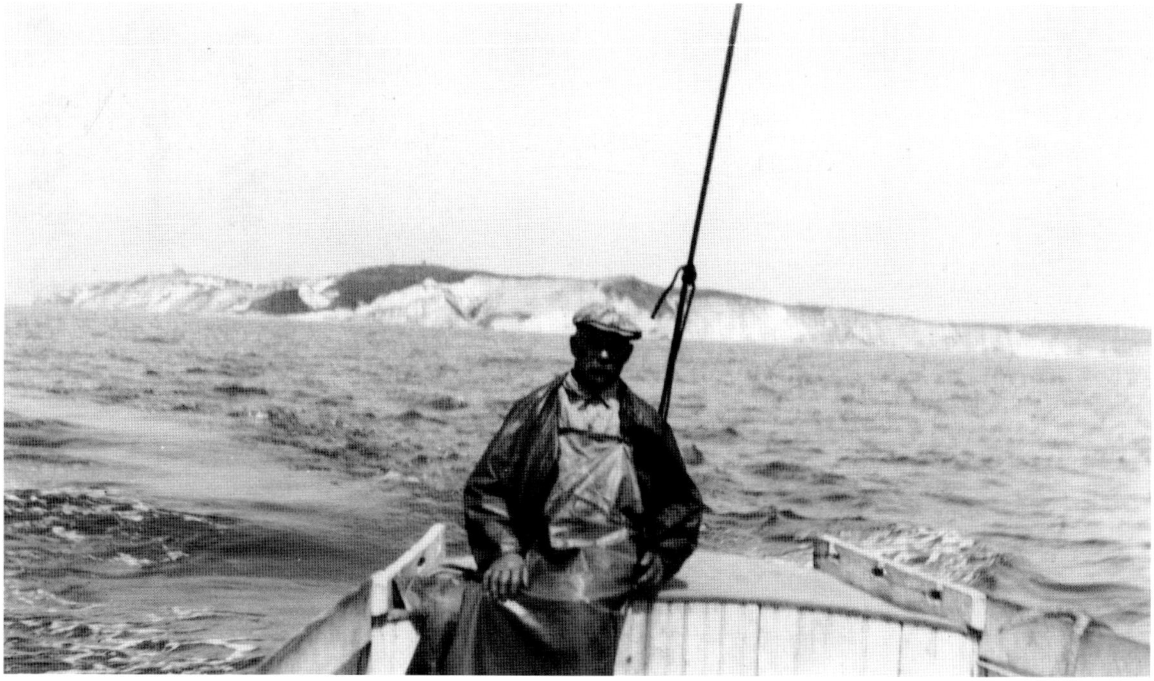

Harry Reed started out as a doctor and teacher. In the 1930s, he opted for a change of pace and scenery, embarking on a new career as a lobsterman in Menemsha. He is posed in his oilskin apron in this 1960 photograph, with the Gay Head cliffs visible in the background.

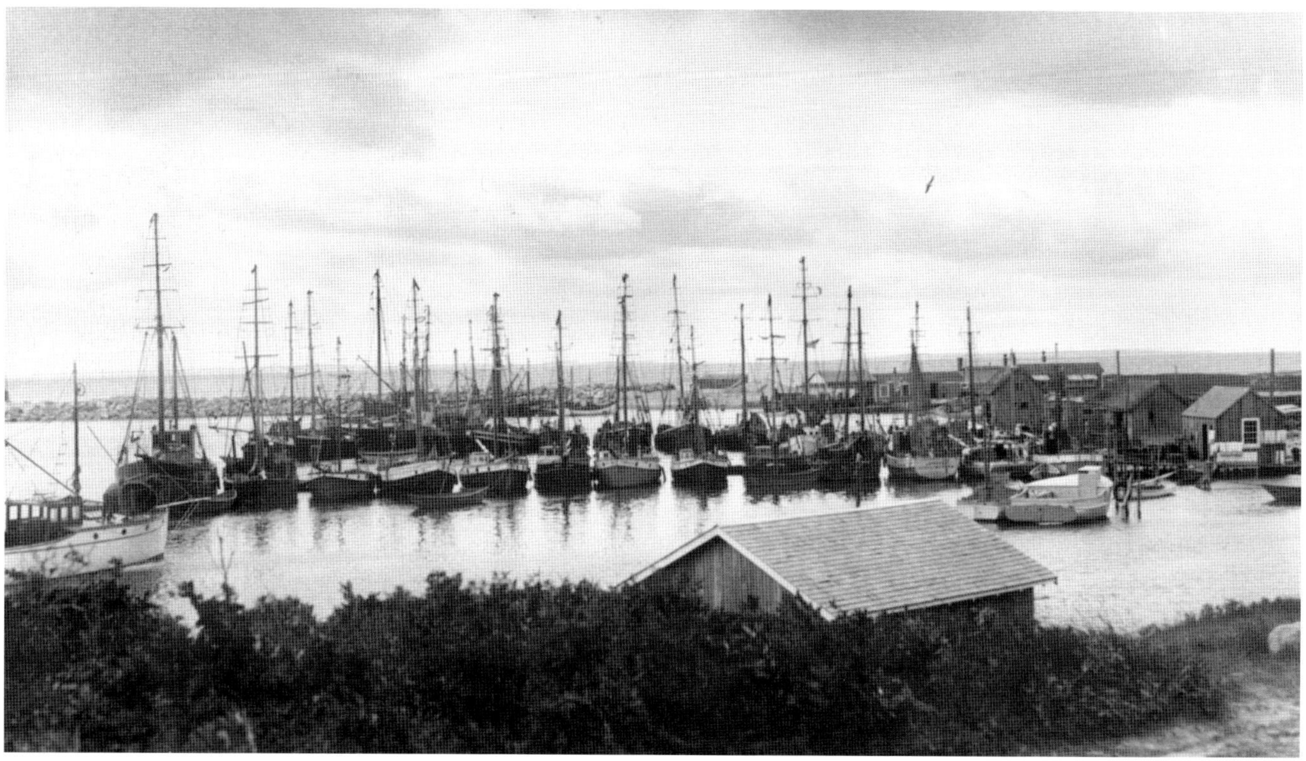

Menemsha is the embodiment of a picturesque fishing village, but it has also been a working fishing port for more than a century. In the early 1900s, when swordfishing was at its height, a sizeable fleet of schooners tied up at Menemsha. Later, fishermen took advantage of engine-powered boats and hired pilots to spot swordfish for them.

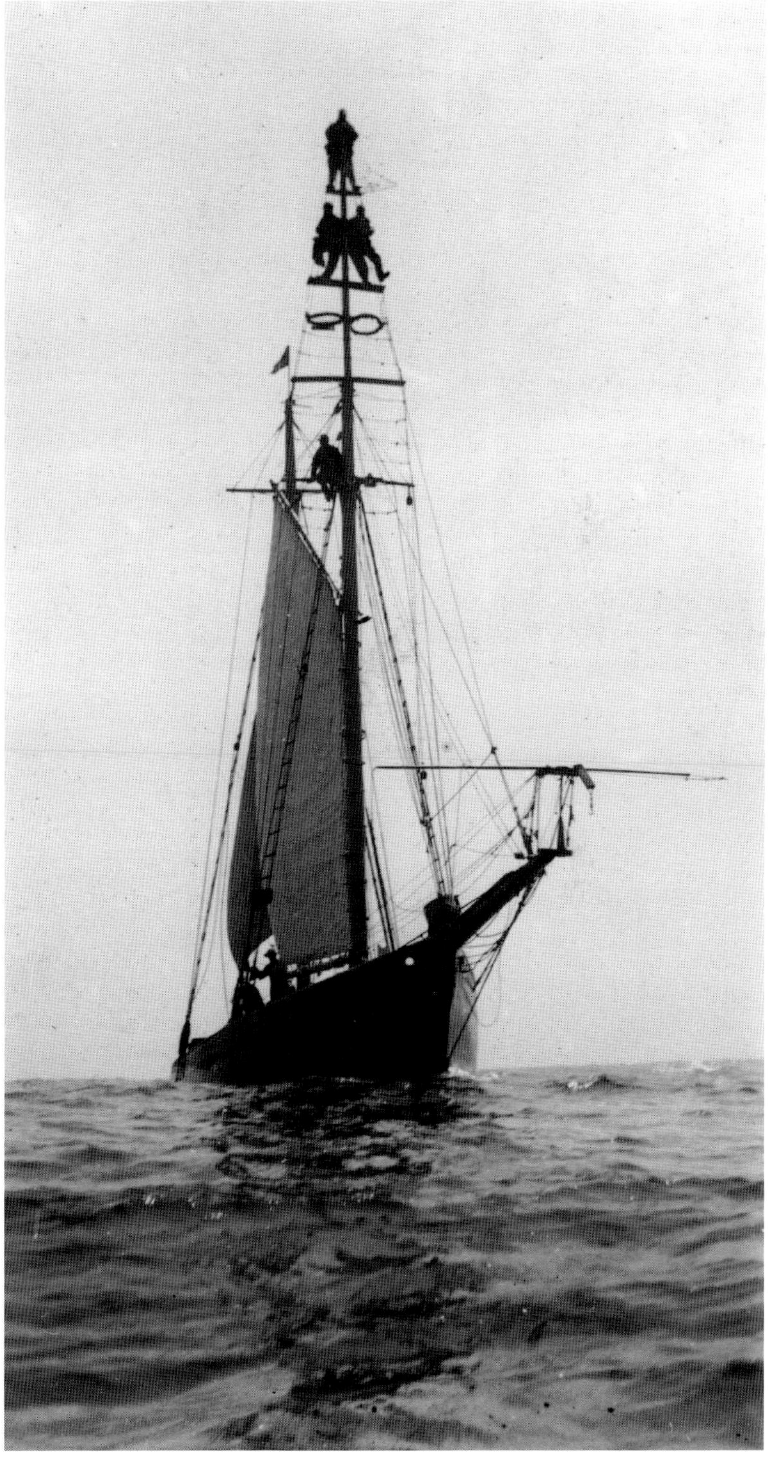

In this obviously posed and beautifully composed photograph taken from a nearby dory, the crew stands atop the mast of the swordfishing schooner *Hazel M. Jackson*. Based in Edgartown, the *Hazel M. Jackson* was skippered by Bob Jackson. For many years, he went out on two-week trips to the abundant fishing grounds of Georges Bank, between Cape Cod and Nova Scotia. These could be difficult and dangerous, and they had to be profitable to be worth the effort. Jackson was quoted in a 1936 *Vineyard Gazette* article as saying, "I don't think I'll go another year." The article continued, "The six fish of Jackson's last, broken trip, were small, weighing only 700 pounds. Eight days of rough seas at the start of the trip were too much of a drain for the steward George Paul's strength. The steward held to his cooking duties in the rolling craft until the weather eased off, when he turned in, exhausted. Mr. Paul was discharged from the Marine Hospital this week." (Photograph by Audrey M. Richard.)

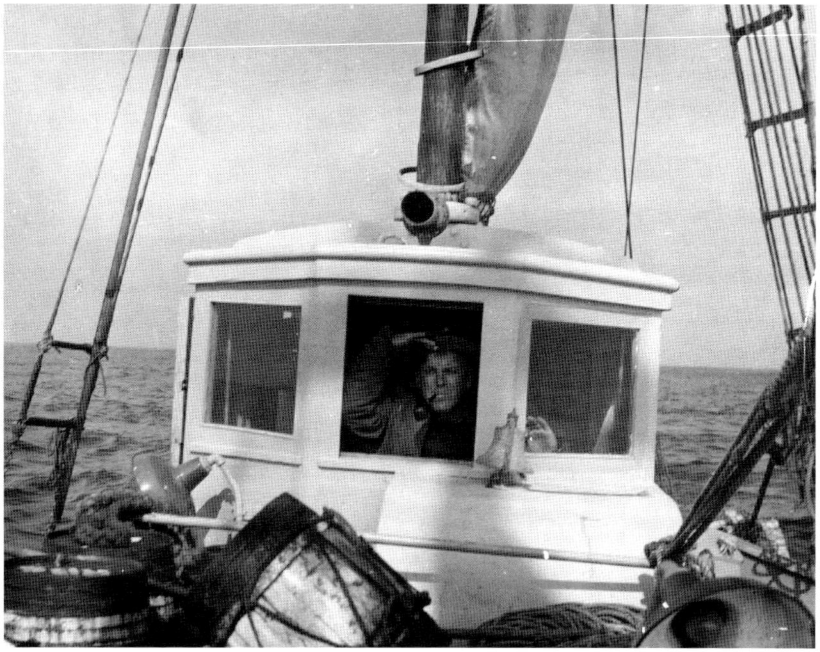

The name of this fisherman on the swordfishing schooner *R.B. Slenson*, seen here off Noman's Land in the summer of 1948, was not recorded. Some of the gear used for fishing is visible in the foreground of the photograph, including floating barrels and electric lights to illuminate the deck and the water around the schooner.

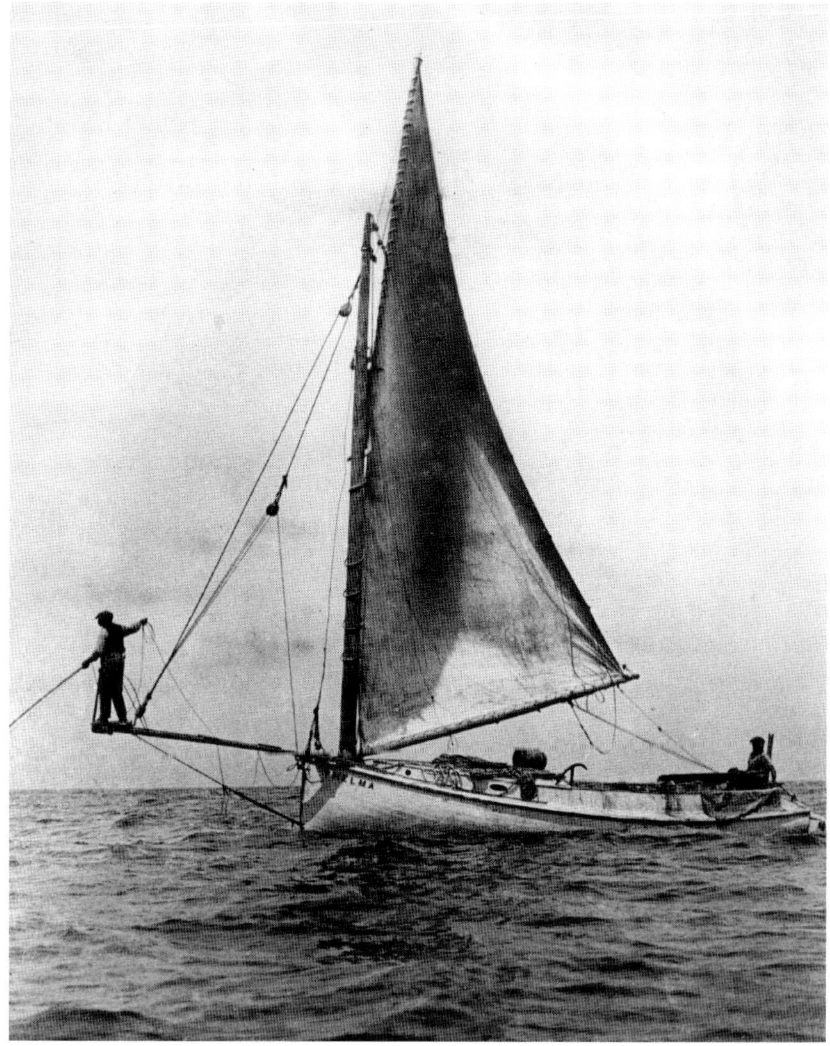

The catboat *Thelma* was based in Vineyard Haven and also fished out of Menemsha. In this photograph from 1915 or 1916, Charles B. Cleveland stands as the striker on the pulpit. His son Rodney V. Cleveland of Vineyard Haven is at the helm. The pulpit is supported by a block-and-tackle arrangement that was also used to hoist the swordfish onto the boat.

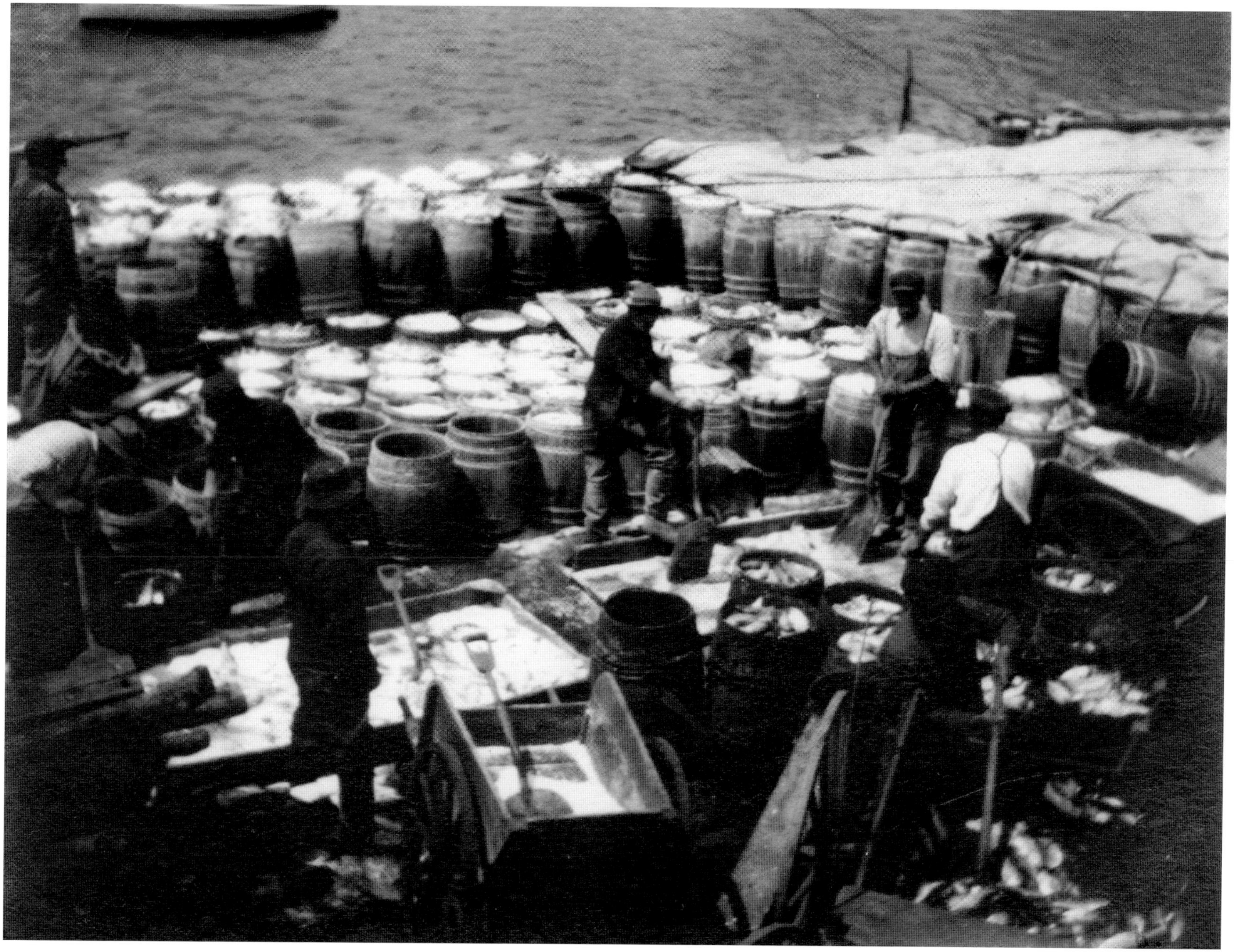

During the Civil War, while in camp in Virginia, Edgartown's Charles Macreading Vincent wrote, "A man can't get along and grow very fat on Government rations alone, especially when he has a delicate appetite and is so situated that he is deprived of the staff of life, that is to say, Herring." Here, 2,800 pounds of Mattakesett herring awaits transport to market on Osborn's Wharf in Edgartown. (Photograph by Walter S. Osborn.)

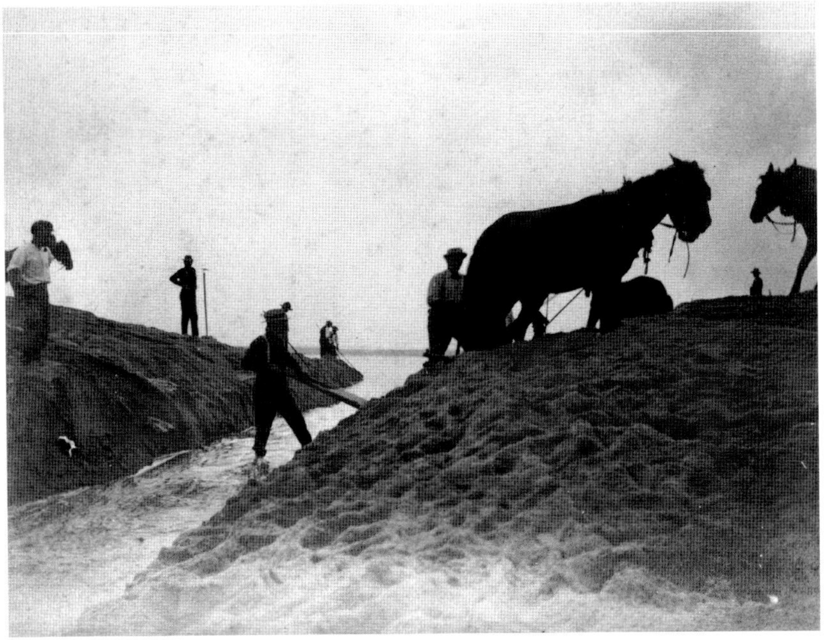

The great ponds were, and still are, periodically opened to the sea to control the water levels. In earlier days, opening the ponds at the right time of year also allowed herring to come through to be caught. A herring fishery was operated at Mattakesett Creek in Edgartown for more than 100 years. Other towns also did this. This late-1800s or early-1900s photograph shows the opening of Tisbury Great Pond.

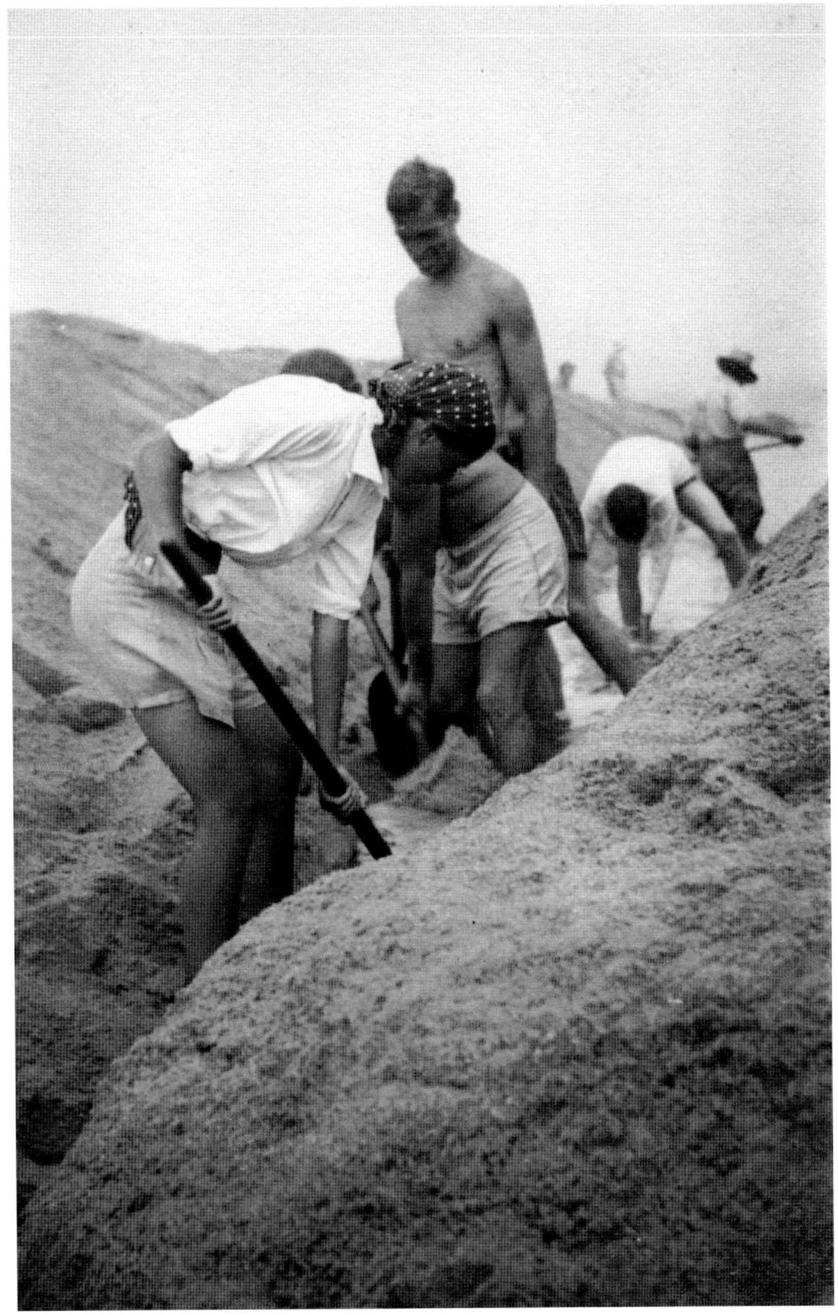

In 1933, Tisbury Great Pond was opened by a group of men and women who, in the traditional manner, shoveled the sand away by hand. Before long, thousands of herring, also called alewives, began to rush through the opening. (Photograph by Peg Knowles.)

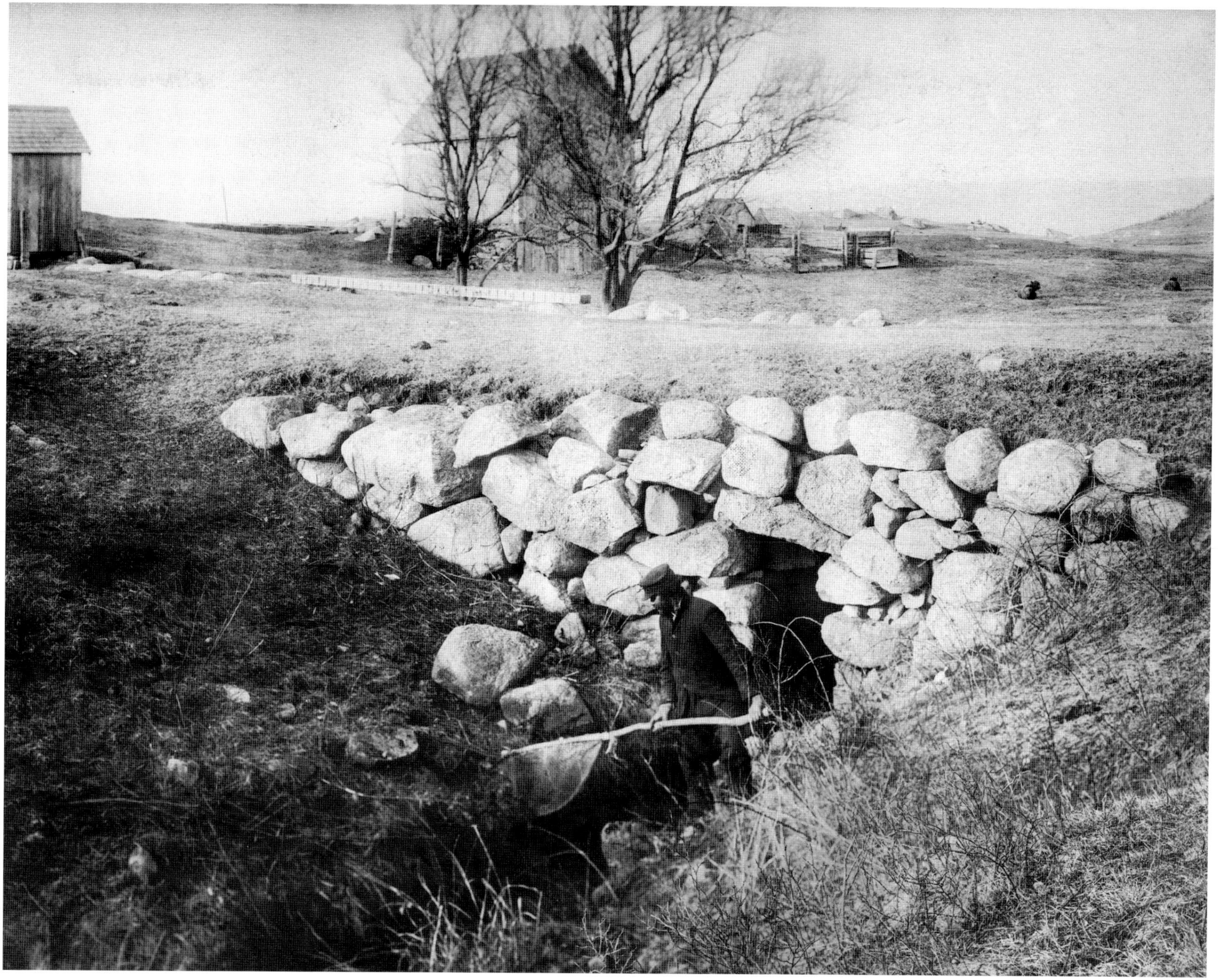

In this undated photograph from Gay Head, a man is using a dip net to catch herring. Here, herring were trapped by a weir, a fence-like wooden obstruction placed across the stream where they were trying to swim. This allowed them to be easily scooped up with a dip net.

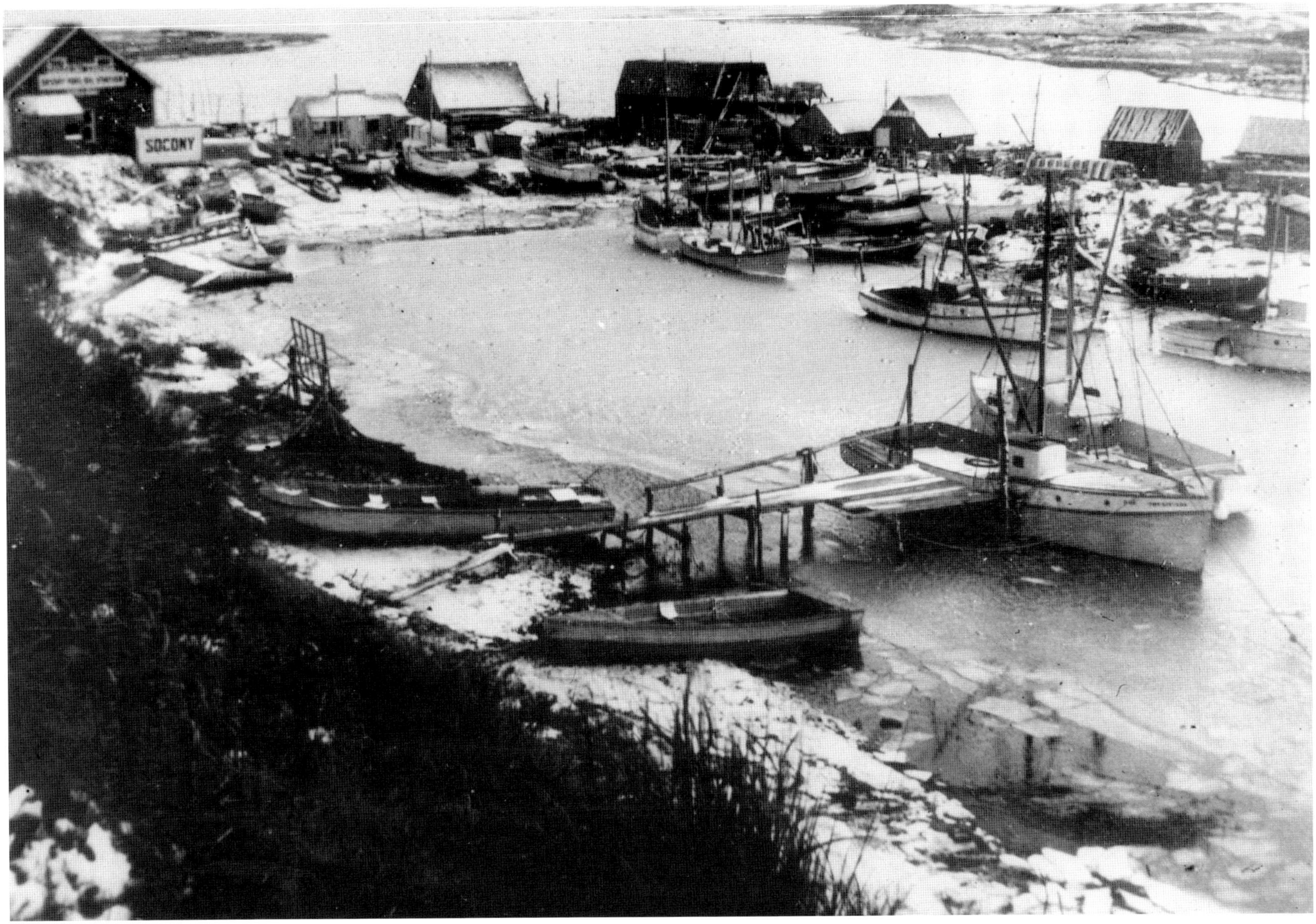

Here, *Two Sisters* is tied up at Ralph Tilton's dock in Menemsha. Snow and chunks of ice floating near the shore indicate that this undated photograph was taken in the winter. The configuration of the buildings place the date before the hurricane of 1938.

OPPOSITE: This late-1800s photograph of a farm on Indian Hill in West Tisbury shows a common up-island arrangement of farmhouse, barn, and walls made from stones that were cleared from the fields. Farmers worked around boulders left behind by the retreat of the glacial ice sheet 18,000 years ago. (Photograph by Henry Platt.)

TWO

LAND AND COMMUNITY

Farmers worked the Vineyard lands and raised livestock, though it could be a difficult and lean living. By no means assured of prosperity, they often combined several jobs in order to subsist. It was common for men to ship out on whaling or trading voyages and then return to help out on the farm for a while, or to have several trades in succession. One such man was William Jernigan (1728–1817) of Edgartown. He apprenticed to a builder and then worked at that trade for seven years before going to sea for a decade. When he returned, he engaged in trading land, and then he farmed and traded, all before the age of 60.

Agriculture left its mark on the land. Growing crops required fields, and sheep farming required pastures, which were often defined by walls made from the stones cleared away from the fields. Though pastures, stone walls, and sheep farms remain today, early photographs commonly show many more cleared areas that are now fully wooded.

Every town had its own post office and at least a small store for the convenience of its residents, but some Vineyarders who lived outside the larger towns had to travel to Vineyard Haven or Edgartown, which had the busiest downtowns. There they could find more goods and services.

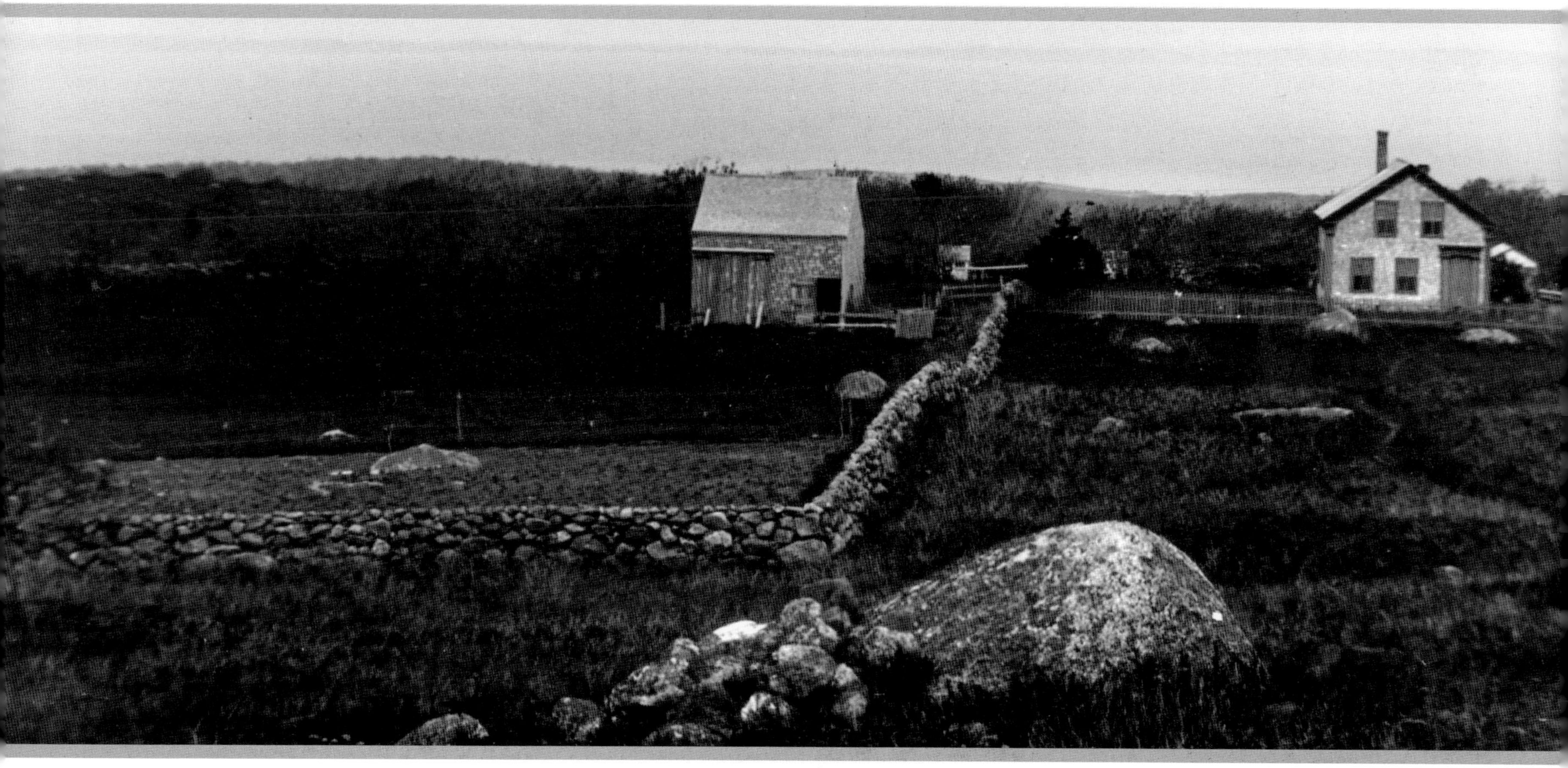

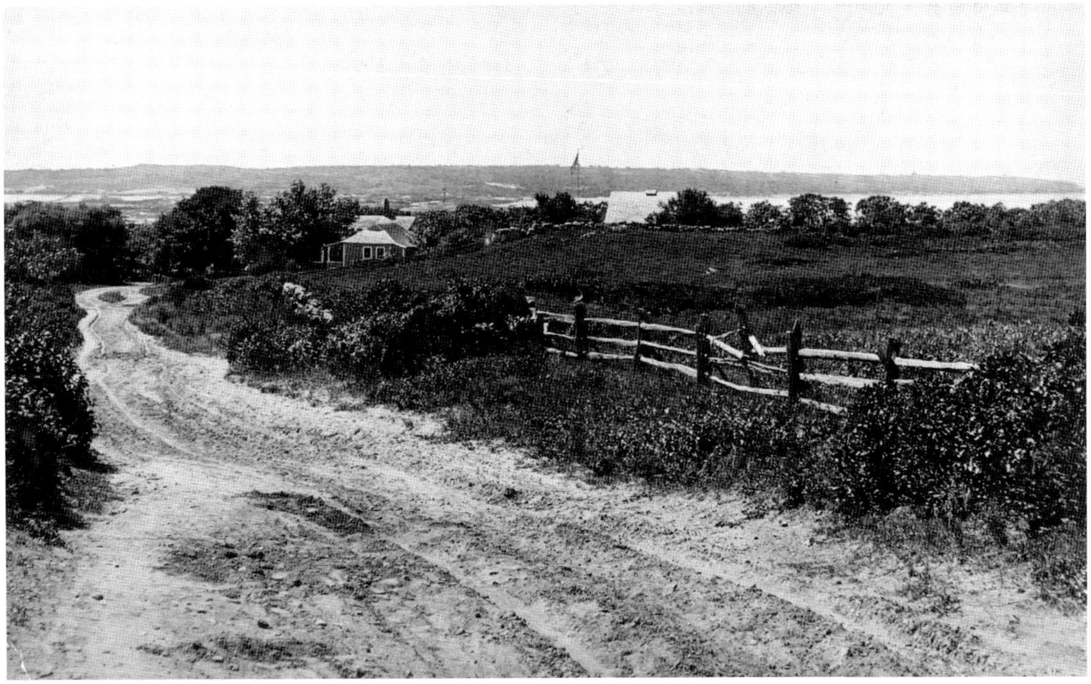

The note scrawled on the reverse of this photograph reads, "Creek Hill before hard surfacing." A traveler does not need to go far on Martha's Vineyard to encounter winding and deeply rutted dirt roads. In the 1800s and early 1900s, it was even more difficult to get from place to place. This necessitated allowing for a lot of time to journey even the short distances between towns. Creek Hill overlooks Menemsha Creek.

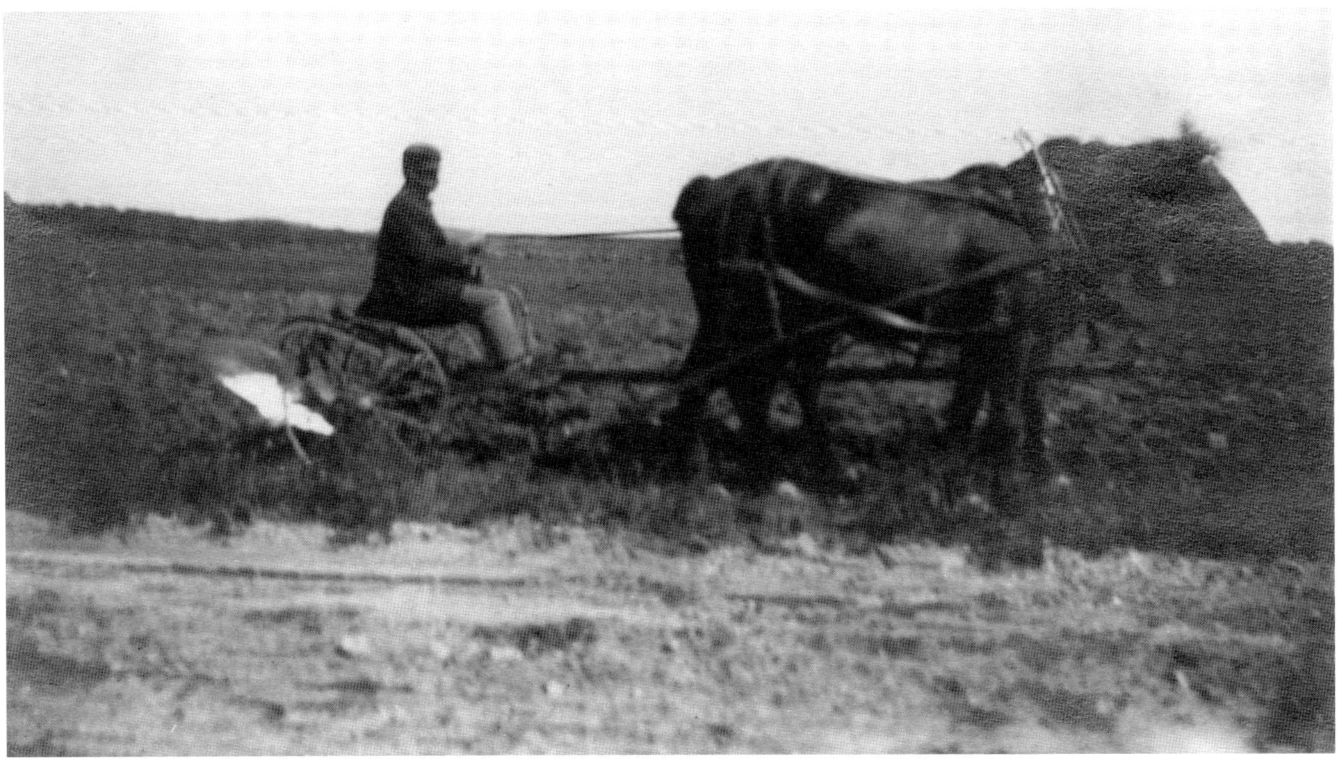

In its early years, Seven Gates Farm, in West Tisbury, was both a retreat for the family of Harvard professor Nathaniel Shaler and a working farm. Beginning in 1887, Shaler purchased several contiguous farms totaling 1,600 acres. Seven Gates, named for the number of gates Shaler had to pass through to get to his house, had a dairy and produced food crops. (Photograph by Jeannette Ogden Thomas.)

Chilmark's town hall stands at Beetlebung Corner, the quiet center of a small town. When the building was constructed in 1897, the town's population was less than 300. Farming and fishing were the primary occupations. The beginning of a seasonal population increase had begun as well, with a few wealthy off-islanders coming to summer estates in the area.

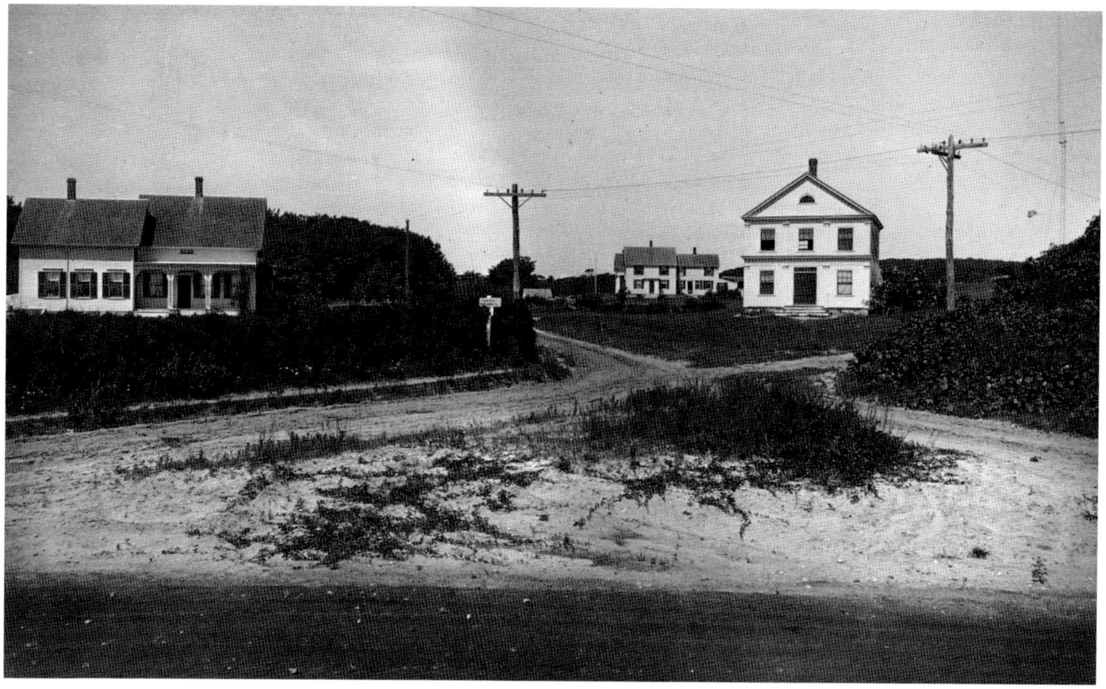

Gardiner Hammond built this complex of house and outbuildings at Squibnocket, the southwestern tip of the island. The treeless vista in this 1939 photograph is typical of many sites on Martha's Vineyard in the 1800s and early 1900s that subsequently became more heavily wooded as farming began to play less of a role in the island economy.

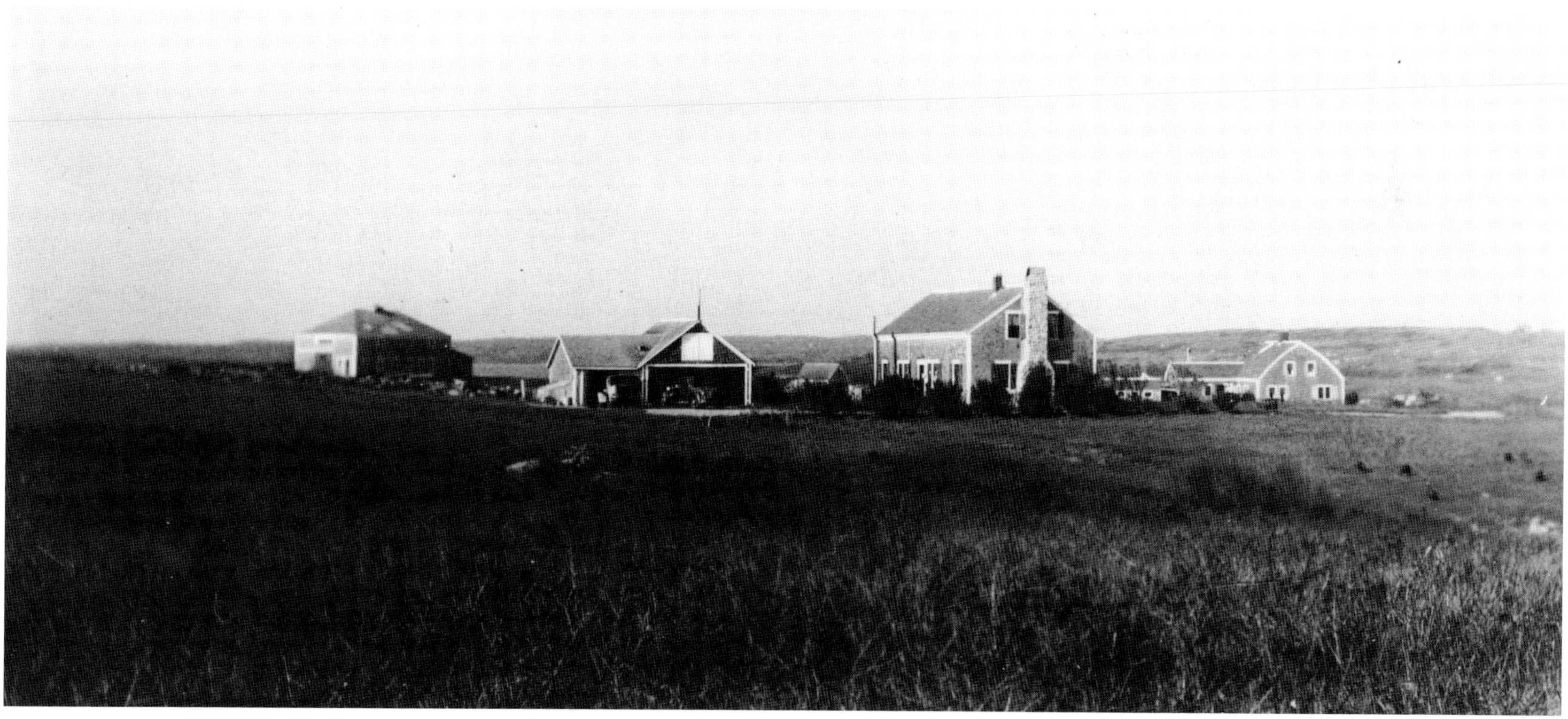

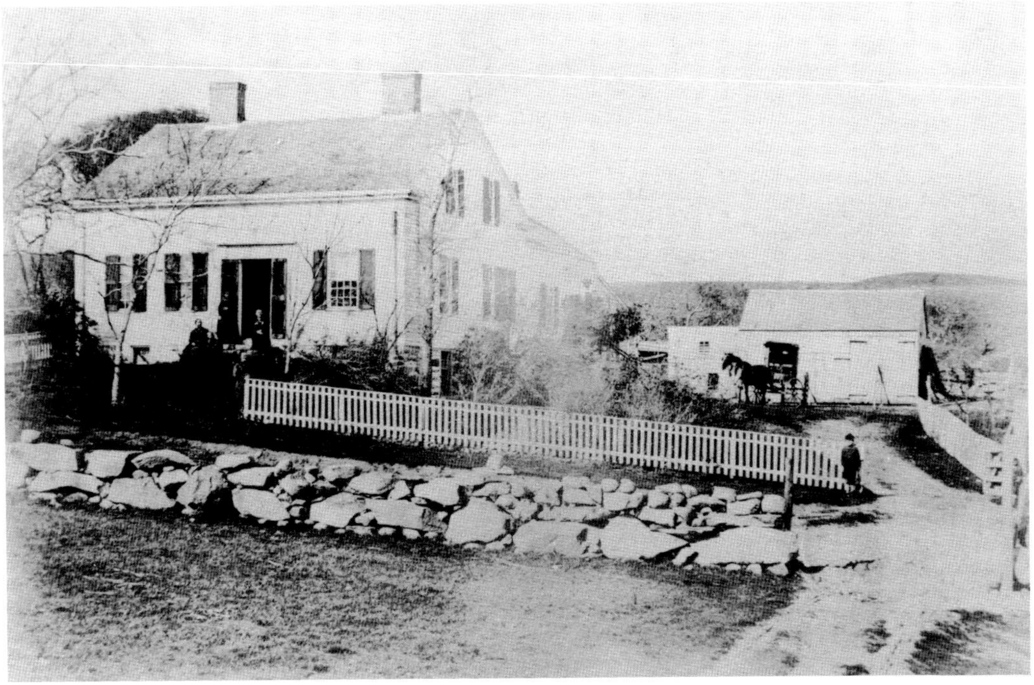

The Tilton house, on Chilmark's Middle Road, dates from the 1700s. The 1850 census shows 15 Tilton households in Chilmark. The occupations recorded for the heads of household were almost evenly divided between farmer and mariner. Often, younger men in farming households were listed as mariners, suggesting that it was common for men to go to sea before settling on the farm.

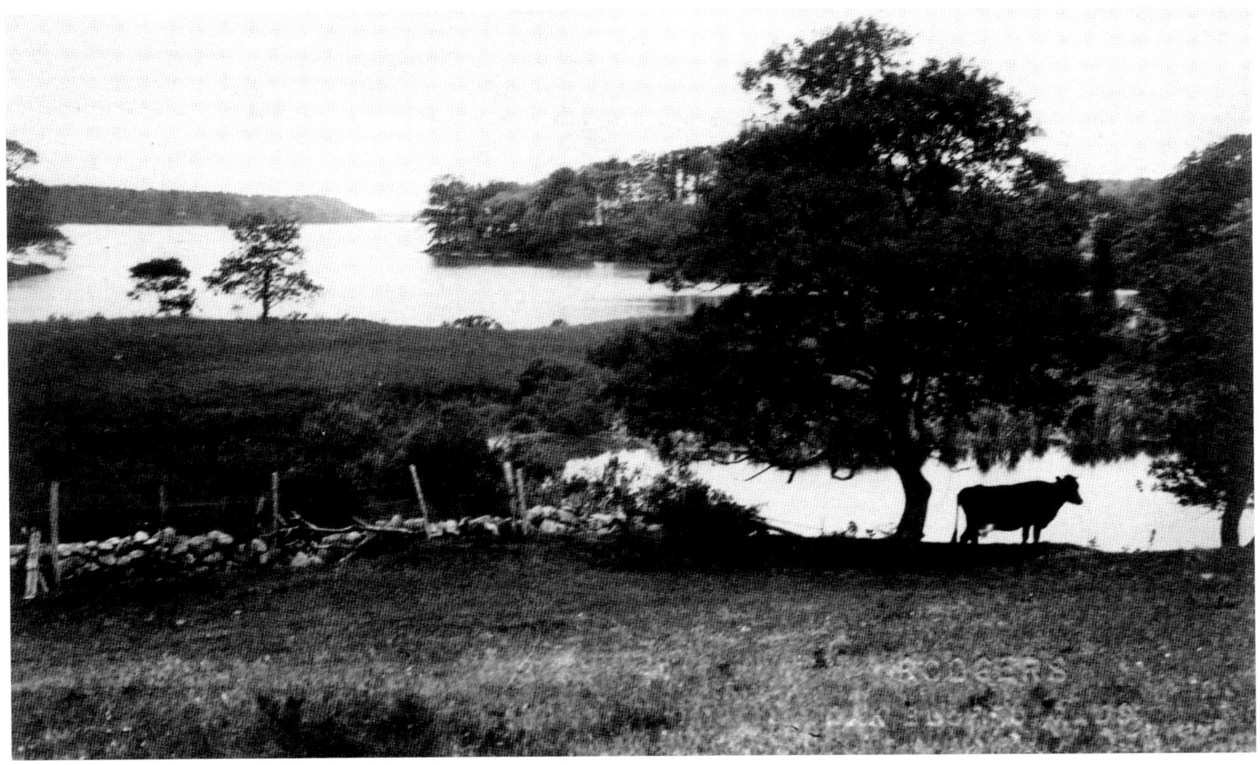

The busy and relatively populous harbor region of Tisbury (Vineyard Haven) overshadowed the rural character of the southern part of the town. In 1884, West Tisbury successfully separated from Tisbury to form a new town with a government that it felt would better represent its agrarian priorities. But this did not mean that Tisbury was no longer a farming community, as this image from Tashmoo, in the northwest part of the town, shows. (Photograph by Stanley E. Rodgers.)

By 1916, the telegraph and the automobile had reached West Tisbury, albeit by a dirt road. But the clear fields, fences, and barns are evidence that farming, especially sheep farming, remained a vital part of up-island life. To the growing number of summer residents who chose to settle here, the area's remoteness was one of its attractions. (Photograph by H.M.Wood.)

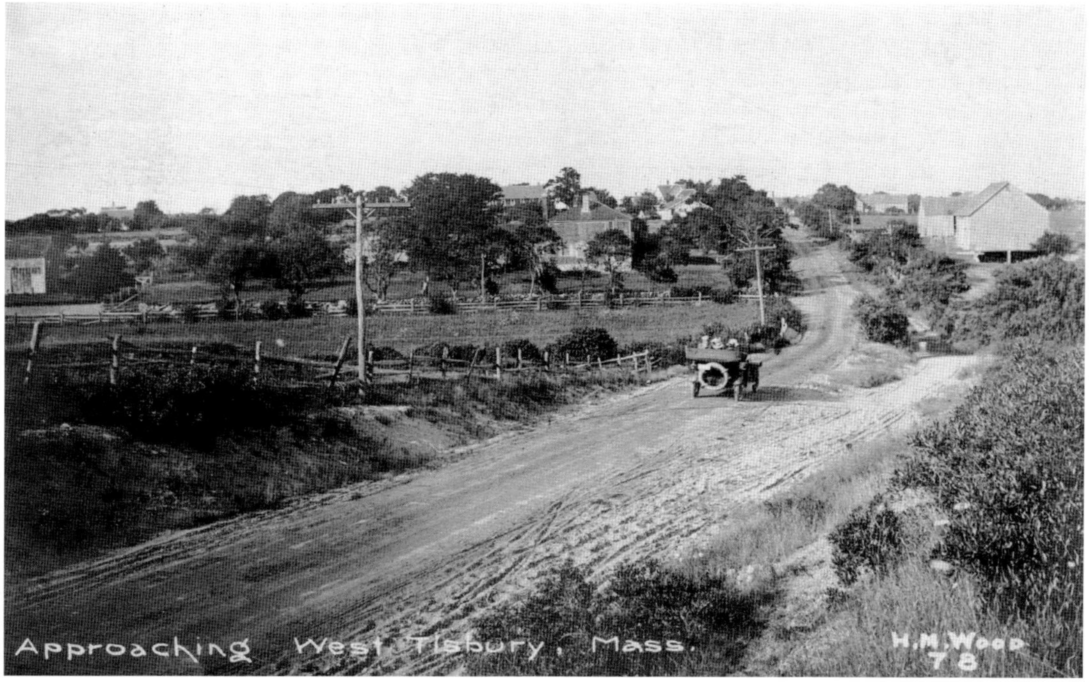

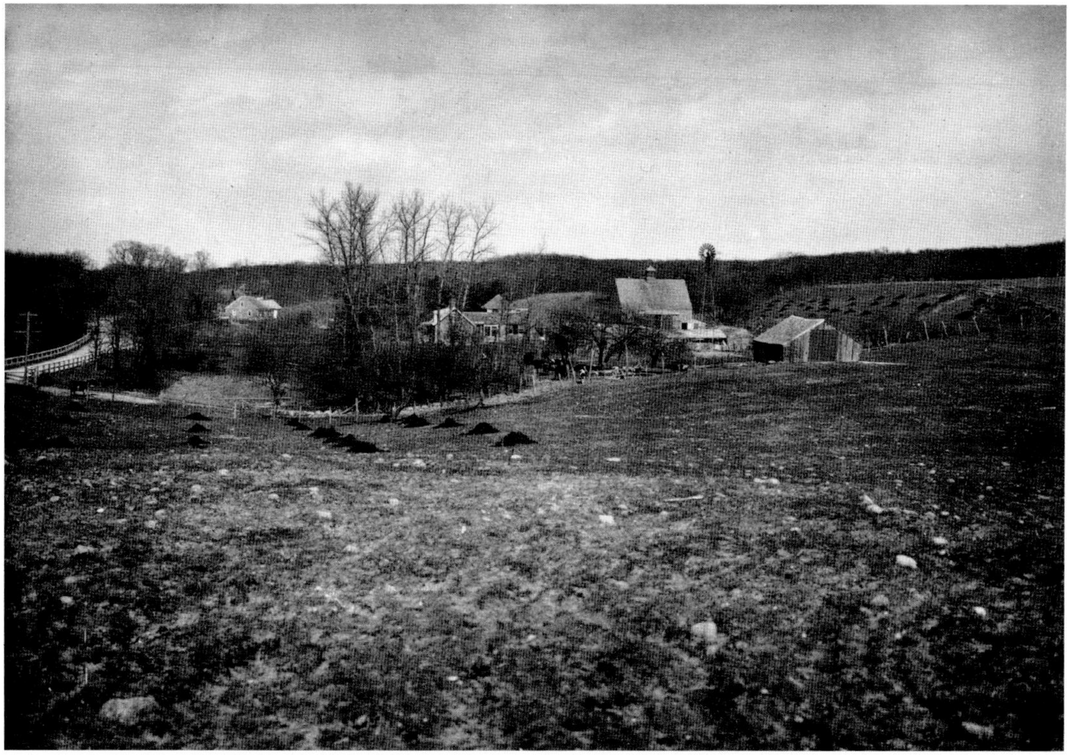

This Vineyard Haven property on State Road was farmed in the past by members of the Norton, Tilton, and Mayhew families. Later, it was owned by Mai Fane. It is now part of the Martha's Vineyard Land Bank as the Tisbury Meadow Preserve.

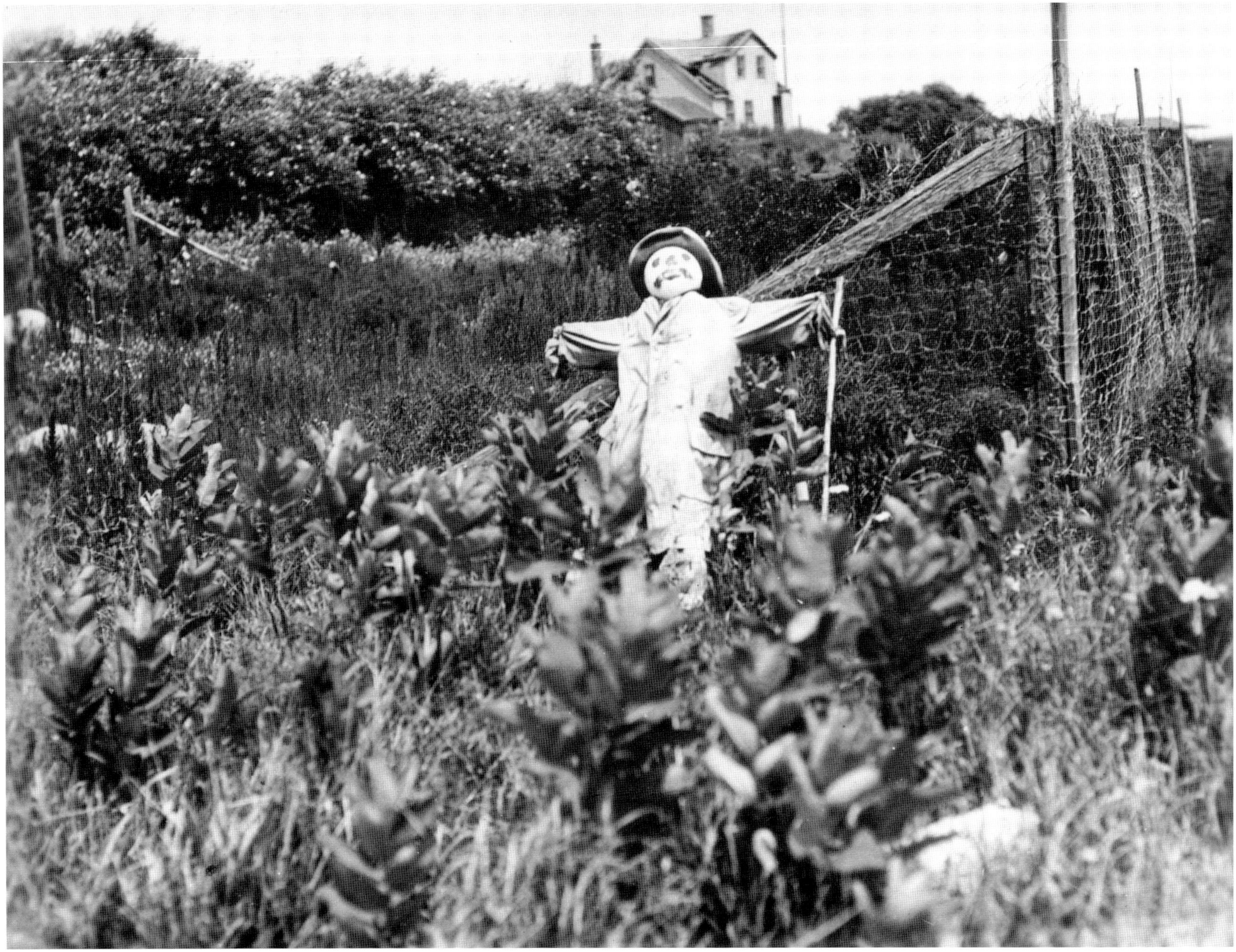

On Noman's Land, the Wood family truly dwelt apart. The family worked as caretakers for the island's owner, Joshua Crane, of Dedham. They grew food for themselves in addition to their fishing and livestock farming. By the 1920s, growing food was no longer a strict necessity for many Vineyarders, but it remained important for the very few who lived on this small island, which is south of the Vineyard and part of Chilmark.

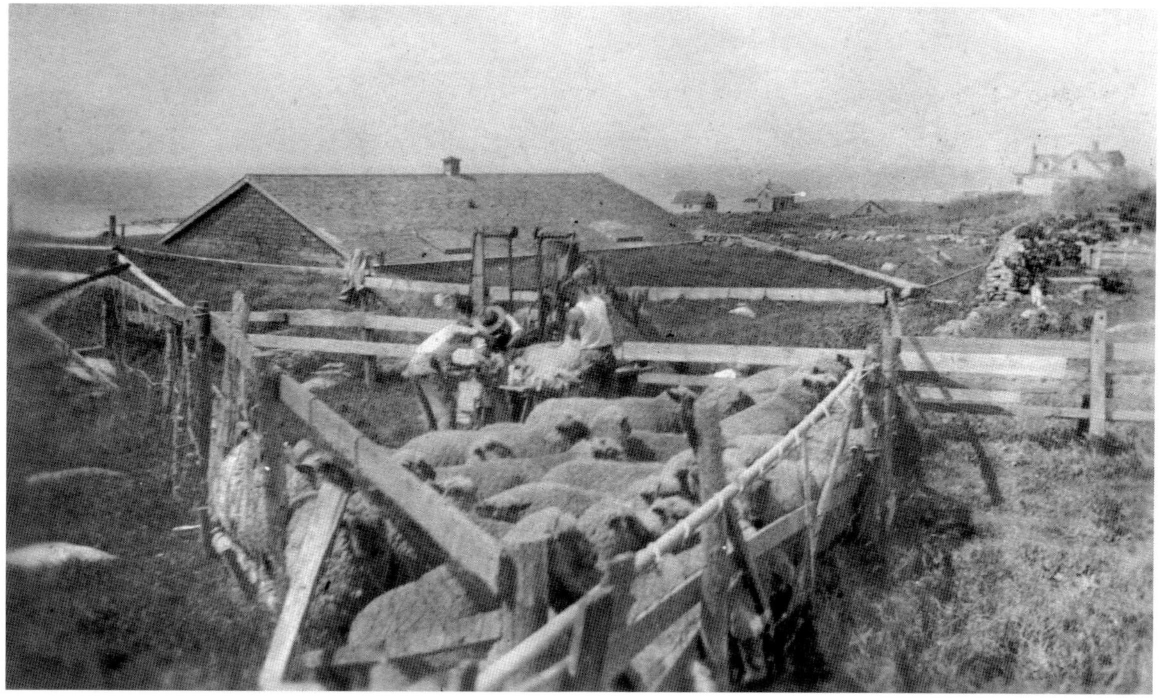

When shearing time came in June 1930, the sheep that had roamed Noman's Land were herded together and sheared in their pen. They can be seen in the photograph above huddling as far as they could from the men who wielded the clippers. Once the wool was bagged, it was loaded onto a horse cart to be taken to the *Flit*, Ralph Wood's powerboat. In the photograph below, Bertrand and Cameron Wood await the *Flit*, which would take the wool on the next leg of its journey to market.

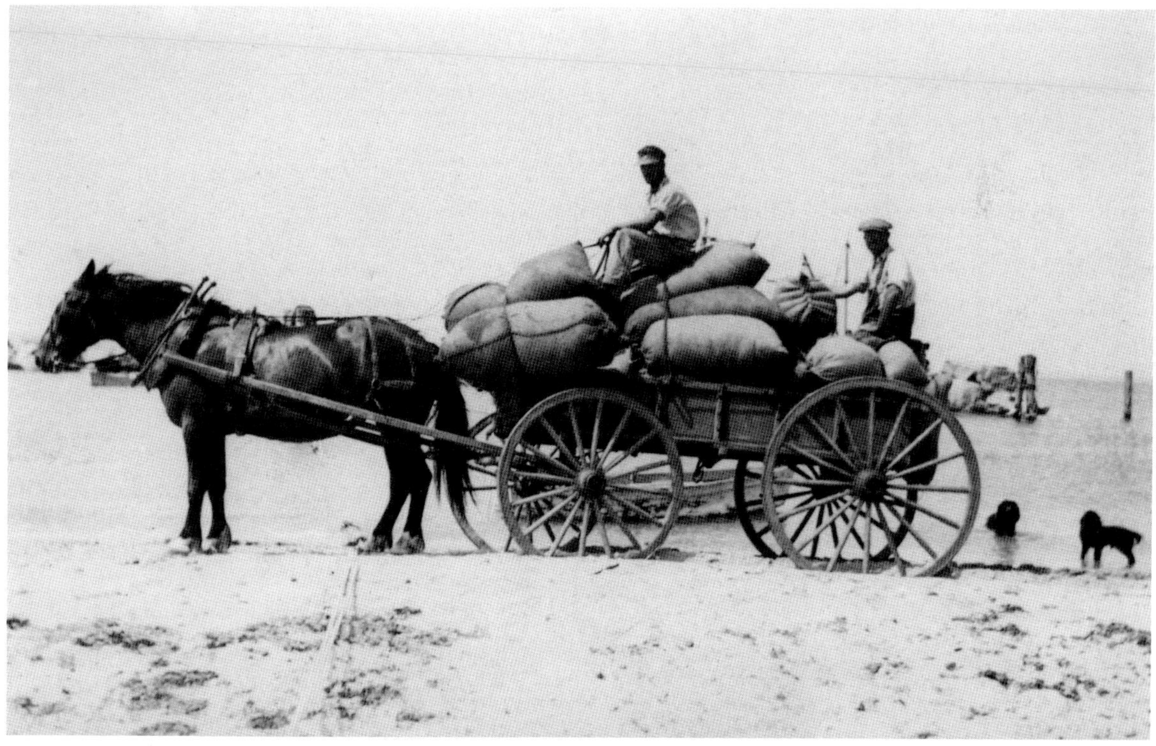

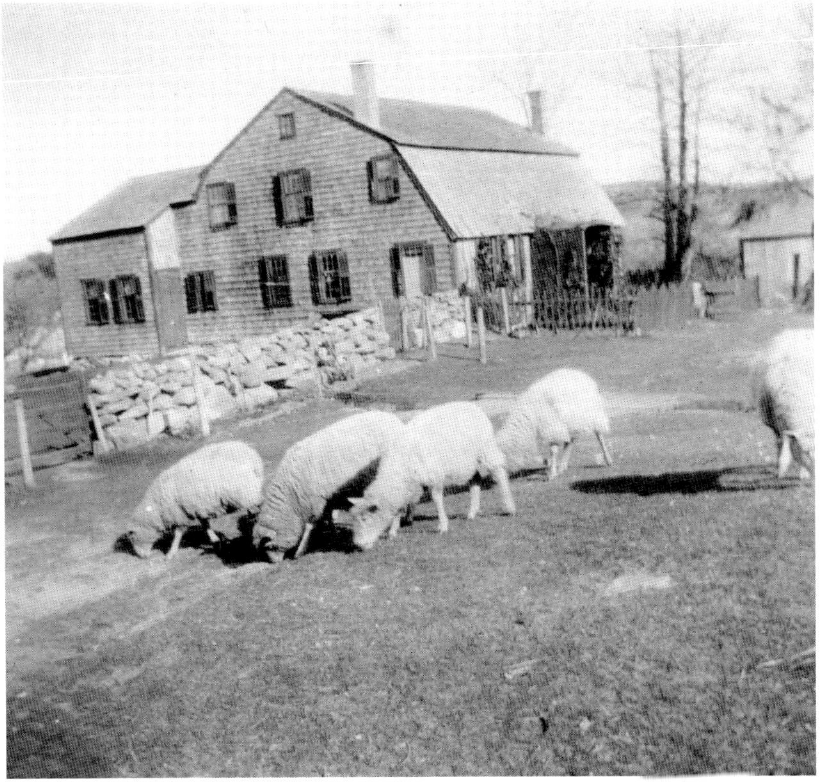

Sheep graze near the Skiff house in Vineyard Haven around the 1920s. The rocky Vineyard soil made growing crops difficult, but it was fine for grazing sheep. One of the few Revolutionary War incidents that occurred on the island was Grey's Raid, which resulted in British forces seizing 10,000 sheep and 3,000 oxen. Sheep farming continued to be an important contributor to the island's economy through the 1800s.

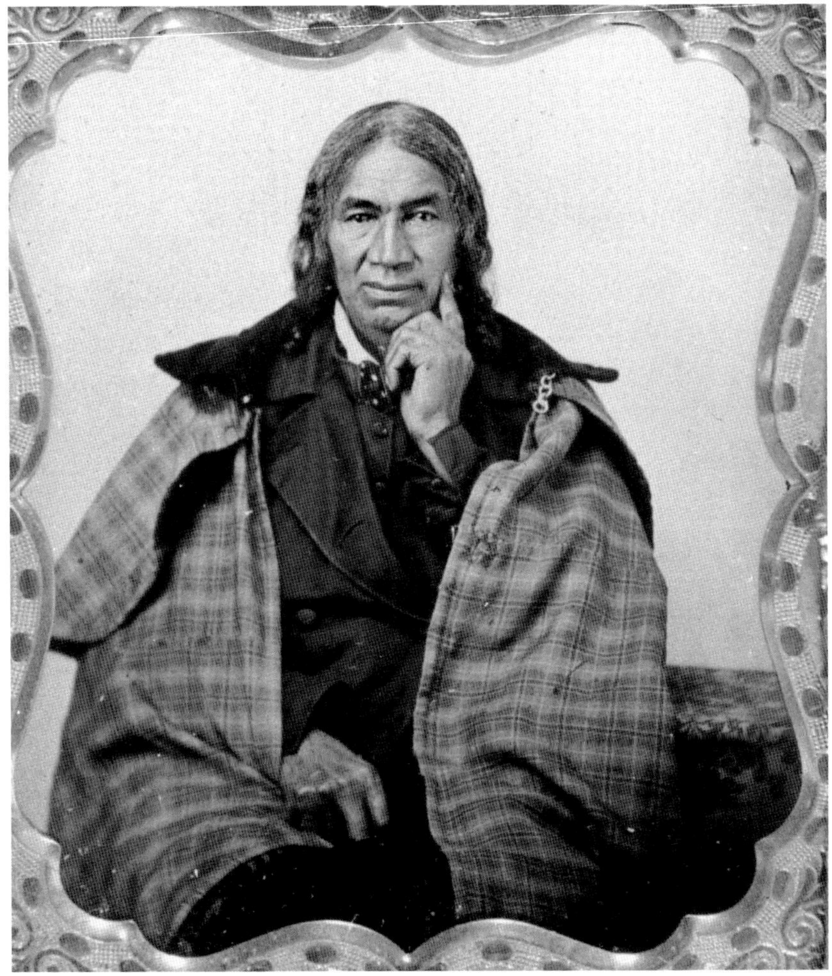

Simon Johnson (1794–1875) is listed in the 1871 Massachusetts census as a farmer, weaver, and laborer. A combination of skills and occupations was common among Vineyarders, who often adjusted their work to the season. A member of the Wampanoag tribe, Johnson was a deacon of the Baptist church in Gay Head (Aquinnah), where he lived.

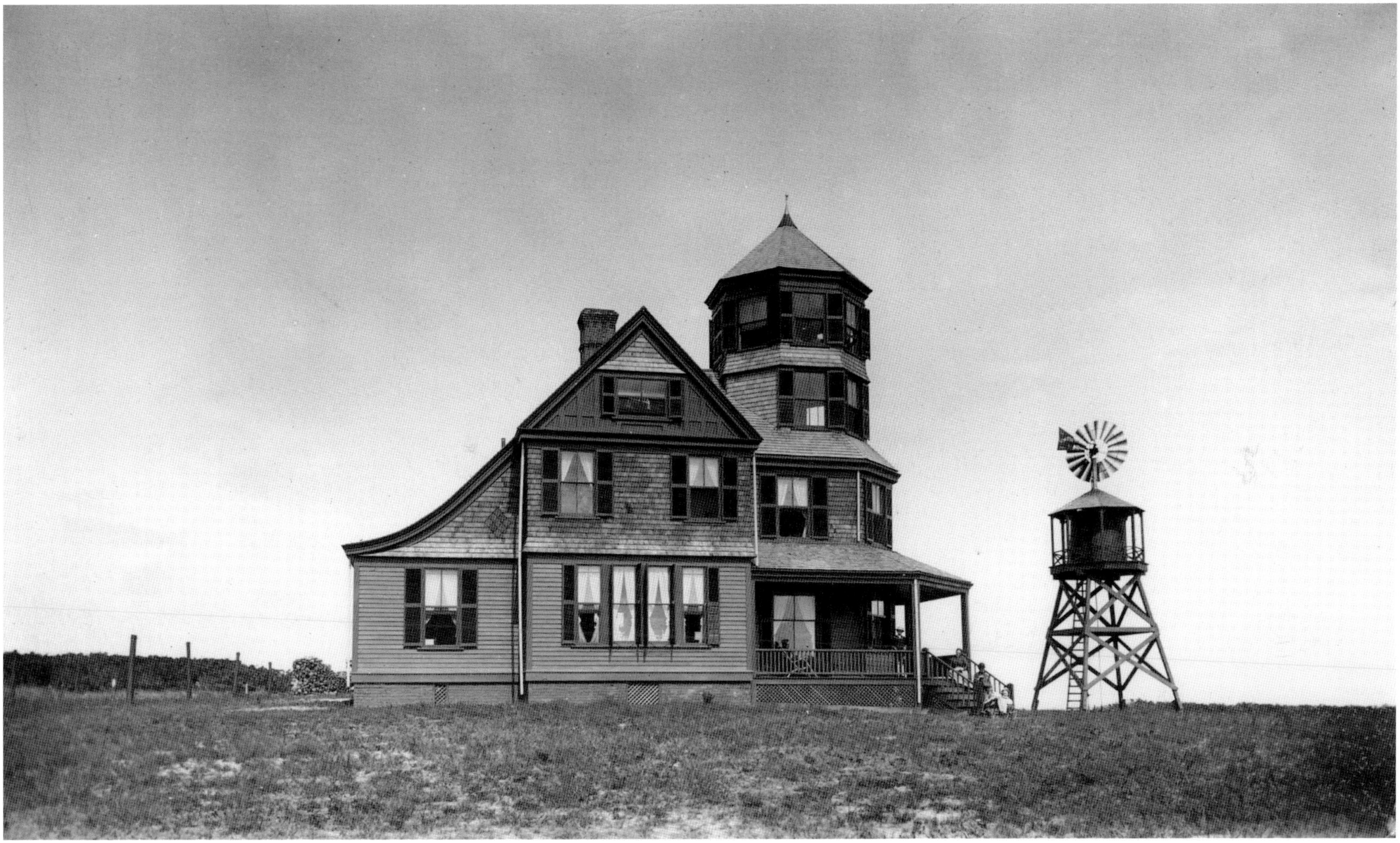

The Weston house was built in 1892, as Chappaquiddick was becoming a summer haven. Part of the town of Edgartown and often reachable only by ferry, Chappy maintained its remote character even as the town and harbor bustled right next to it. A Wampanoag settlement remained in place on Chappaquiddick well into the 1800s.

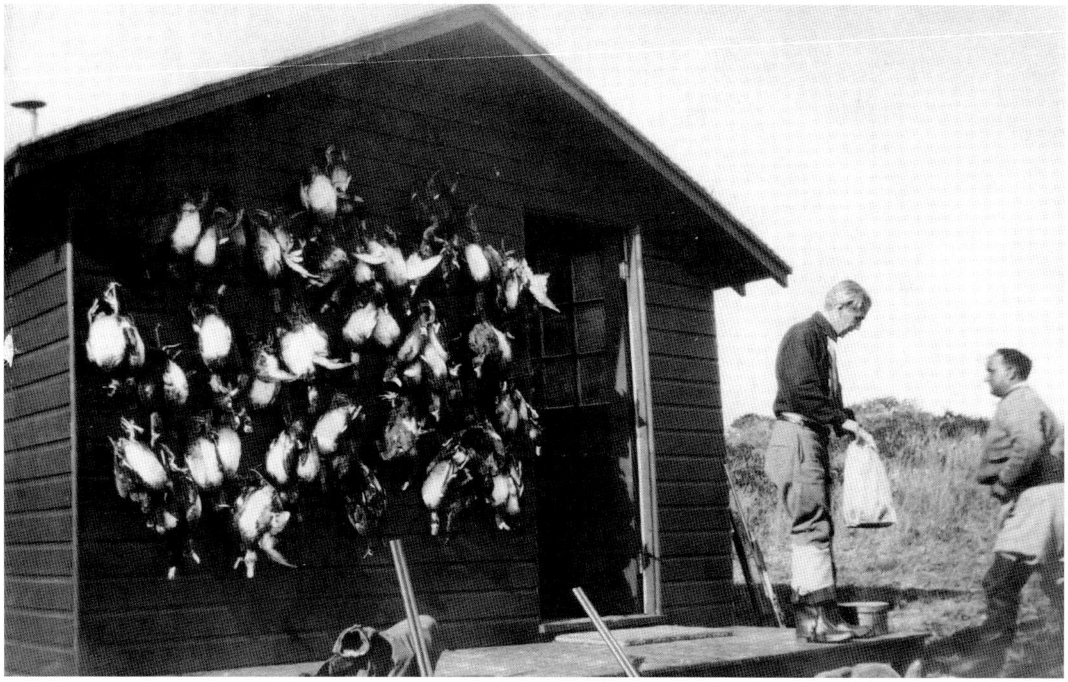

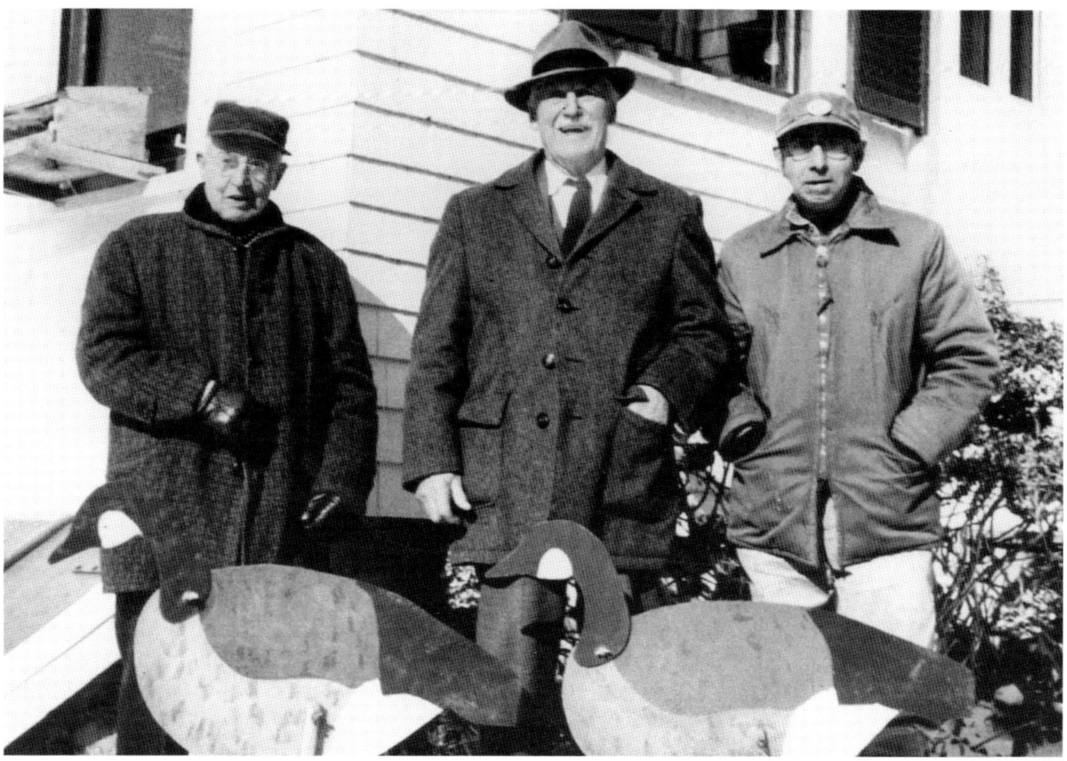

Hunting was more than a sport for the year-round residents of Martha's Vineyard; many relied on wildfowl for food. The island, located on the birds' major migration route, offered ample wetlands where decoys could be placed to lure them from the sky. Until the practice was outlawed in 1918, some hunters were also market gunners who shot hundreds of wildfowl and sent them to Boston for sale. But there was sport-hunting as well. Gunning camps were built near the great ponds. The photograph above shows Bruce Corcoran (left) and Rod Cleveland (right) after a successful hunt in West Tisbury in the early 1920s. Below, from left to right, Tom Pease, Herbert C. Hancock, and Eugene F. Rogers, all of Vineyard Haven, pose with a pair of Canada goose decoys.

Businessman Daniel Fisher built this mill in West Tisbury in 1858 to supply his Edgartown hardtack factory with flour. Hardtack was a staple food on long sea voyages because it is not as perishable as other foods. By milling island-grown wheat on Martha's Vineyard, he was able to get his product from field to sailor without sending it off-island at any point in the process.

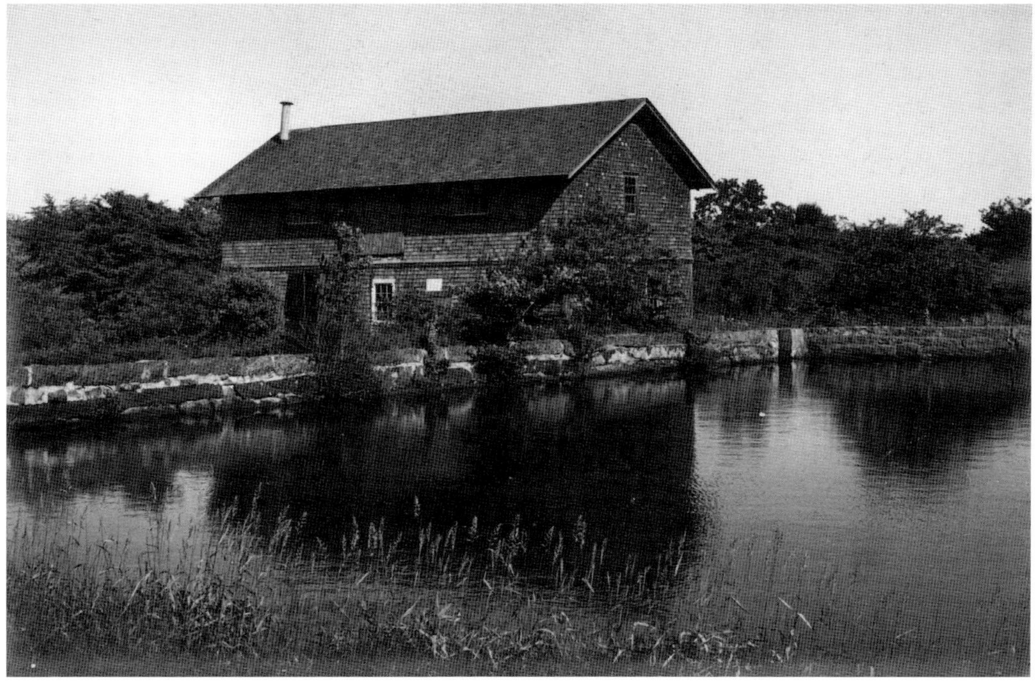

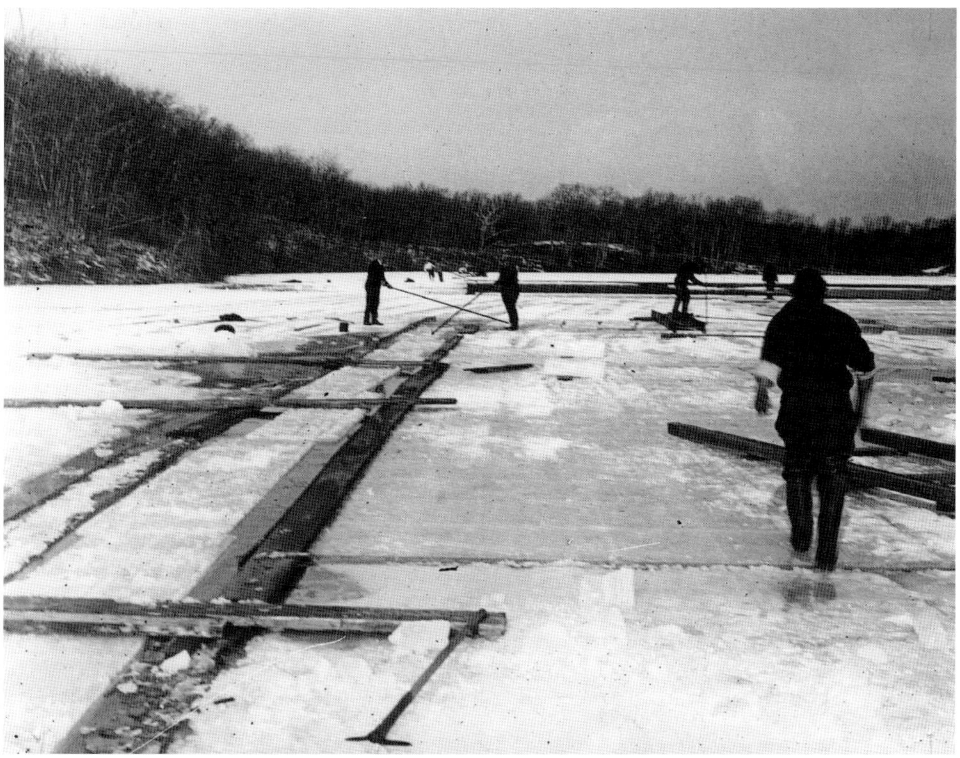

Ice was harvested from several of the island's ponds before mechanical refrigeration was available. Icehouses, including the one at Old House Pond in West Tisbury, stored the large blocks until summer, separated with layers of saw dust. This allowed islanders and the businesses that catered to tourists to stock their iceboxes all summer long.

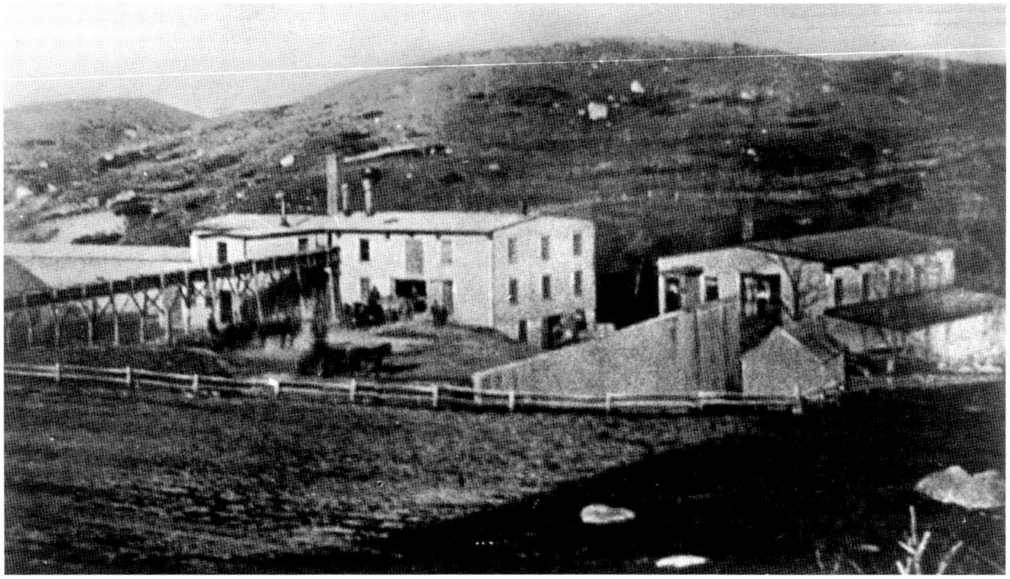

In 1850, Hiram and Francis Nye of Falmouth built a paint mill in Chilmark. They ground white, yellow, and red pigments from clay deposits found near the shore. They also had a paint store on Main Street in Tisbury that was destroyed in the fire of 1883.

The brickworks in Chilmark were located near the shore to take advantage of the clay deposits and to allow easy transport of the finished bricks by boat. They were sited in the Roaring Brook area. This photograph was taken from a hill opposite a boardinghouse where the workers stayed. (Photograph by Richard or Charles Shute.)

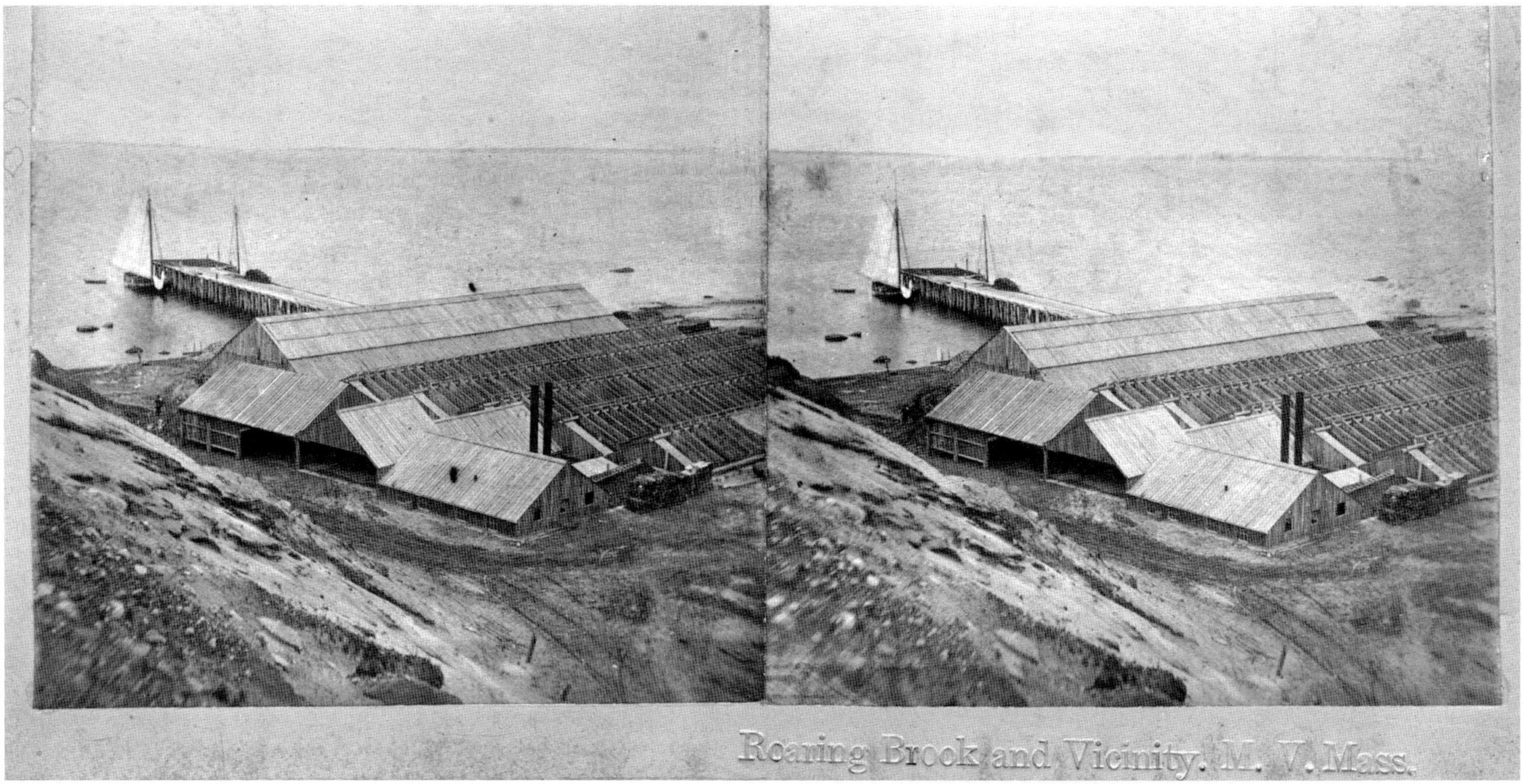

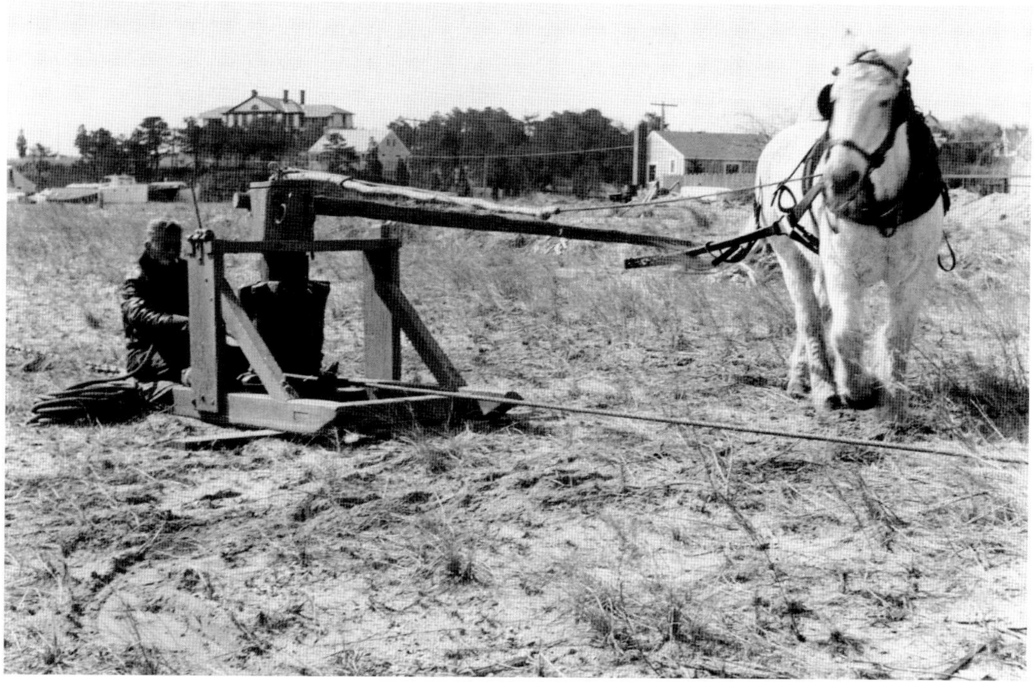

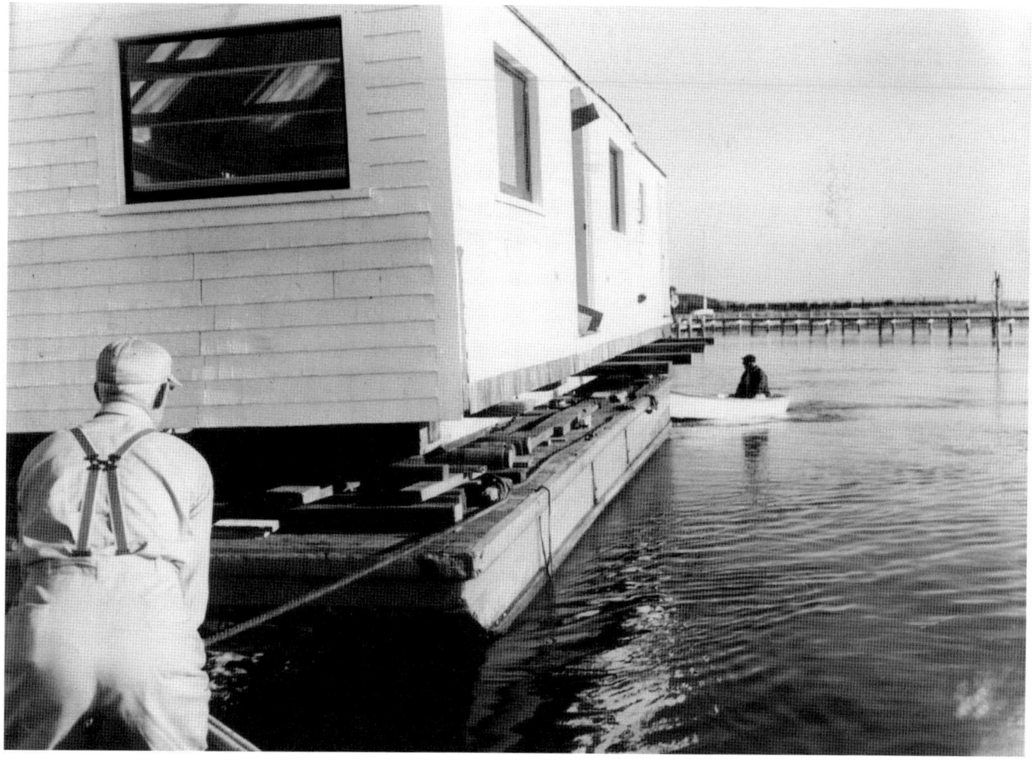

House moving was a common practice on Martha's Vineyard. Above, Tom De Costa operates a capstan, a machine he used to move houses. It consisted of a wooden cylinder that was turned by his horse, Jerry. The rope wound around the capstan, pulling the house as it got shorter. The particular house being moved has not been identified, but the Marine Hospital on the hill beyond proves that it was in Vineyard Haven. Below, a house is being moved over water from Chappaquiddick to Edgartown. Both photographs were taken around 1950.

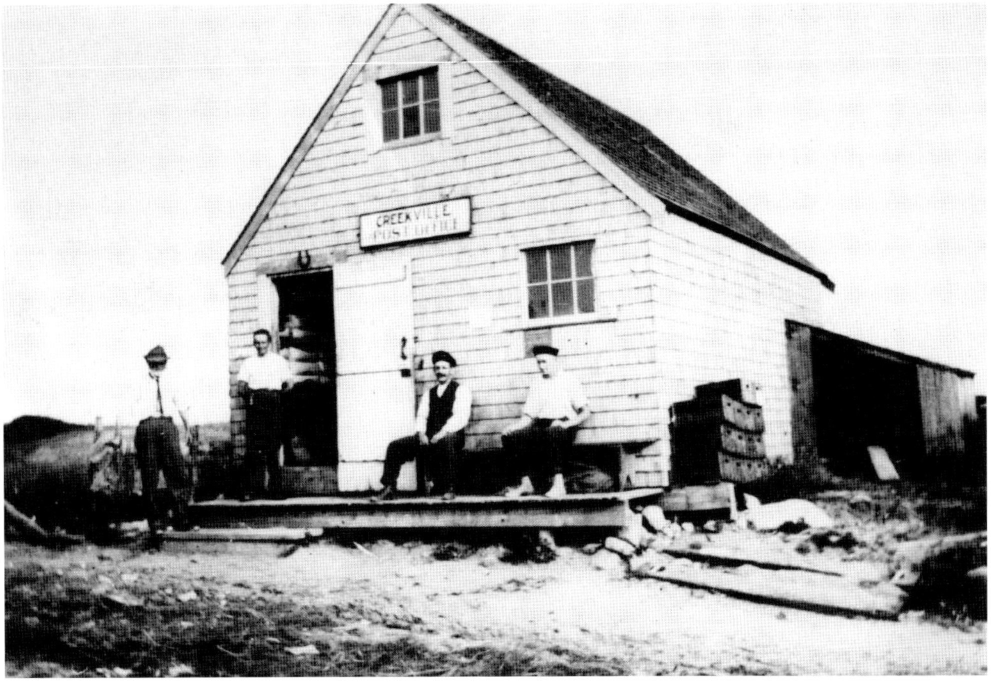

Menemsha was called Creekville until 1910. Even though it was small, it had its own post office. Only after an opening was dredged between Vineyard Sound and Menemsha Pond and a stone jetty was put into place did the town turn into a working fishing village. This view is from around 1900.

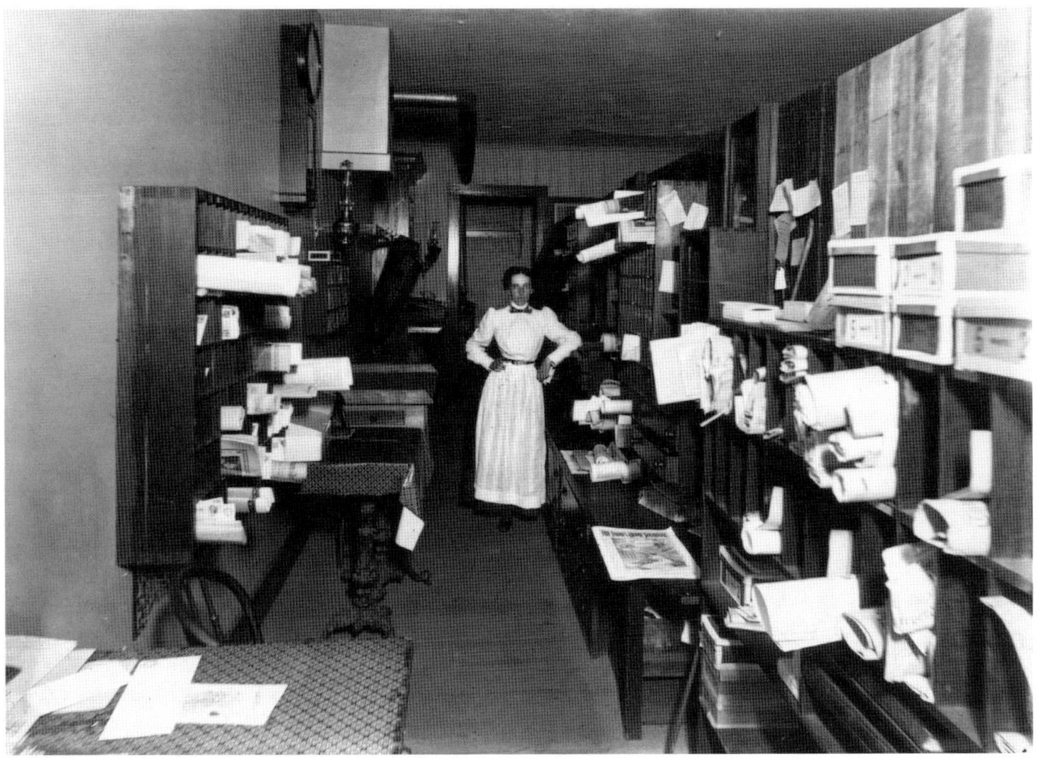

Mary Addlington, seen here at work, was the postal clerk for Edgartown in the late 1800s and early 1900s. She was responsible for sorting and distributing the letters and the many newspapers and periodicals Edgartown residents subscribed to in order to stay connected to the world. One of these, the *Ladies' Home Journal*, can be seen on the table in front of her.

The North Tisbury Post Office displays the once-familiar blue-and-white Bell Telephone sign, indicating that there was a public phone available for long-distance calls. When the town of Tisbury split in 1892 to create West Tisbury, the part of town known as North Tisbury was included in the new town of West Tisbury.

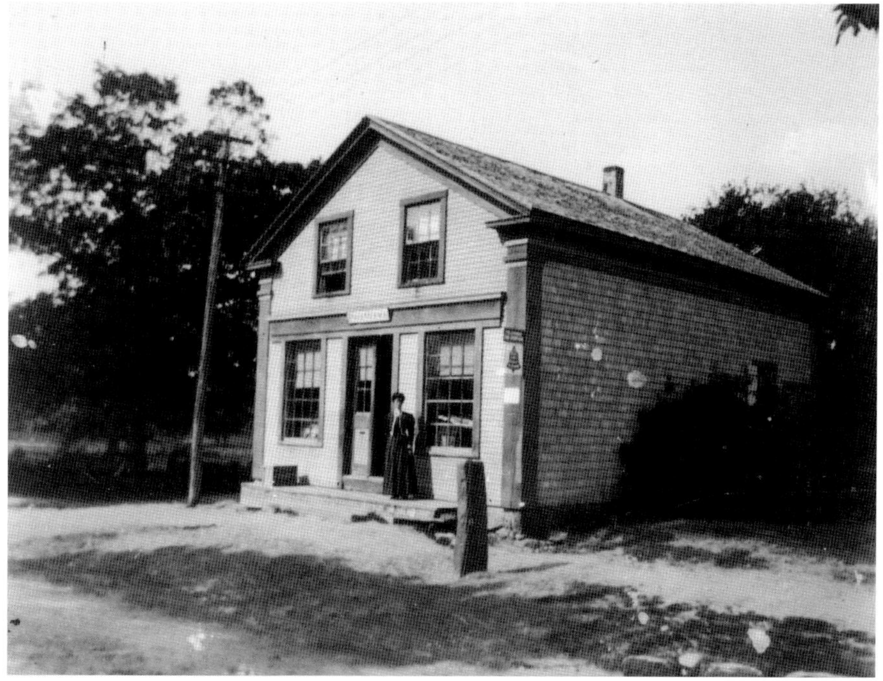

Alley's General Store in West Tisbury has been in business under one name or another since 1858. Opened by Nathan Mayhew and taken over by his sons, Sanderson and Ulysses, after his death in 1867, the store became known as S.M. Mayhew Co. In 1946, the store became Albion, Alley & Co., and, in 1964, its name was changed to Alley's.

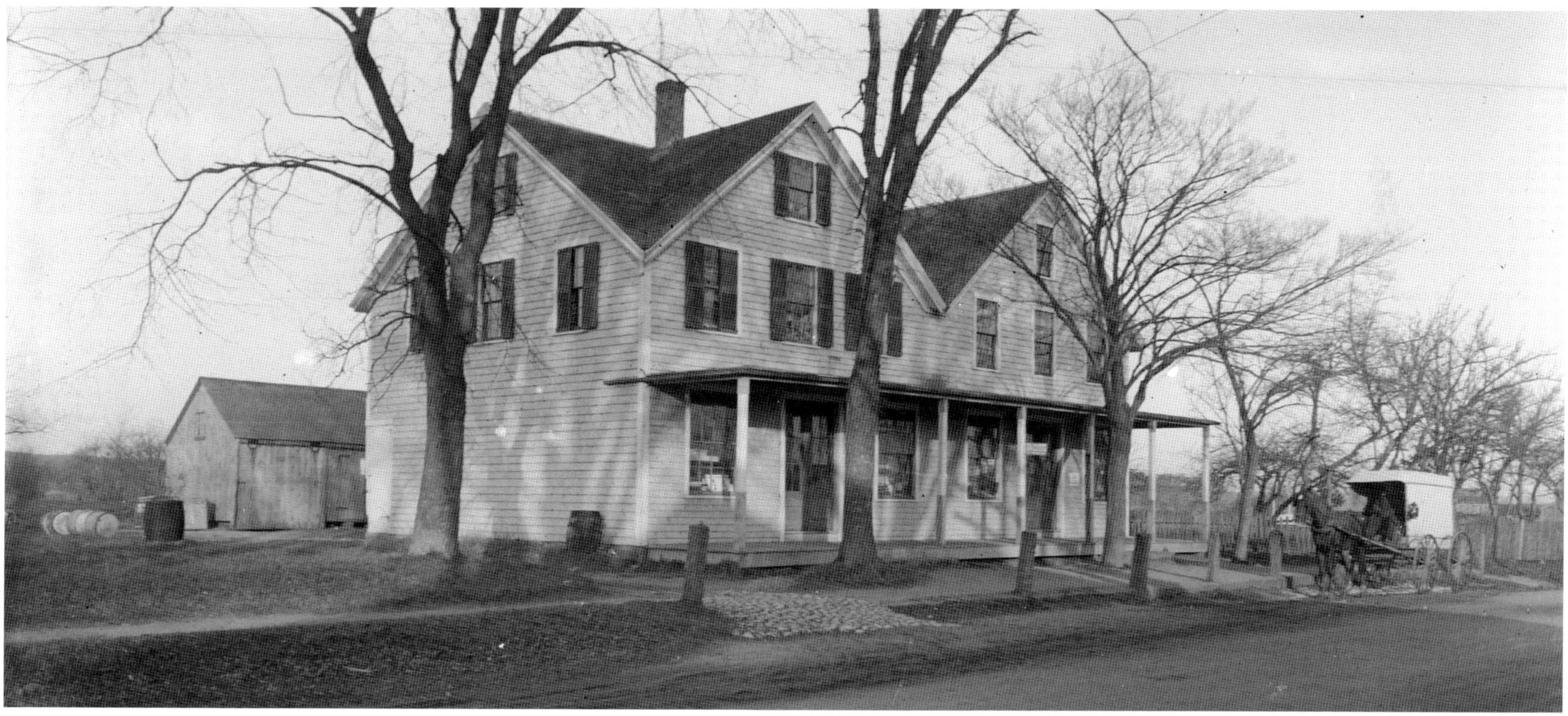

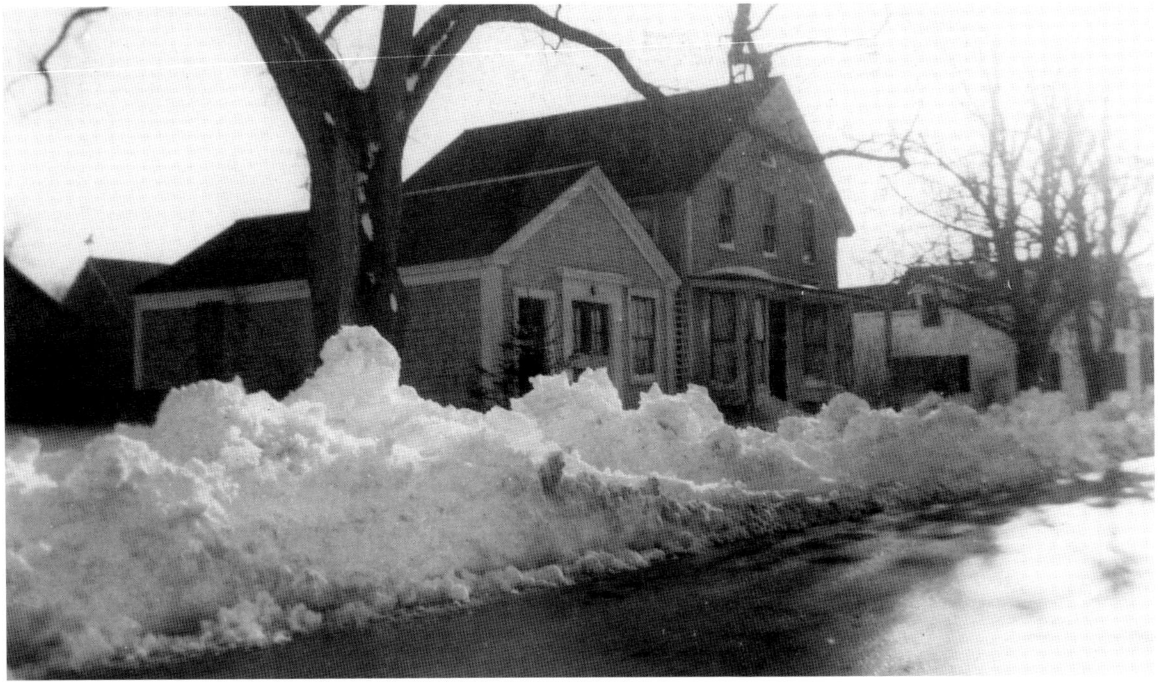

George G. Gifford opened his store in West Tisbury in the late 1800s and ran it until the mid-1900s. He sold home goods, farming products, and feed and grain. After the store had been closed for years, his son reopened it in the 1970s. This photograph, taken after a deep snowfall, shows the store before gas pumps were installed.

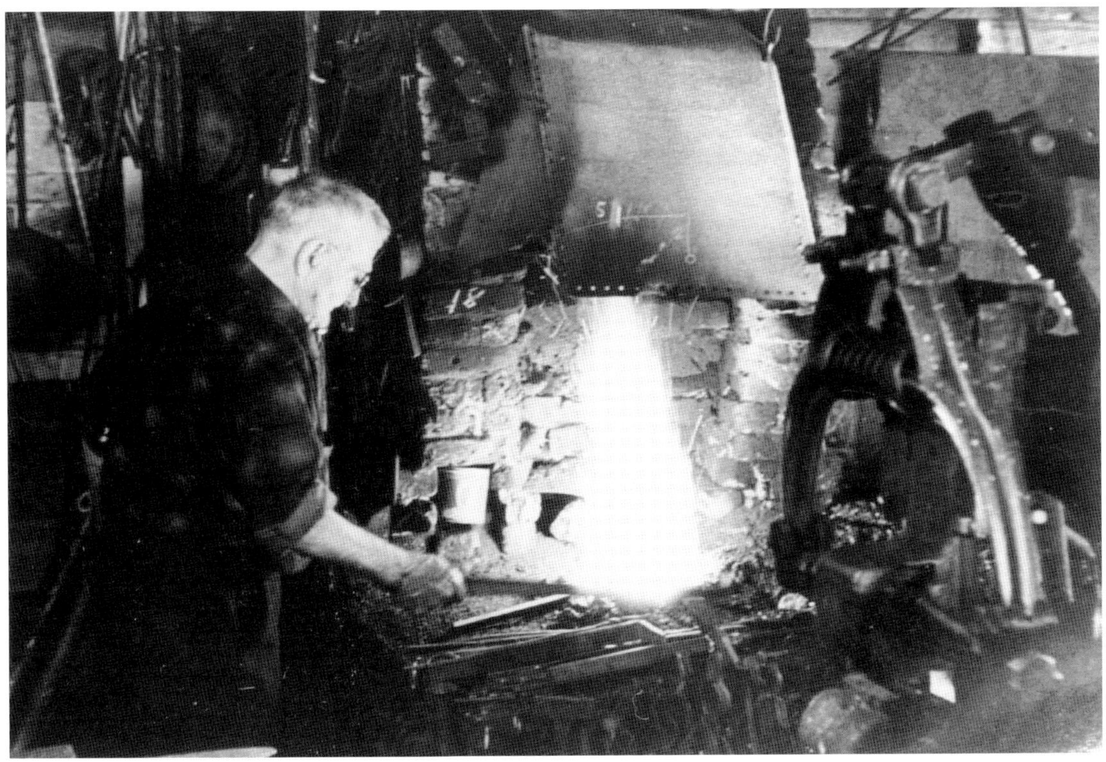

Orin Norton ran his blacksmith shop on Dock Street in Edgartown until his death in 1961. He supplied the community with farming and fishing tools for 60 years. In a 1961 *National Geographic* article about Martha's Vineyard, he is described as "grizzled and powerful, blunt of speech, afraid of nothing." He was also innovative, designing and making a novel quahog rake, for which he received a patent in 1906.

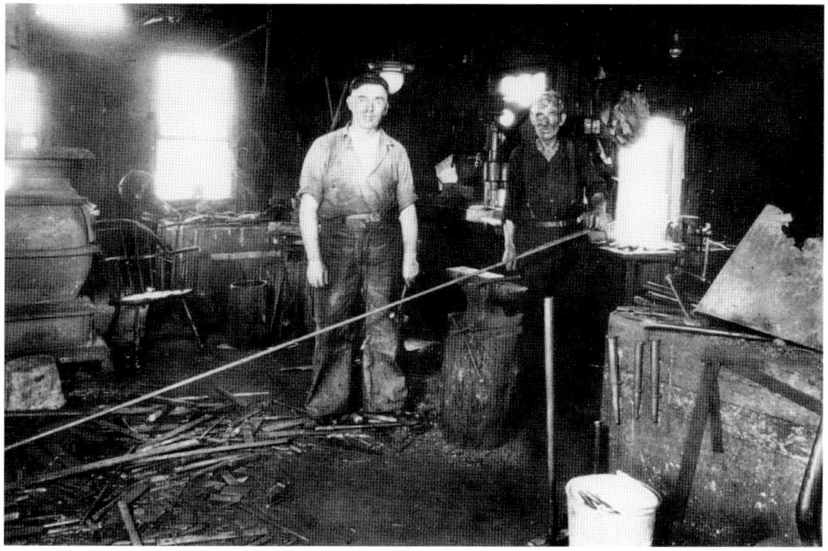

Ed Colleton (left) and Elmer Chadwick pause from their work in Chadwick's blacksmith shop in Tisbury (Vineyard Haven). The shop was located off Beach Road in an area known as Duarte Village. Chadwick worked in the early 1900s making andirons and other ironwares as well as repairing and making replacements for car parts. In 1983, Duarte Village became the site of Tisbury Marketplace.

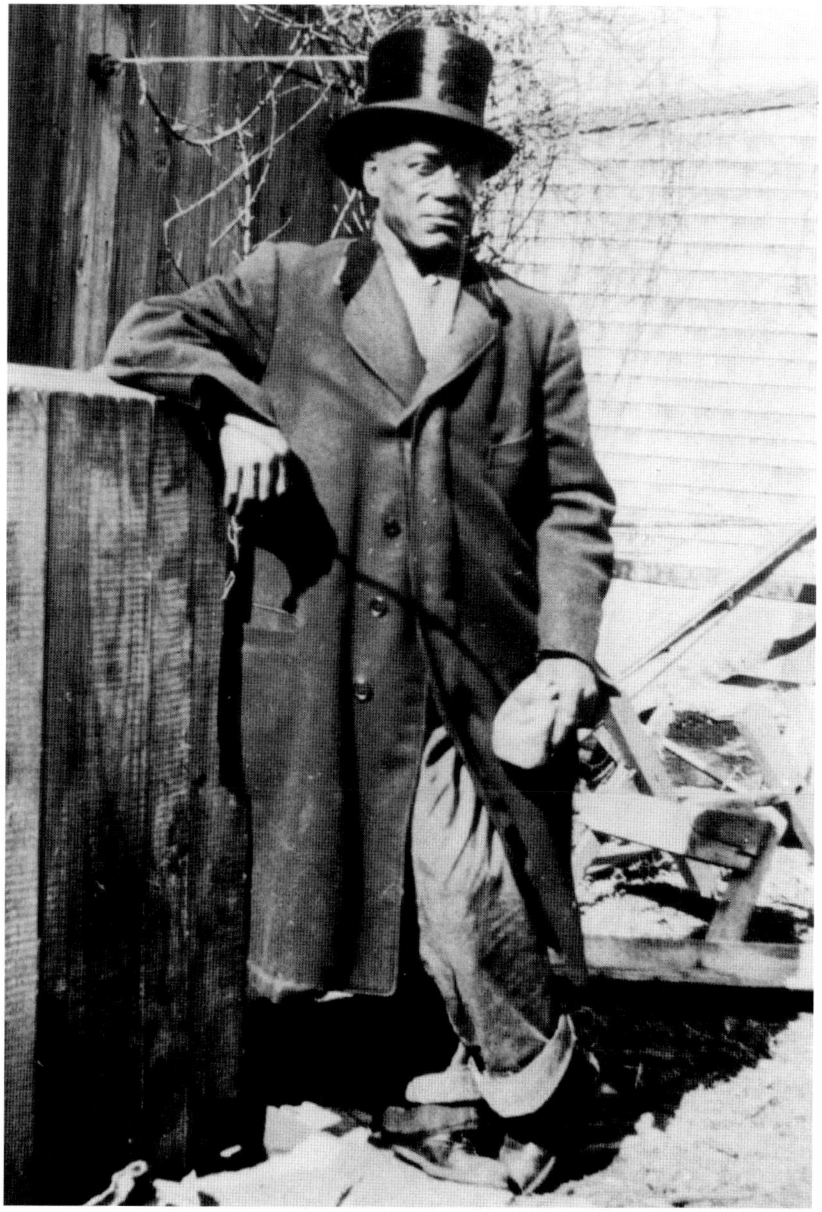

Local historian Stan Lair recalled Ben Taylor as living in Vineyard Haven in "a little room on one side of Renear's Stable." He continued, "We'd go in and sit around and chew the rag with him. Ben was a real nice fellow. He had a shoeshine stand he'd put out front in the summer." Ben Taylor died around 1940.

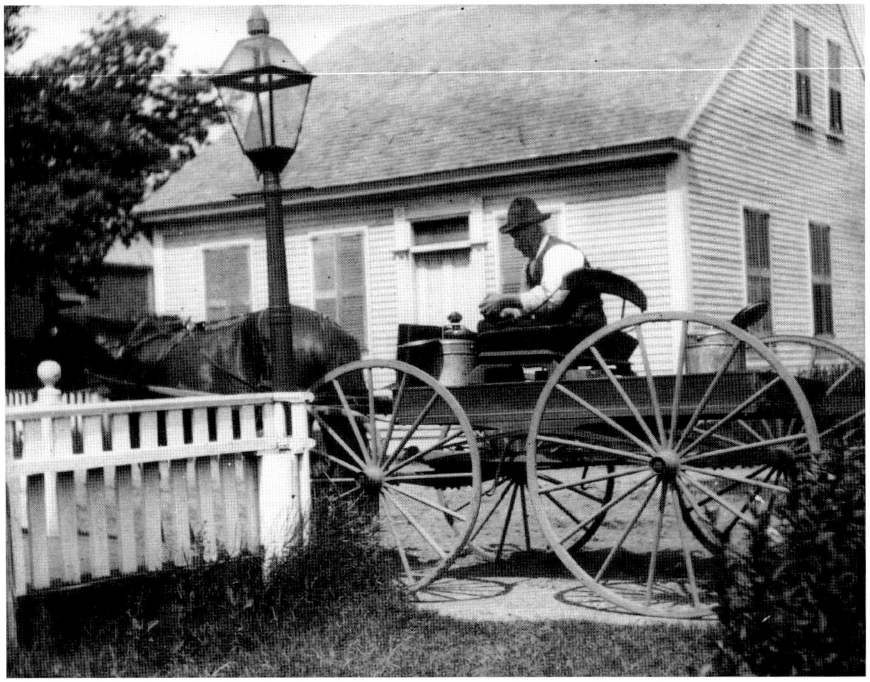

Martin Van Buren Norton worked as a lamplighter in Edgartown. In this photograph from 1903, he is filling a streetlamp with oil before placing it in the protected lantern on the lamppost. Norton's twin brother was named Andrew Jackson Norton, prompting a newspaper reporter to quip that their father was obviously not a Republican.

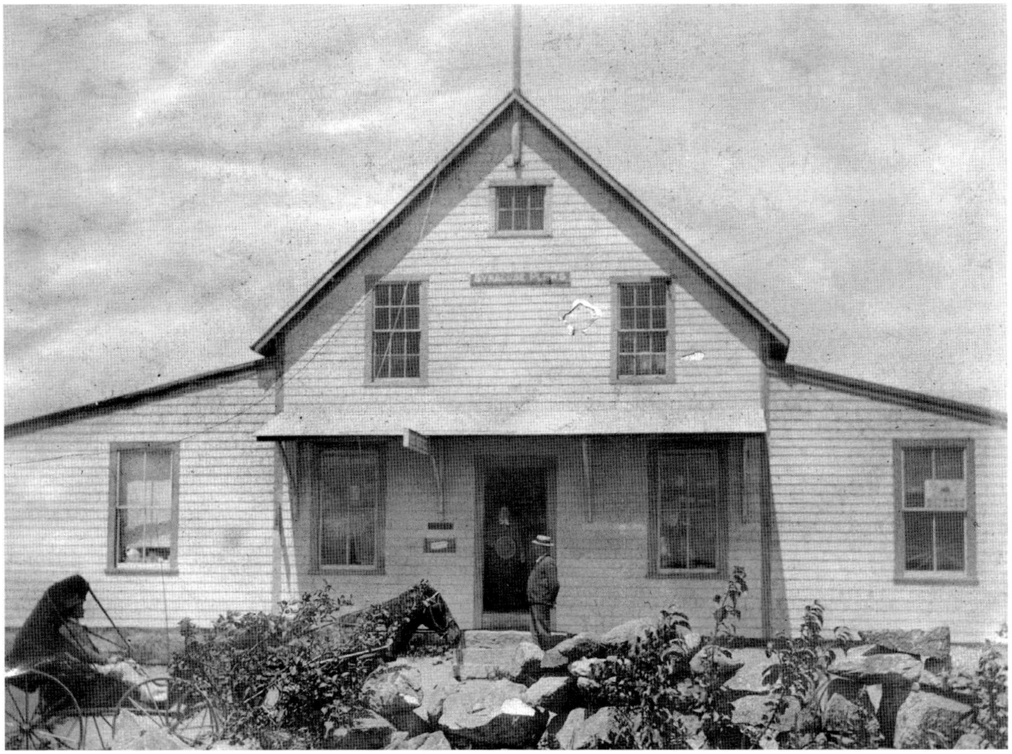

In a 1907 directory, E. Elliot Mayhew advertised himself as a "Dealer in Stoves, Furnaces and Ranges, Hardware, Wooden Ware, Tin Ware and Kitchen Furnishing Goods. Groceries, Farming Tools, Fertilizers, Paints, Dry Goods, Crockery. In fact, dealer in almost everything." His Chilmark store was established in 1875 and is seen here around 1900.

In August 1883, a fire started in the Crocker harness factory on Main Street in Vineyard Haven. It spread rapidly. By the next day, all of the buildings on both sides of Main Street had been destroyed, from Nye's Paint Store, north of Union Street, to the Mansion House hotel. Without firefighting equipment of its own, Vineyard Haven was unable to fight the flames until help arrived from Cottage City.

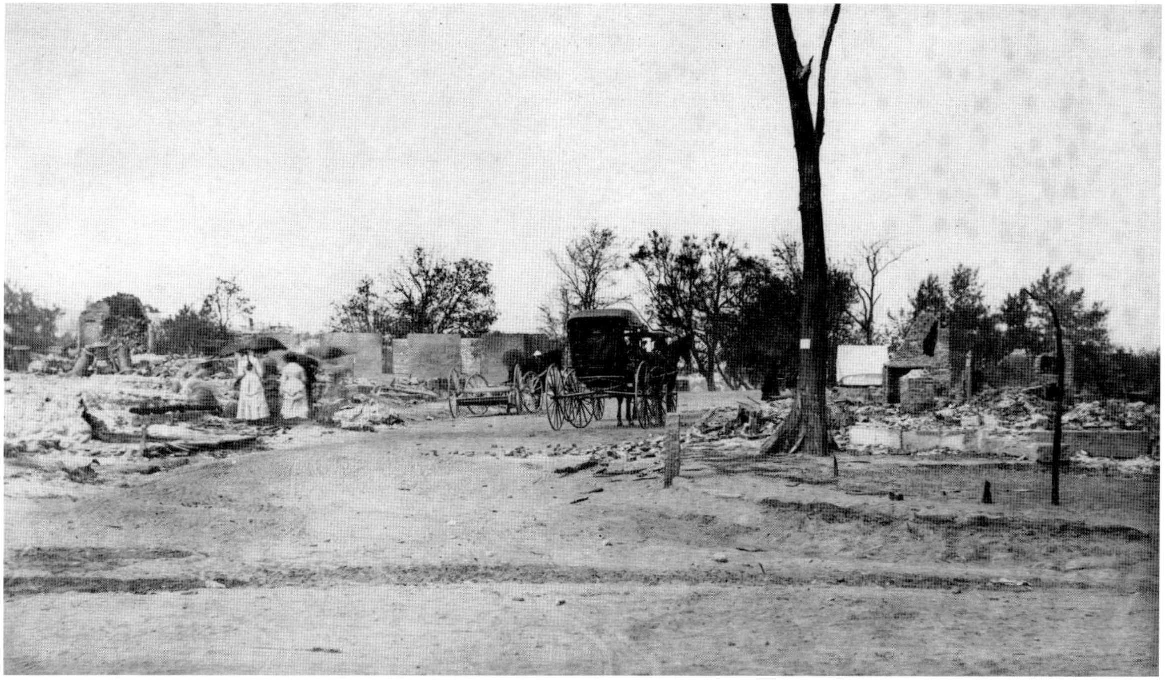

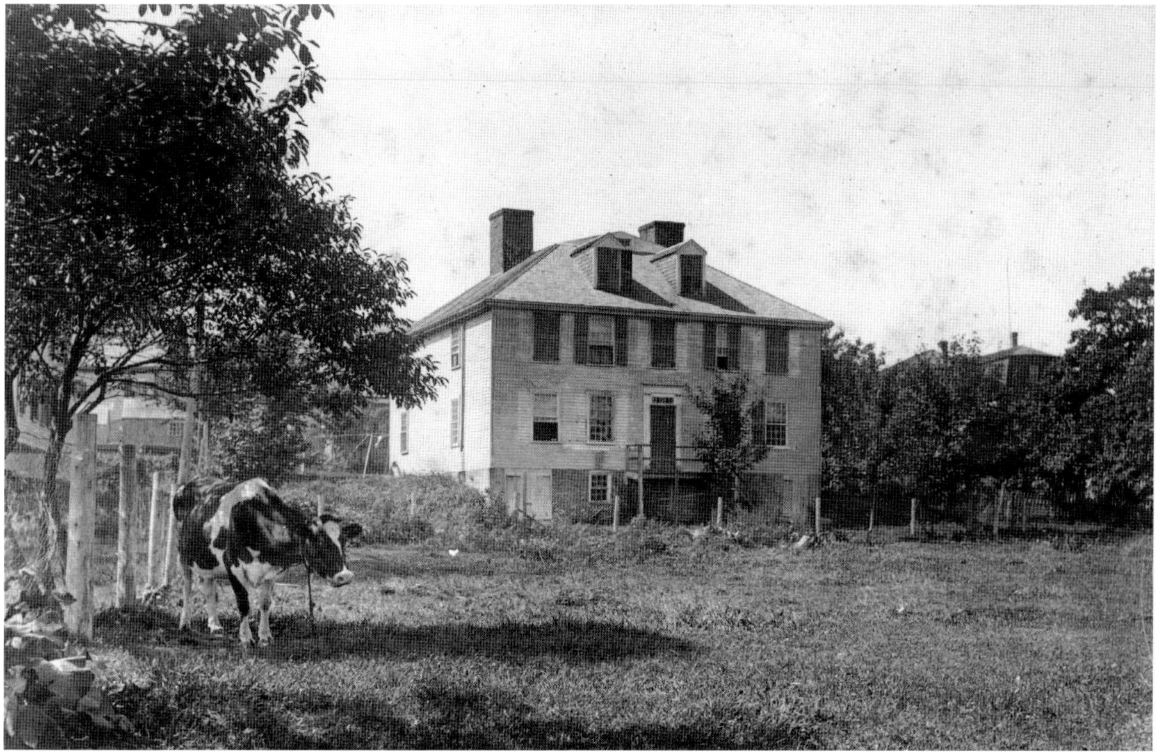

Abraham Chase built the Great House in Holmes Hole (Vineyard Haven) around 1720. It stood on a site between the current Stop & Shop and the Tisbury police station for 200 years, surviving the fire of 1883, before it was moved to West Chop. In its day, Chase probably operated a tavern in the building.

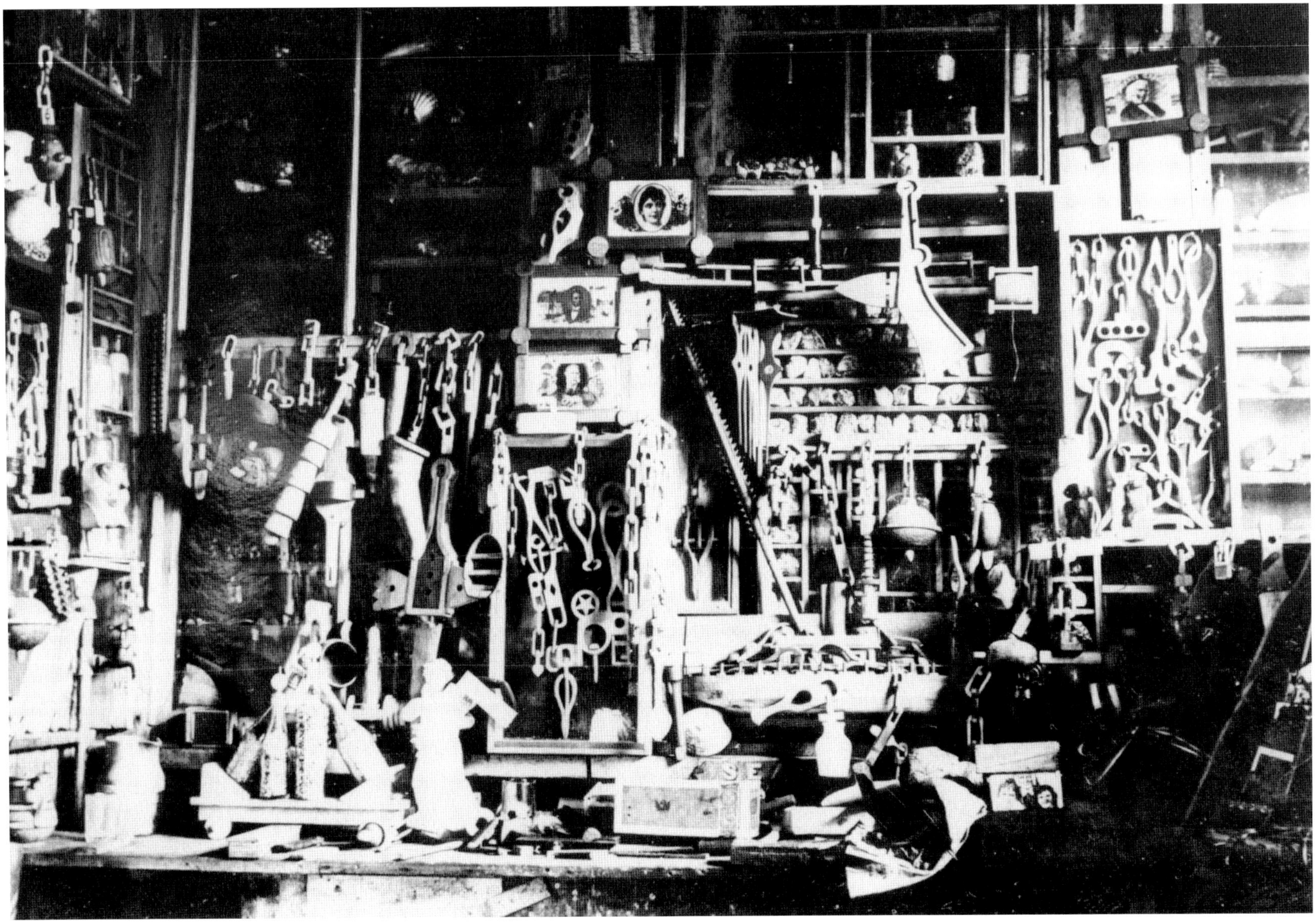

"Ben Chuck" Dexter (1830–1907) was an eccentric man who ran an ice cream parlor decorated with his wood carvings. The shop, on Main Street in Vineyard Haven, was destroyed by the fire of 1883, but he opened a new one a year later. It is not clear whether this photograph shows Dexter's old or new shop.

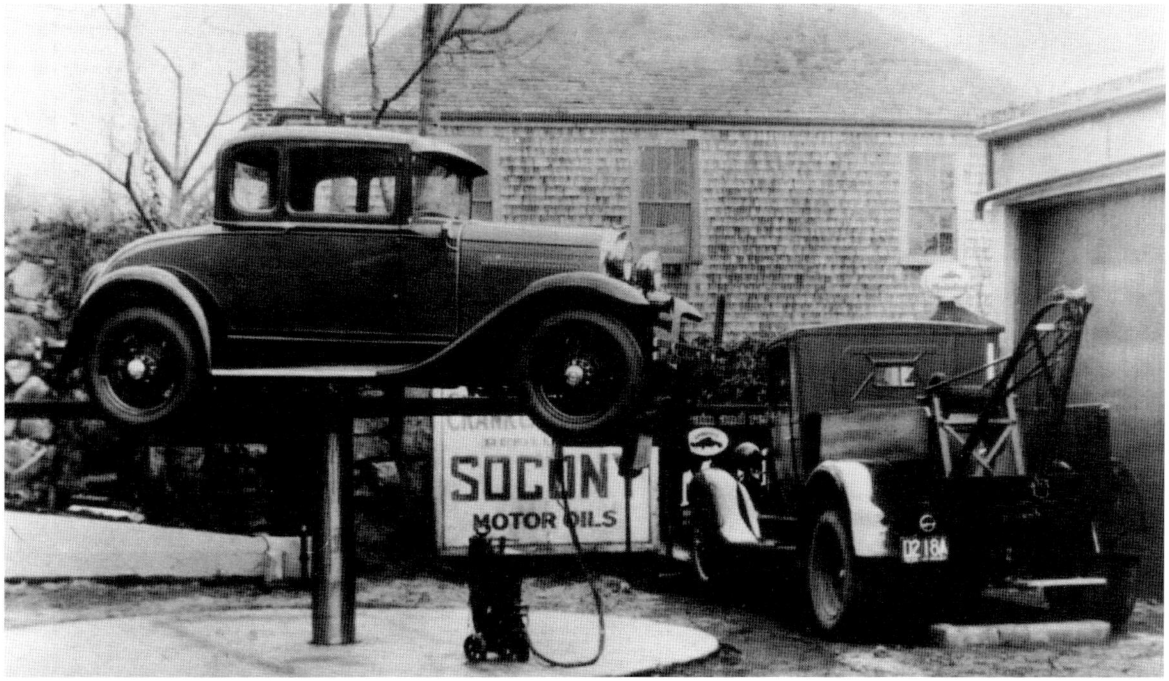

Renear's Garage was on Church Street in Vineyard Haven. It occupied a complex of buildings that provided a number of services, including auto repair, sales, a storage garage, and a Socony (Standard Oil Company of New York) gas station. This photograph was probably taken around 1930.

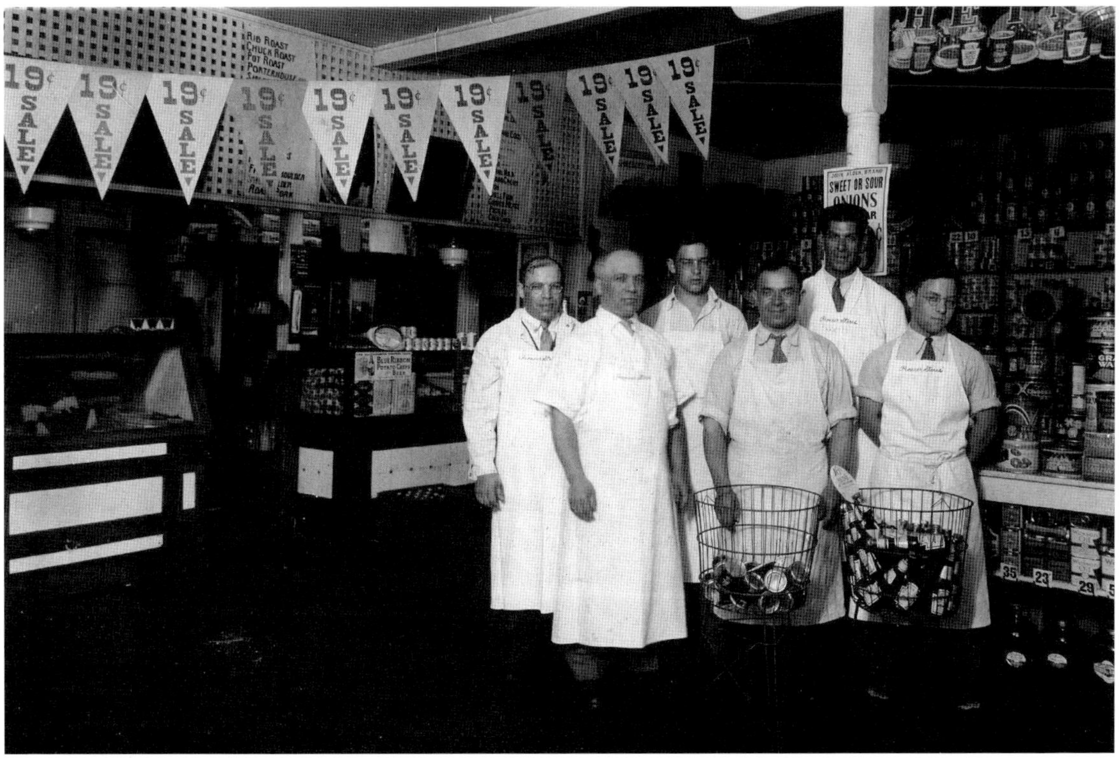

In the early 1900s, Sam Cronig, a Jewish immigrant from Lithuania, moved to Martha's Vineyard to work on a farm. In 1917, he convinced his two brothers to move to the United States. Together, they opened a meat and grocery store on Main Street in downtown Vineyard Haven.

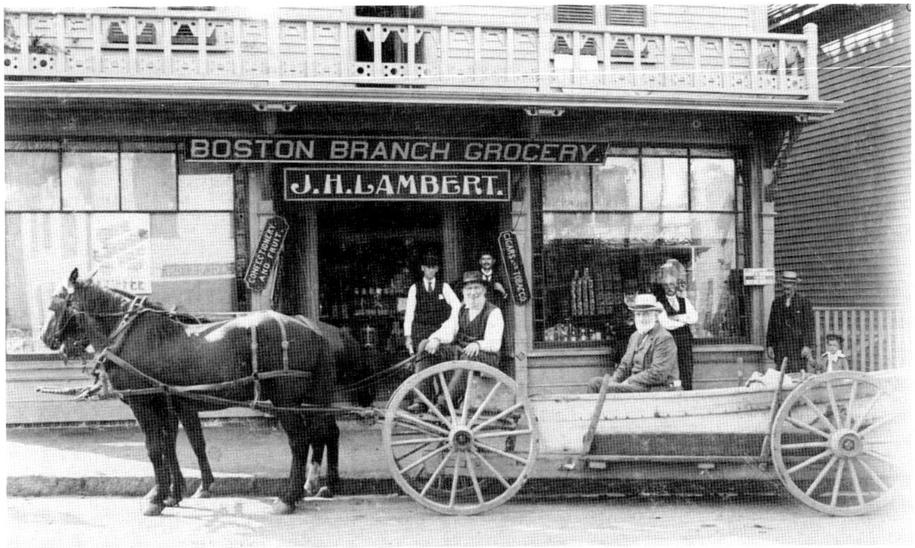

J.H. Lambert's Boston Branch Grocery stood on the corner of Spring and Main Streets in Vineyard Haven from 1893 until 1895, replacing his dry goods store, which had been in the building for 10 years. John Lambert, the proprietor, stands here with his arms folded in front of the window on the right. The others are unidentified. The store occupied a building that replaced the Baptist church, destroyed in the 1883 fire.

Around 1900, when this photograph was probably taken, Main Street in Vineyard Haven boasted a harness shop. The harness shop was in the space formerly occupied by the J.H. Lambert Store.

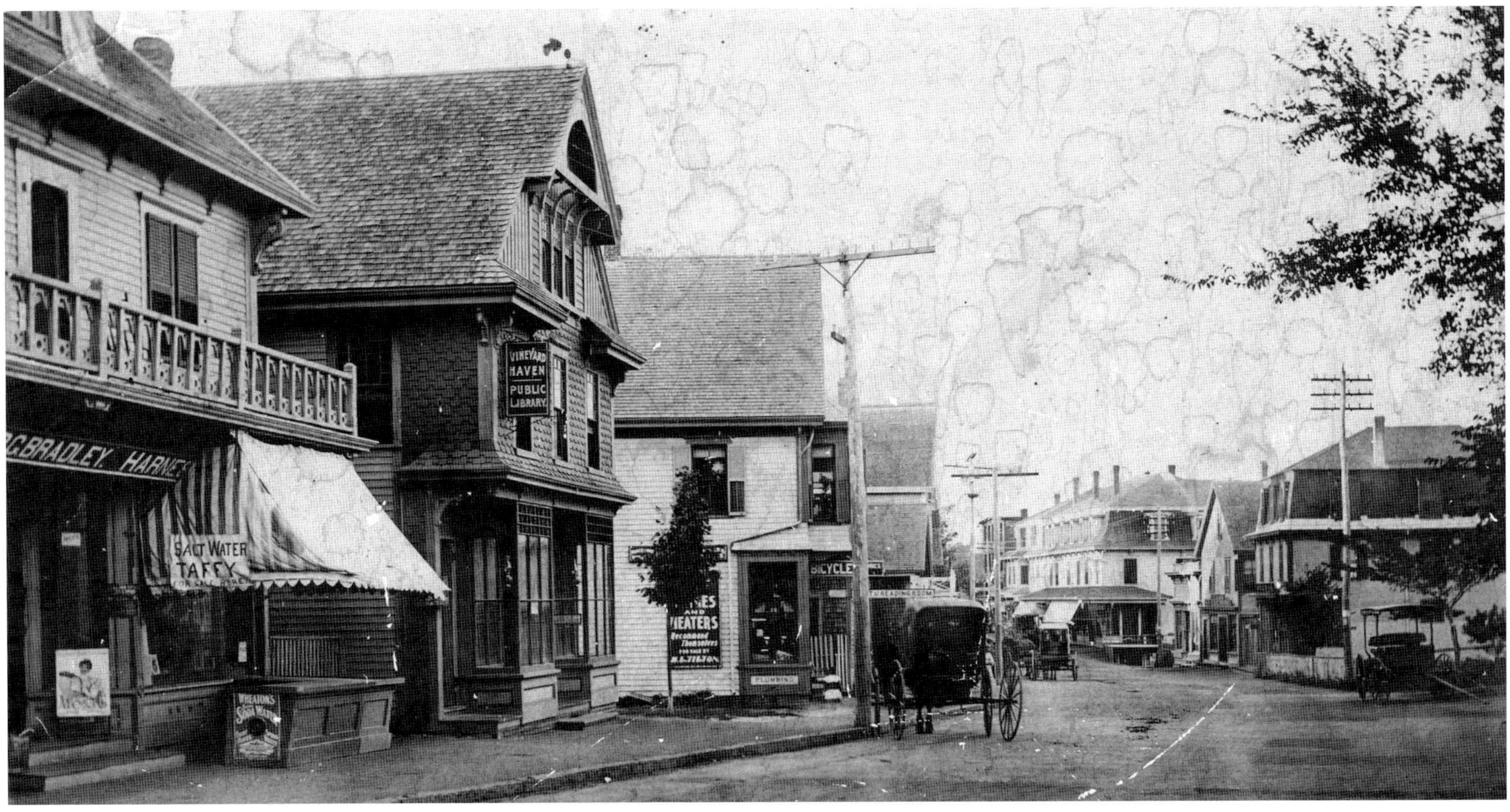

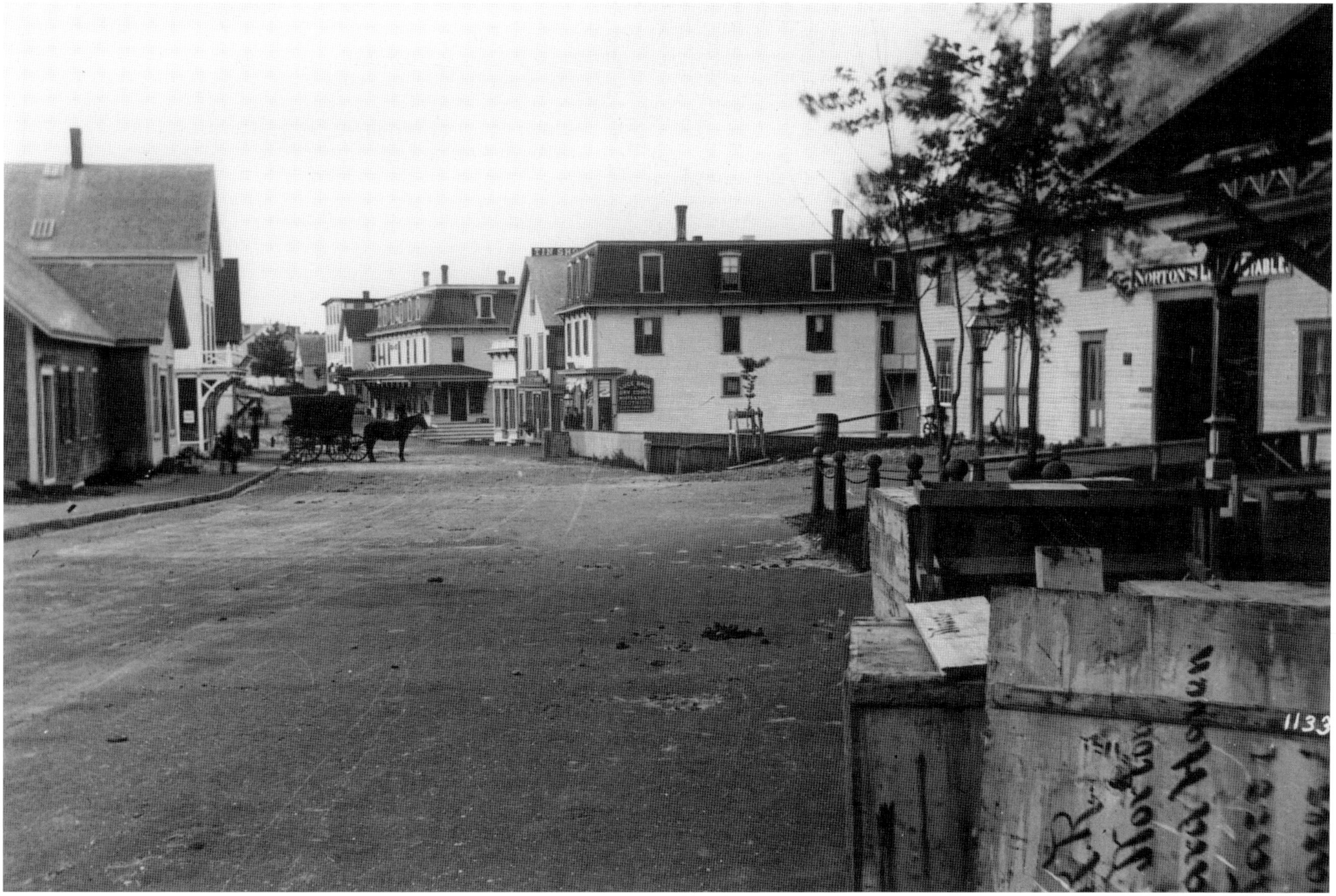

Norton's Livery Stable was located on Main Street in Vineyard Haven around 1900. The building still stands today. It has been occupied by several businesses, including the Bowl and Board and, most recently, the Bunch of Grapes bookstore. (Photograph by Harry Platt.)

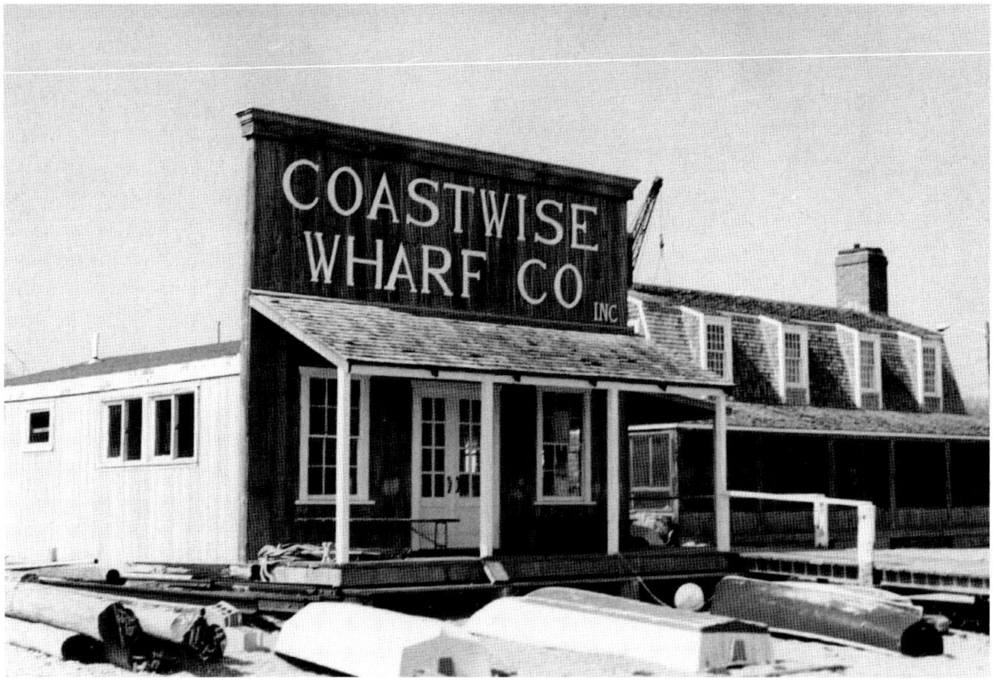

The Black Dog Tavern opened in Vineyard Haven in 1971 and quickly became a landmark business on Martha's Vineyard. In this early photograph, it is to the right of a Coastwise Wharf Co. building. The Black Dog now has several shops and cafés across the Vineyard in addition to the original tavern shown here.

The bridge connecting Vineyard Haven to Oak Bluffs extends over the opening between Vineyard Haven Harbor and the Lagoon. It has been replaced several times. According to Charles Banks's 1911 *History of Martha's Vineyard*, "The present drawbridge on the 'Beach Road' connecting Cottage City, spans an opening into Lagoon Pond, which was made about 60 years ago."

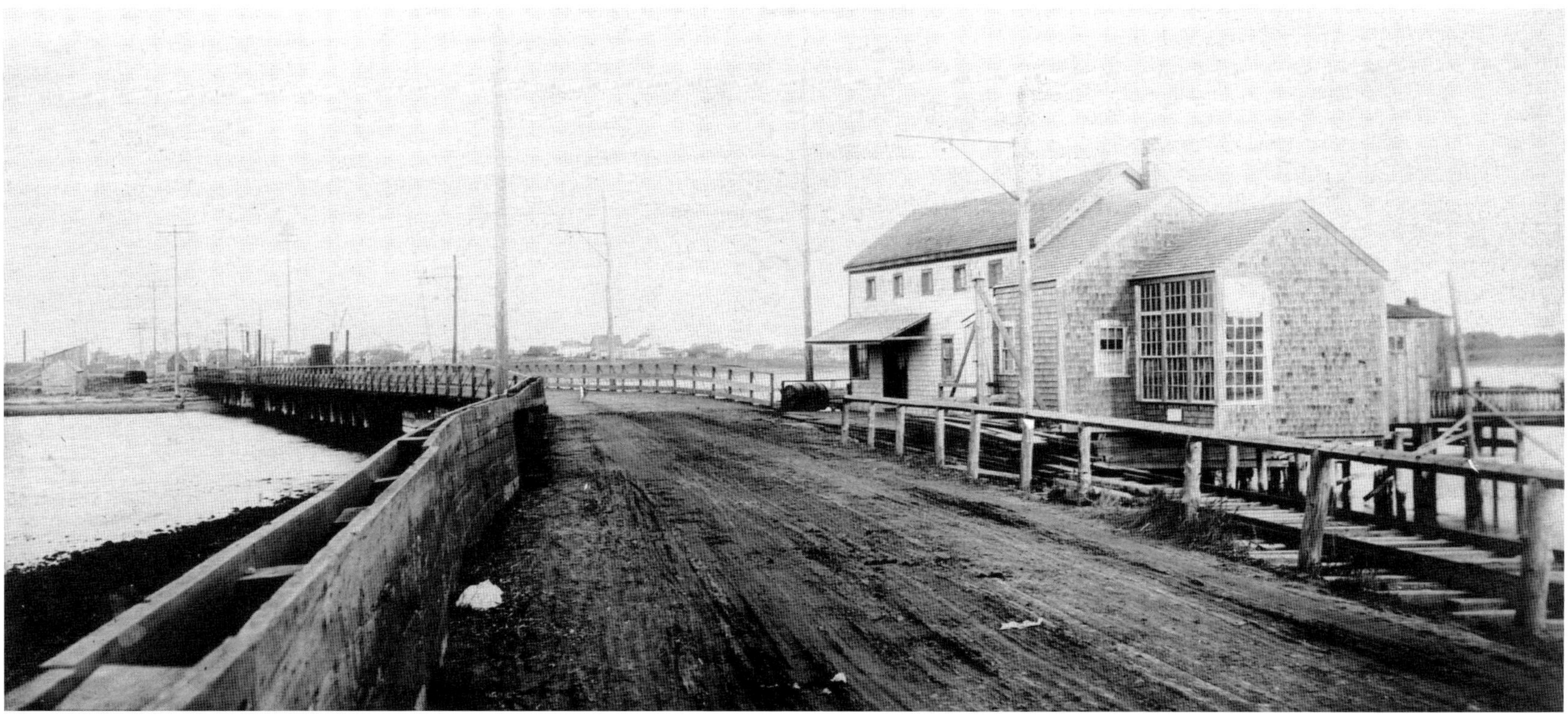

Circuit Avenue, the main commercial street in Oak Bluffs, is seen here on a quiet day around 1890, possibly in the off-season or early morning. Flags are flying, but the only signs of life are one man and a solitary horse cart. The large building on the right is the Island House hotel. Across the street from it is the Pawnee House. The cigar shop in the front advertises "No Fancy Prices."

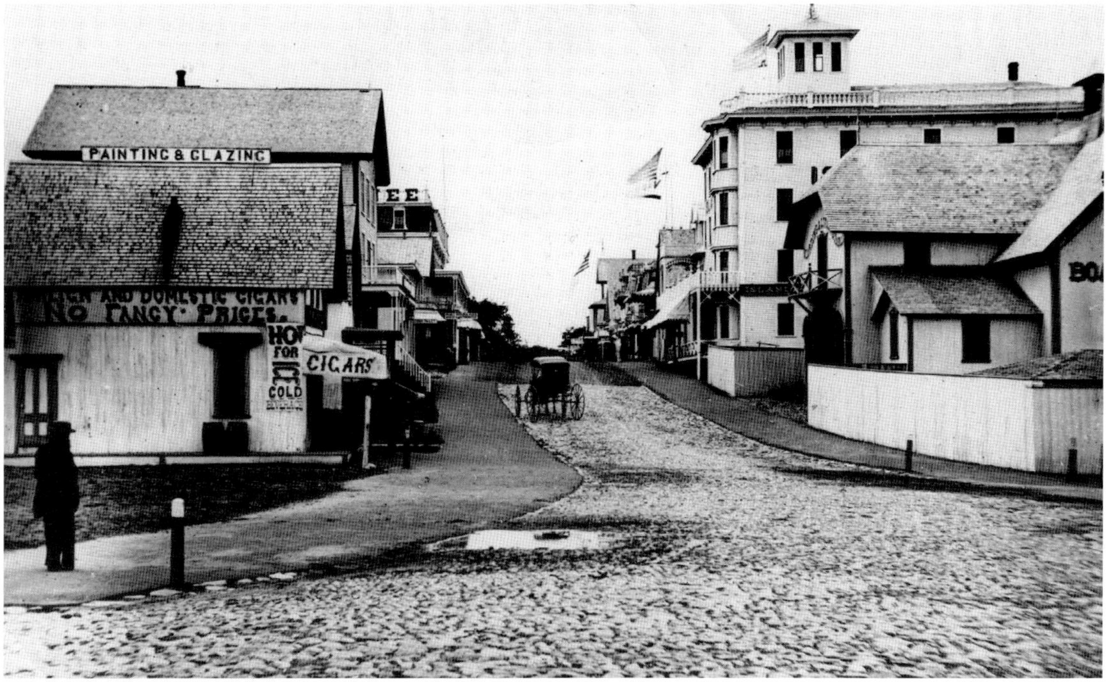

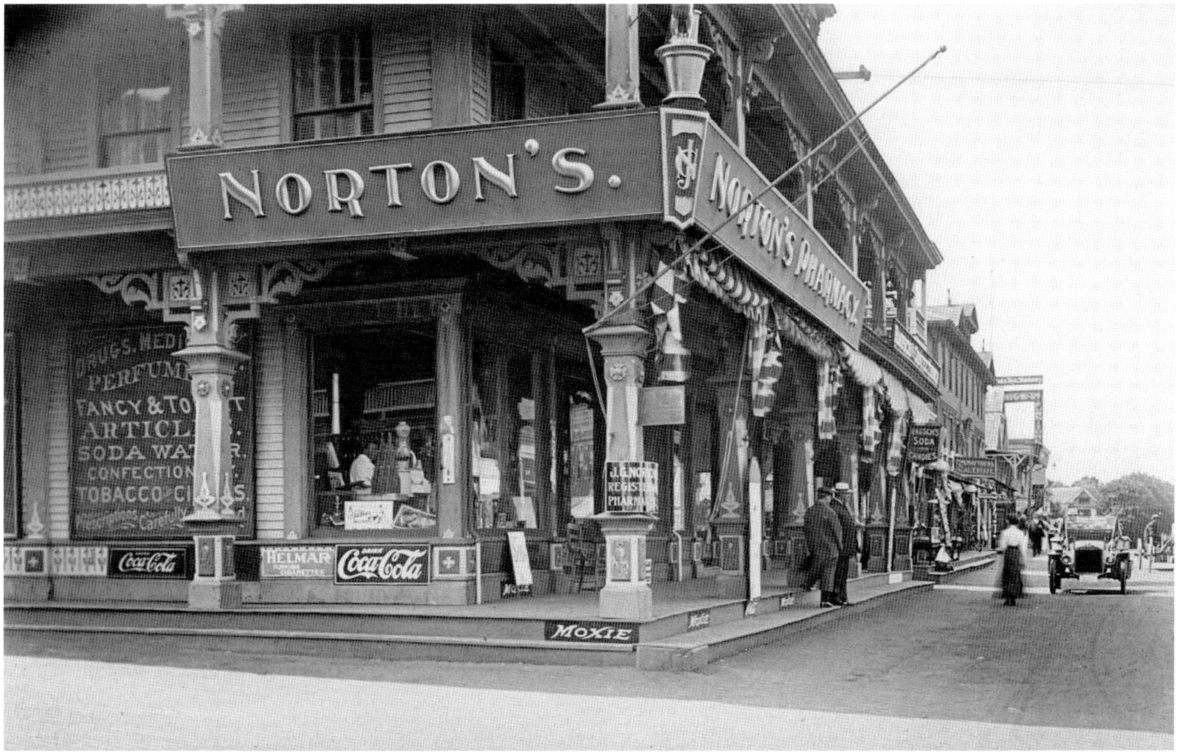

Norton's Pharmacy, on Circuit Avenue in Oak Bluffs, shared the ground floor of a hotel, the Metropolitan House, with Rausch's Ice Cream Parlor. In addition to offering the services of registered pharmacist J.G. Norton, the store sold perfume, fancy and toilet articles, Turkish cigarettes, Coca-Cola, and Moxie. Though by the time this photograph was taken around 1915, both Coca-Cola and Moxie were being sold as soda pop; they were both originally marketed as medicine.

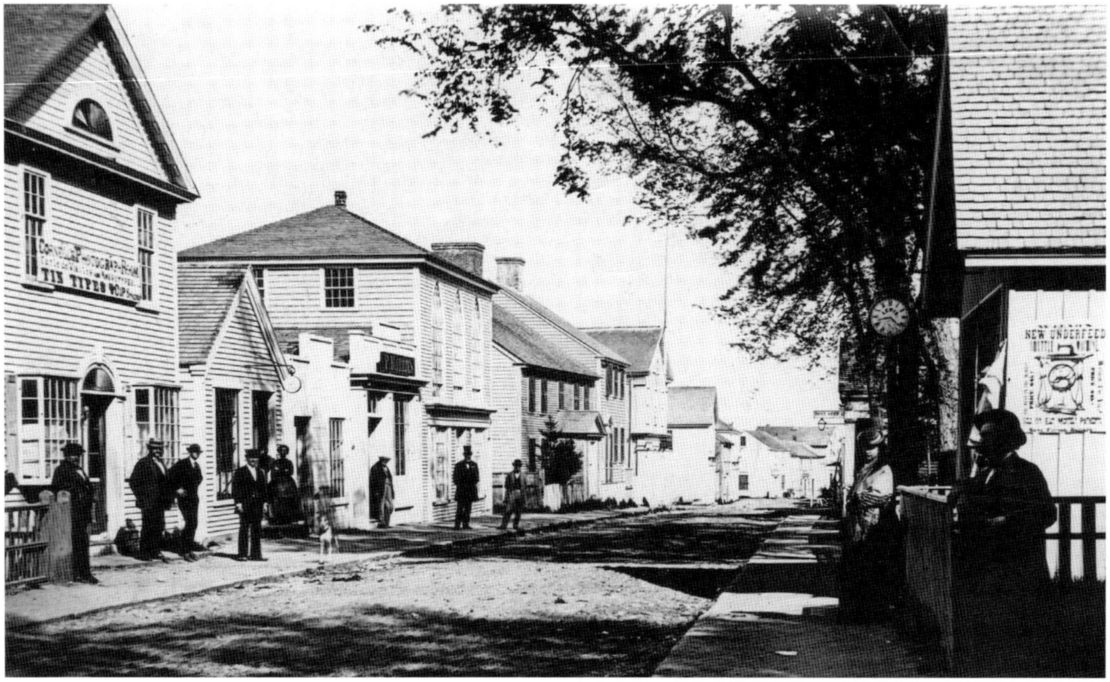

Most of the buildings in this view, looking east down Main Street in Edgartown around 1890, still stand today, though none of the businesses in them have survived. Cornell's Photograph Room is the first building on the left. This shop advertised *carte de visites*, ambrotypes, and tintypes.

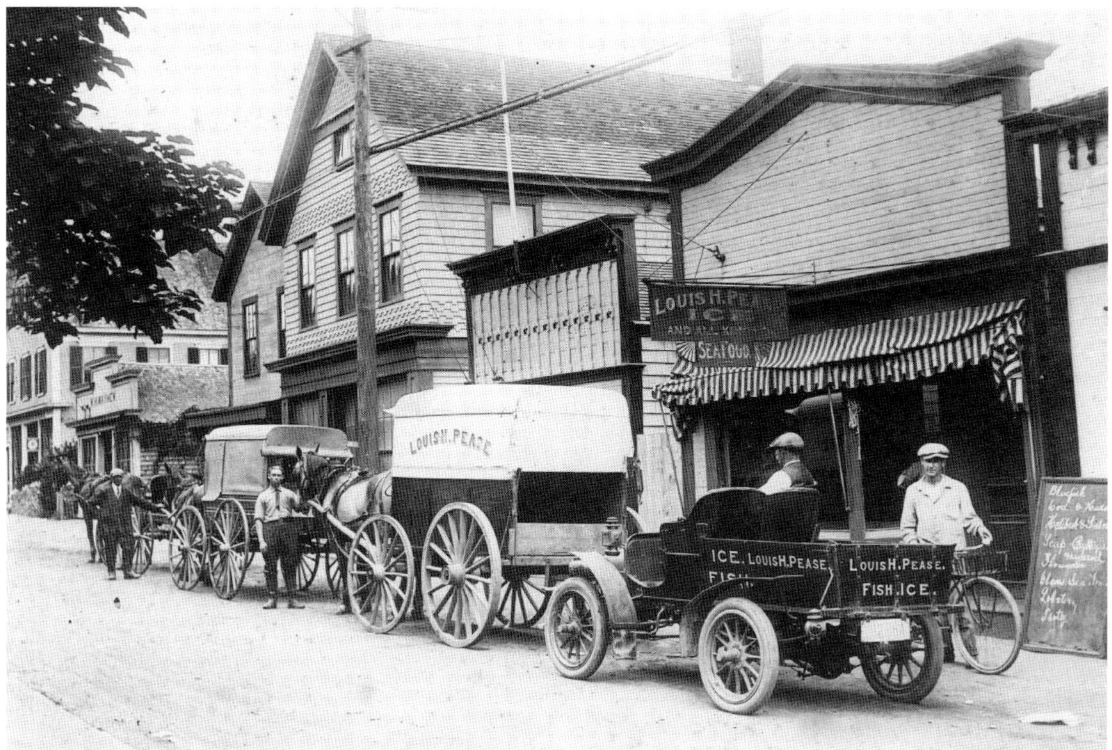

North Water Street in Edgartown was the location of Louis Pease's fish market. In this view, which appears to be from the first decade of the 20th century, the business's three delivery wagons and one delivery car are lined up in front, attesting to the efficiency and service its customers could expect.

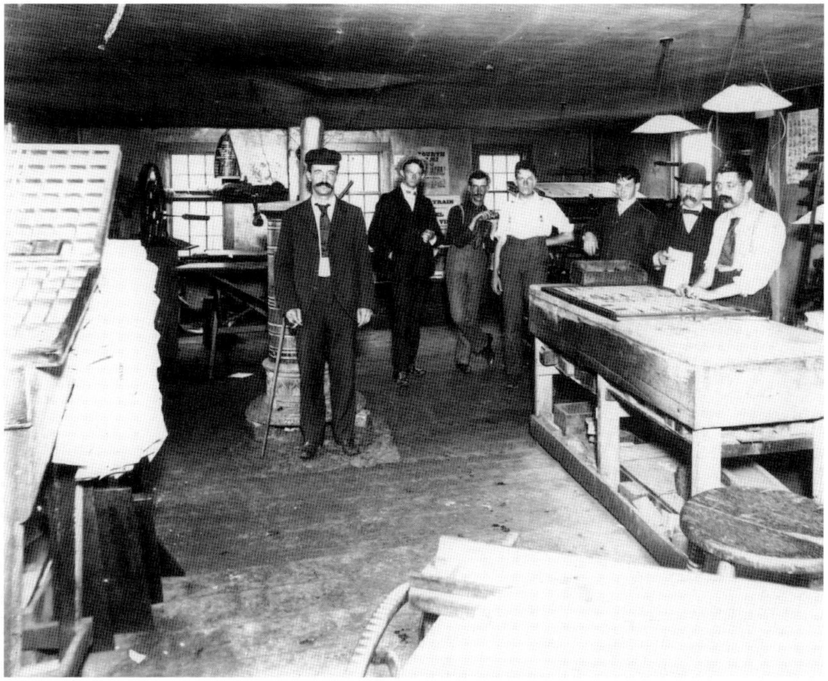

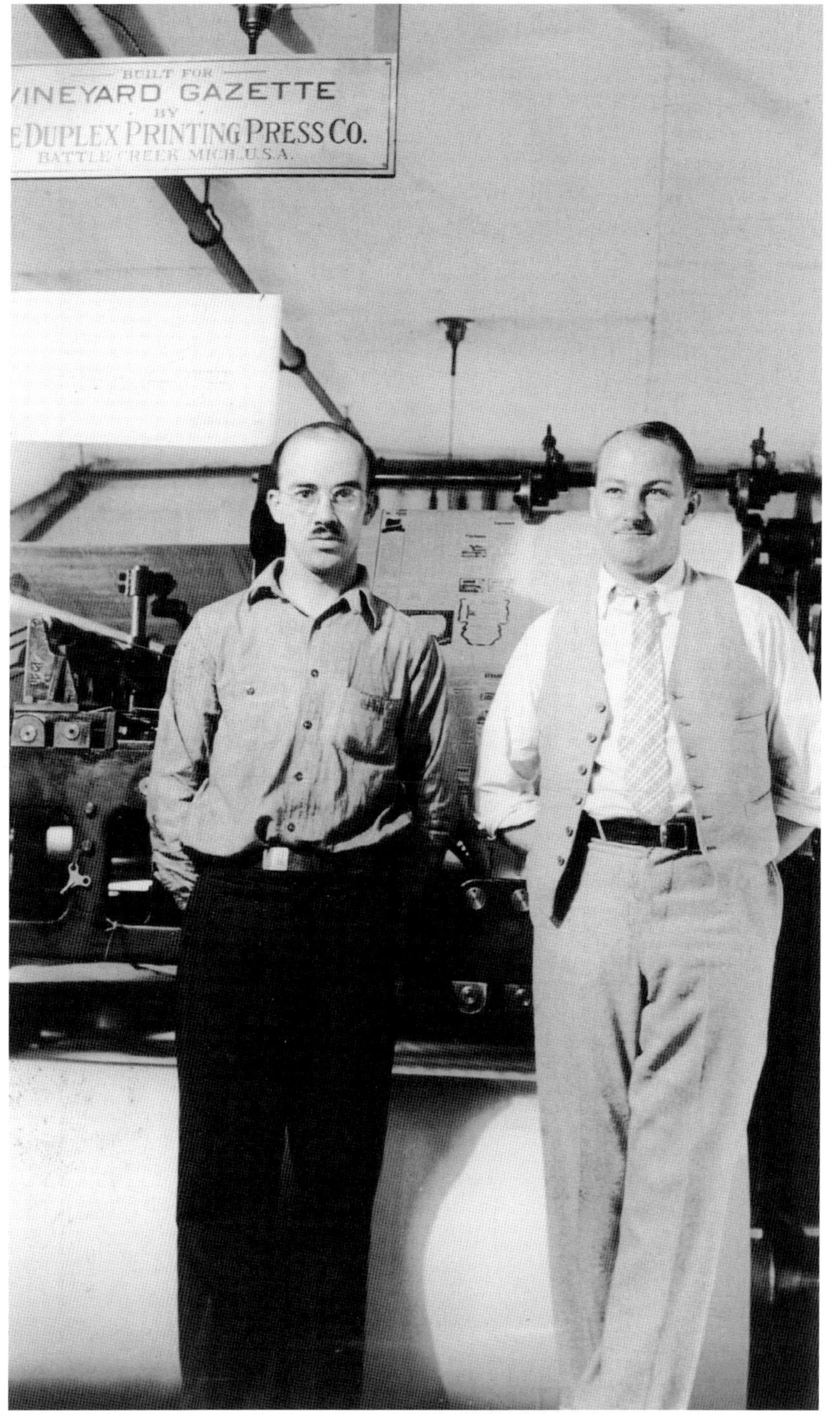

The *Vineyard Gazette* was founded in 1846 by Edgar Marchant and has been in business ever since. Formerly located at the corner of Main and North Water Streets, it has moved more than once, but it has always remained in Edgartown. Above, the staff of the newspaper poses in the 1870s or 1880s near the large wooden table where type was set. The men in the picture are not identified. At right, the names and jobs of the two men photographed in the *Gazette* office around 1935 were carefully recorded: "Everett M. Gale, primary pressman and also operator; and William Roberts, manager and genius of the production end of the Vineyard Gazette. These two constitute the back office staff."

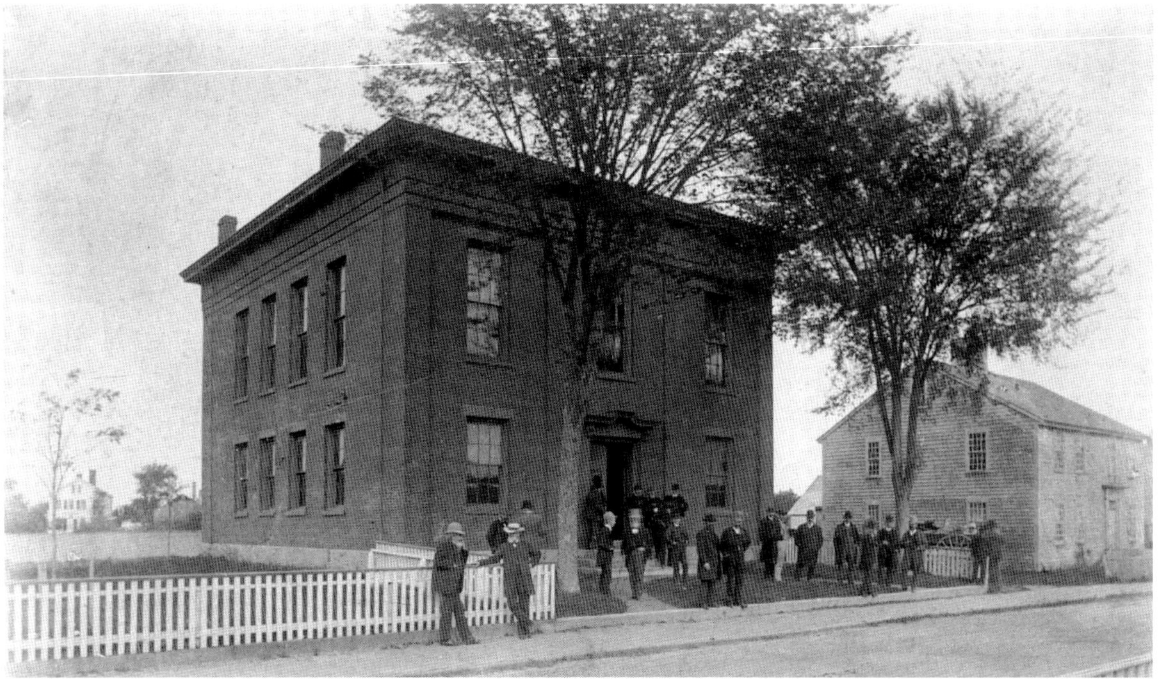

The Dukes County Courthouse was built in 1858 and is seen here around 1892. About 40 years later, Laura Jernegan Spear (seen as a child on page 11) helped identify some of the men standing in front of the building. On the left is Capt. William Crowell, and next to him is Capt. Jared Jernegan, Laura's father. Judge McIlvaine wears a top hat and carries a cane. (Photograph by Richard Shute.)

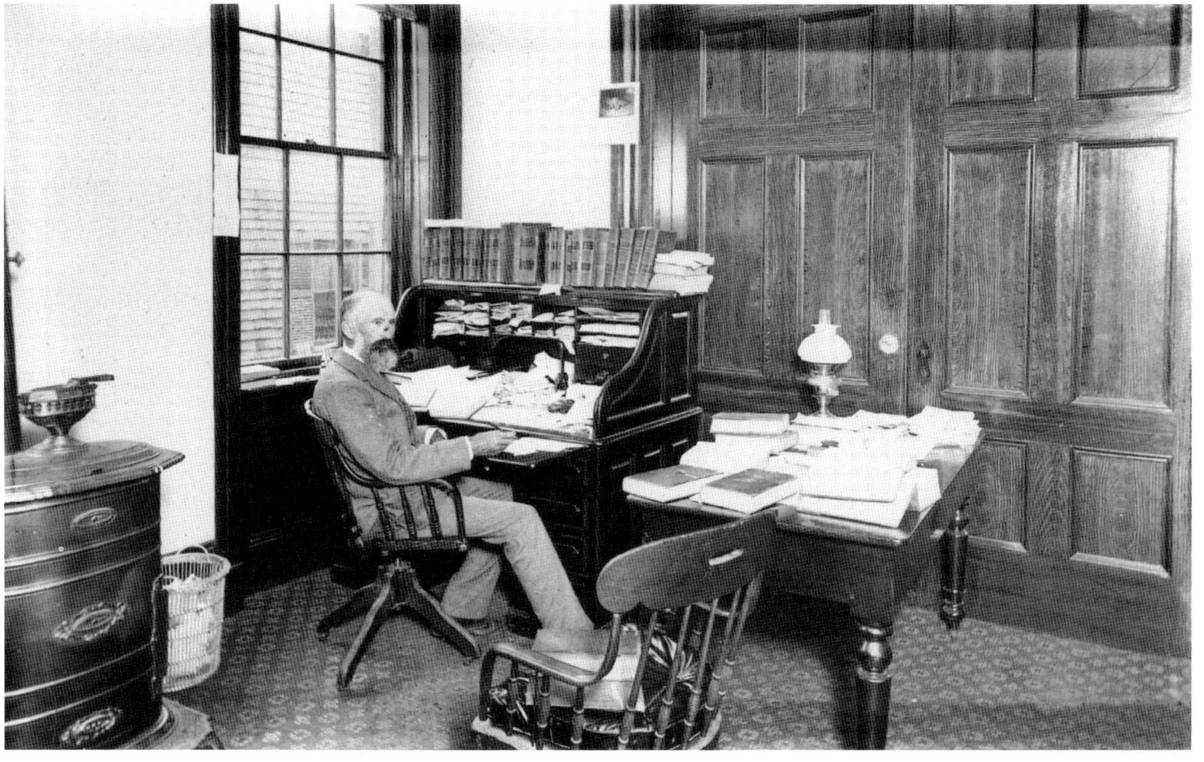

Beriah Hillman was born in Chilmark and attended high school at Dukes County Academy. He served in the Civil War, attended Bridgewater Normal School, returned to the island to teach, and was elected to local and state office. In 1887, he was appointed trial justice for Dukes County. Later, he became the register of probate and was admitted to the bar. Hillman is seen here in his office in the Dukes County Courthouse.

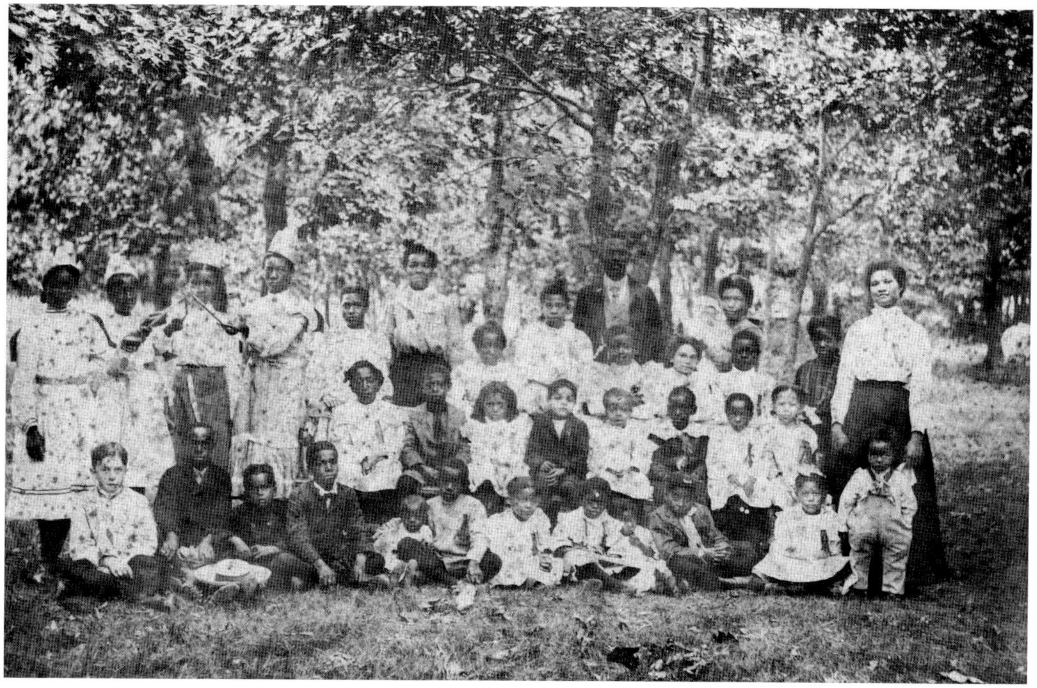

Bradley Memorial Church was started in Oak Bluffs by the Reverend Oscar Denniston (standing in the back row in the dark jacket) in 1907. The church was the first on the island to serve both the African American and immigrant populations. Reverend Denniston and his family ran the church for nearly 50 years.

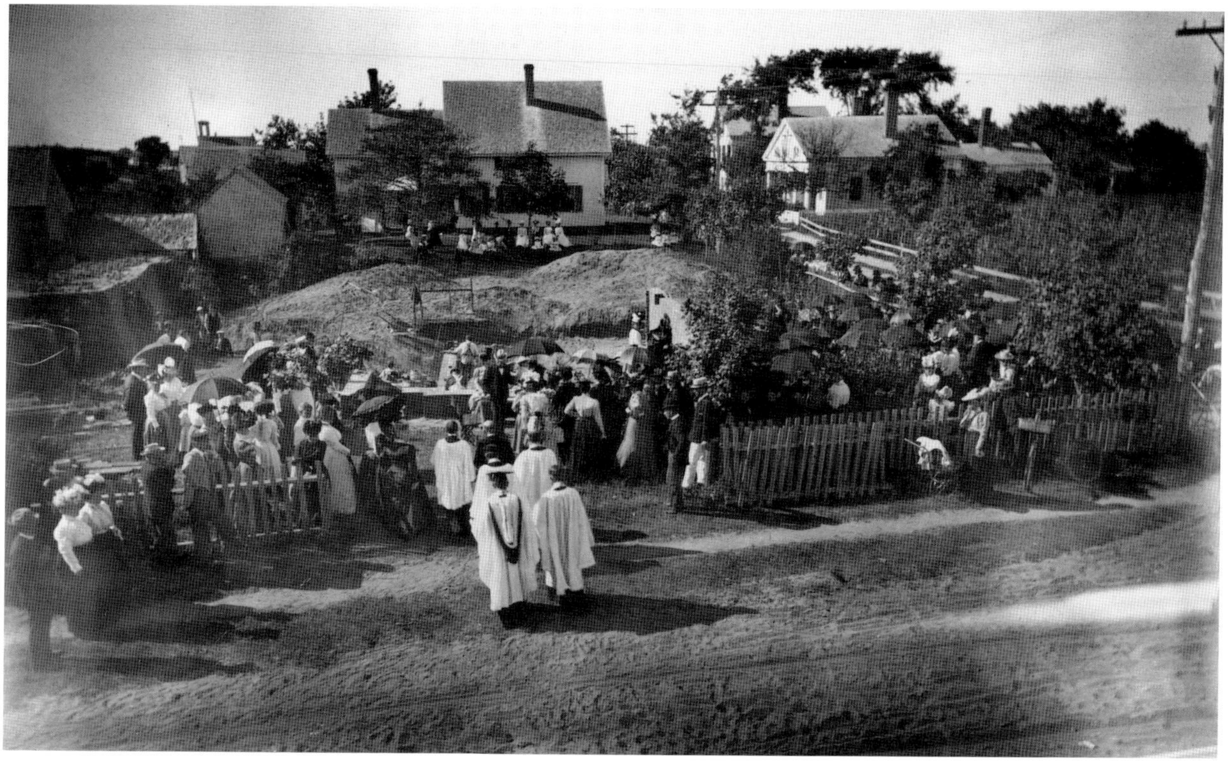

The cornerstone for St. Andrew's Church, at the corner of Winter and Summer Streets in Edgartown, was laid in 1899. Observers gathered all around the edges of the site to watch the ceremony. (Photograph by Richard Shute.)

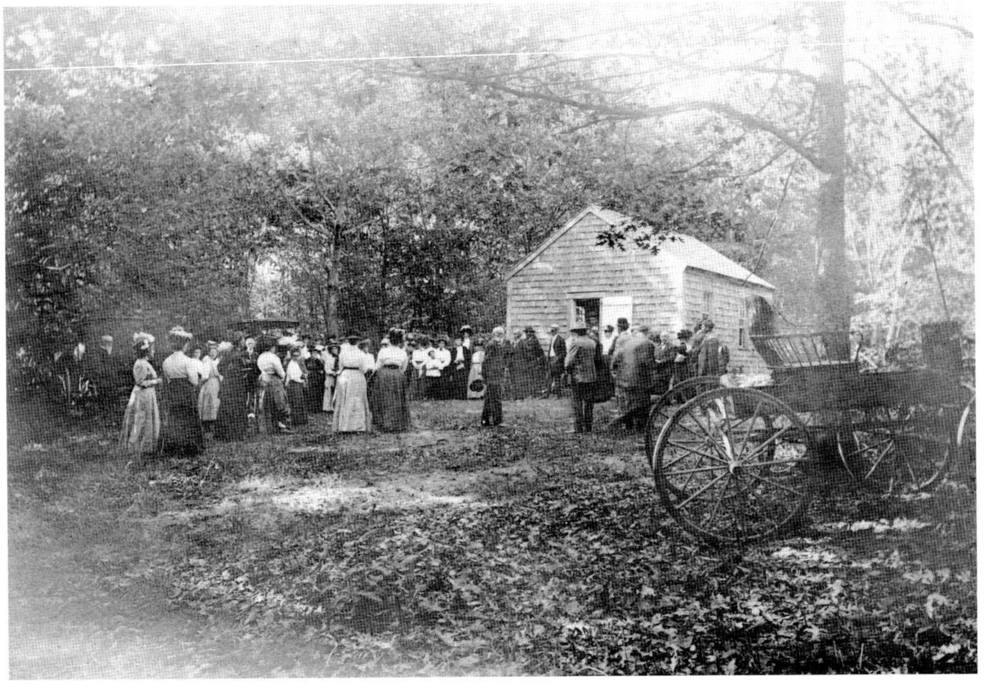

Christiantown Meeting House, also called the Mayhew Chapel, was originally built as a place for Wampanoag tribal members who had converted to Christianity. Located in West Tisbury, it is named for Thomas Mayhew Jr., the island's first missionary. The chapel in this photograph was built in 1829, replacing a much earlier structure.

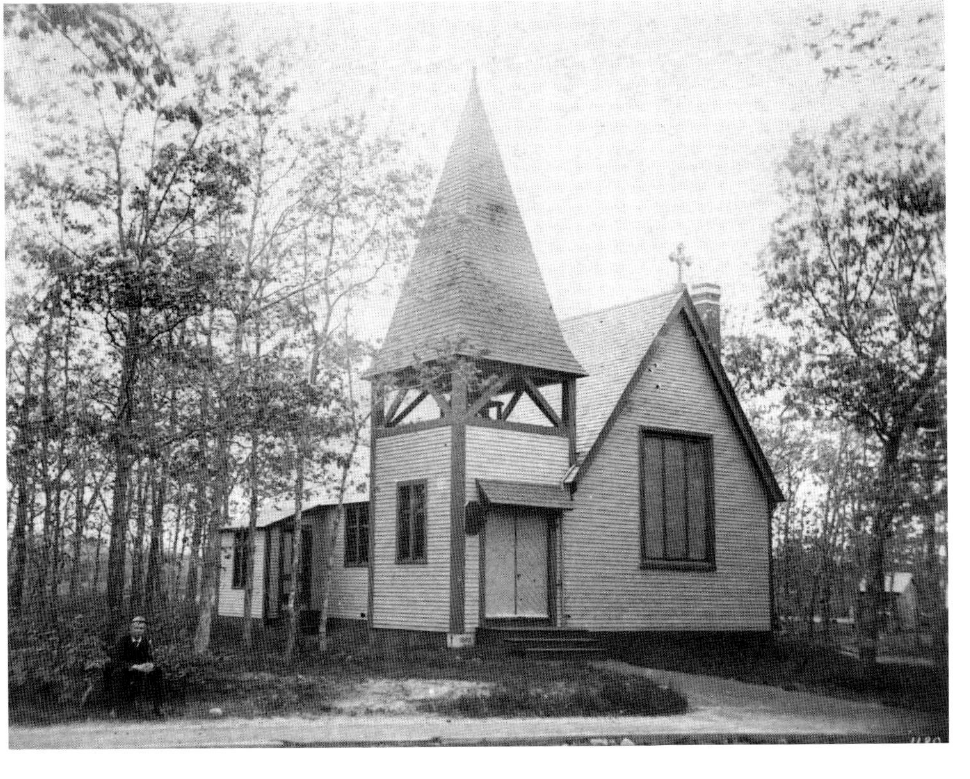

Grace Episcopal Church stands on the corner of Woodlawn and William Streets in Vineyard Haven. This building was constructed beginning in 1882. In 1999, a stained-glass window depicting Bishop John Melville Burgess, the first African American elected as a diocesan bishop in the Episcopal Church and a Martha's Vineyard resident, was installed in the church.

The Dukes County Academy opened in West Tisbury in 1837 with Leavett Thaxter as its first teacher. The building is now the West Tisbury Town Hall.

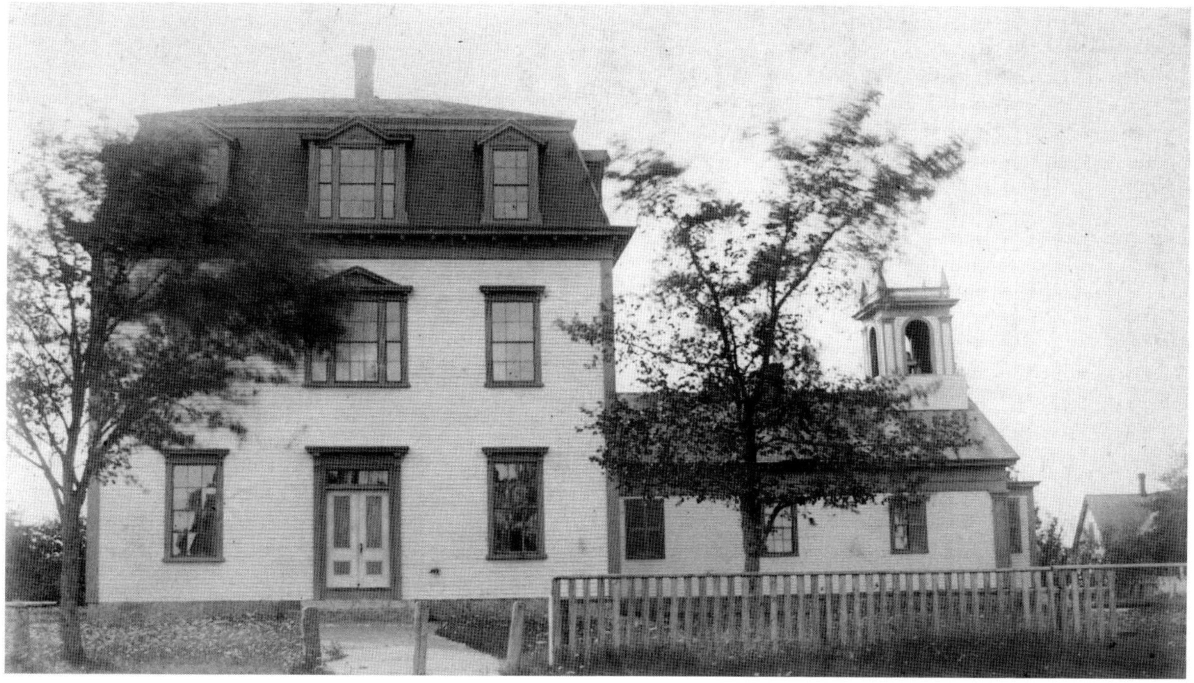

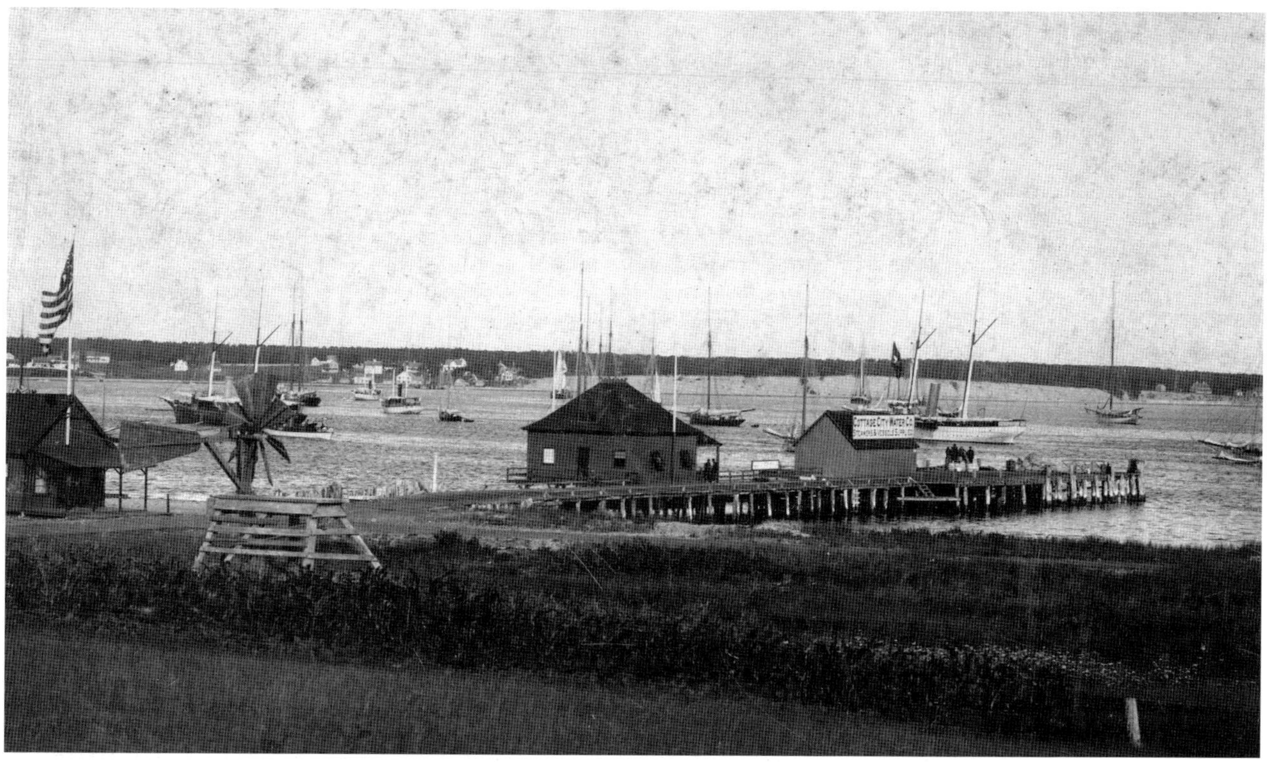

The Cottage City Water Company on New York Wharf supplied water to vessels. It was located past East Chop on the Vineyard Haven side of town. A windmill is visible in the foreground. Wooden windmills like this, or taller, were often constructed on the Vineyard. (Photograph by John N. Chamberlain.)

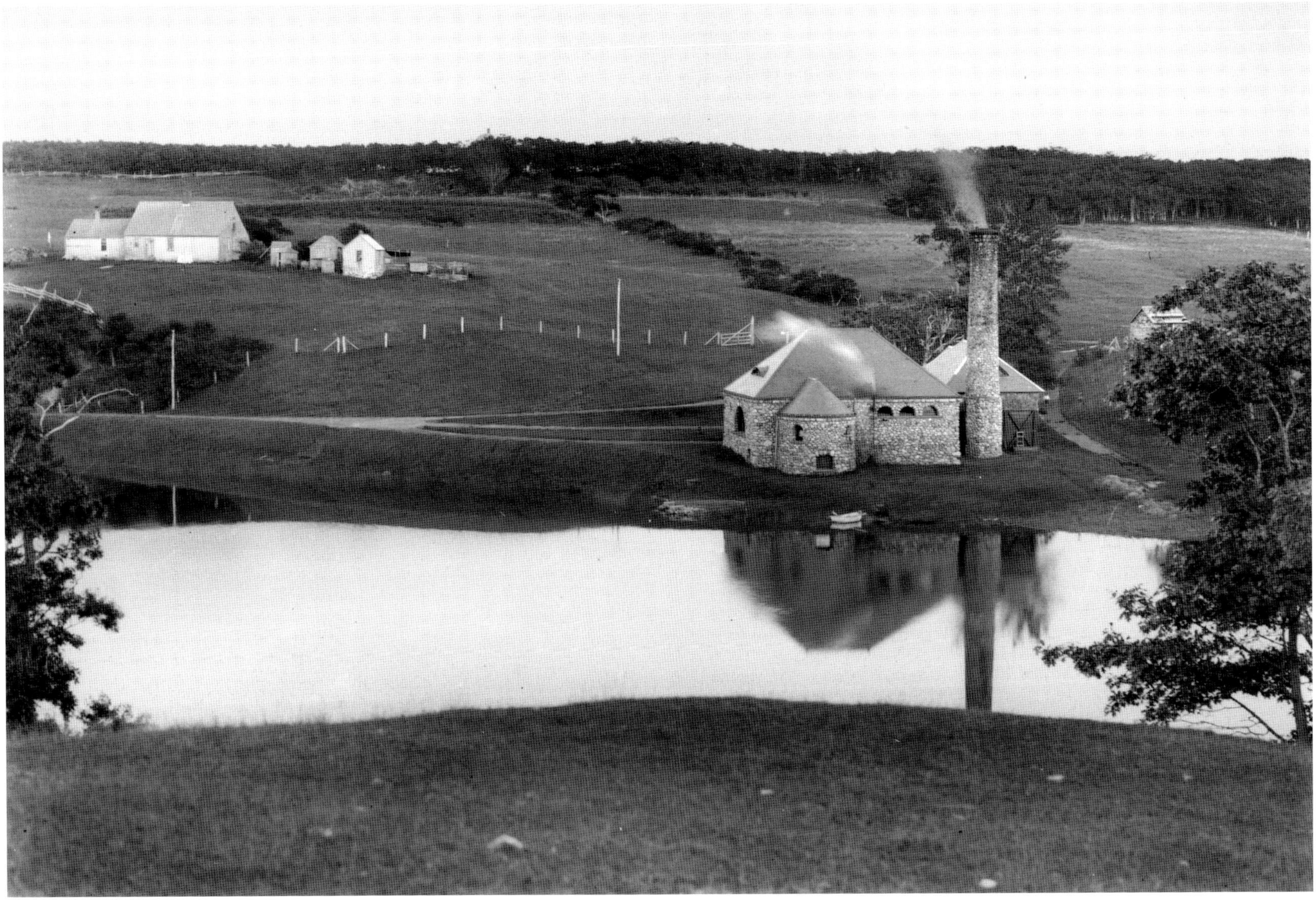

Oak Bluffs Pumping Station, near the southern part of the Lagoon, still provides some of the freshwater used by that town. Constructed in 1890, it is the oldest continuously operating pumping station in Massachusetts. Another pumping station of similar appearance still stands in Tisbury at Tashmoo.

OPPOSITE: This group from around 1900 gathers near the entrance to the Oak Bluffs wharf. Despite the physical changes that have taken place over the years, the summer scene has had one consistent feature for a century and a half: crowds of people wait. They are expecting visitors, are at the end of a trip, or perhaps are just beginning a trip off the island.

THREE

ENCHANTED ISLE

Martha's Vineyard grew from a small year-round population of less than 4,000 in 1840 to about 16,000 in 2010. But that number does not reflect the enormous surge in population that occurs in the summer months. On any given summer day, there may be 75,000–100,000 people enjoying the pleasures that the Vineyard has to offer or working for businesses that cater to the crowds. The idea of Martha's Vineyard as a vacation spot began to take hold in the mid-1800s with the two different—and, sometimes, even competing—impulses of resort and retreat.

The Methodist camp meetings that began in the part of Edgartown that later became Oak Bluffs introduced a new population to the island. Erastus P. Carpenter recognized the potential to capitalize on these visitors by creating the Oak Bluffs Land & Wharf Company in 1866. The company built the Sea View House hotel and laid out a development where people could build vacation houses. Before long, the town boomed, leaving quiet Edgartown behind.

In 1912, Charles Shearer opened Shearer Cottage to lodgers in order to provide a welcoming place for African American vacationers. This marked the beginning of Oak Bluffs as a popular resort for African Americans, including such luminaries as Harry Burleigh, Loïs Mailou Jones, and Adam Clayton Powell Jr. Author Dorothy West summered in the Highlands neighborhood of Oak Bluffs for many years and lived there year-round in the last years of her life.

At the same time, people began to discover the Vineyard as a retreat where they could find relaxation away from the hustle of Boston and New York. Settling for the summer in quiet areas in and out of the towns, they returned year after year, creating their own communities and blending in with year-round residents. Sometimes, the attraction became so strong that they decided to move to the island permanently.

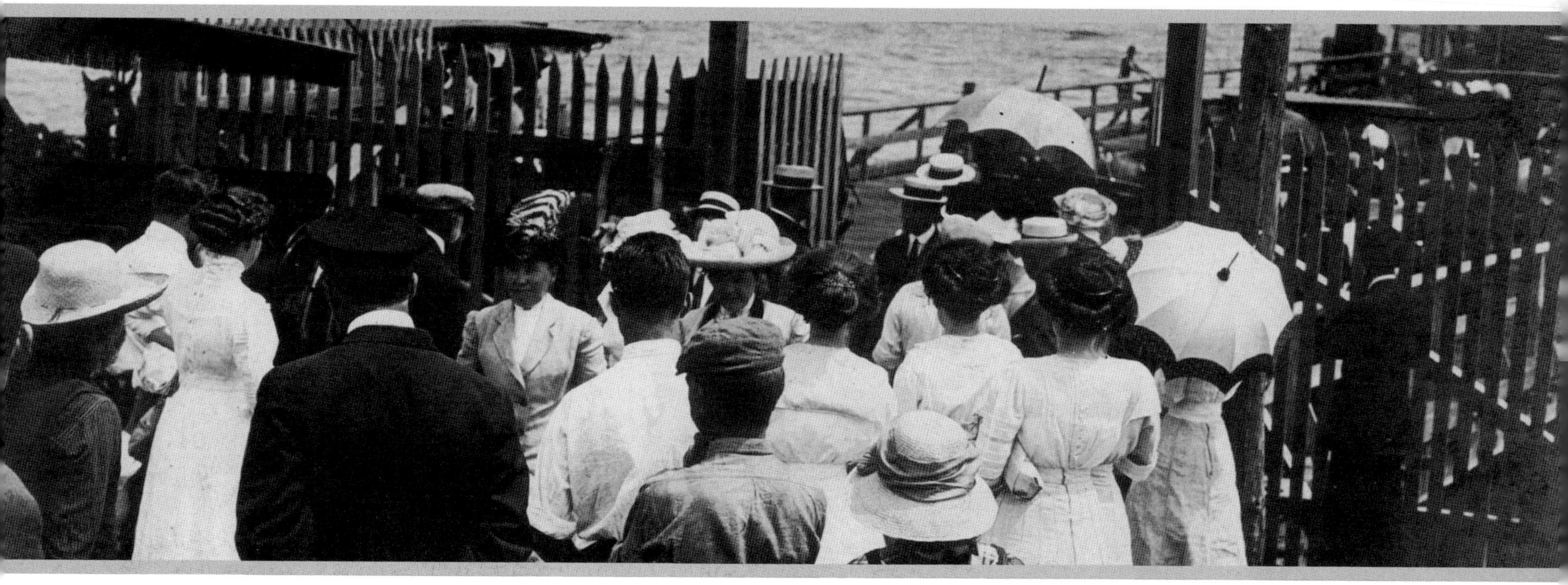

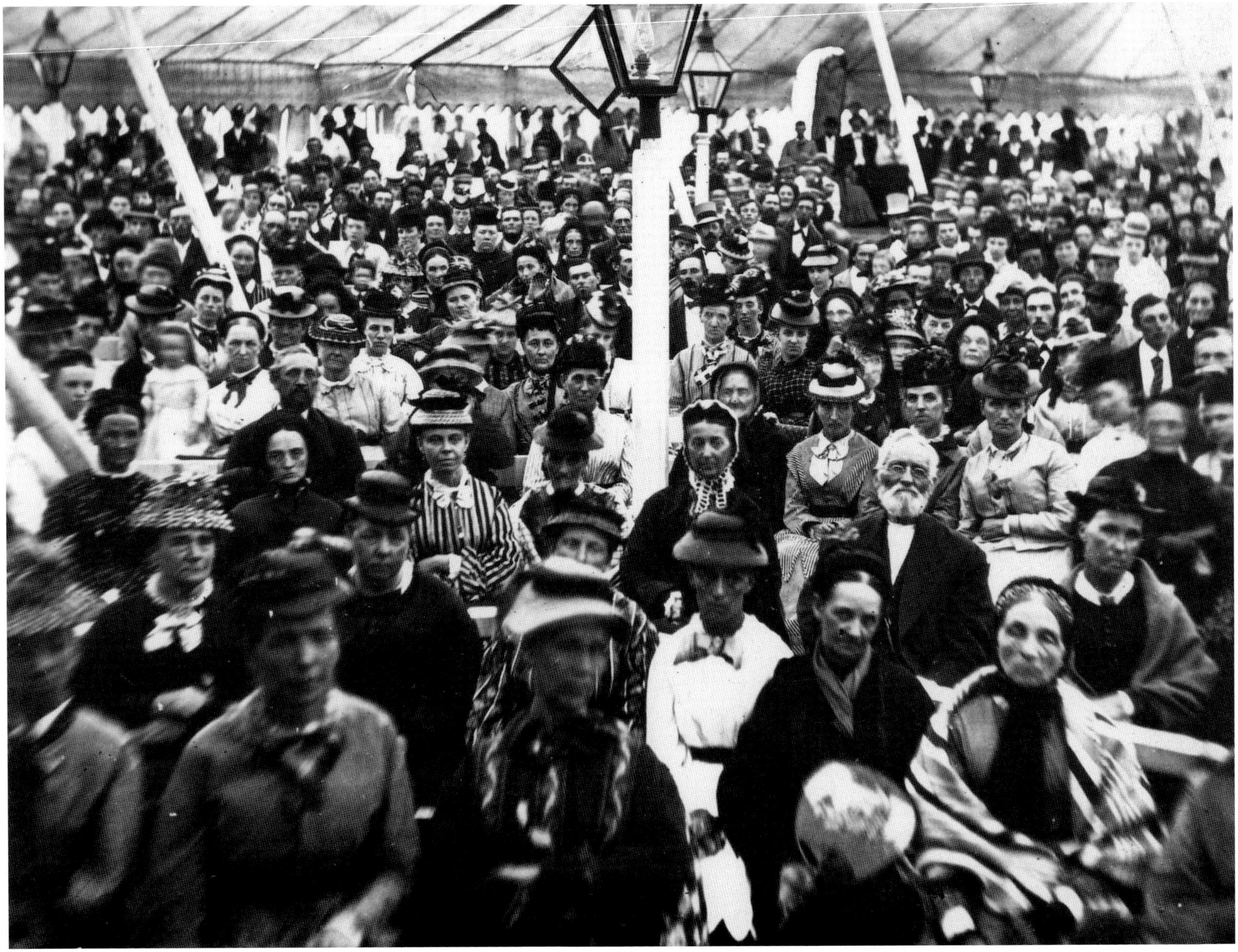

Martha's Vineyard as a popular vacation destination began with religious revivalism. The first Methodist camp meeting on the island was held in West Chop in 1827. One of the attendees, Jeremiah Pease, helped organize Wesleyan Grove in the Eastville part of Edgartown in 1835. From a modest beginning of 9 tents, it grew to 200 tents in 20 years. For a week to 10 days in August, the faithful thronged to the camp meeting for intense periods of worship and fellowship.

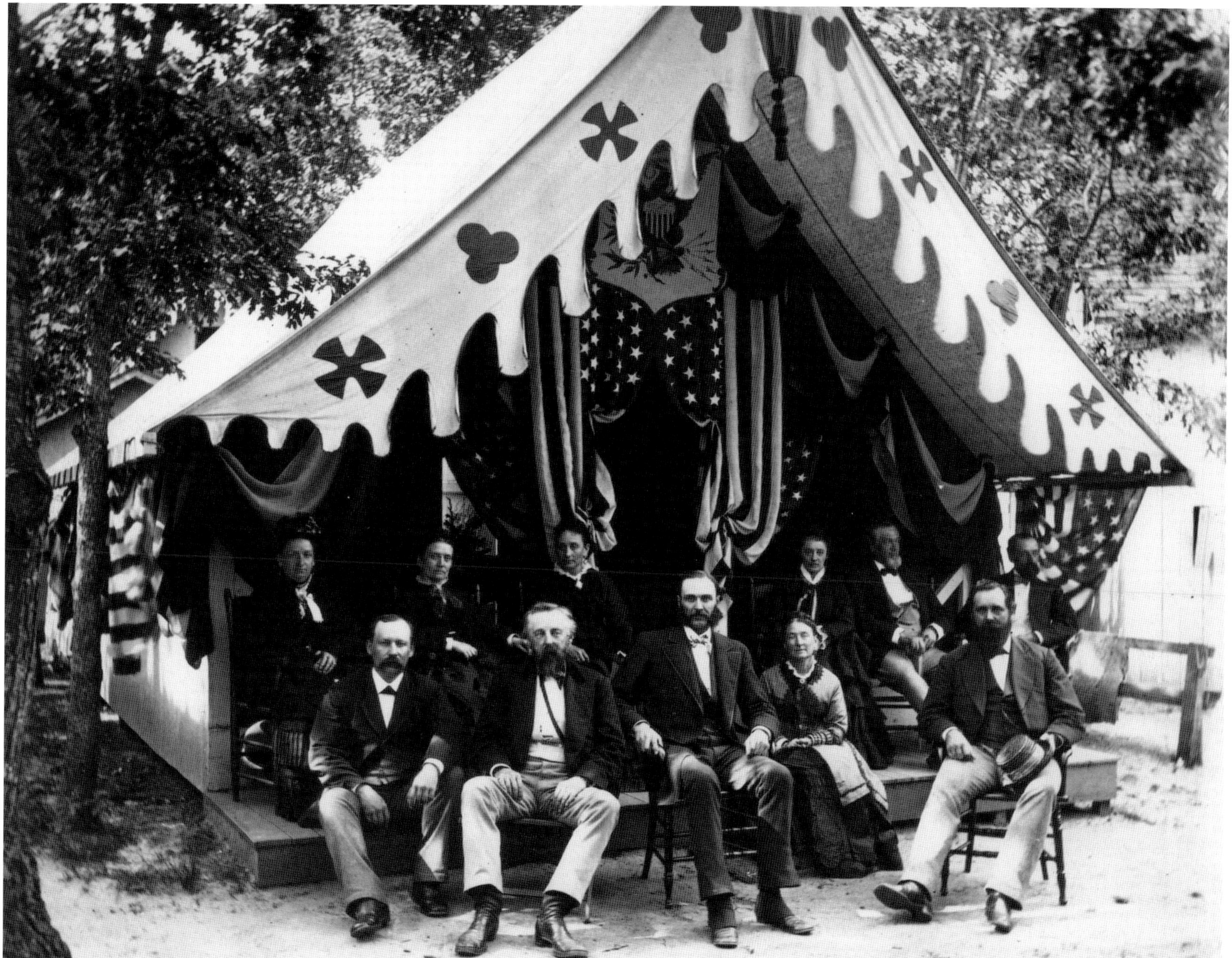

At first, camp meeting attendees stayed in tents. During the camp meeting of 1868, a total of 570 tents were pitched at Wesleyan Grove. Some of them were quite plain, but some, like this one, had ornamental edging along the roof, a detail that was later recalled in the gingerbread-style cottages that followed.

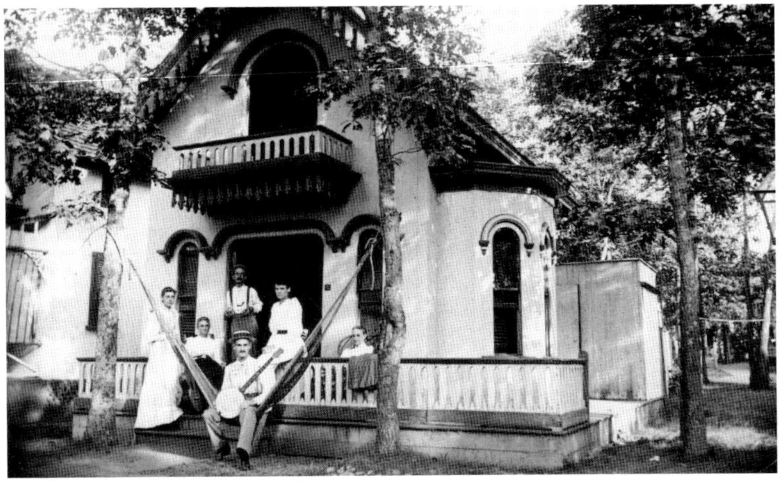

Cottages began to replace tents in the 1860s. The change prompted one writer in an 1873 issue of *Harper's New Monthly Magazine* to exclaim, "What a wonderful collection of tiny houses strewn about helter-skelter, like toys forgotten by children! . . . You may peer into tents that have done duty in the Army of the Potomac, and find the familiar contrivances of the old soldier brightly bedecked by the tasteful handiwork of his wife. You may gaze boldly into the open doors of the most aristocratic homes without giving offense. It is said that in the crowded season as many as forty thousand people dwell in those cottages by the sea." Dr. Elizah Packard's cottage is seen at left, and Cornell's Gallery, which rented rooms and sold "fancy goods," is below. (Below, photograph by Josepah W. Warren.)

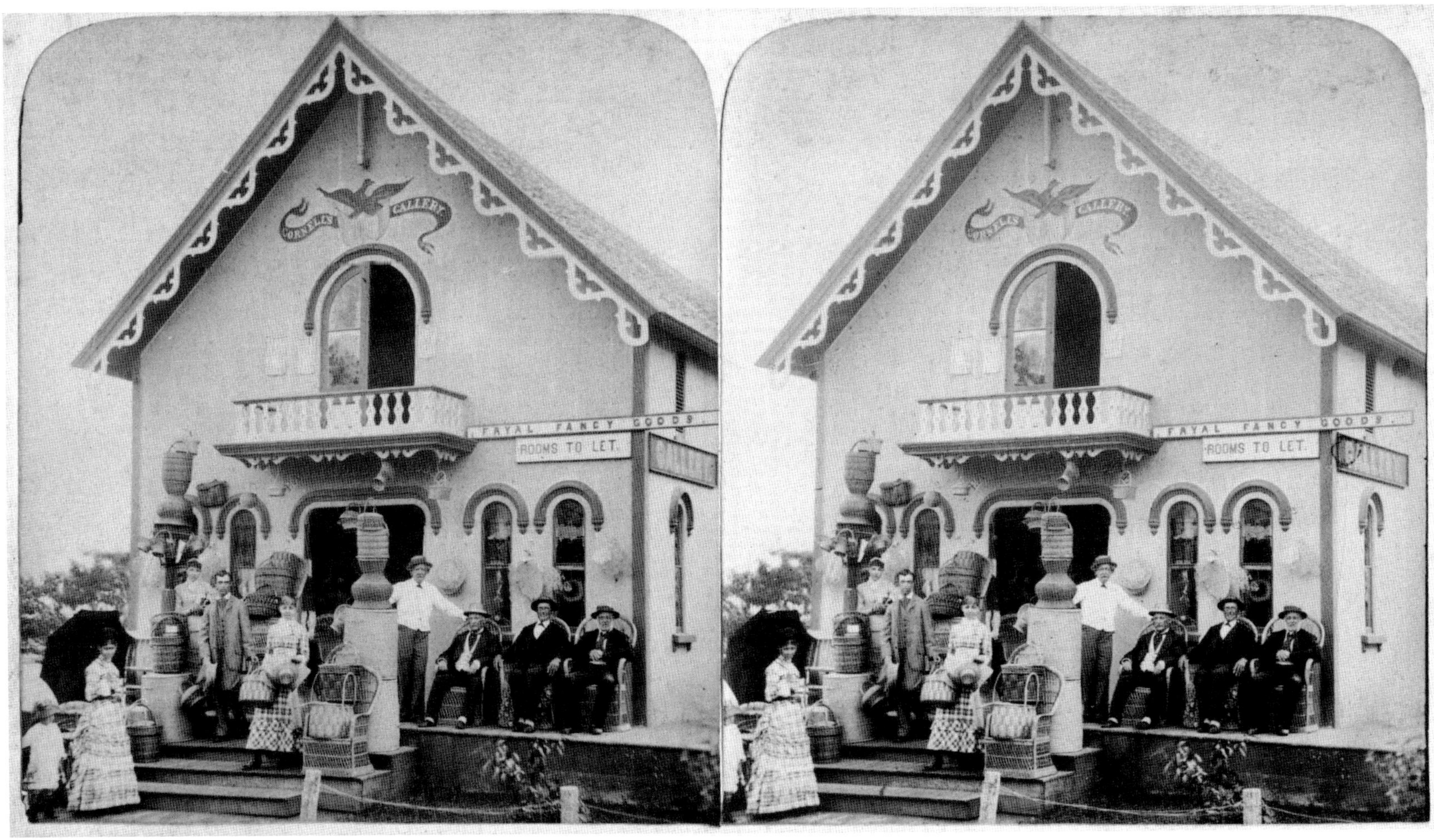

The *Island Home* belonged to the New Bedford, Martha's Vineyard & Nantucket Steamboat Company and ferried passengers to Martha's Vineyard from about 1886 to about 1895. Seen here arriving at the Oak Bluffs ferry wharf, the side-wheel steamer met trains in Woods Hole and New Bedford that brought passengers from Boston and New York.

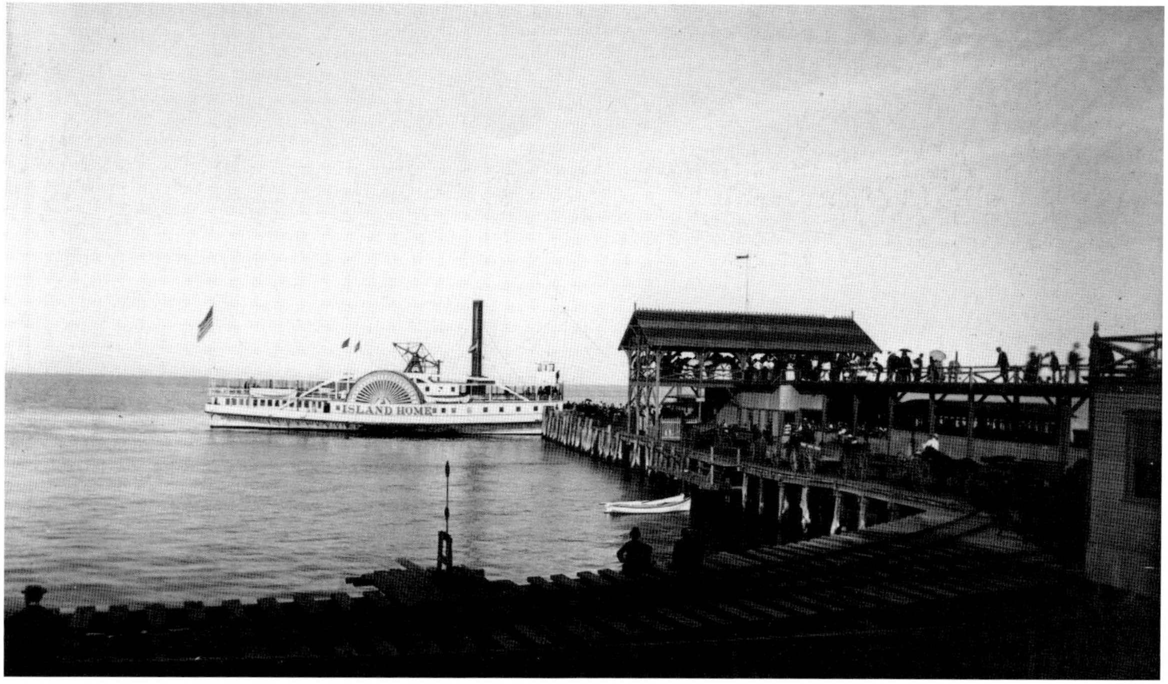

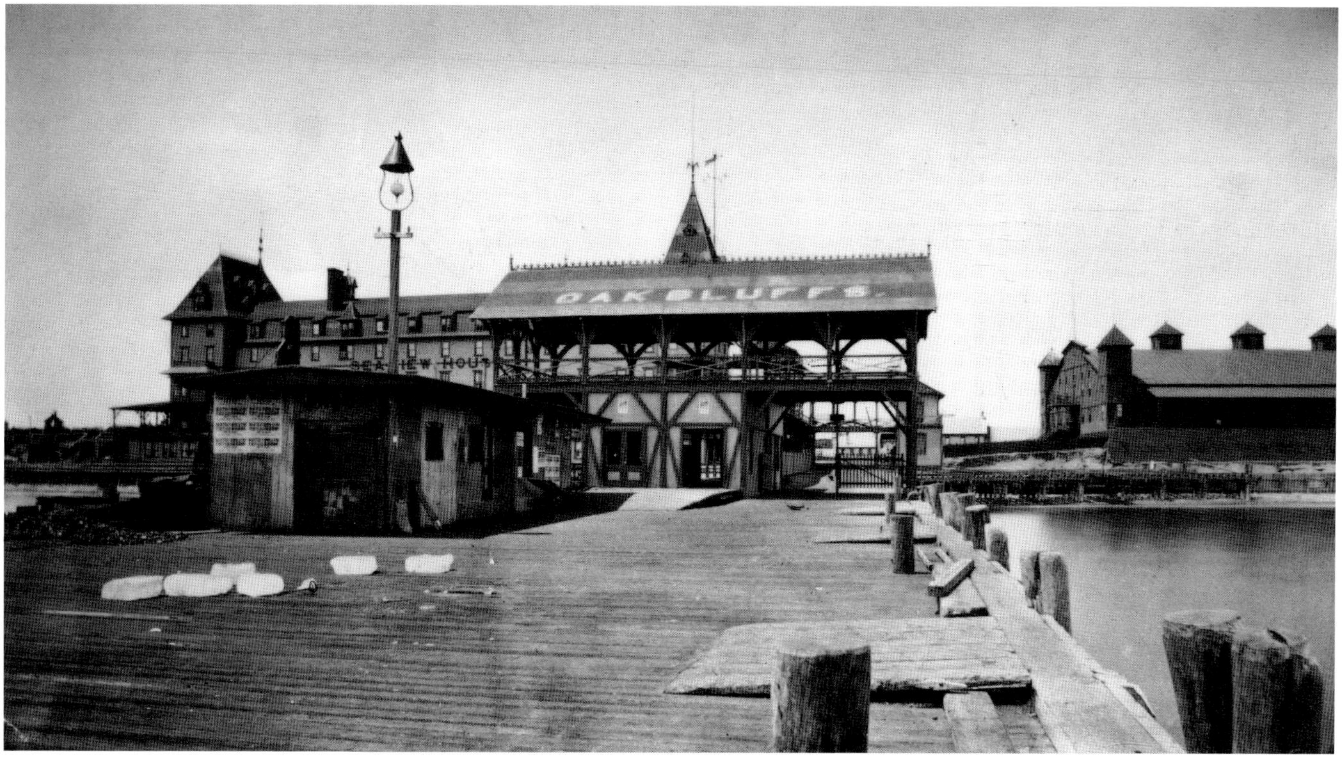

Blocks of ice, necessary for the summer needs of ice cream parlors and resort hotels, sit on the wharf in Oak Bluffs, probably in the early morning of a summer day before the arrival of the next boat full of visitors. The roller-skating rink on the right dates this photograph to between 1879 and 1892.

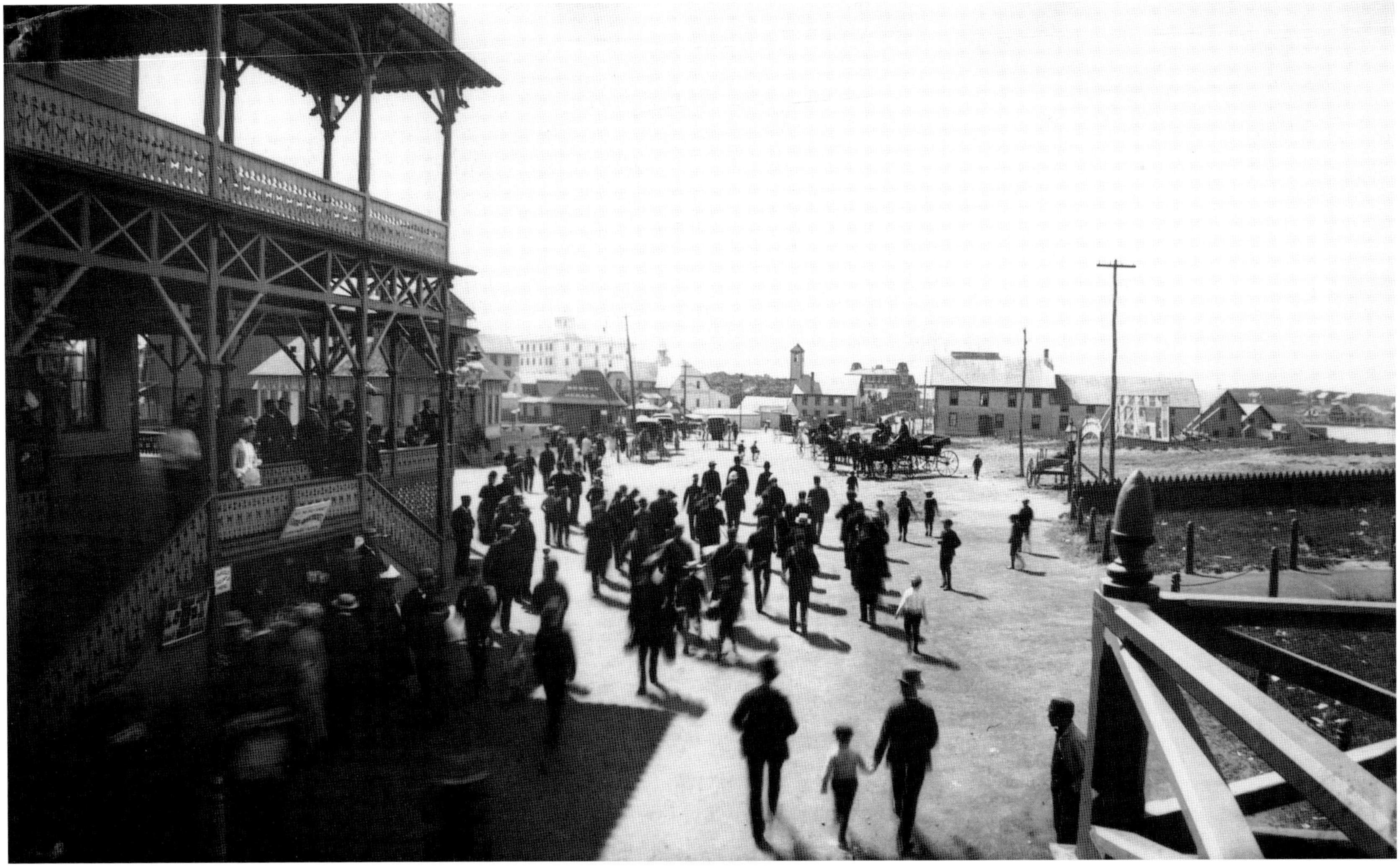

Looking up Oak Bluffs Avenue from the wharf in the 1880s, this photograph shows the rapid growth that had occurred over just a decade or so. In 1873, *Harper's New Monthly Magazine* warned, "Simplicity is fast disappearing. Tall, pretentious, and gaudy structures are going up as dwellings and hotels that will ere long take away from the camp meeting the great charms of lowliness and humility. If it should once become fashionable, its doom is sealed."

The Central House hotel stood in Montgomery Square in the campgrounds. The gingerbread decoration along its eaves echoed the fanciful cottages nearby. It was built in 1866 as the Dunbar House, but the name was changed in 1870. The child on the right in the center of the photograph appears in several of Shute's tourist photographs, suggesting that he was hired. (Photograph by Richard Shute.)

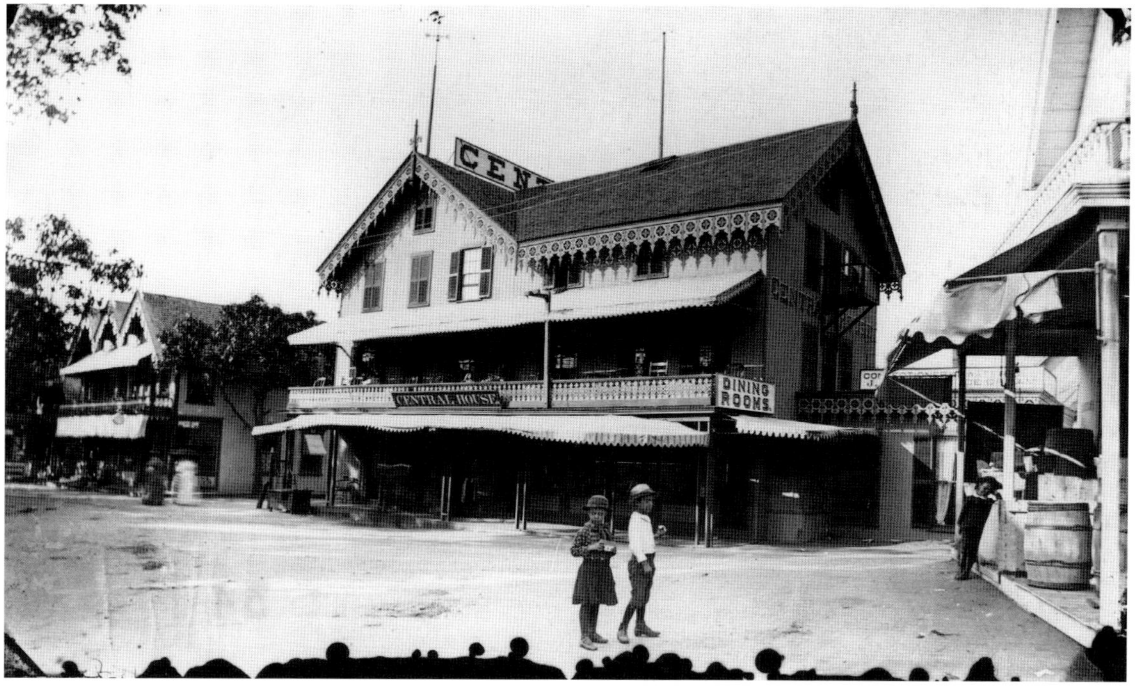

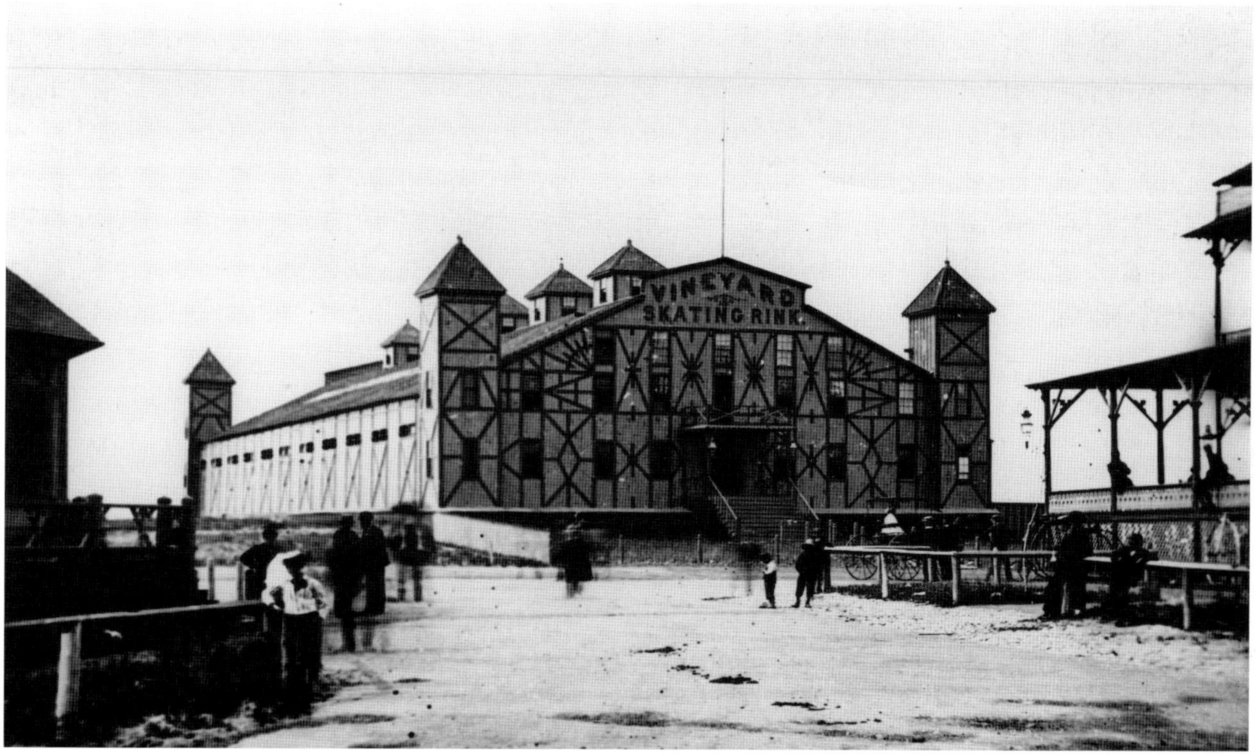

The Vineyard Skating Rink in Oak Bluffs was built in 1879 by Samuel Winslow of Worcester. It was the site of concerts and dances as well as roller-skating. In September 1892, the nearby Sea View House burned down in a conflagration that caused irreparable damage to the skating rink as well. The rink was never rebuilt. (Photograph by Richard Shute.)

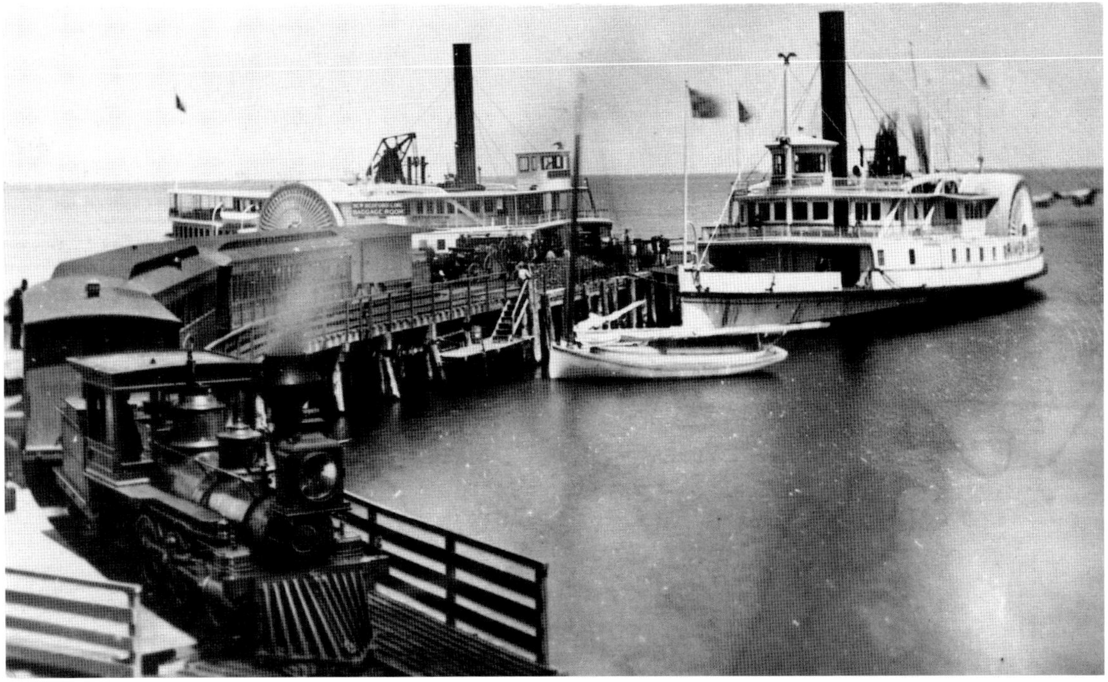

The Martha's Vineyard Railroad was built in 1874 as an attempt by Edgartown and private investors to siphon off some of the success of Cottage City (Oak Bluffs). It ran the nine miles between Cottage City and Katama, where a new grand hotel, the Mattakeset Lodge, was built to accommodate the hoped-for vacationers. At the time, Cottage City was still part of Edgartown, but there was growing resentment in the prosperous new development towards the old town. This would lead to the separation into two towns in 1880.

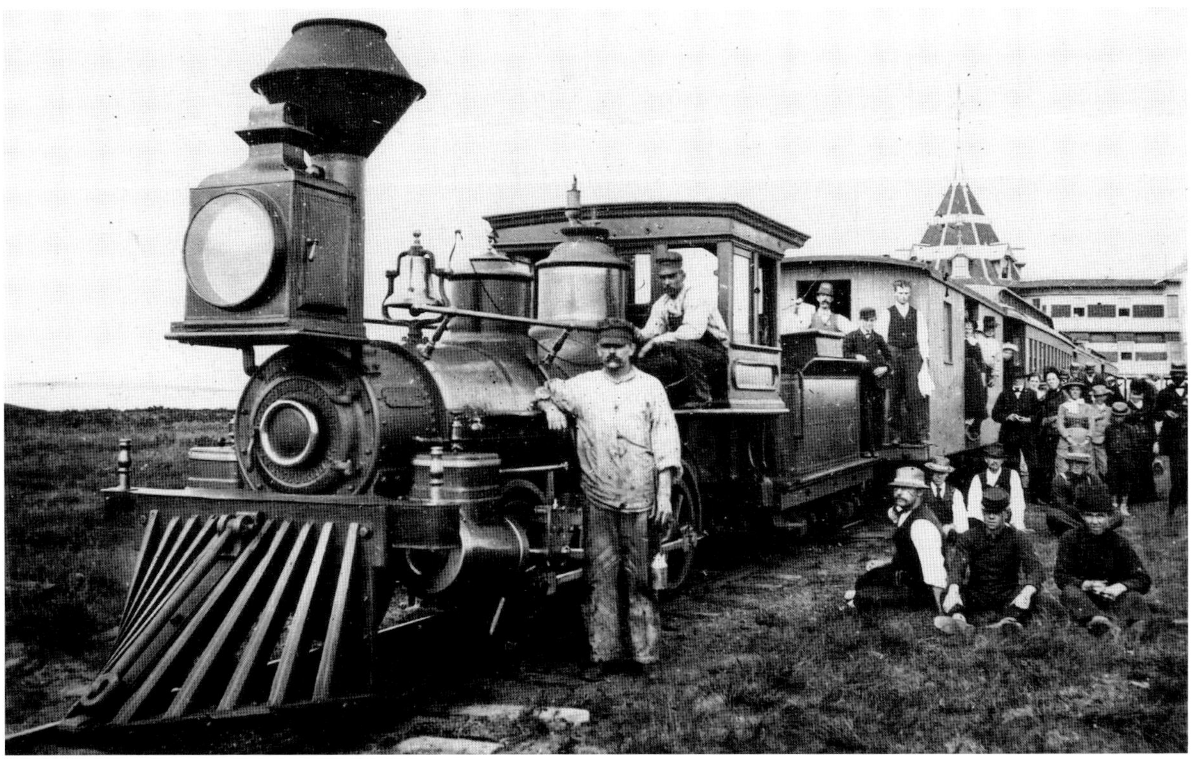

The railroad, never profitable, finally closed in 1895. The Mattakeset Lodge was even less successful, only lasting until 1879. Here, the crew and passengers stand near the train and its engine, the *Active*, in front of the lodge. (Photograph by Richard Shute.)

The lookout tower, or observatory, offered a fine view of Oak Bluffs and its surroundings. It was part of a complex of structures on the shore just east of Ocean Park along Sea View Avenue that included boardwalks and bathhouses where beachgoers could change their clothes. The access from the street to the tower included a pavilion and a covered walkway over the railroad tracks.

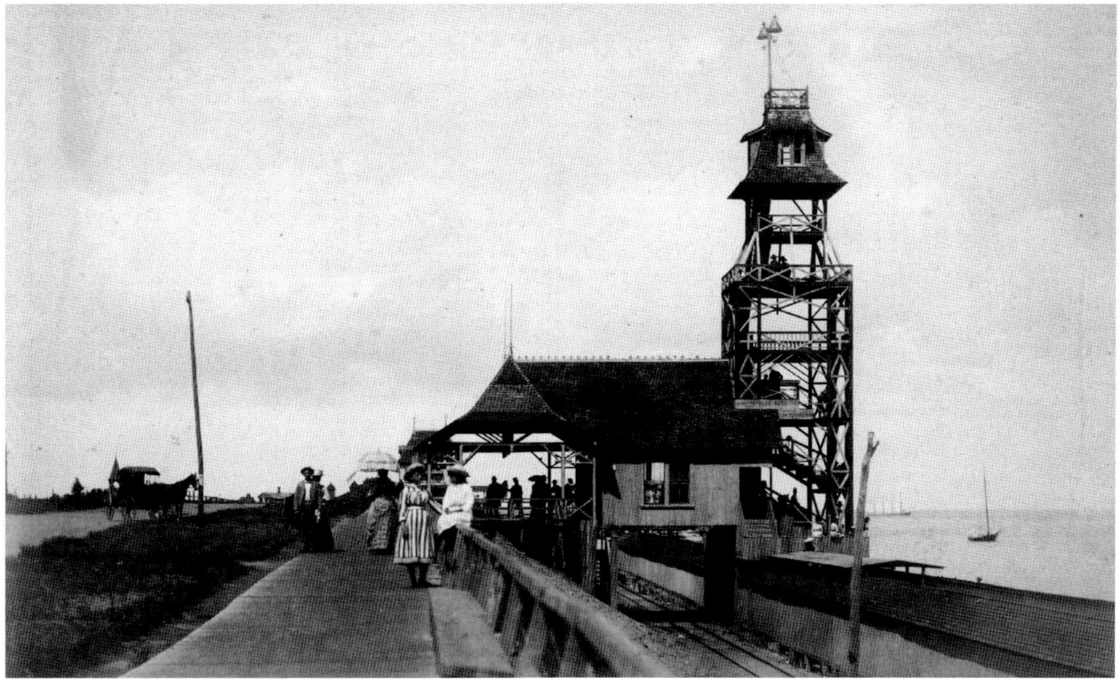

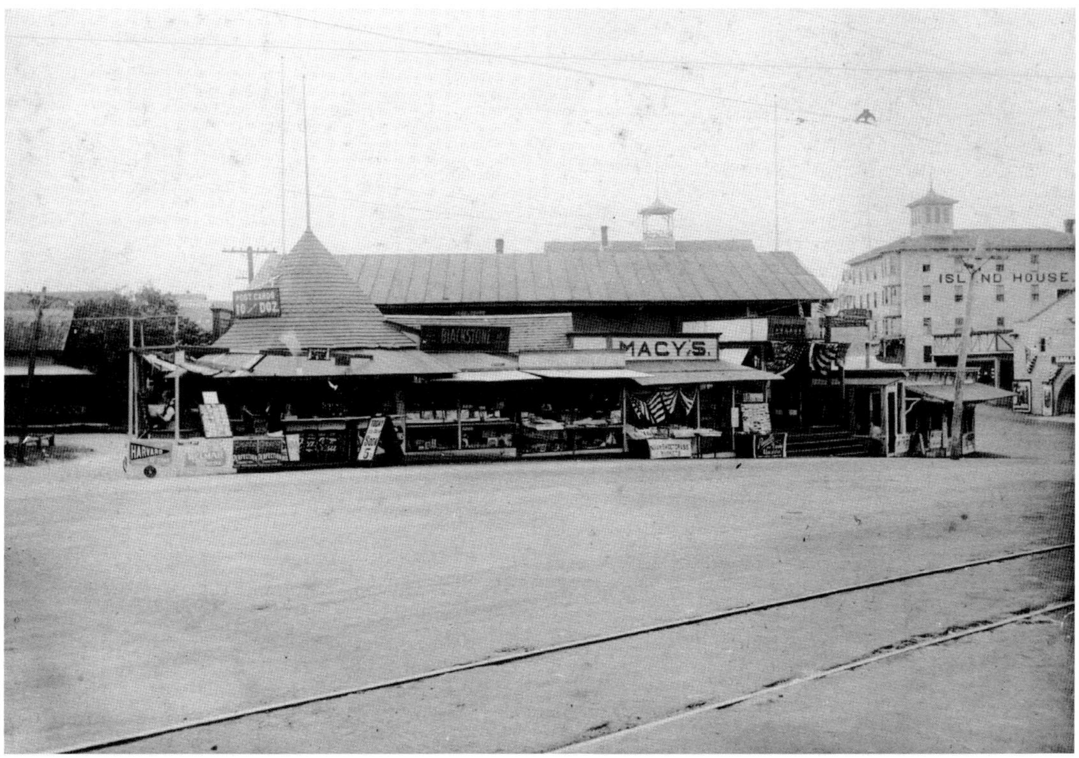

Trolley tracks can be seen in the foreground of this early-1900s view of the intersection of Lake and Circuit Avenues in Oak Bluffs. The Island House hotel is on the right. The shops are filled with goods designed to appeal to tourists, including postcards and "Indian Sweet Grass baskets."

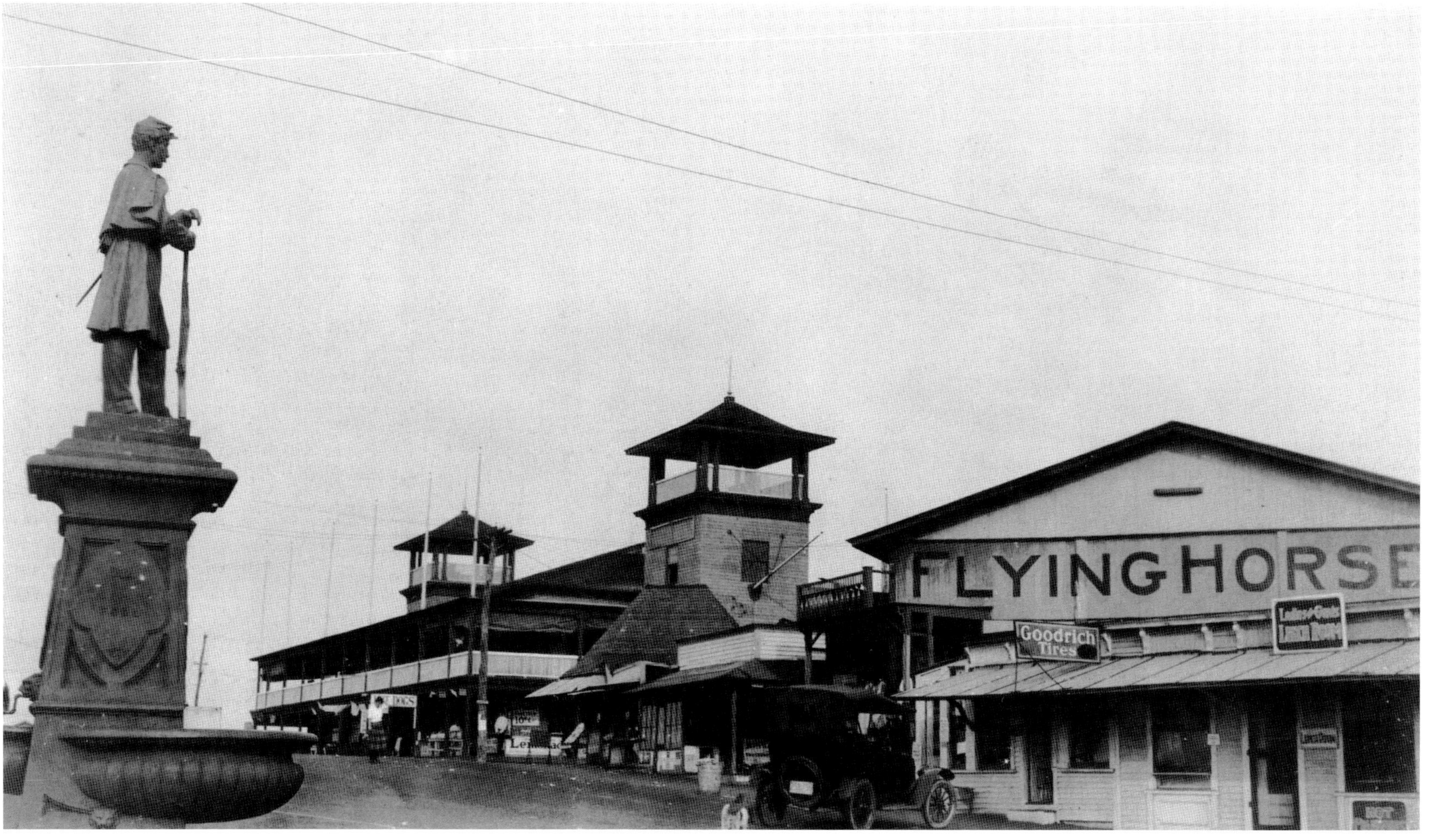

This photograph from the early 1900s shows the original location of Oak Bluffs' Civil War statue on Circuit Avenue. It was erected in 1891 with funds raised through the efforts of Charles Strahan, a Confederate veteran of the Civil War who came to the island to publish the *Martha's Vineyard Herald*. The statue was moved to its current location near Ocean Park in 1930. The Tivoli dance hall (center), originally called the Cottage City Casino, stood from 1901 to 1964. Bandleader and songwriter Will Hardy wrote "Tivoli Girl" to capitalize on the popularity of the dance hall. The Flying Horses Carousel was moved from Coney Island to Oak Bluffs in 1884. Constructed by Charles Dare in 1876, the carousel is still operational and retains its original wooden horses. Many generations of riders have tried to catch the brass ring on their Flying Horses Carousel rides.

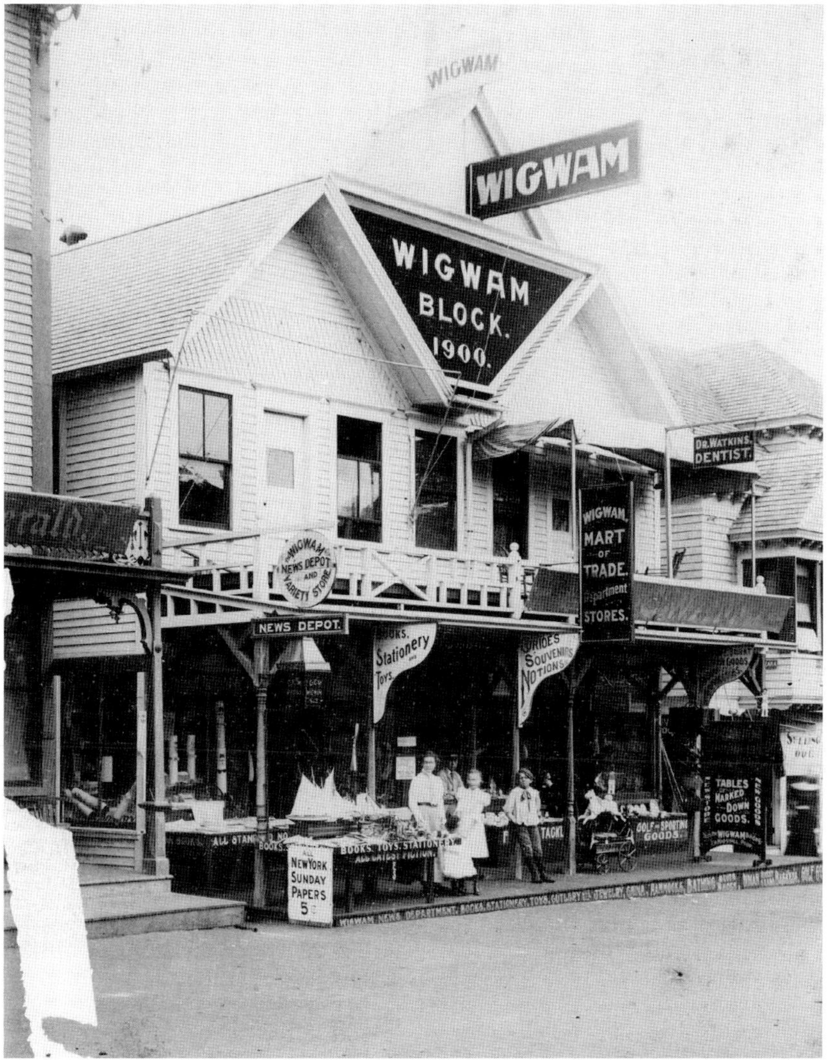

The Wigwam Block, built in 1900, was the home of Marshall's department store. It sold newspapers, books, sporting goods, fishing tackle, toys, souvenirs, bathing suits, notions, Indian novelties, and burnt leather goods, among other things. (Photograph by A.W. Pierce.)

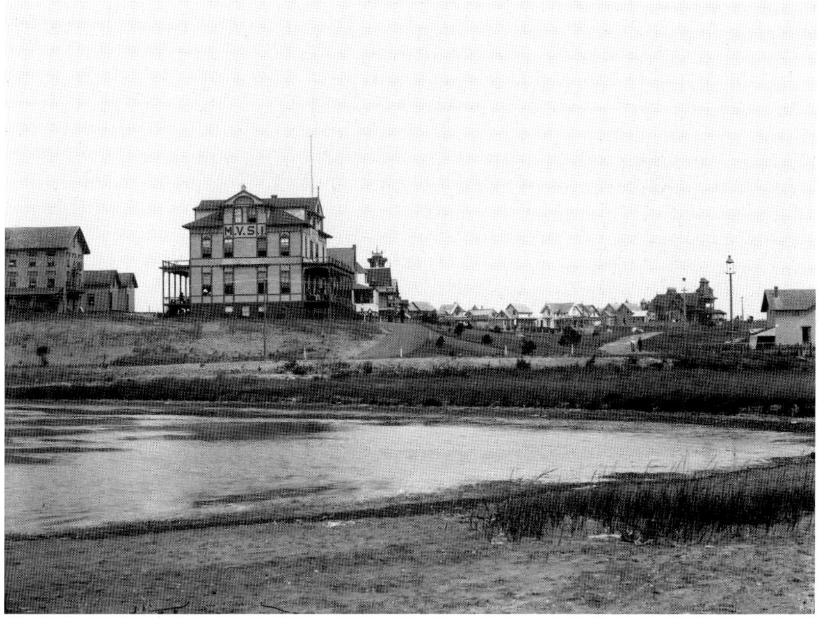

In 1878, Homer Sprague, a summer resident and the headmaster of Girls High School in Boston, founded the Martha's Vineyard Summer Institute. Located on a bluff in the Highlands area of Oak Bluffs, the school offered instruction in history, mineralogy, music, art, and other subjects. By 1890, enrollment was at 700, but it rapidly declined after 1900. The Martha's Vineyard Summer Institute closed in 1906. (Photograph by John N. Chamberlain.)

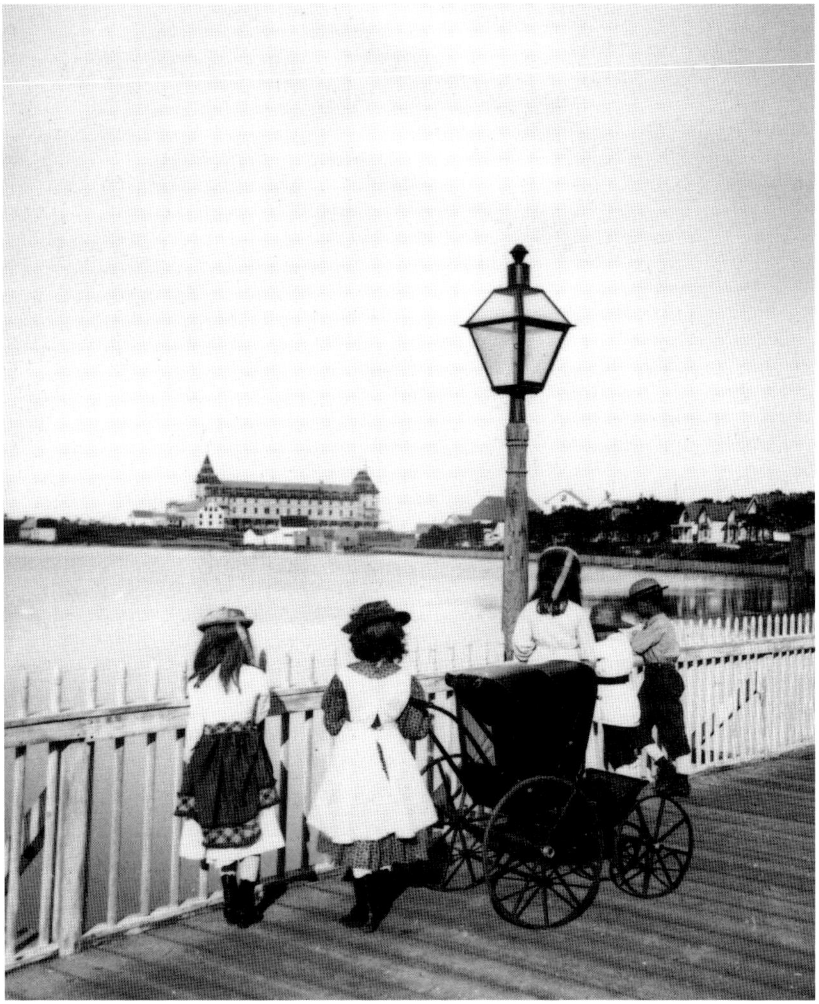

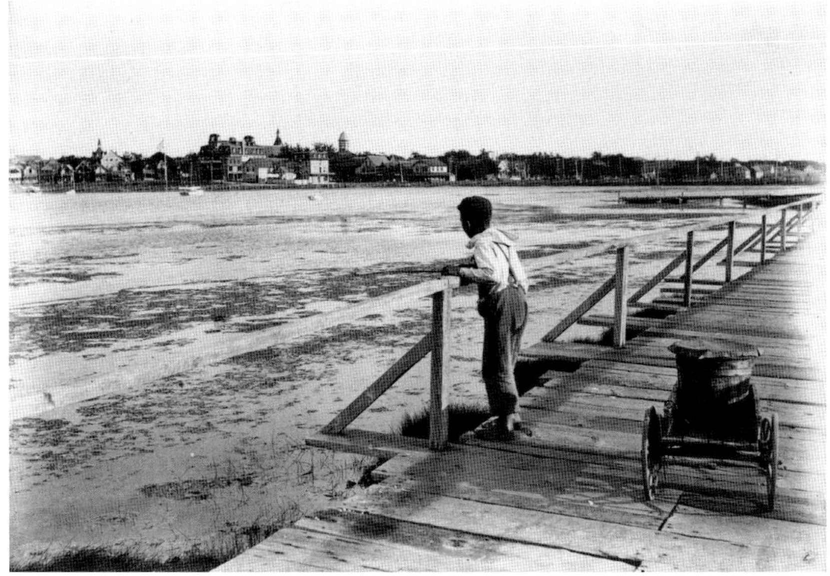

The Shutes had a photography studio in Oak Bluffs during the summer season, where they sold stereo views to vacationers. In addition to their popular whaling series (see page 20), they staged picturesque photographs designed to evoke reminiscences of the town's memorable views. The two on this page, both from the late 1800s, are typical. At left, two boys and a trio of prim and starched little girls with their doll's carriage gaze toward the Sea View House from the Jordan Crossing, which separated Lake Anthony from Sunset Lake. Above, a studiedly scruffy local boy has been posed in a similar position.

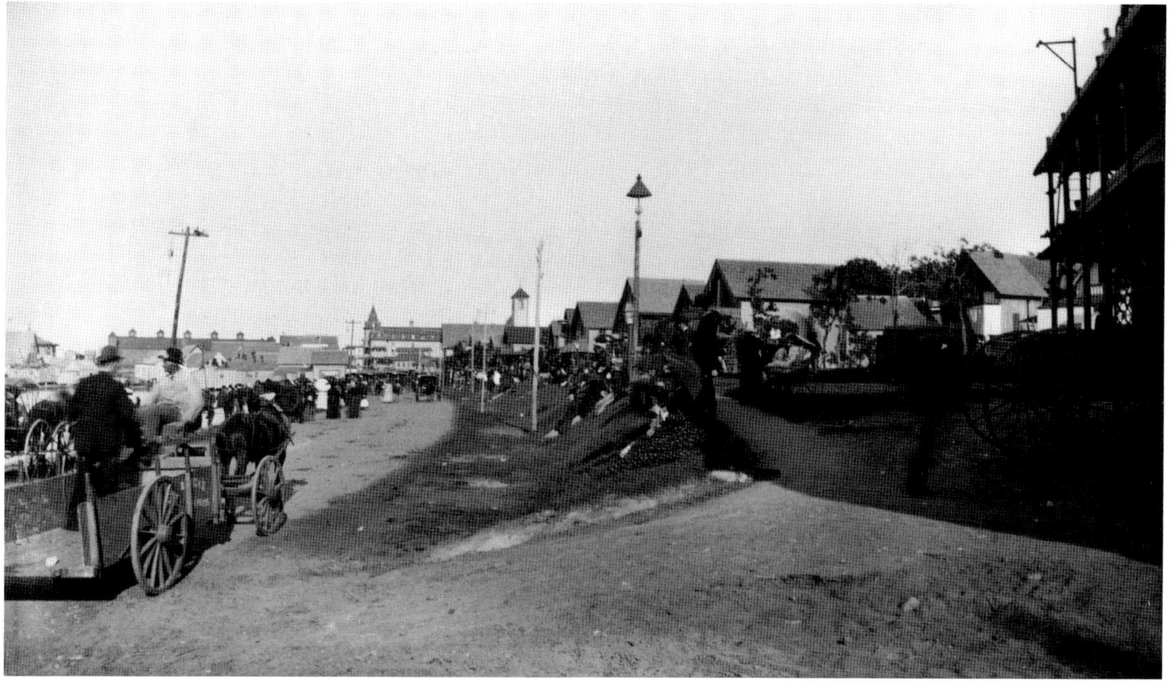

In the 1880s, the view from the front of Wesley House, on Lake Avenue in Oak Bluffs, encompassed Lake Anthony (now the harbor) and, in the distance, the skating rink and the Sea View House.

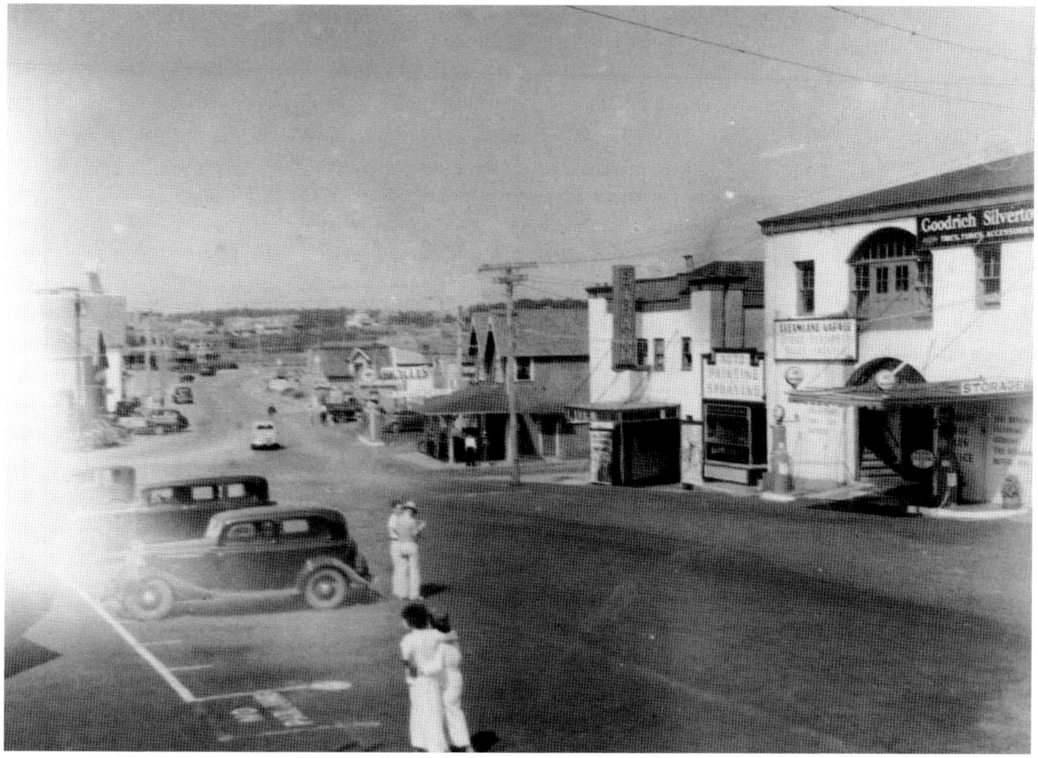

By the 1930s, Oak Bluffs Avenue had changed quite a bit from the days of horses and dirt roads. Space was made for parking automobiles on the street, and the Dreamland Garage, seen here on the far right, had gas pumps and room to store one's car.

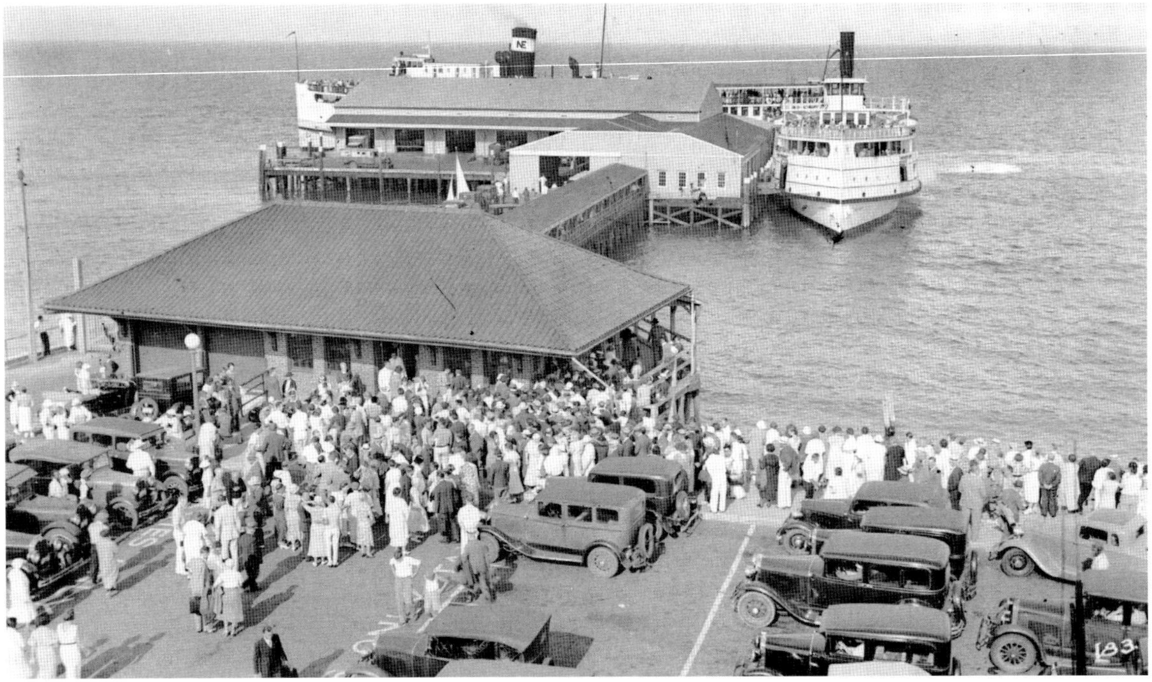

Continuous development combined with wear and tear meant that the Oak Bluffs ferry wharf underwent many transformations over the years. The addition and removal of the railroad tracks, the building and tearing down of ticket offices and waiting areas, and repairs and reconfigurations all left the waterfront looking quite a bit different in the 1920s than it had just a few years earlier.

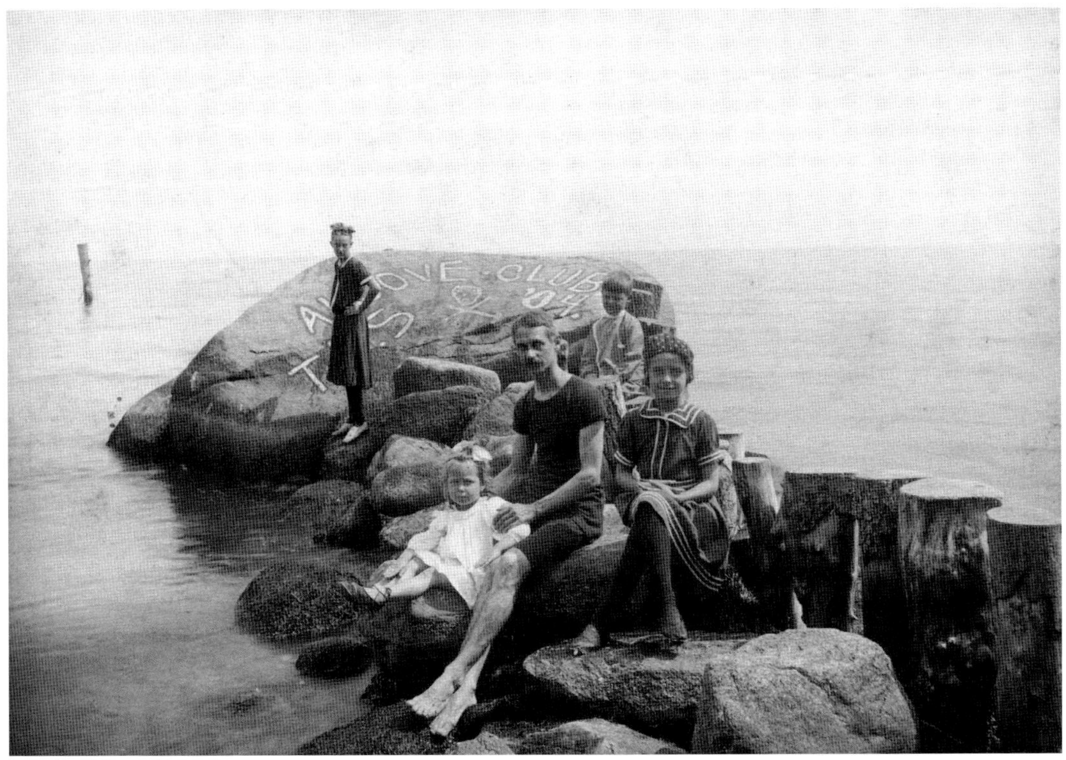

Lovers Rock, off the beach in Oak Bluffs, was a popular place to pose for pictures. It often had an inscription of some sort on it, but in this photograph, the writing appears to have been added or enhanced on the negative. The date of 1904 and a drawing of skull and crossbones are apparent. The rest of the writing is illegible. The rock was buried by the town in 1973. (Photograph by W.B. Douglas.)

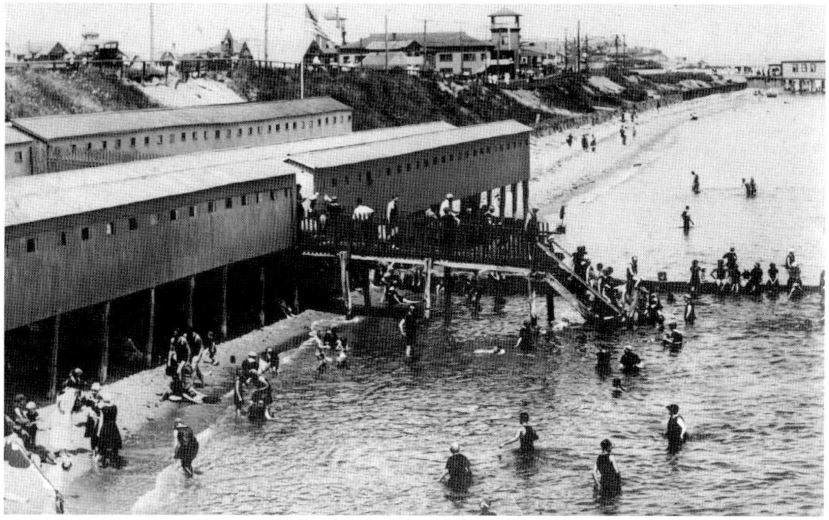

Long rows of changing houses lined the beach in Oak Bluffs, allowing bathers to slip into their wool swimsuits in privacy. This photograph was probably taken from the top of the observatory. (Photograph by Stanley E. Rodgers.)

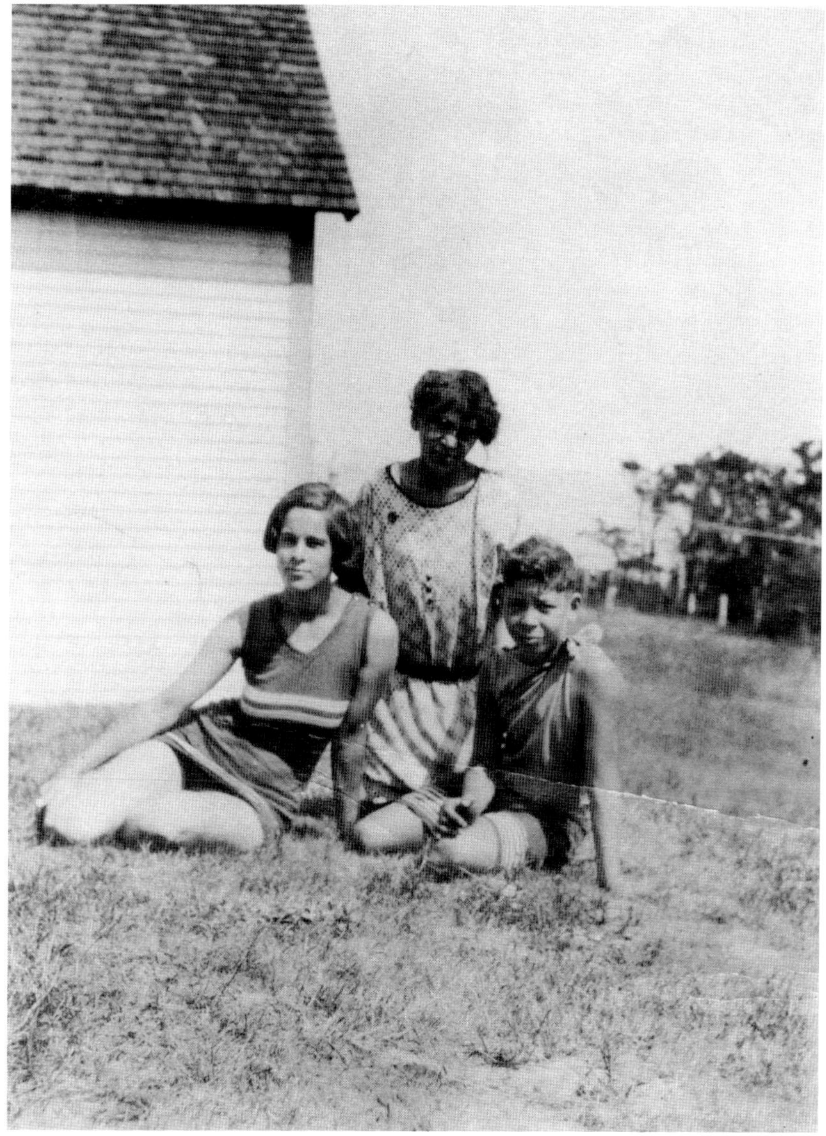

The woman kneeling in the center of this snapshot is identified as Edwina Douglas. It appears to have been taken in the 1930s. Martha's Vineyard became a popular vacation spot for wealthy and middle-class African Americans, especially after 1912, when Charles and Henrietta Shearer opened Shearer Cottage, the first African American–owned guesthouse on the Vineyard.

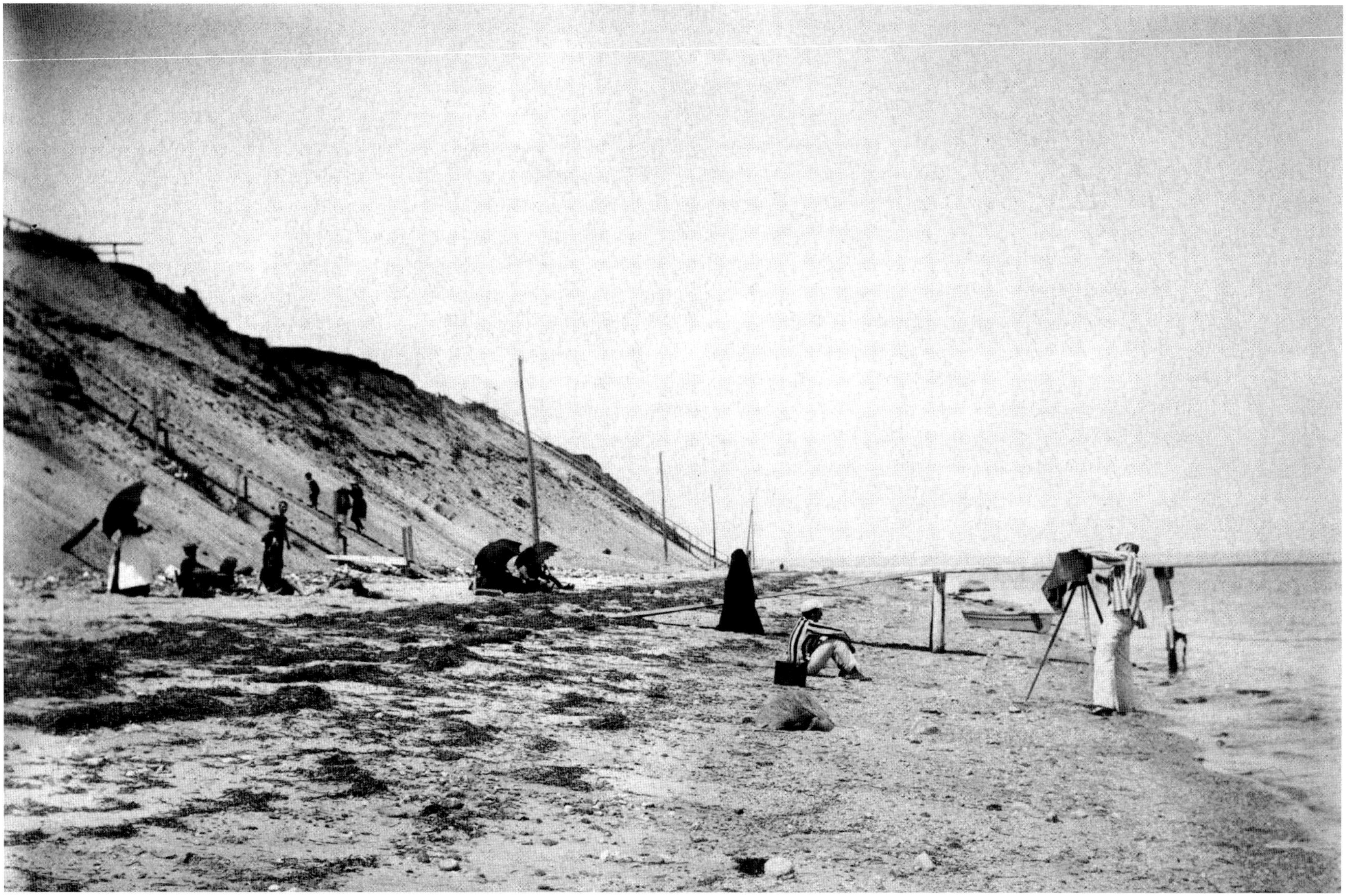

The Highlands are part of Oak Bluffs to the west of the busier resort area. There was a Baptist tabernacle in the Highlands, and it also had its own wharf and beaches, including this one. The relatively few bathers at the Highlands beach may be because of the very steep stair down the hill. To the right, a photographer is at work near the shoreline.

Crowded beaches filled with bathers who may not have been good swimmers required the services of lifeguards. This unidentified guard worked on the beach in Oak Bluffs in the early 1900s.

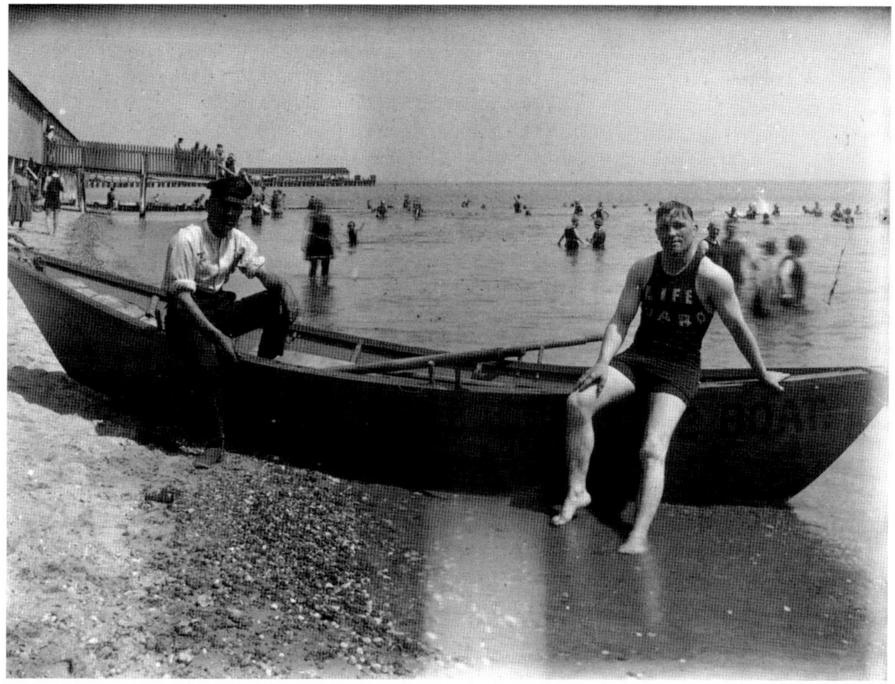

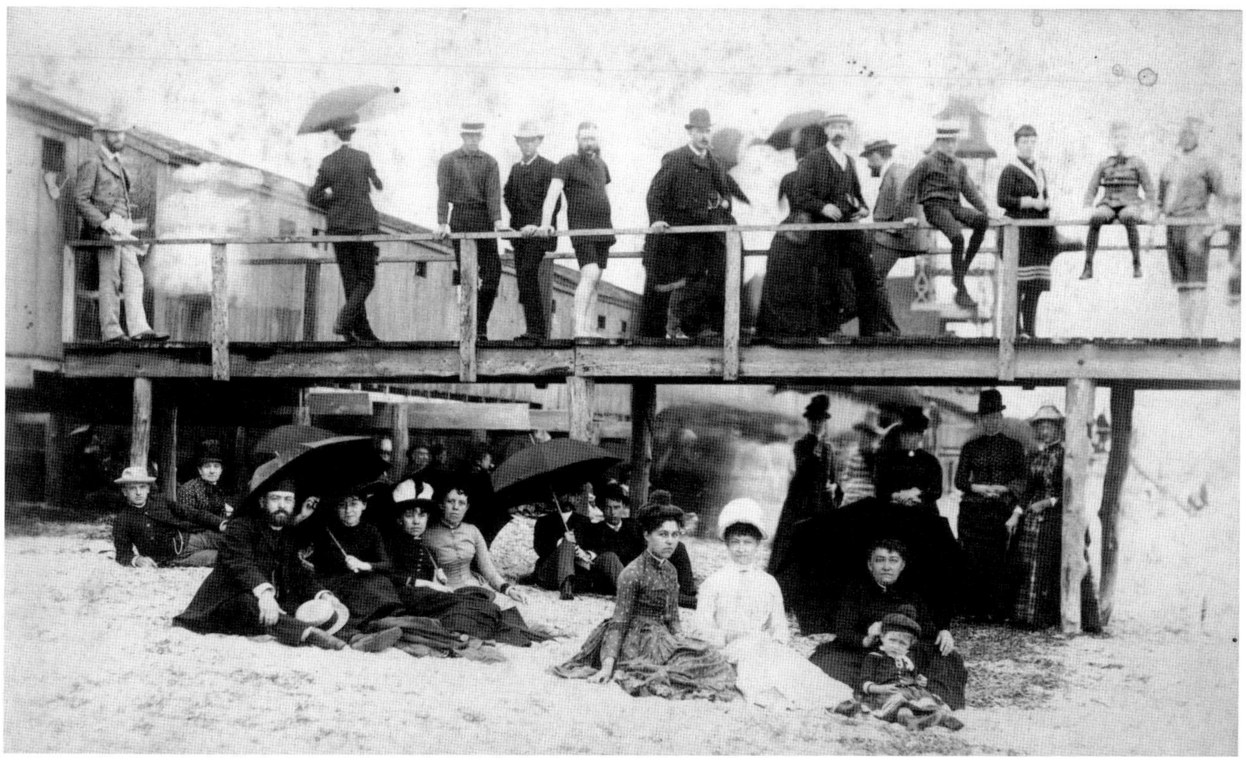

Few of the beachgoers in this photograph of Smith Pier, on the Bathing Beach in Cottage City, are wearing bathing suits. It was common to go to the beach fully clothed in suits or dresses. Sun protection was provided by hats, umbrellas, and by sheltering under the pier. (Photograph by John N. Chamberlain.)

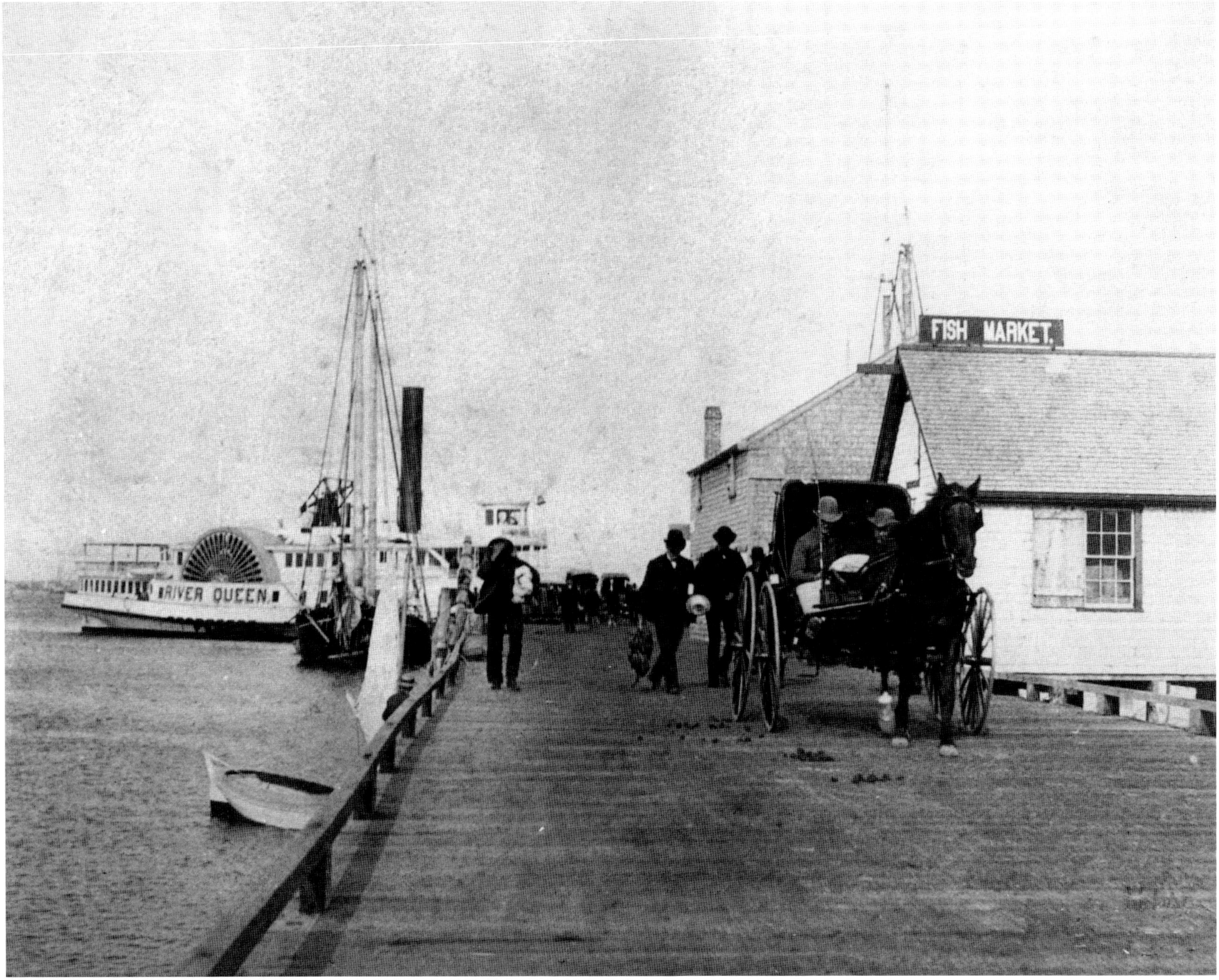

Oak Bluffs was not the only ferry stop on Martha's Vineyard. Vineyard Haven is, and has long been, the main year-round ferry terminal. One of the men who has disembarked from the *River Queen* in this photograph, which probably dates from the 1870s, is carrying a bunch of bananas.

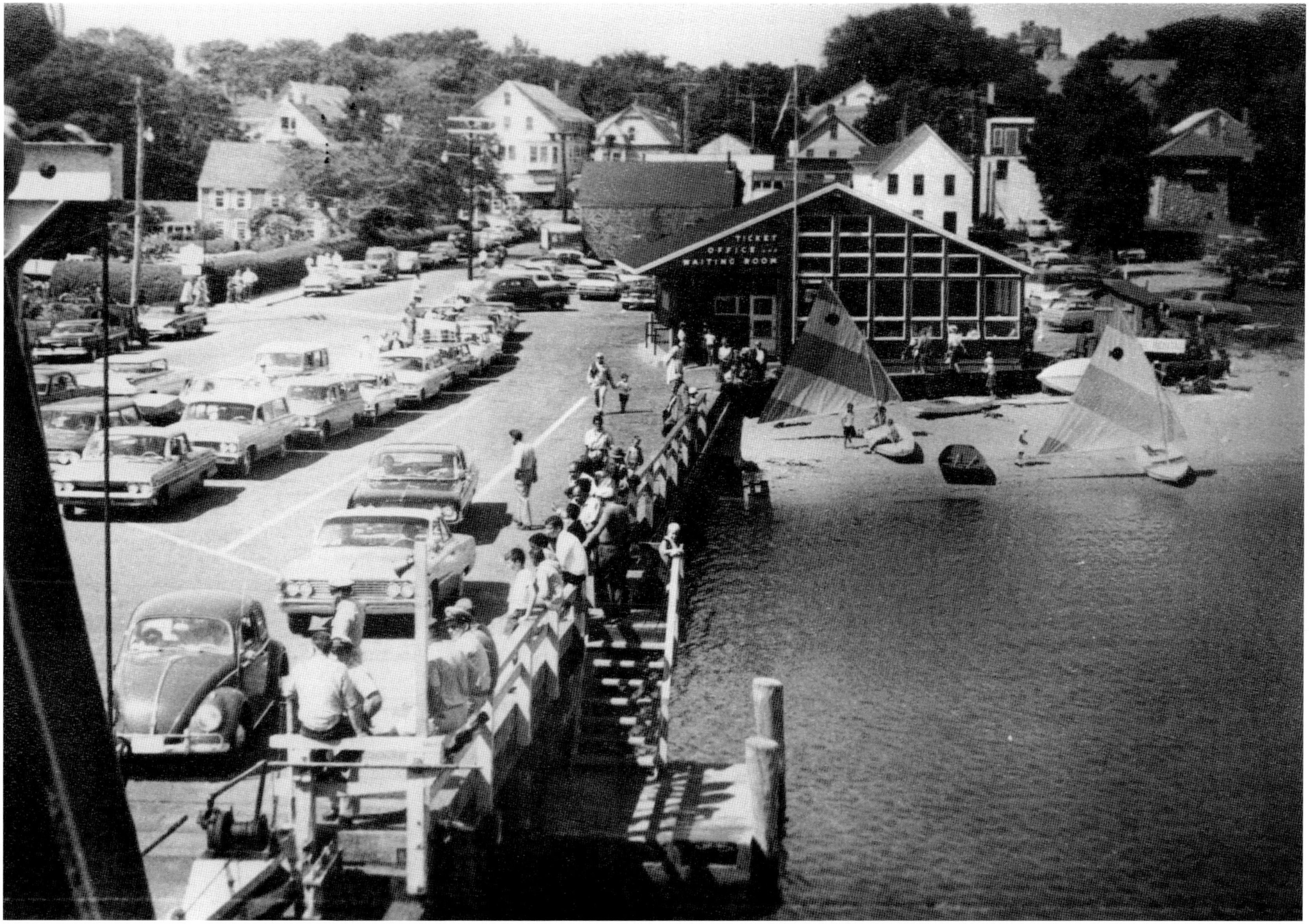

By the 1960s, horses had given way to automobiles. This photograph was taken from the window of a ferry at the wharf in Vineyard Haven. It shows the modern ferry terminal and cars lined up to board the ferry. This ferry terminal was torn down in 1994 and replaced with another in a location nearby.

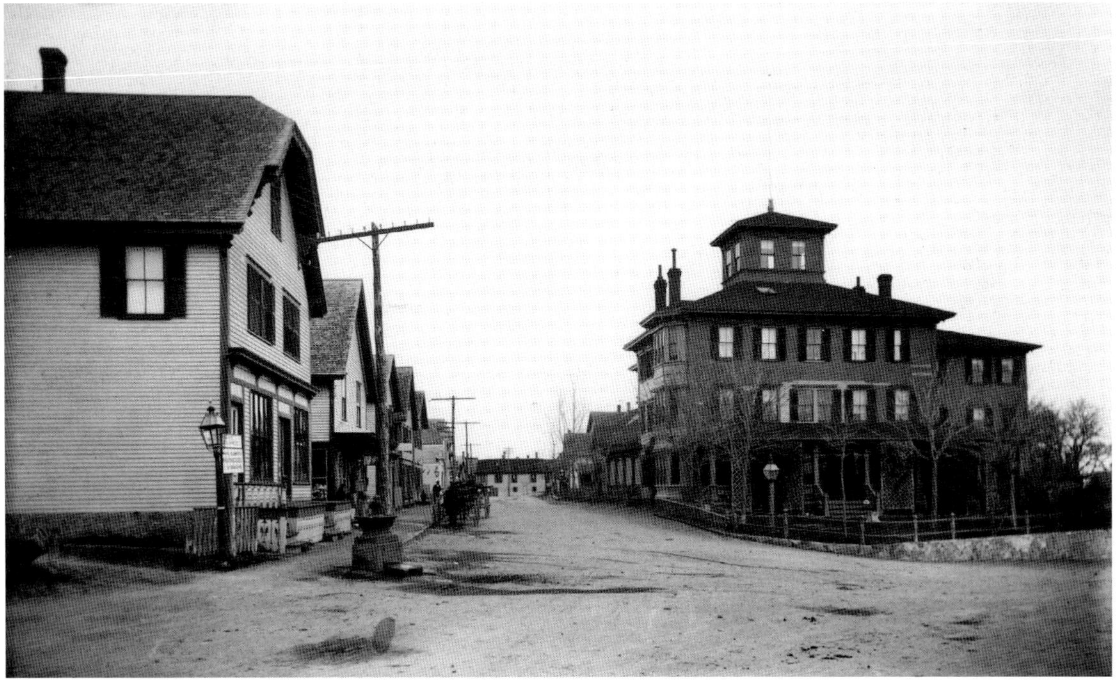

Vineyard Haven's Mansion House burned in the fire of 1883 and was immediately rebuilt in the fashionable Italianate style. A 1915 guidebook advertised the hotel as "Under the management of Mrs. Samuel Look, who has conducted the house for the past forty years."

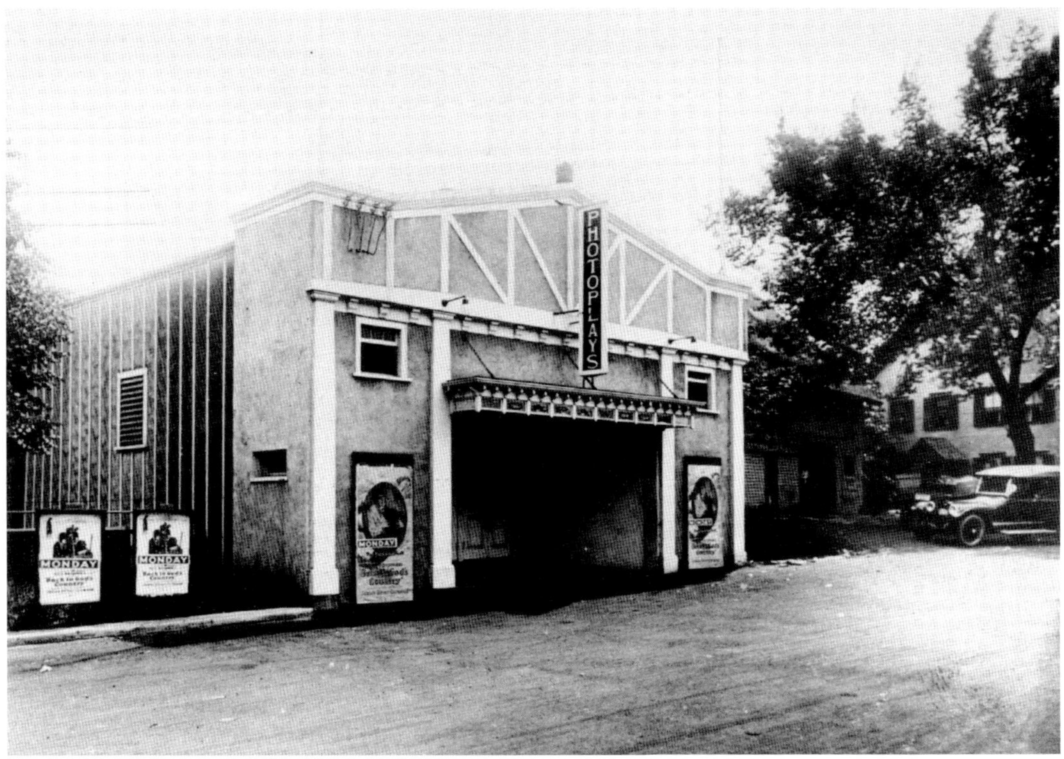

Back to God's Country was the photoplay showing at the newly built Capawock Theater in 1919. Located on Main Street in Vineyard Haven, the theater showed first-run movies that attracted both vacationers and islanders, providing entertainment year-round.

Souvenir ships in bottles were sold in this small shack on the shore of the Lagoon near the old Marine Hospital in Vineyard Haven. The two men are not identified, but the photograph is dated May 26, 1948. The shack still stands today.

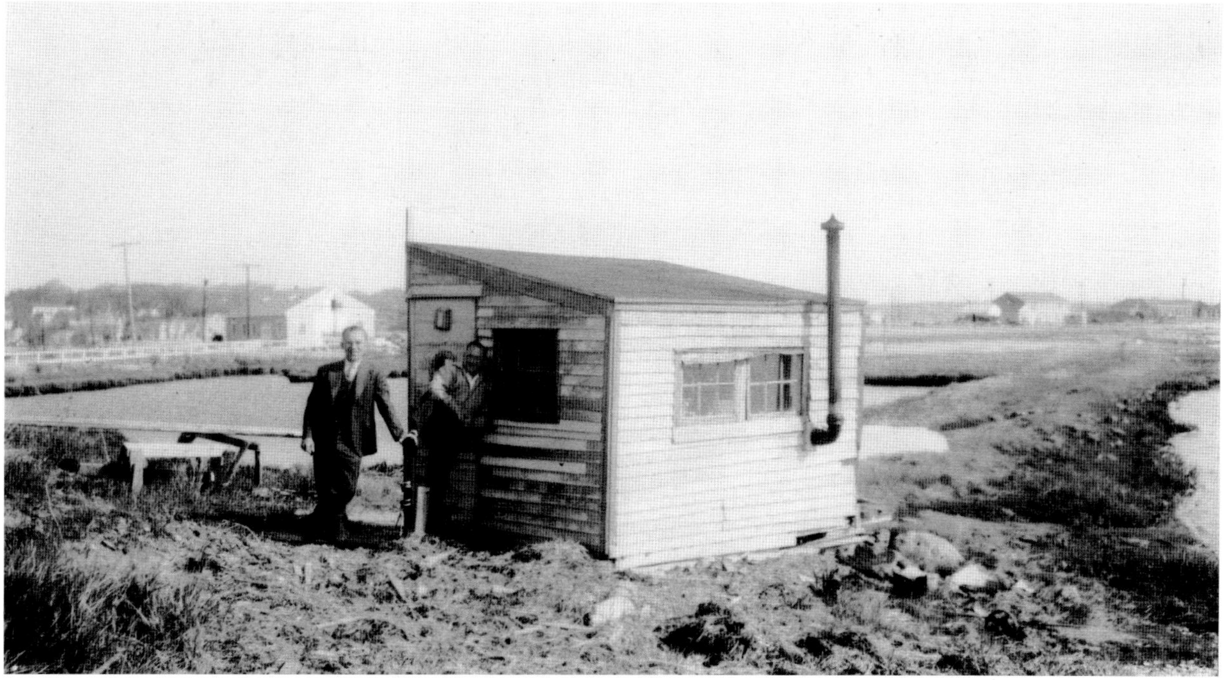

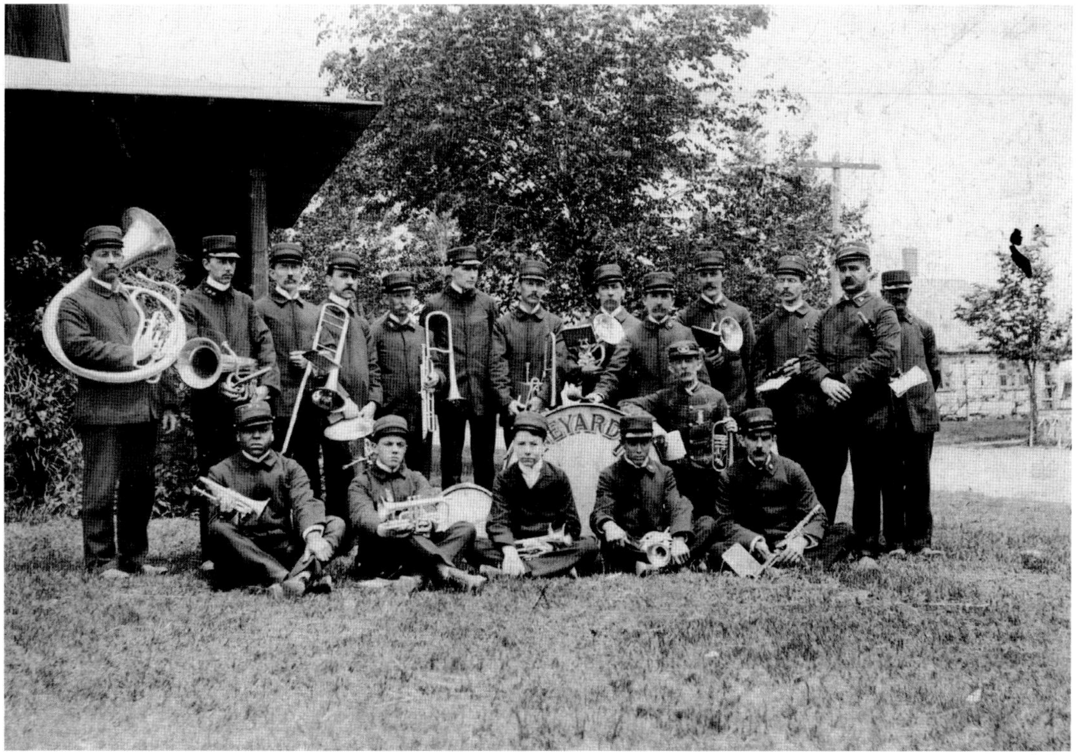

The Vineyard Haven Town Band posed on May 30, 1899. Their names are a mixture of familiar island names with some not heard as often. Pictured are, from left to right, (sitting) Forman, Peakes, Norton, Norton, and Lair; (standing) Johnson, Luce, Ames, Foster, Smith, Dutcher, Weeks, Merry, Shugrove, Lair, Wilkinshon, Cleveland, and Trecherman. Kneeling next to the drum is the Edgartown photographer Richard Shute.

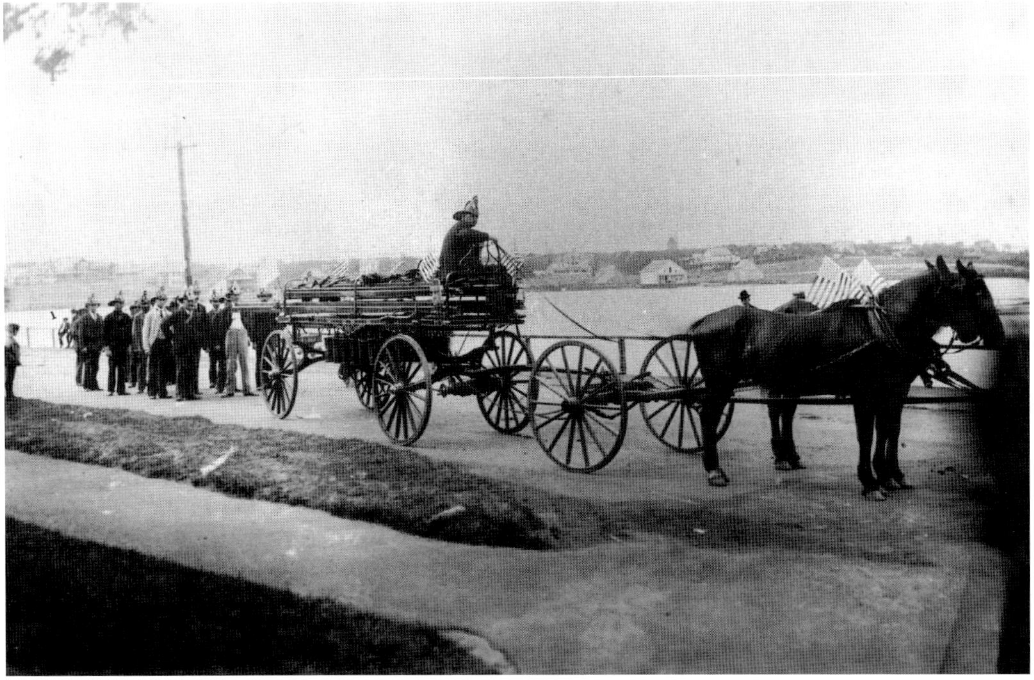

Island fire companies have long marched in patriotic parades. In Edgartown, firefighters still push the historic hand-drawn Button Pumper in the Fourth of July parade. Here, the Vineyard Haven Fire Department awaits the beginning of a May 30 parade in Oak Bluffs around 1900. Walter Renear is at the reins.

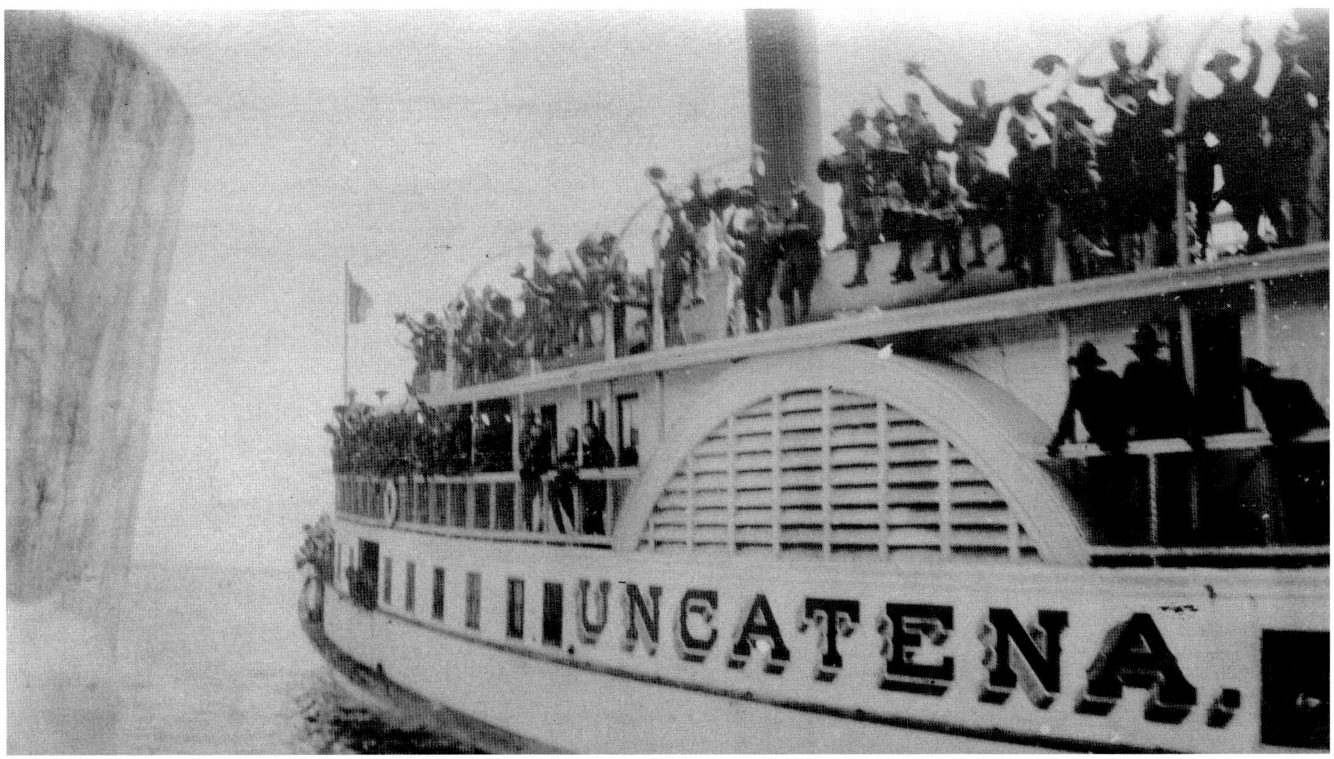

Vineyarders have served in the military throughout the country's history. During World War II, there was combat training in Lambert's Cove, and Noman's Land was used for bombing practice. Before World War I, there was a training camp, Camp Crocker, in Katama. The soldiers are seen here arriving (or departing) on the ferry *Uncatena*. (Photograph by Kathleen Vincent.)

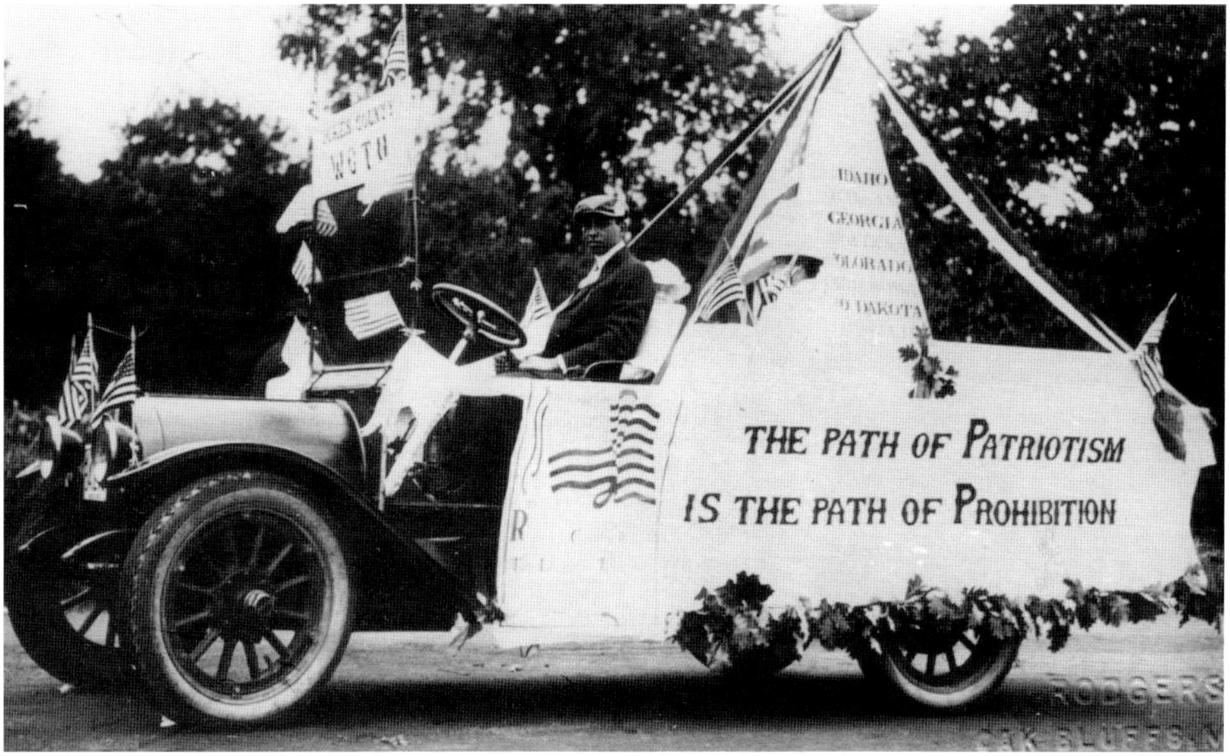

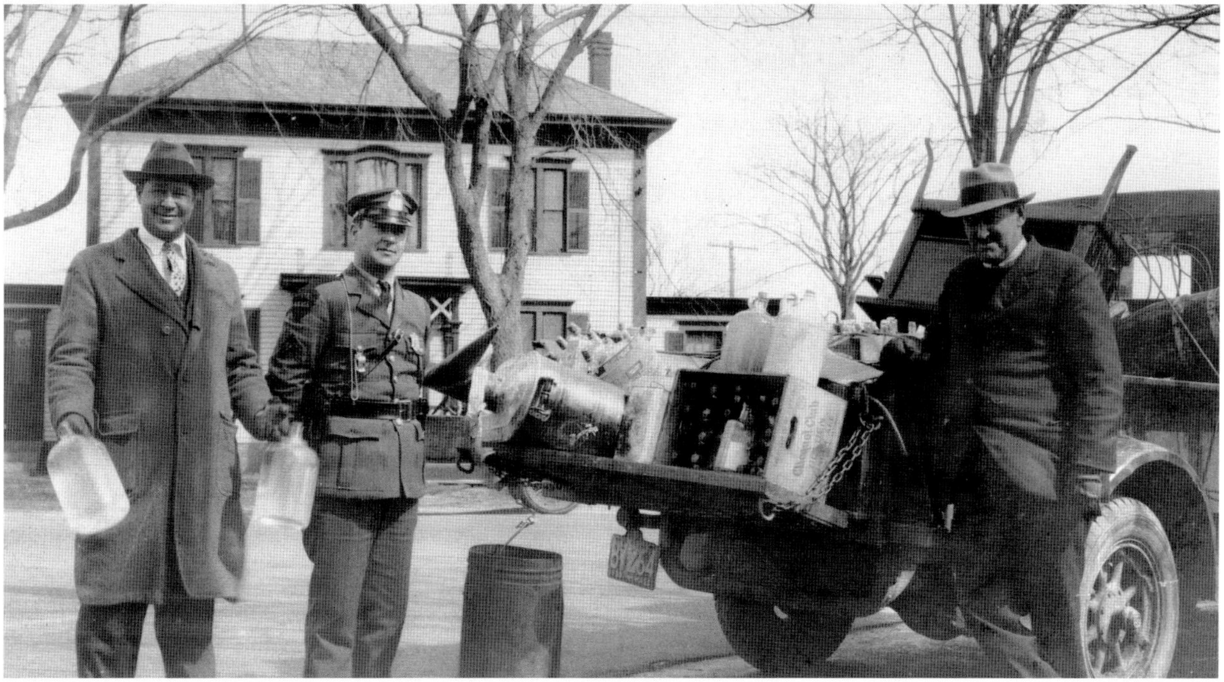

Temperance took an early foothold on Martha's Vineyard. The newspapers carried many announcements for men's temperance meetings, and the Women's Christian Temperance Union (WCTU) was strong in the 1800s and early 1900s. Even after Prohibition was repealed in 1933, Chilmark, West Tisbury, and Vineyard Haven remained dry. But that does not mean people who wanted alcohol had trouble finding a drink. Above, Joe Andrada drives a WCTU float in a parade in the 1920s. Below, authorities pose in front of the Edgartown jail with jugs of moonshine and a still, presumably seized during Prohibition.

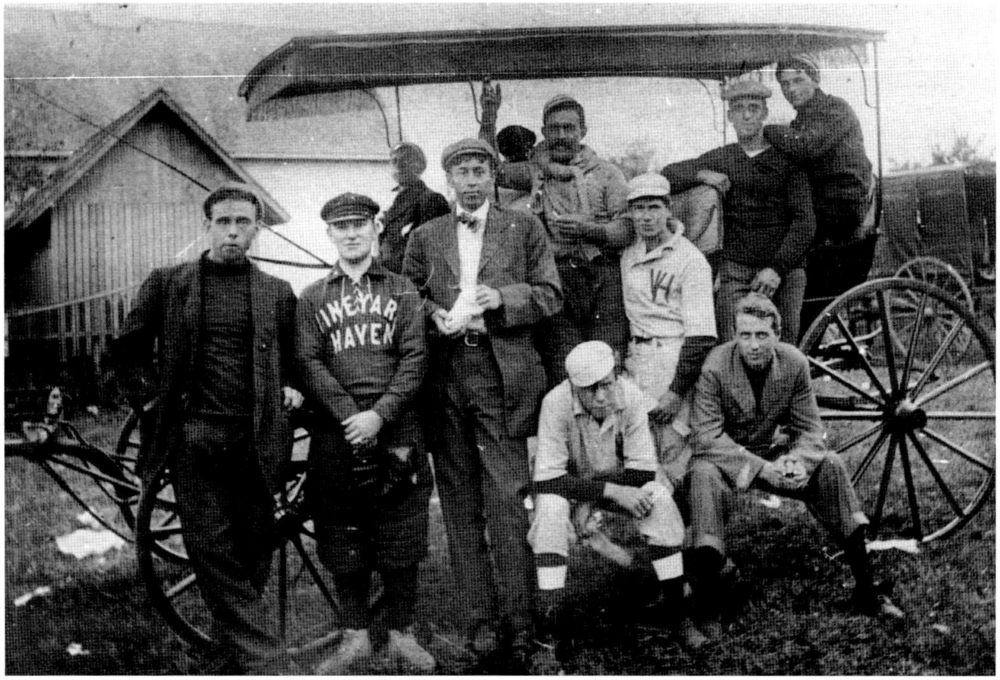

Members of a Vineyard Haven baseball team from the late 1800s pose near a fringe-topped wagon. The team members are, from left to right, (sitting in front) Ed "Iceberg" Smith and Ralph Look Sr.; (standing) Ed Colton, Charles "Duffy" Vincent, unidentified, Peter Lynch, unidentified, Ben Norton, and Jack Bumpus. The driver was John Johnson.

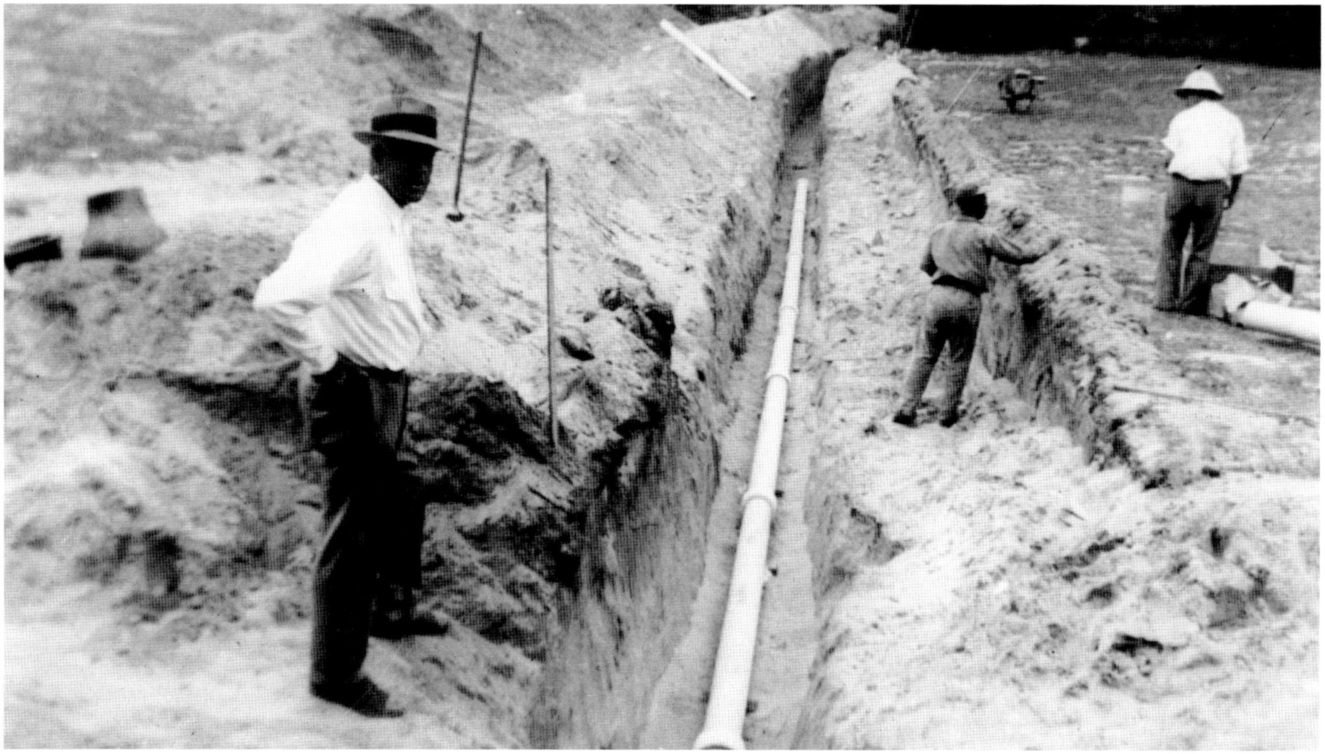

Mink Meadows Golf Course was four years away from opening when Robert Bigelow (left) was inspecting the laying of its irrigation pipes in 1935. The course was located on Bigelow's property in West Chop. When he conceived of the idea for the course before the Depression, Bigelow was quoted as saying, "Martha's Vineyard is destined to become the greatest summer resort on the New England coast."

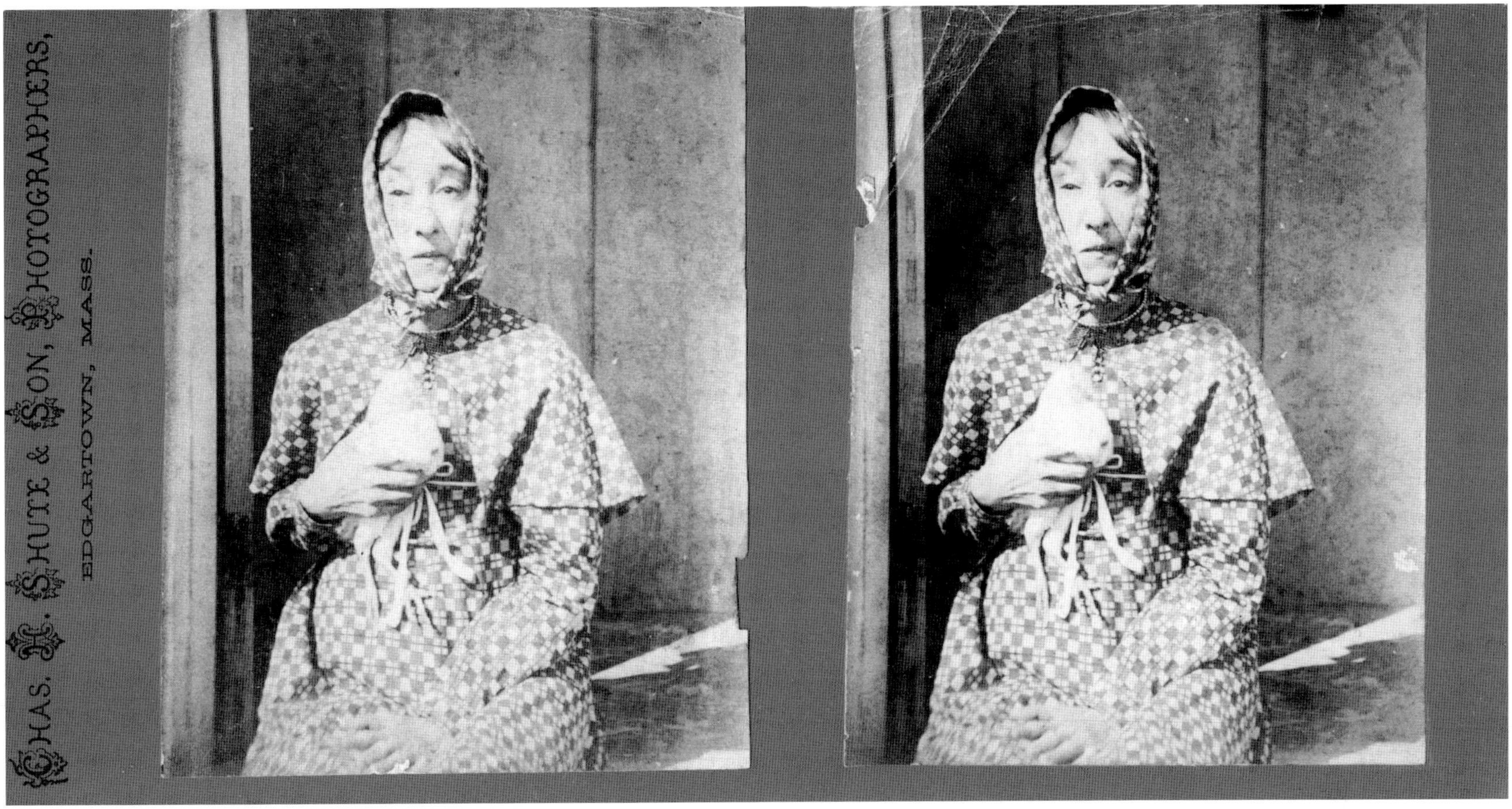

Nancy Luce (1814–1890) lived in West Tisbury with her cow and her hens, which she gave fanciful names like Teedie Lete, Pheba Peadeo, Letoogie Tickling, Jaatie Jafie, and Ada Queetie. She wrote plaintive poetry about her chickens and her illnesses, and she sold photographs of herself to tourists who stopped by her house to gawk at her eccentricities on their way to see the Gay Head cliffs. (Photograph by C.H. Shute & Son.)

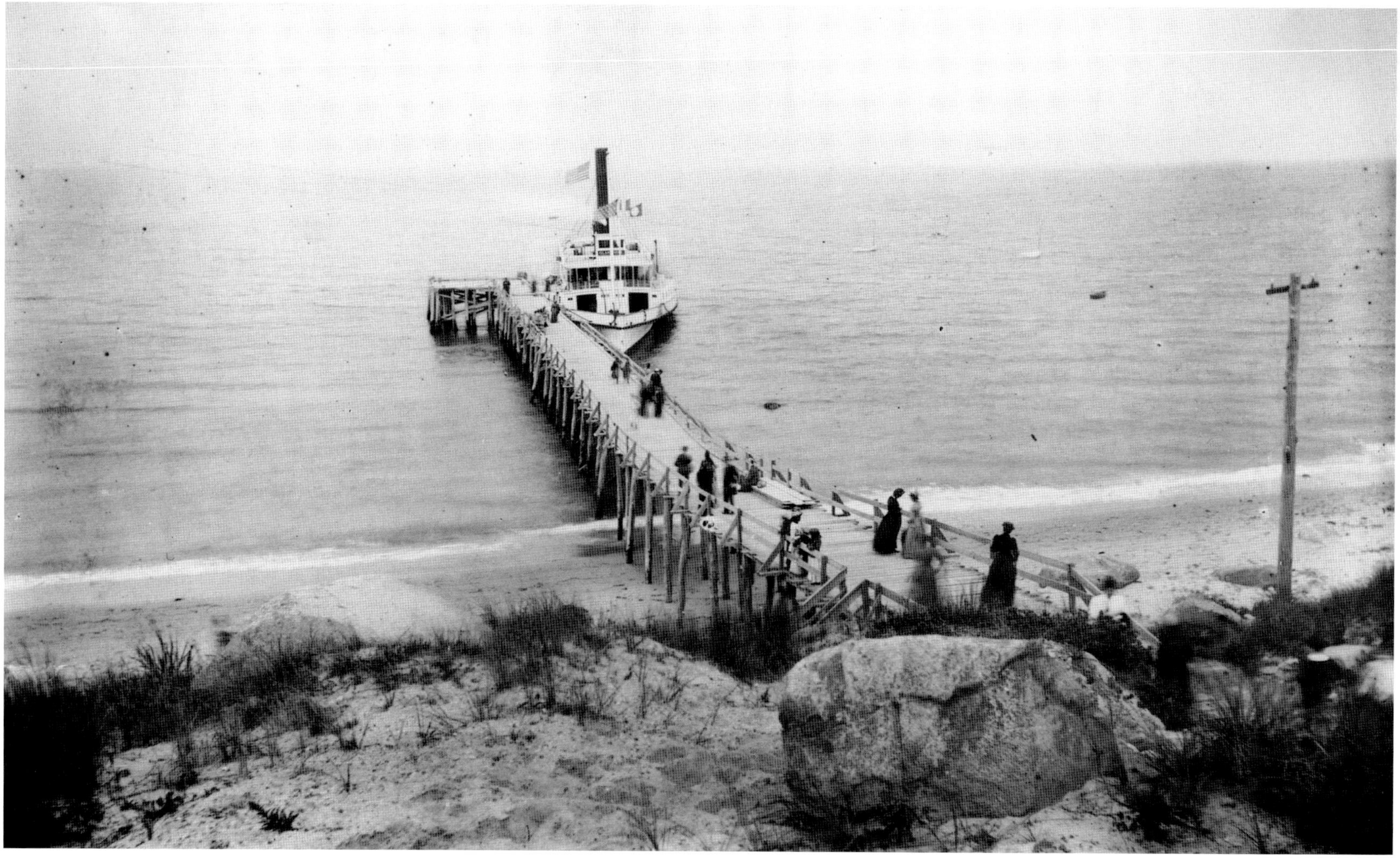

An excursion to Gay Head was a necessary day trip for anyone who wanted to see the striking streaks of red, yellow, and white clay of the cliffs overlooking Vineyard Sound, an experience that could not be duplicated anywhere else. Excursion boats carried passengers to the wharf at Gay Head (Aquinnah), where they could find a place to view the cliffs or take an oxcart up to the lighthouse.

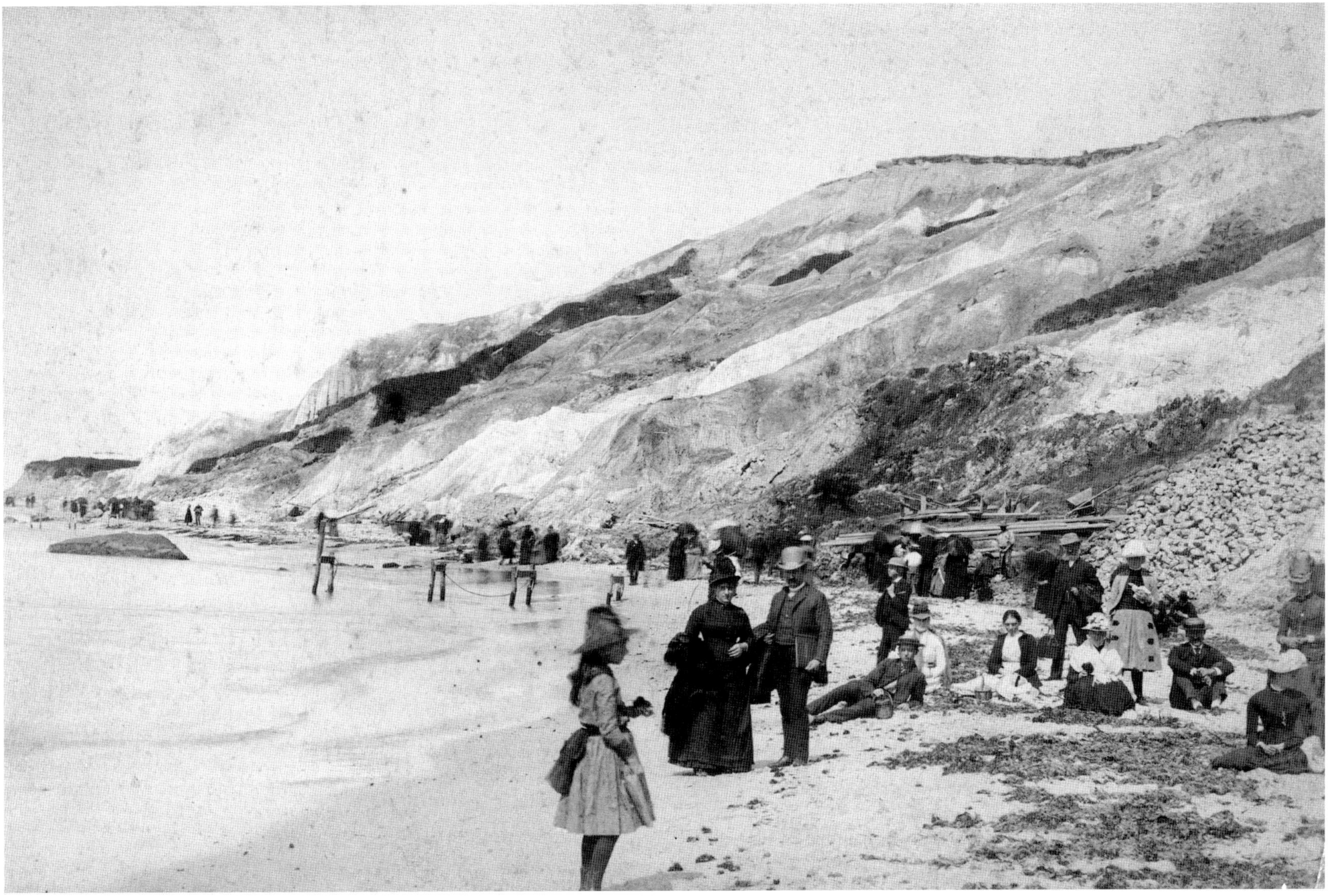

Tourists could view the Gay Head cliffs from the shore and even climb on them and take clay for souvenirs, activities that are no longer permitted. (Photograph by John N. Chamberlain.)

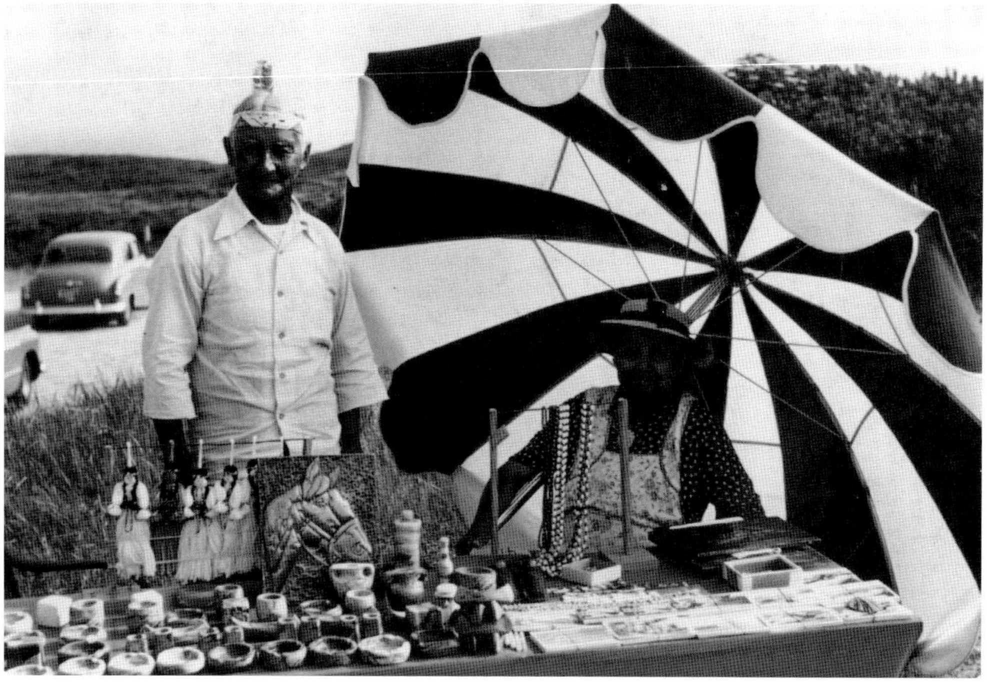

Generations of Wampanoag tribal members made things for tourists to buy on their excursions to the cliffs. Among the most popular were pots made from the multicolored Gay Head clay. Harrison Vanderhoop and his wife, Selina Manning Vanderhoop, are seen here in the 1950s selling their wares at Gay Head (Aquinnah).

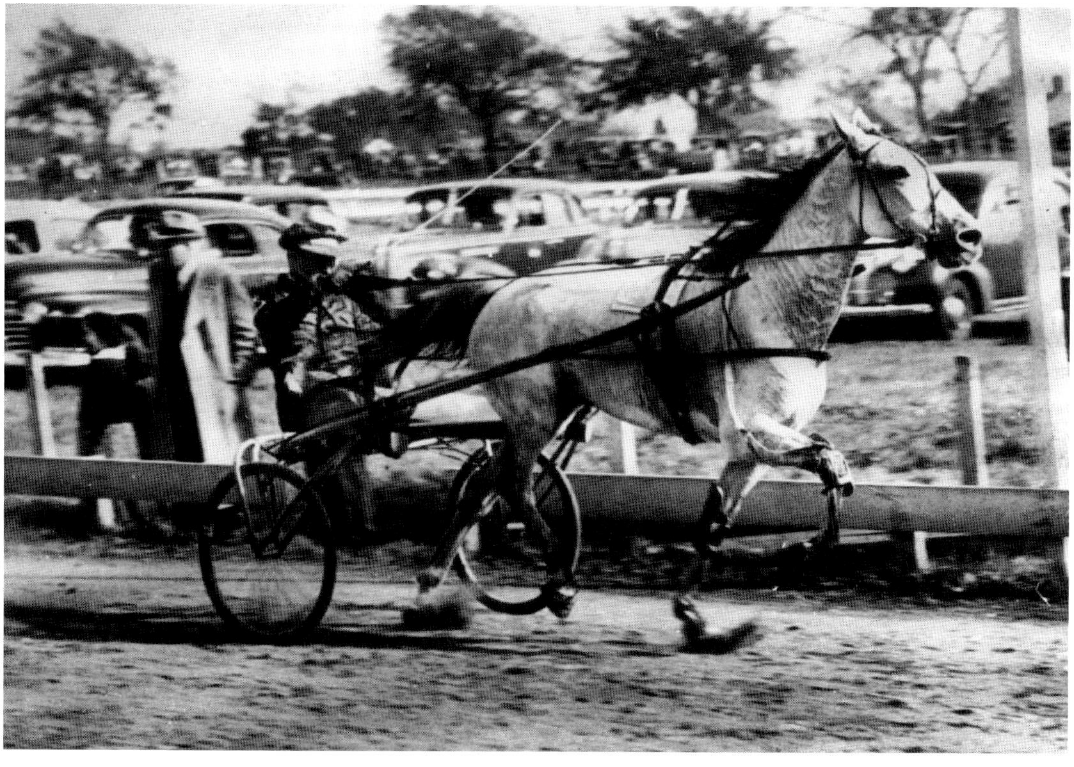

Girdlestone Park was a harness-racing track in Oak Bluffs, in the area near where the regional high school was later built. It was open from the late 1800s until the 1950s. Another track was located in West Tisbury. The sulky driver in this photograph is identified as S.C. Luce Jr., but it is not clear which track he is racing.

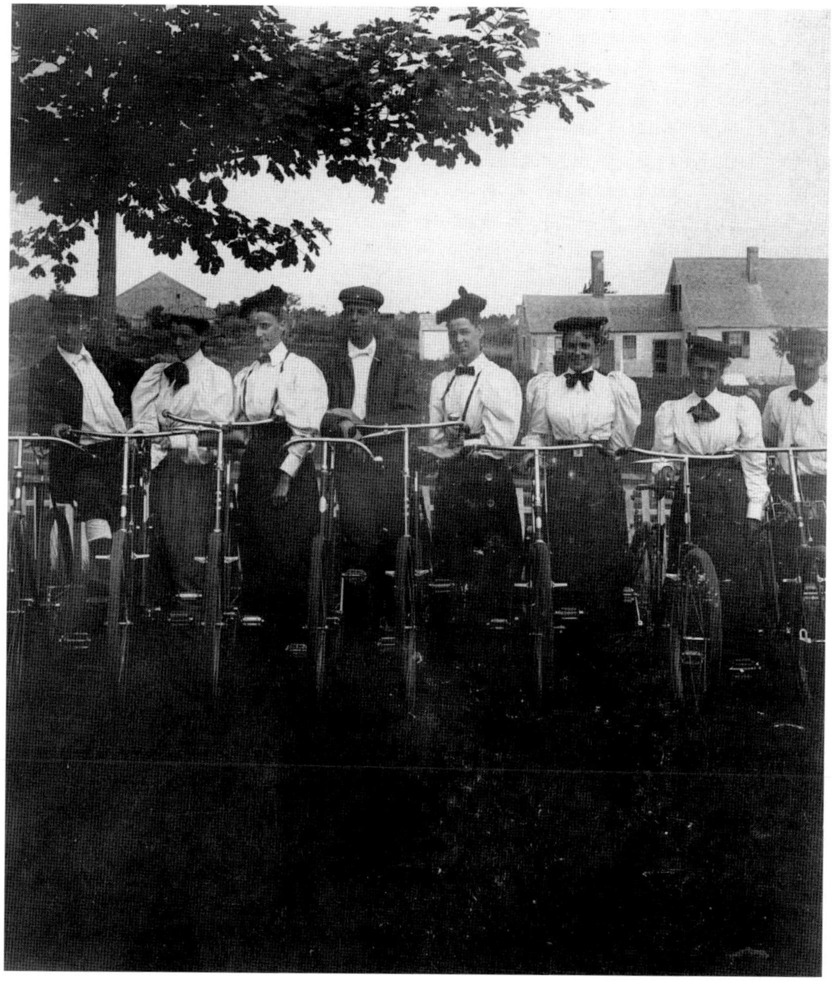

In 1895, Frances Wilder of Melrose, Massachusetts, traveled to Martha's Vineyard with her cycling club for a biking holiday. She entitled this picture "Boston Suits" in honor of the matching outfits the club members wore. (Photograph by Frances Wilder.)

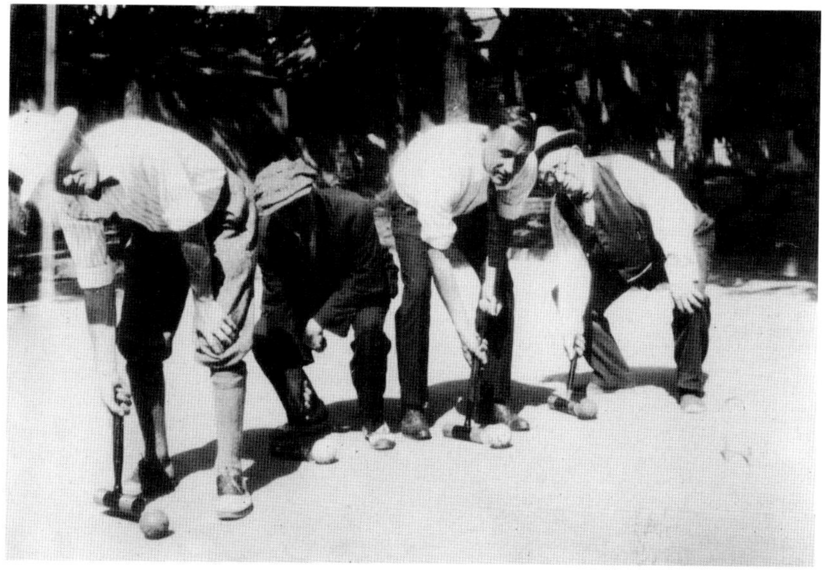

Roque, a variant of croquet, was fashionable on the Vineyard in the early 1900s. It was played with a mallet that had a shorter handle than a croquet mallet, leading to the stooped, almost squatting posture of these men.

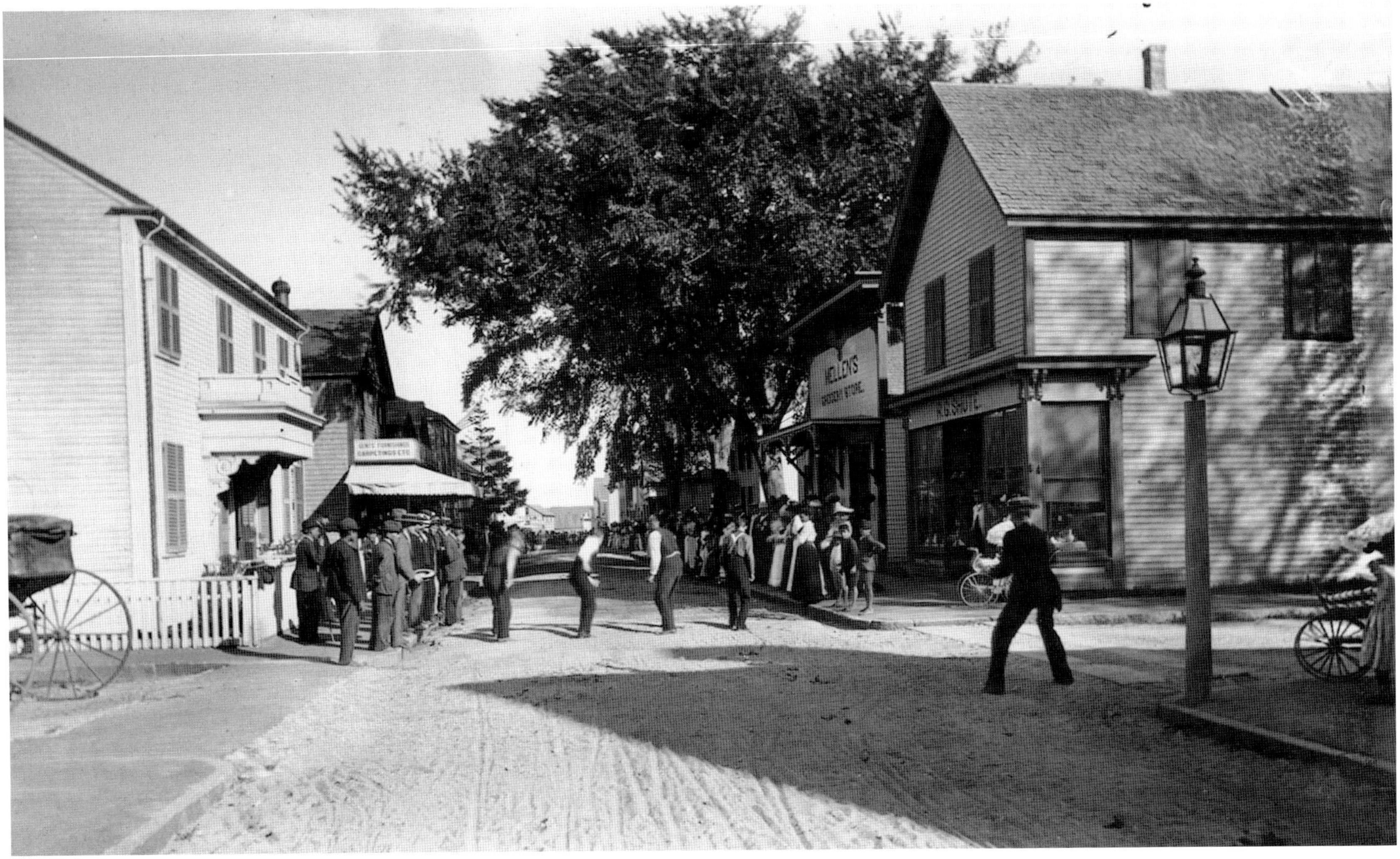

Marcus Jernegan, the brother of Laura Jernegan (see page 11), won this footrace down Edgartown's Main Street in August 1893. It was a 100-yard dash, with two heats and a final. There was also a three-leg race, a potato race (30 potatoes five feet apart, entailing a run of about 4,600 feet), and a greased pig competition. In a greased pig competition, the animal was slicked up and placed in an enclosure. Contestants chased it around, slipping and bumping into each other, to the amusement of the audience (but presumably not the pig). The winner was the young man who caught the pig. (Photograph by Richard Shute.)

The HarborView Hotel has stood in Edgartown since 1891, a time when Edgartown was lagging far behind Cottage City as a magnet for vacationers. Referred to as "a quaint old fishing and whaling town" and "a quiet watering hole," it lacked the crowds that made the newer town so attractive to hoteliers. The grand new hotel hoped to turn that around.

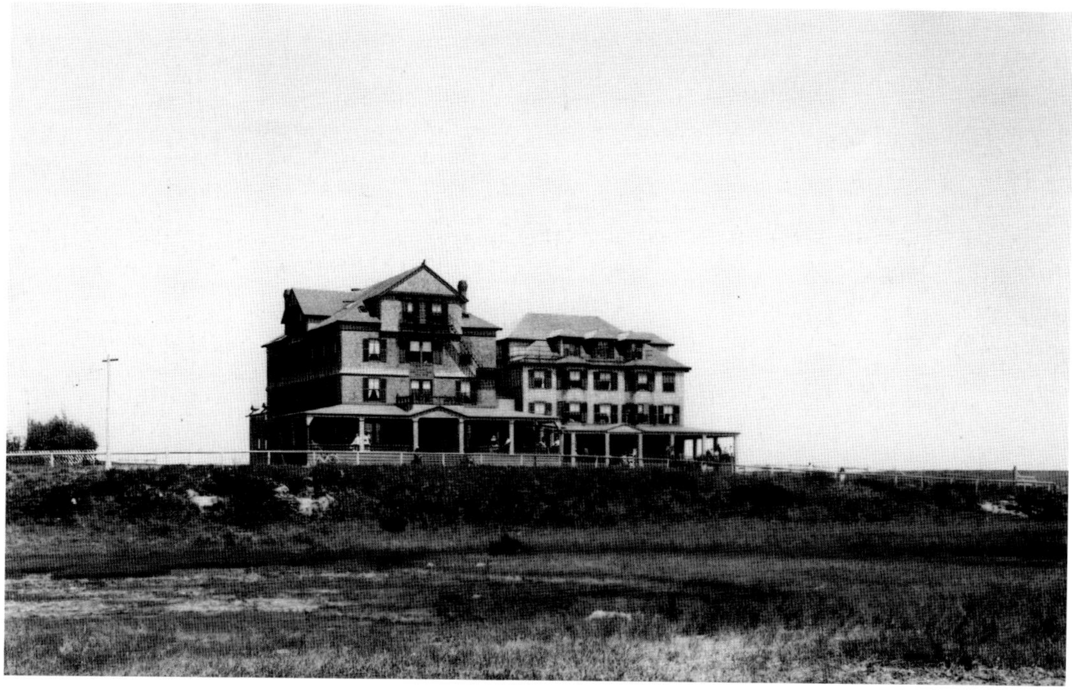

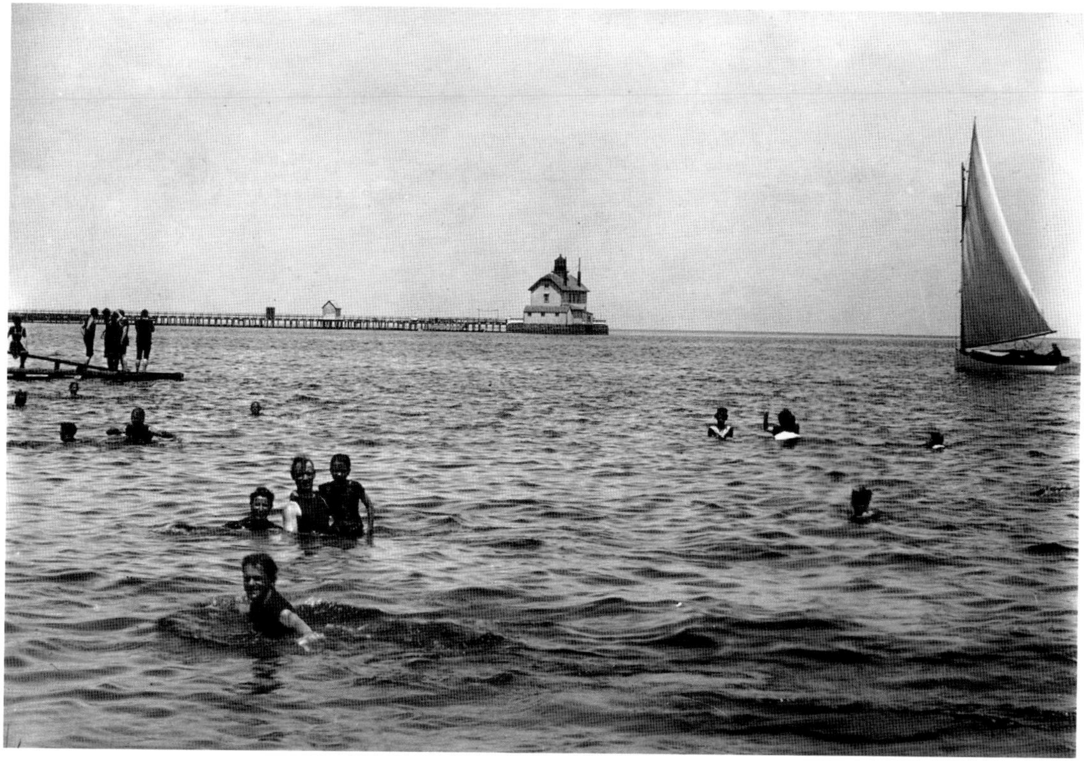

Bathers can be seen here swimming in Edgartown Harbor around 1900. The former Edgartown Light, with its long wooden walkway, is in the background. The current lighthouse is in the same place, but the shifting shoreline has completely surrounded it with sand and the boardwalk is no longer necessary because visitors can walk out to it over the sand.

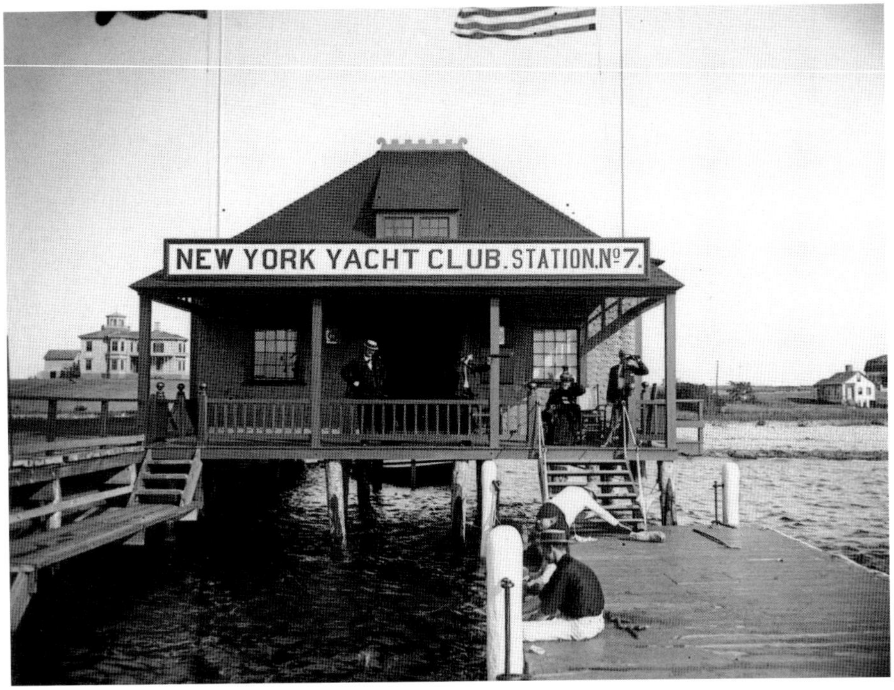

Yacht clubs from off-island had a presence on the Vineyard as well. In 1912, the New York Yacht Club petitioned the Massachusetts Board of Harbor and Land Commissioners for a license to build a pile and timber pier and float stage in Vineyard Haven Harbor in Oak Bluffs. Their petition was granted.

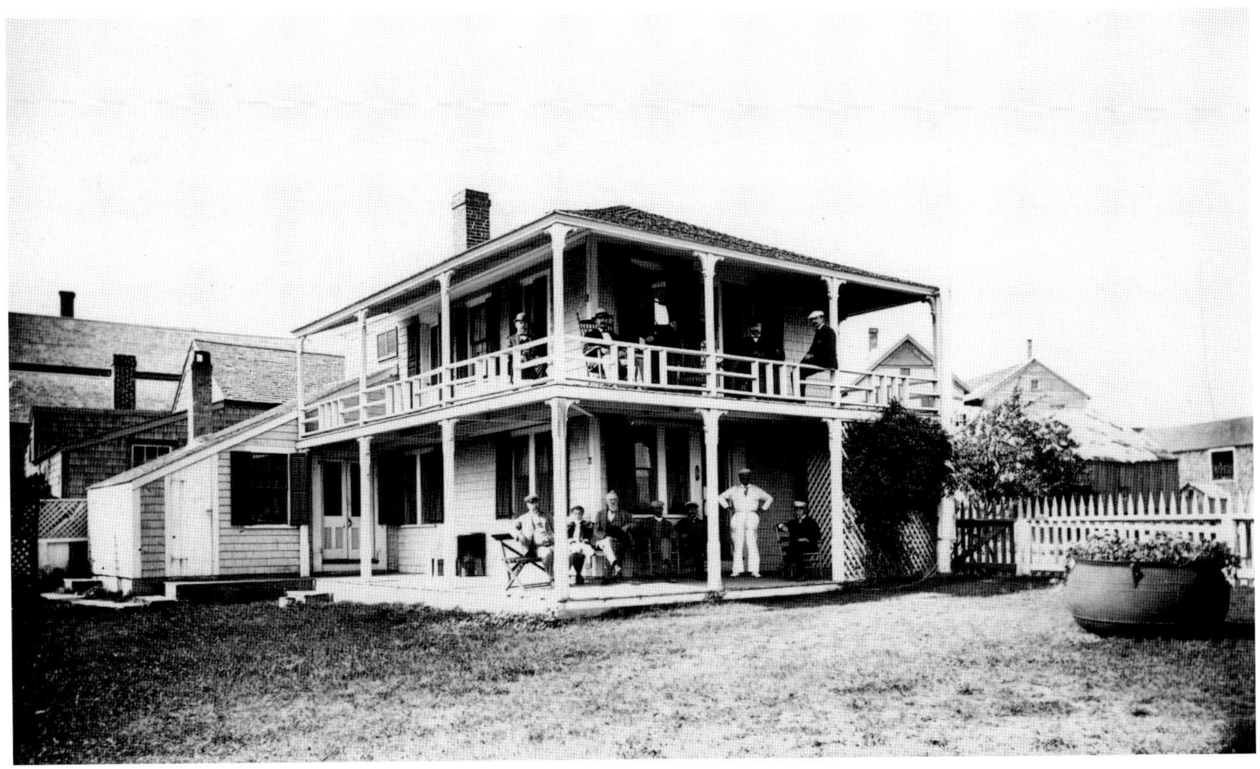

This house was an early home of the Edgartown Yacht Club. It stood on lower Main Street. A remnant of the town's whaling days can be seen in the foreground to the right, where a large try pot, formerly used to render whale blubber into oil on shipboard, has been turned into a garden planter.

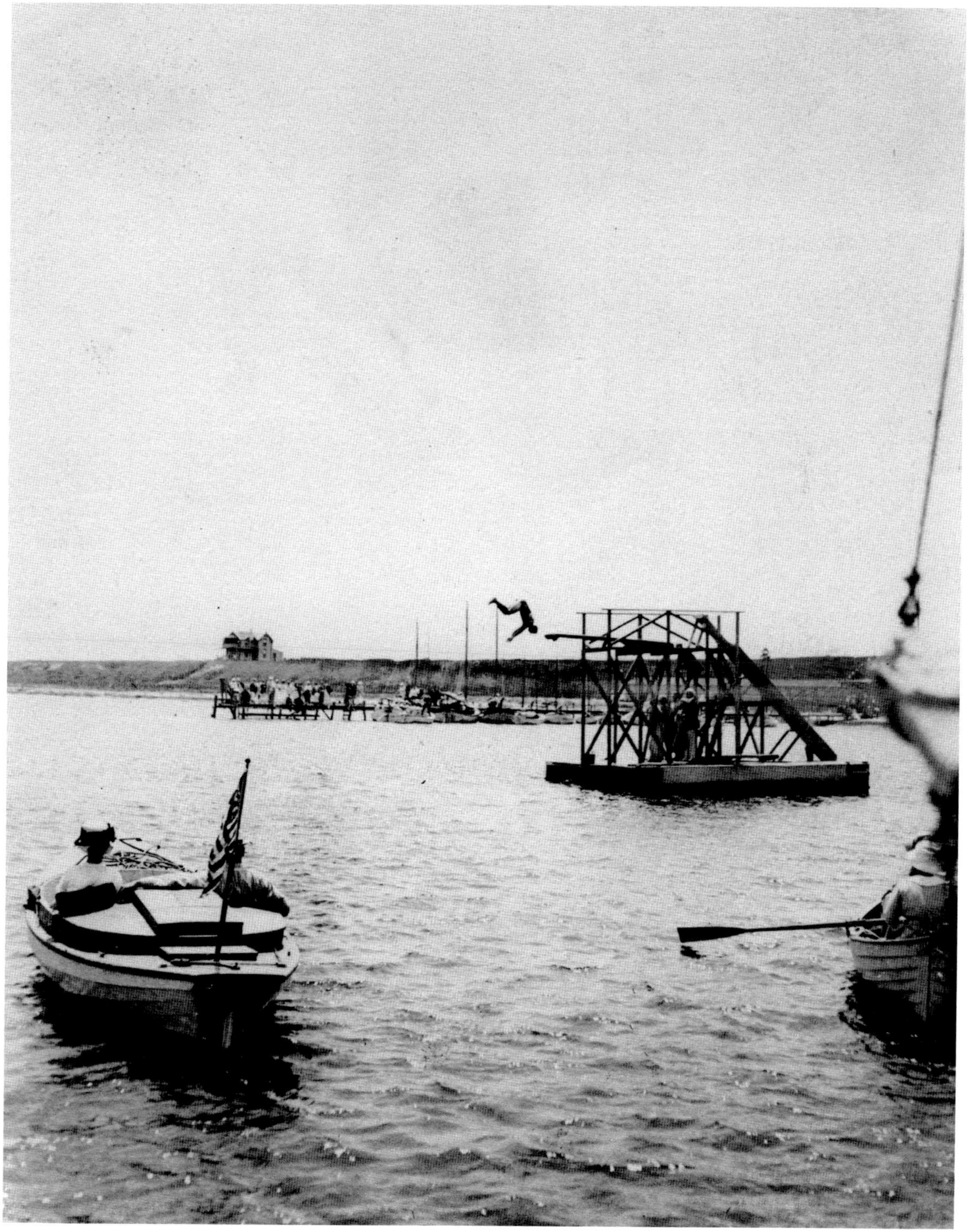

A diver jumps off the elaborate scaffolding on a platform at a 1913 Edgartown water carnival. Entertainment events like this were held occasionally around the island and consisted of diving, swimming, and other water sports. Spectators watched the competition from piers, like the one in the distance in this photograph, and from boats, like the two in the foreground.

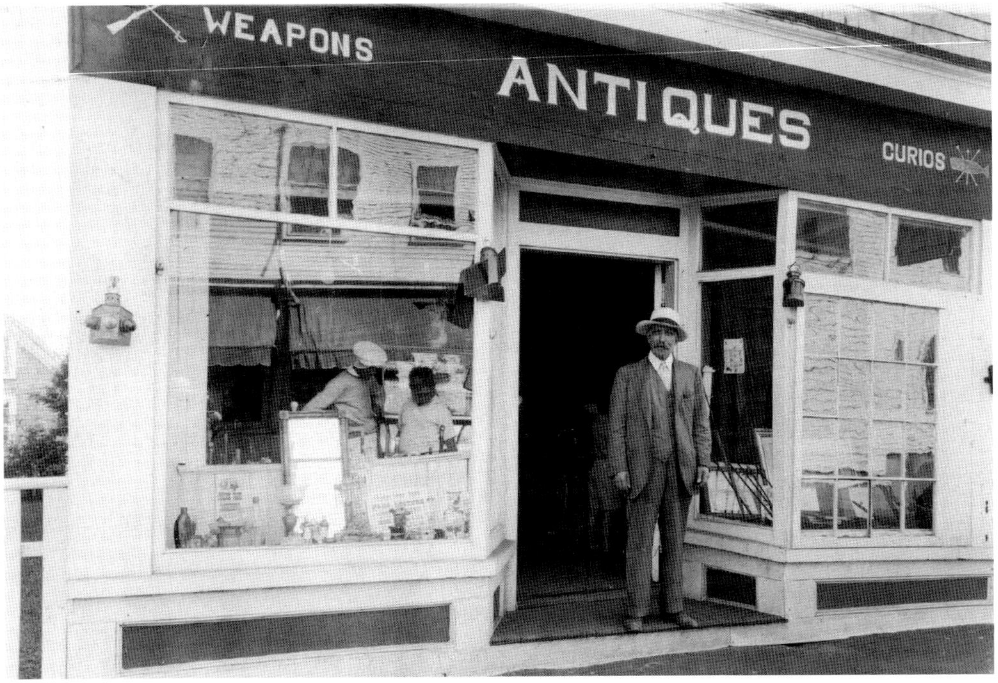

Antiquing was a pleasant vacation pastime in New England, and George Searle purveyed his antique furnishings from a shop on Main Street in Edgartown. The crossed harpoons and whale on the sign indicate that he sold nautical curios, such as scrimshaw. Searle is seen here standing in front of the shop in 1935. The building was torn down in the fall of that year.

This beach on Chappaquiddick is on Edgartown Harbor. On this day in 1906, boys played ball on the shore near the boats and ladies lounged under their umbrellas.

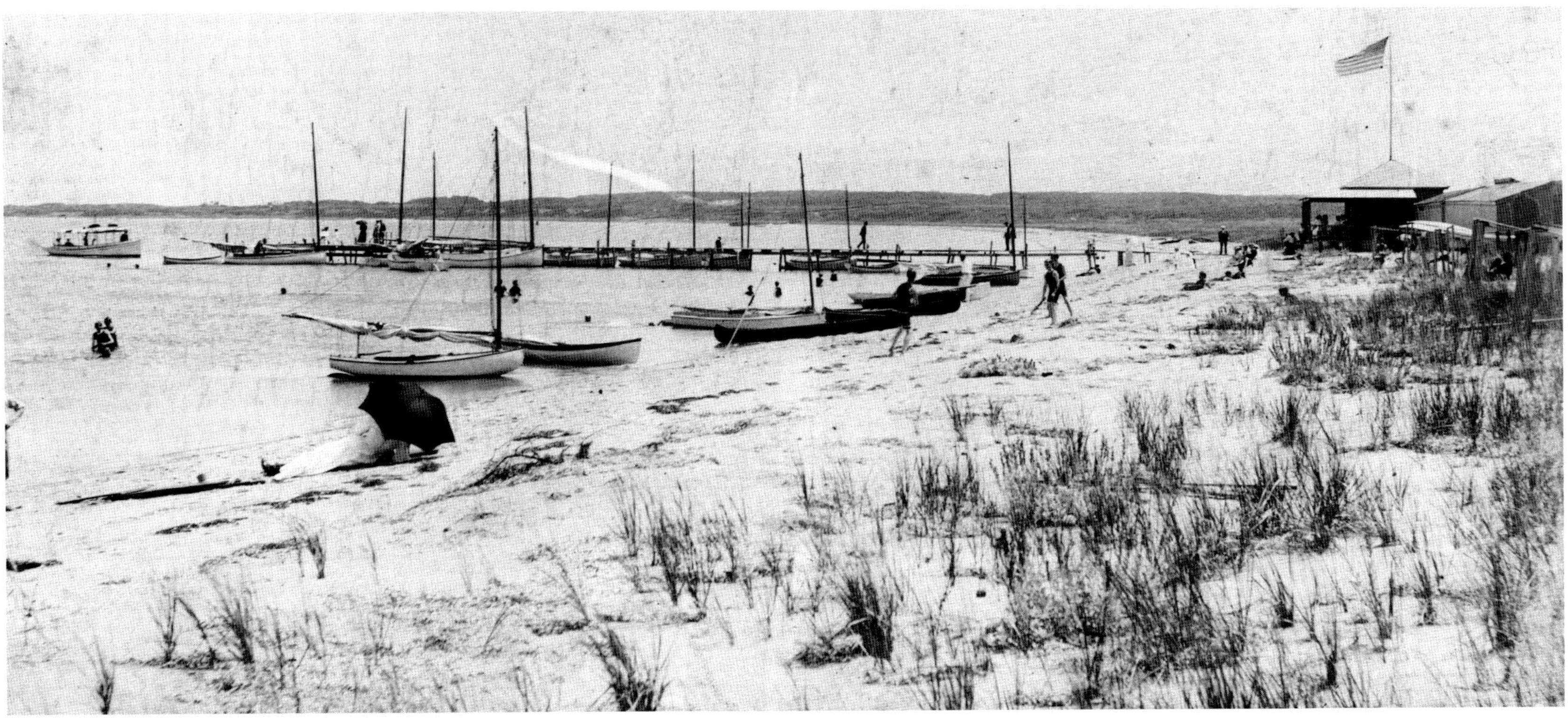

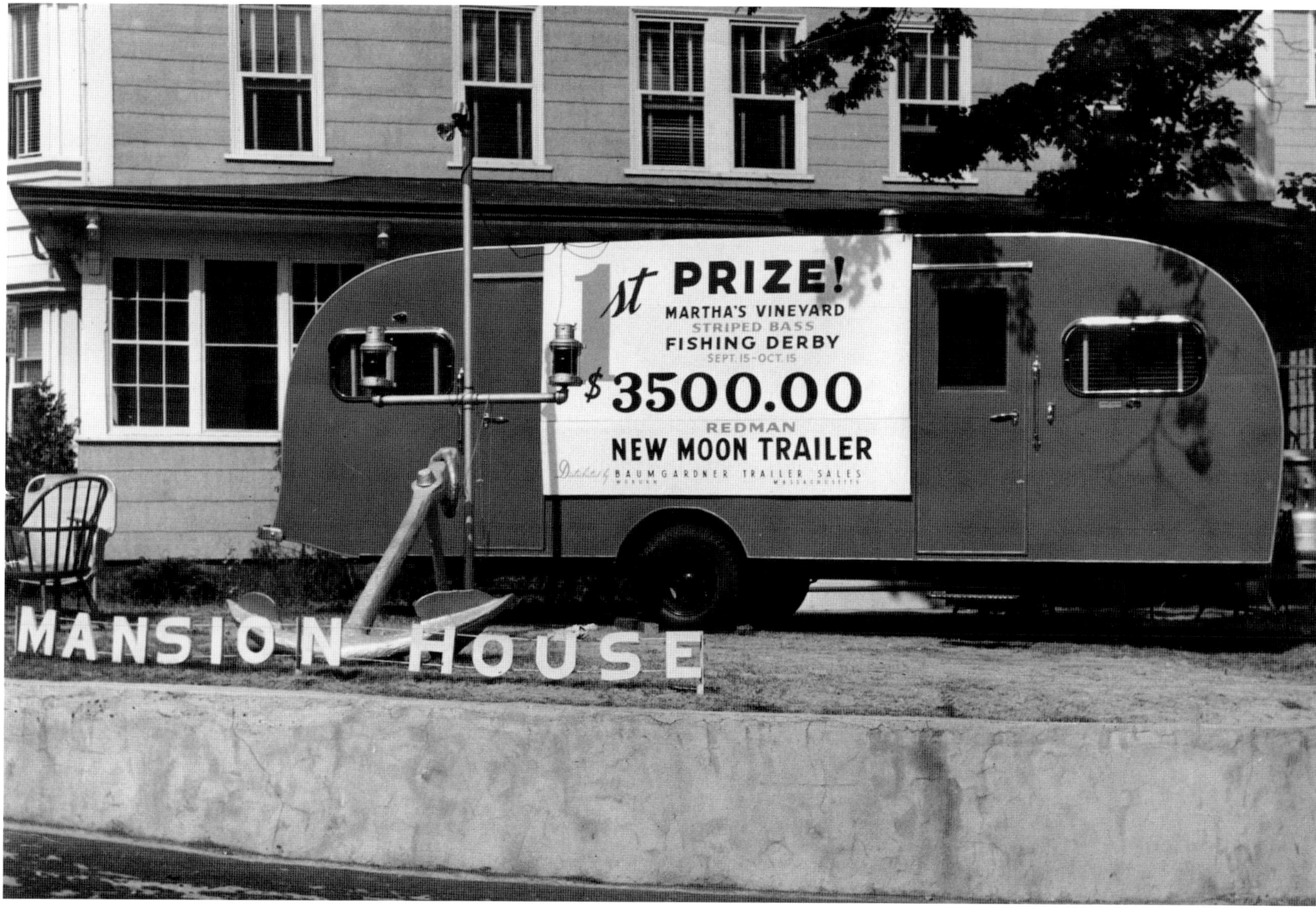

The Martha's Vineyard Striped Bass and Bluefish Derby has been held every fall since 1946. Conceived as a way to attract visitors to the island after the weather began to get cool, it rapidly grew into a month-long competition that brought fishermen, both male and female, back year after year. Prizes have varied over the years and have included boats, tricks, and, at least once, a trailer.

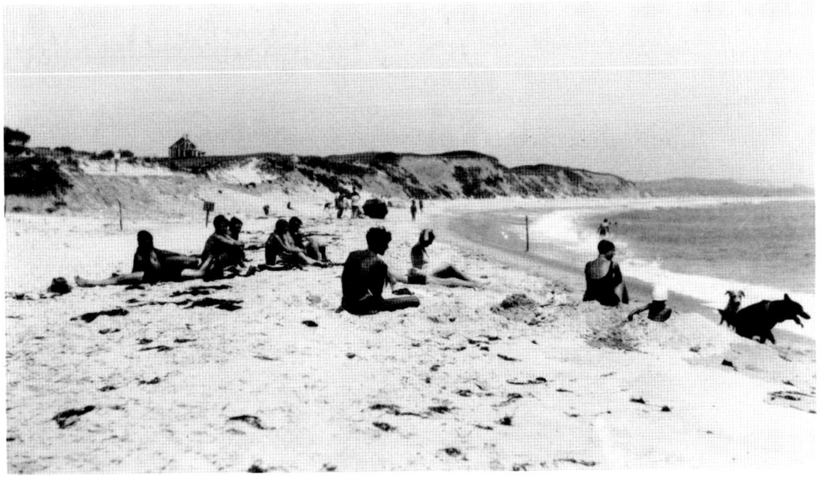

This photograph of Squibnocket Beach in Chilmark from the mid-1900s shows the Nashaquitsa Cliffs in the background. Squibnocket is one of several island beaches that restrict beach access to residents of the towns in which they are located.

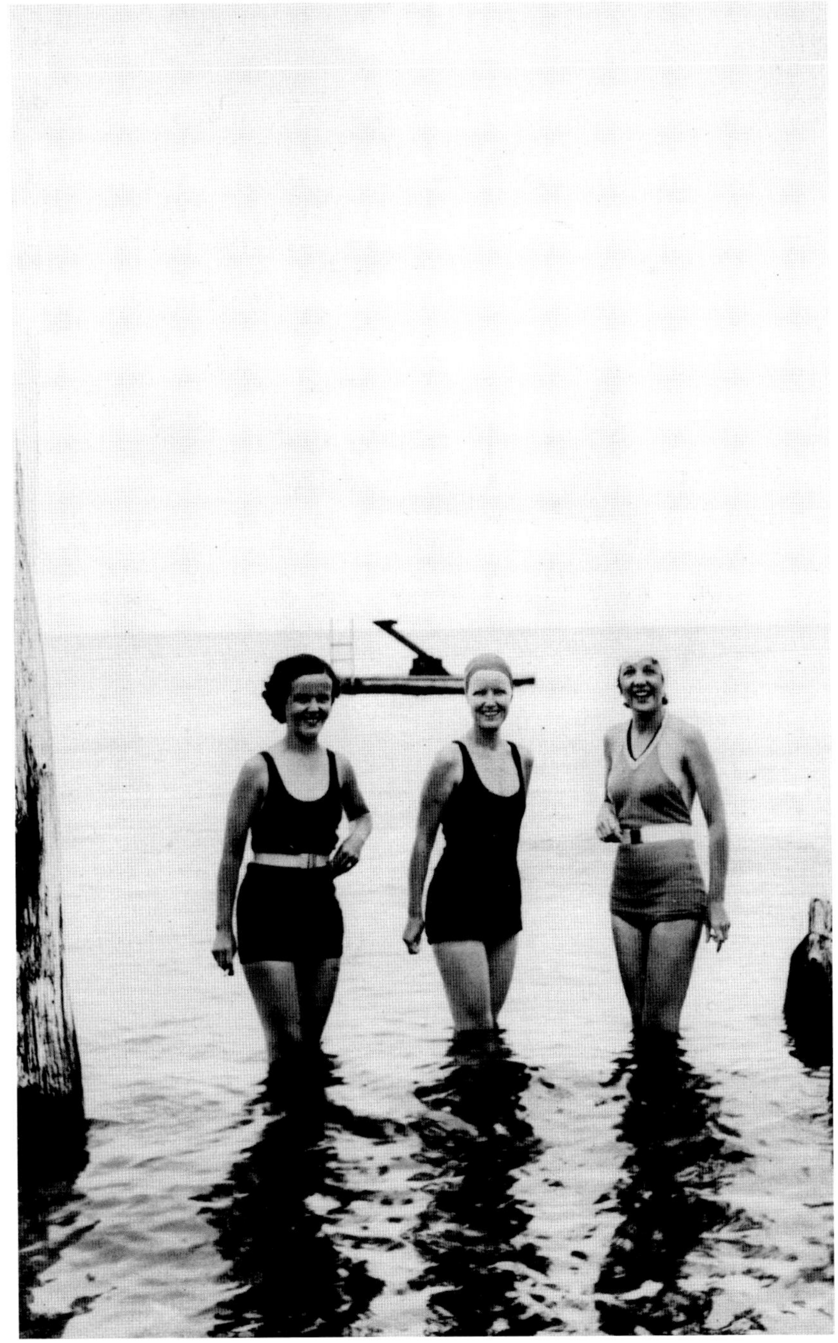

This snapshot dated July 1934 surely resembles countless pictures found in many a vacationer's photo album after a summer trip to Martha's Vineyard. On the back, it is inscribed, "2 aunts, mother in the middle."

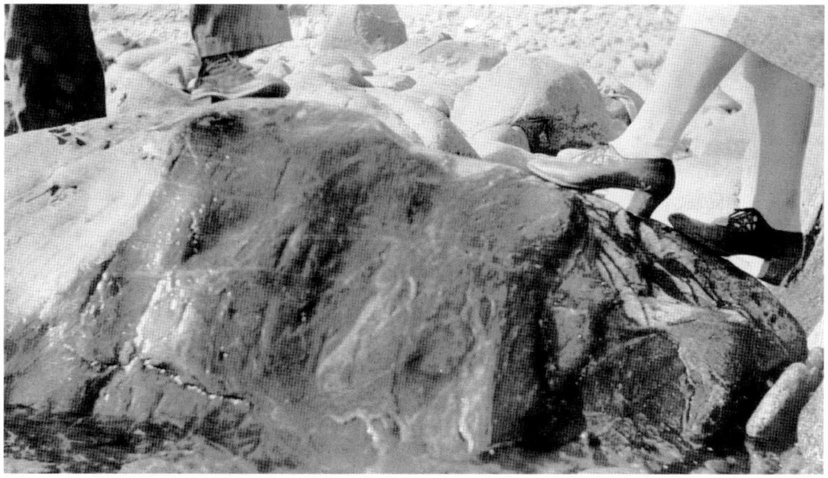

The story goes that in 1926, Joshua Crane, who used to own Noman's Land, discovered inscriptions on this rock near the shore that translate to "Liif Iriksson MI" ("Leif Eriksson, 1001"). Long dismissed as a hoax, the rock nevertheless caught the imagination of people looking for evidence that Vikings visited Martha's Vineyard more than 1,000 years ago.

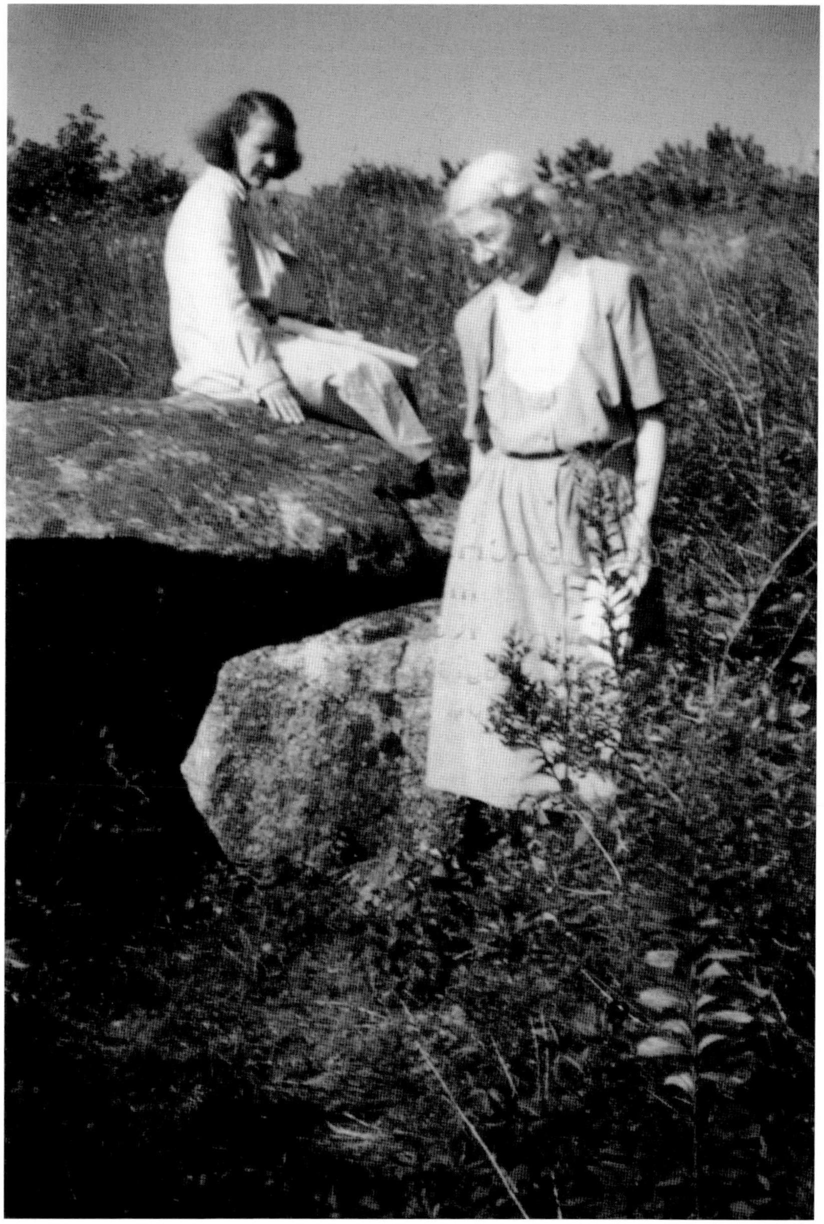

The "Cromlech of Quitsa" is another mysterious formation that archaeologists have demonstrated is not Viking in origin, but that has attracted the curious in search of ancient stories. This photograph of two unidentified women visiting the Chilmark site was taken in 1945.

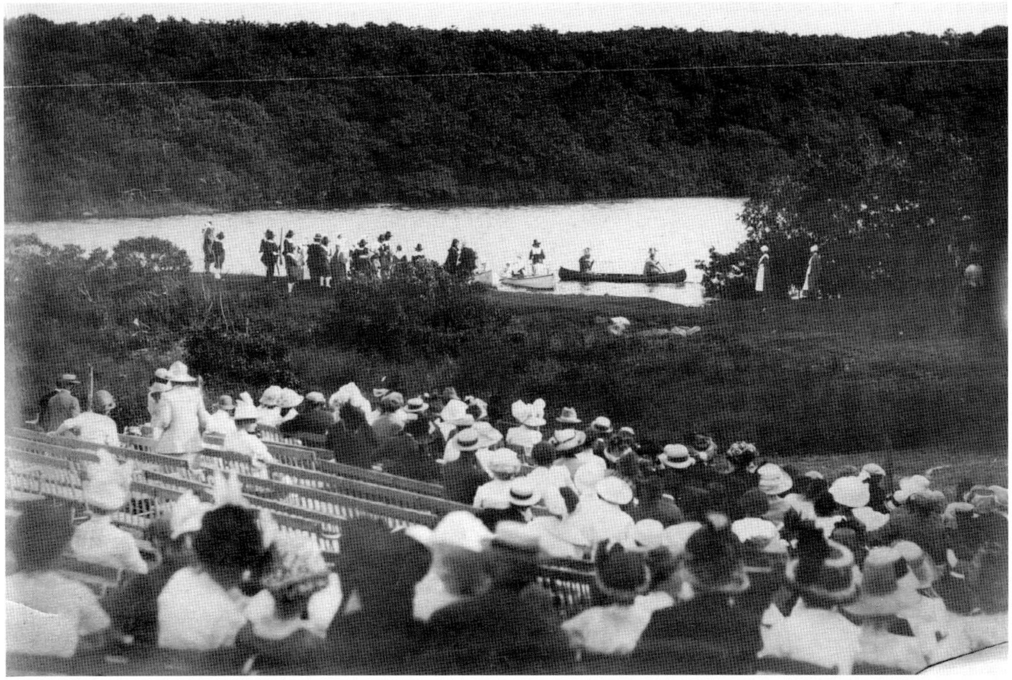

In 1911, Vineyarders got together to put on the first of several historical pageants about Martha's Vineyard. Performed at Allen's Pond in West Tisbury, the event attracted hundreds. This scene portrays the arrival of Thomas Mayhew Jr. in 1642. Because the actors were far from the audience, there was little dialog. The performances consisted largely of gestures and speeches.

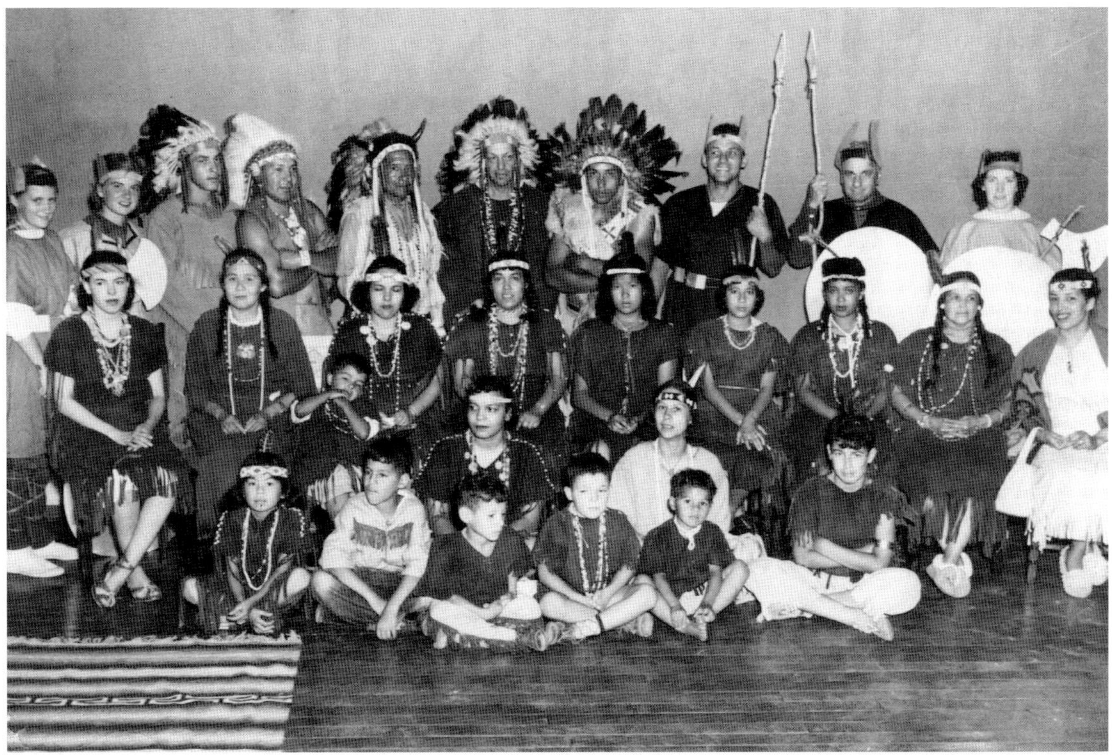

Few members of the Wampanoag tribe were invited to participate in the West Tisbury pageant. Several decades later, however, the tribe produced its own pageant, *Moshup his Family*, based on tribal stories of the island. It was performed at the Gay Head cliffs on August 12, 1955. The family names of the cast members are familiar Aquinnah names: Vanderhoop, Madison, Widdiss, Manning, Jeffers, and Silva. (Photograph by Howell's Photograph Studio.)

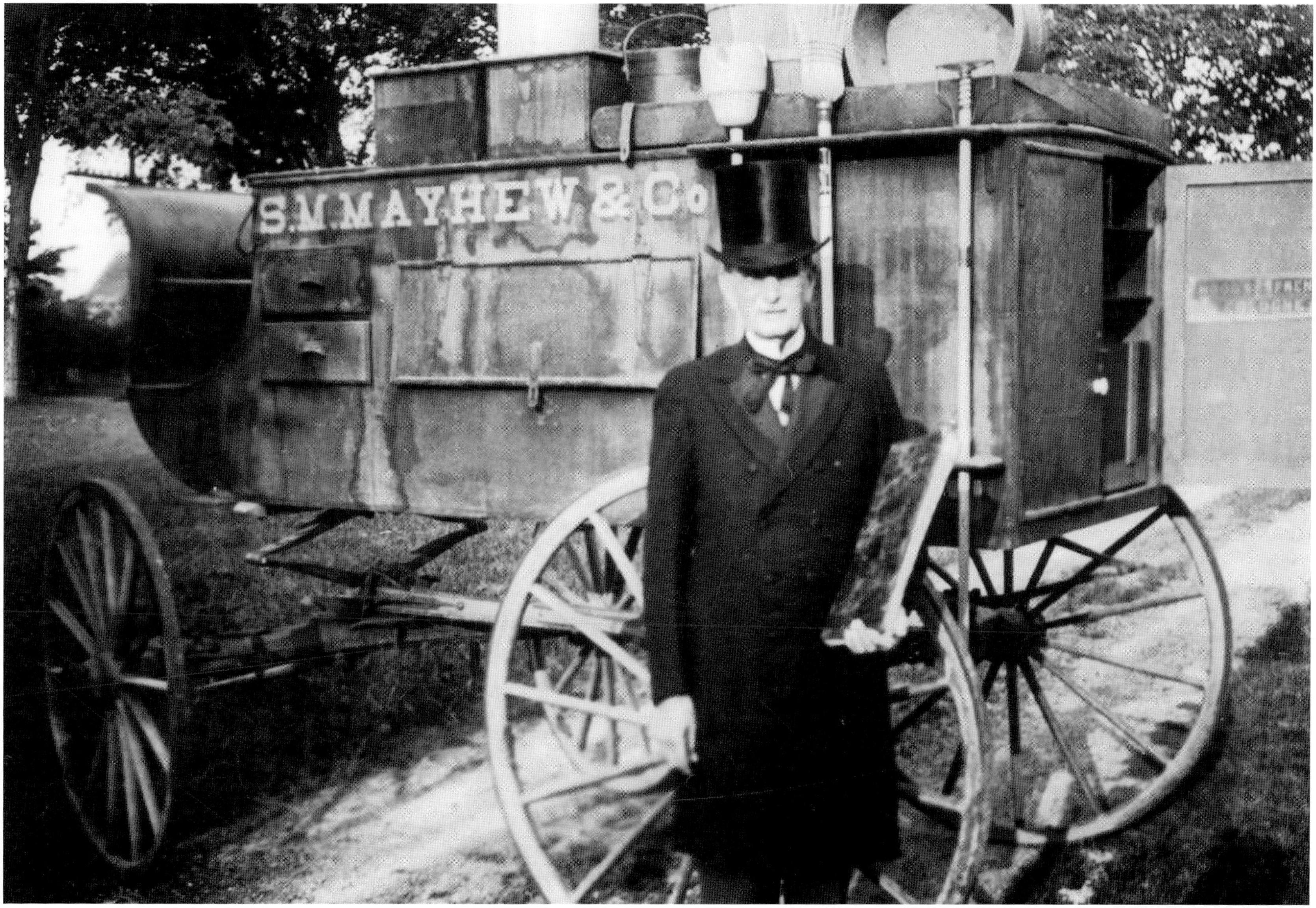

Proud of their heritage, Vineyarders sometimes posed for photographs surrounded by relics of their past. On his 86th birthday, August 16, 1934, Ulysses Mayhew posed in a top hat holding an account book from his family's store and standing in front of the peddle cart used to take goods for sale to rural areas up-island. S.M. Mayhew & Company became Alley's General Store in West Tisbury. The peddle cart is now in the collection of the Martha's Vineyard Museum.

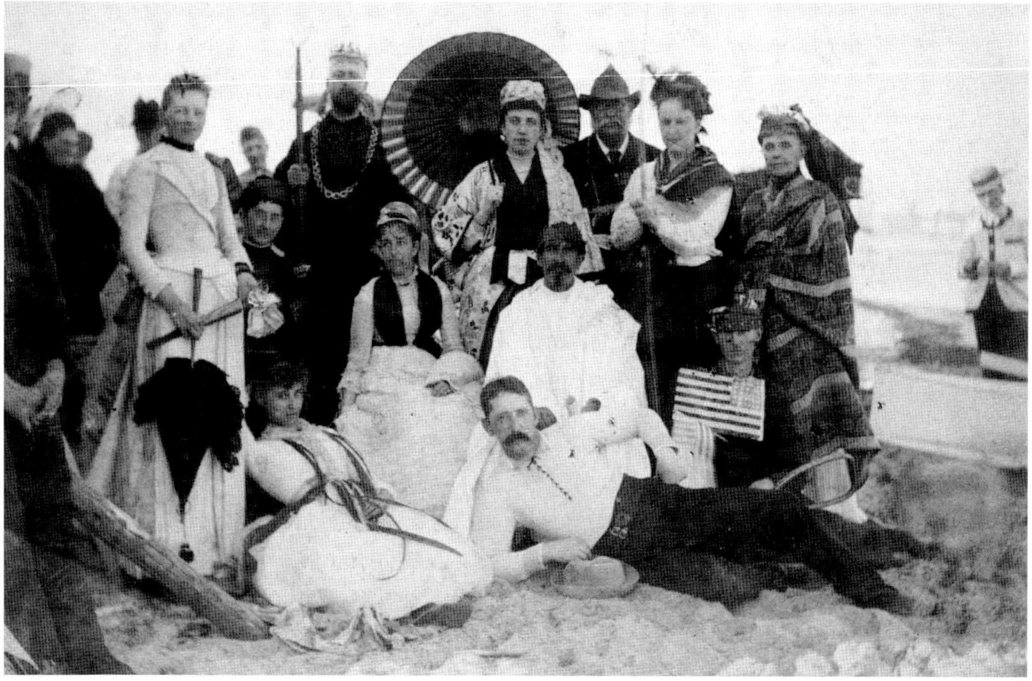

The occasion that prompted these Oak Bluffs beachgoers to dress in costumes is long forgotten. It may have been for a play or a fancy dress party. It was not uncommon for groups of hosts and their houseguests to put on small productions for their own amusement.

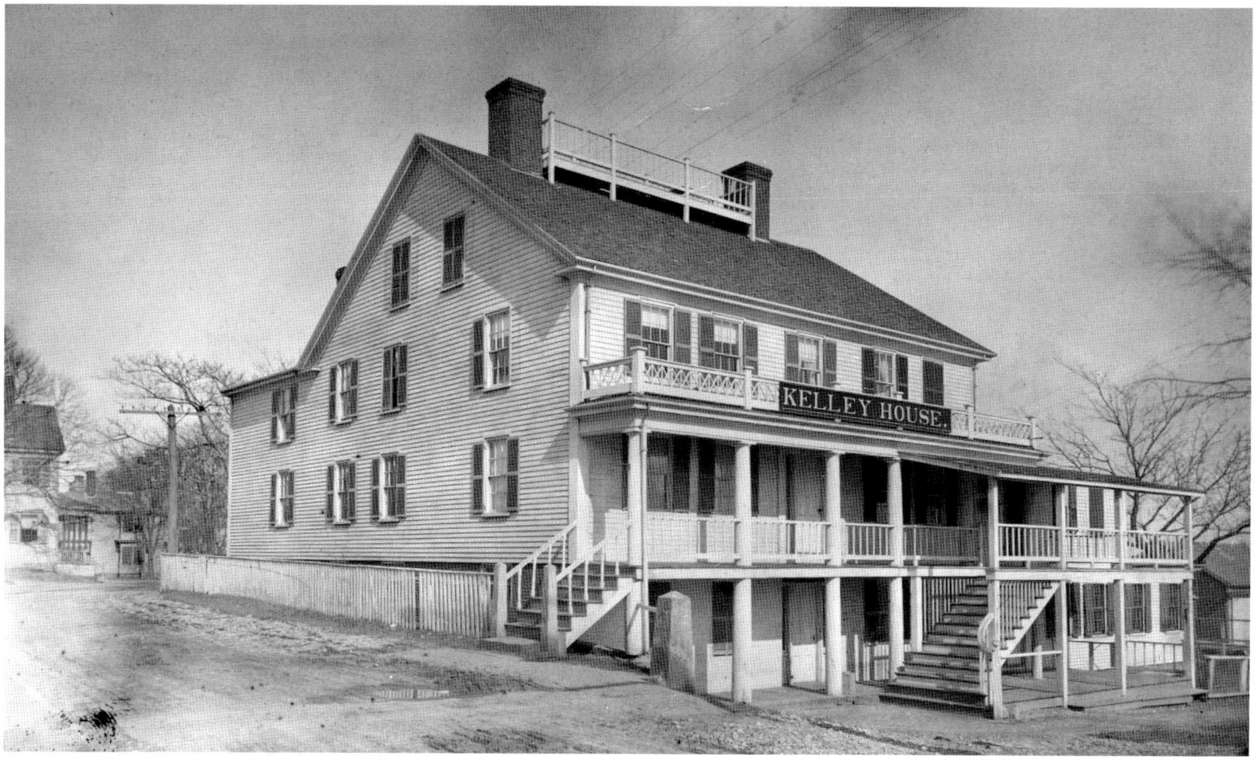

The Kelley House, in downtown Edgartown, was built in 1742. It has operated under several names, including the Marcy House, the Marcy Tavern, the Vineyard House, the Sea View House, and the Great Harbour Inn.

In 1939, Edna Smith started the Open Door Club as a place where Edgartown's black domestic workers could come on their days off to relax, cook meals, socialize, and sing. She is seen here in 1956 with her husband, James Smith. The Open Door Club was located at the Smiths' house, at the corner of Cook and Tilton Streets in Edgartown.

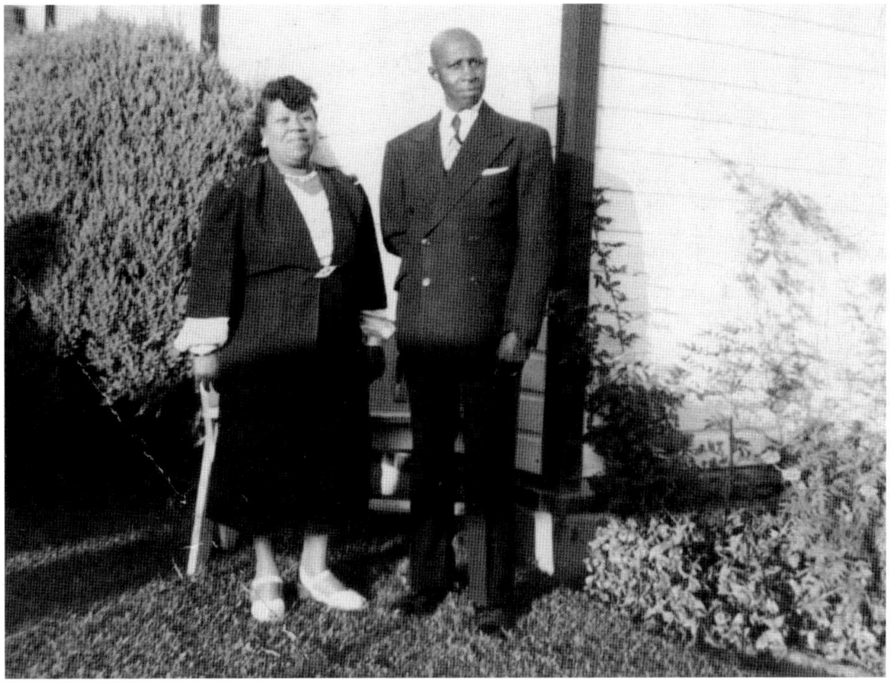

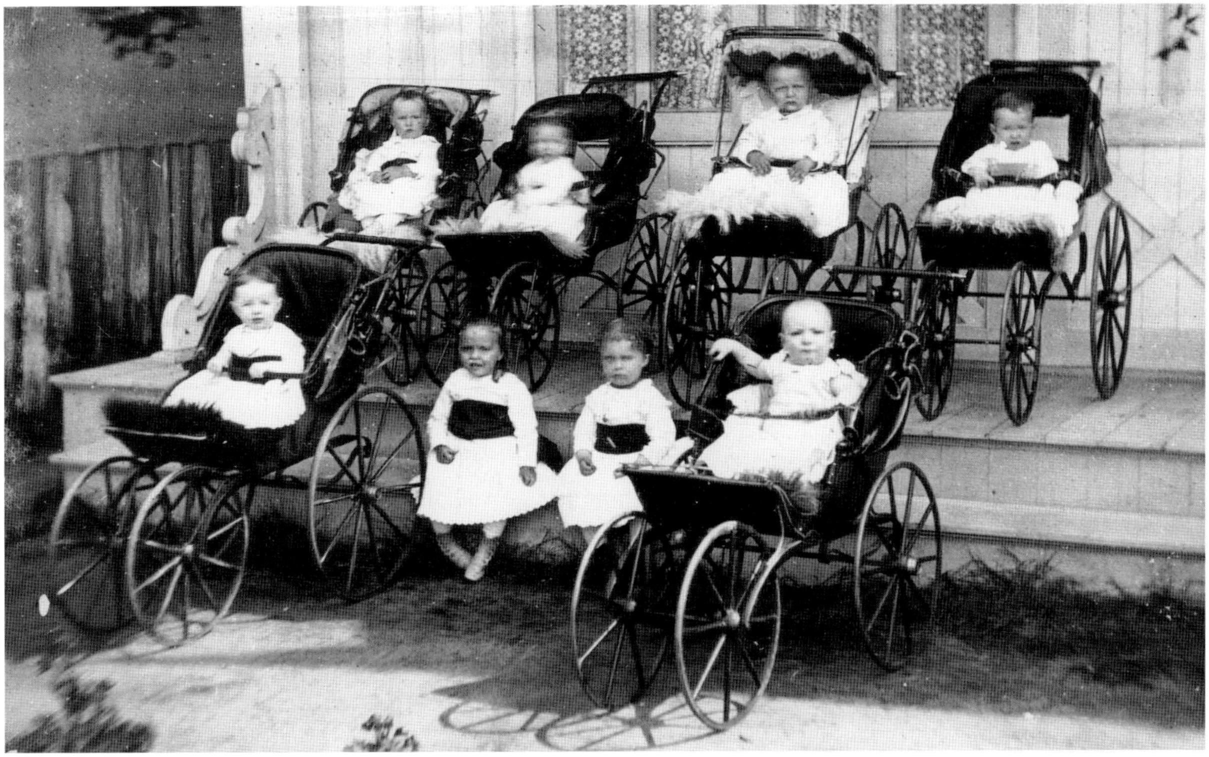

"Pretty Baby" contests were one amusement that periodically took place on the Vineyard. Richard Shute photographed this beauty contest for babies, probably held around 1900, on the steps of an Oak Bluffs cottage home. The names of the contestants were not preserved.

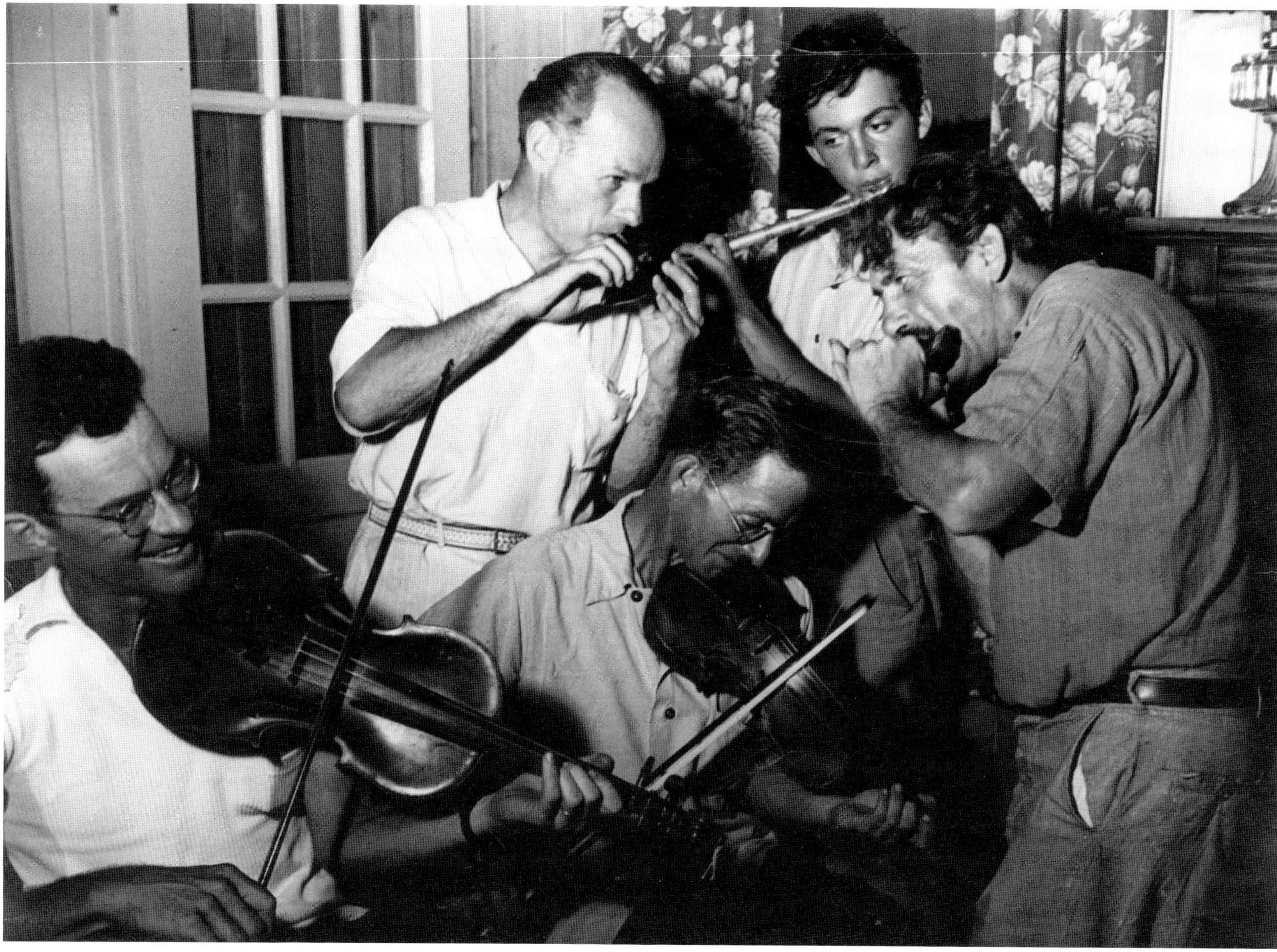

Not everyone who came to Martha's Vineyard for the summer wanted the excitement of a crowded resort. Some preferred a peaceful retreat where they could relax, work, and get to know their neighbors. Here, from left to right, Hollis Smith, an unidentified man, Gale Huntington, T.P. Benton, and Thomas Hart Benton are gathered for an evening of music. The undated photograph appears to be from the 1940s. Gale Huntington is well known for collecting and preserving traditional sea shanties. Thomas Hart Benton was one of the most renowned American painters of his day. (Photograph by Arthur C. Griffin.)

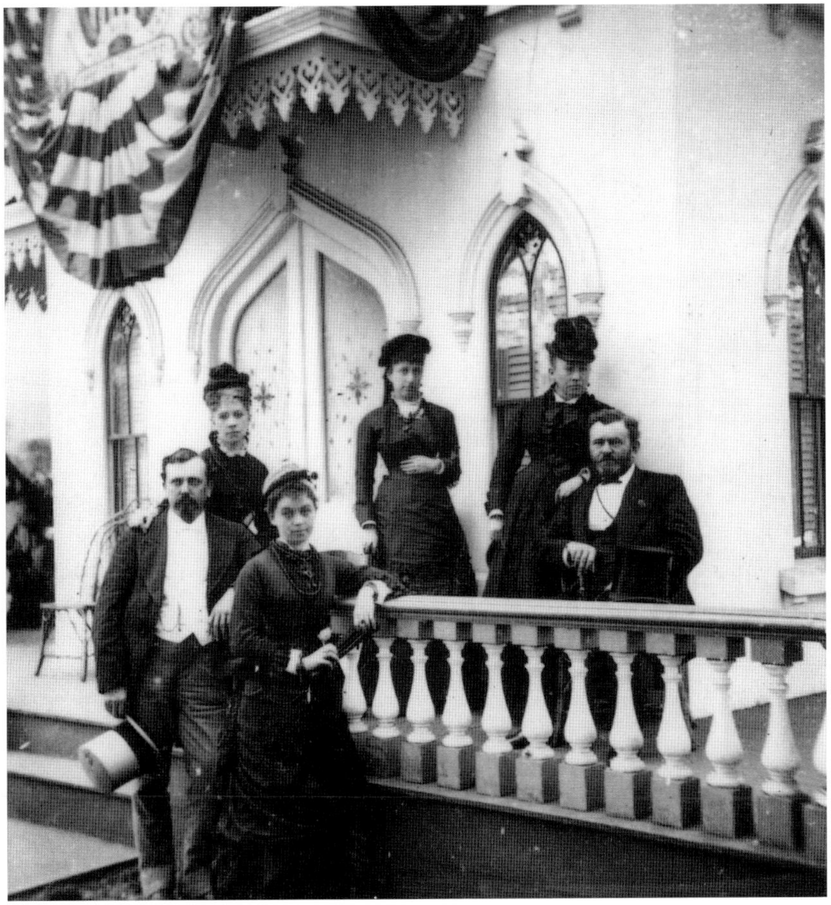

Ulysses S. Grant was the first sitting president to visit Martha's Vineyard. He visited for three days, making excursions to Nantucket, Hyannis, and Naushon. He stayed in the cottage of Methodist bishop Gilbert Haven at the Wesleyan Grove campground in Oak Bluffs. Here, the presidential party poses on the porch of Bishop Haven's cottage. President Grant and his wife, Julia, are on the right. (Photograph by Richard Shute.)

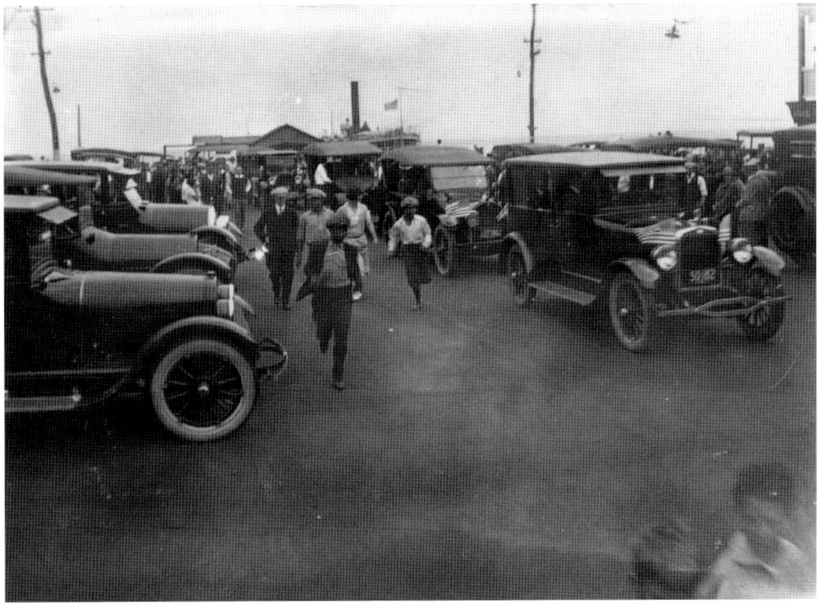

The occasion for this motorcade leaving the Oak Bluffs wharf is not recorded, but it is tempting to speculate that it carried Calvin Coolidge during one of his visits to the island. Though Coolidge did not come to Martha's Vineyard during his presidency, he visited as lieutenant governor of Massachusetts in 1915 and 1917, as governor in 1919, and after his presidency in 1929, staying at least twice at William Butler's summer home in Lambert's Cove.

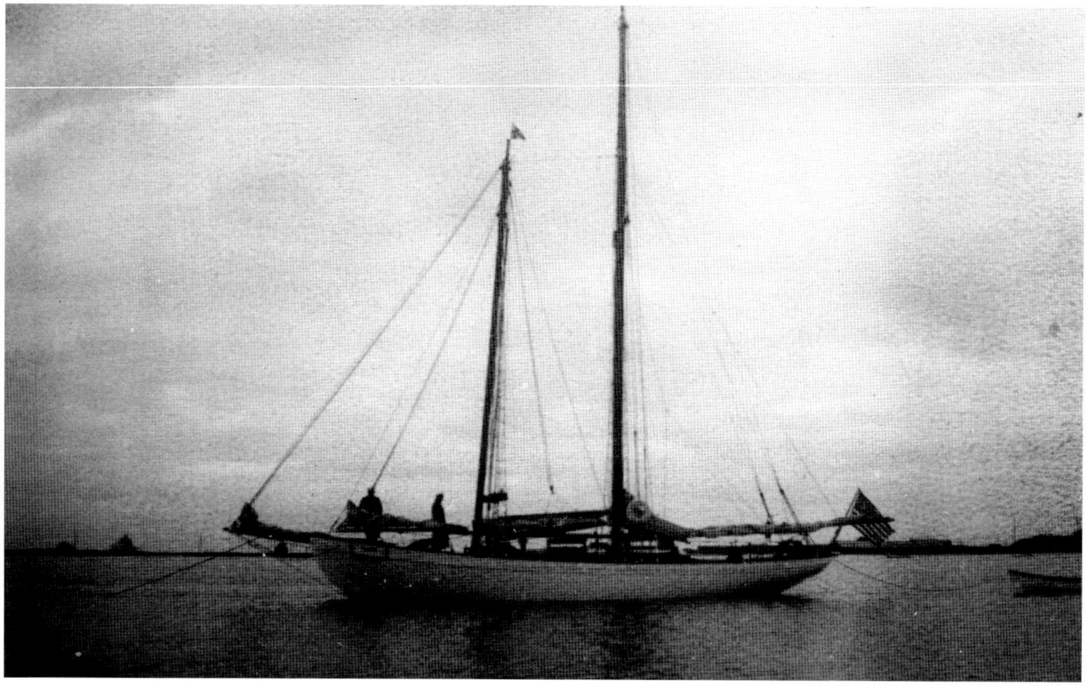

Franklin D. Roosevelt did not vacation on Martha's Vineyard, but he did anchor the *Amberjack II* in Edgartown Harbor when he was sheltering from bad weather during a vacation sail from Rhode Island to Massachusetts on June 18, 1933. Besides Grant and Coolidge, the presidents who visited the island before, during, or after their presidency are Arthur, Kennedy, Nixon, Clinton, and Obama.

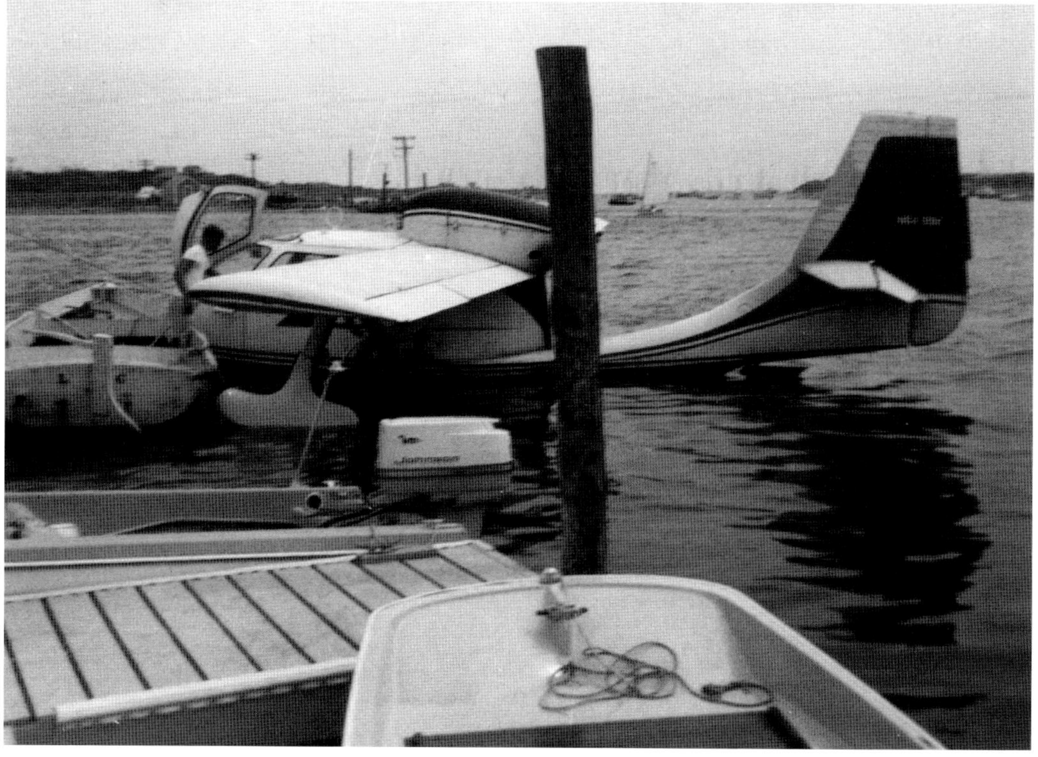

After the invention of air travel, the Vineyard was quickly reachable by plane. Two airfields were established, one at Katama and one in the center of the island during World War II. Private seaplanes, like the one seen here in Edgartown Harbor, were also relatively common sights.

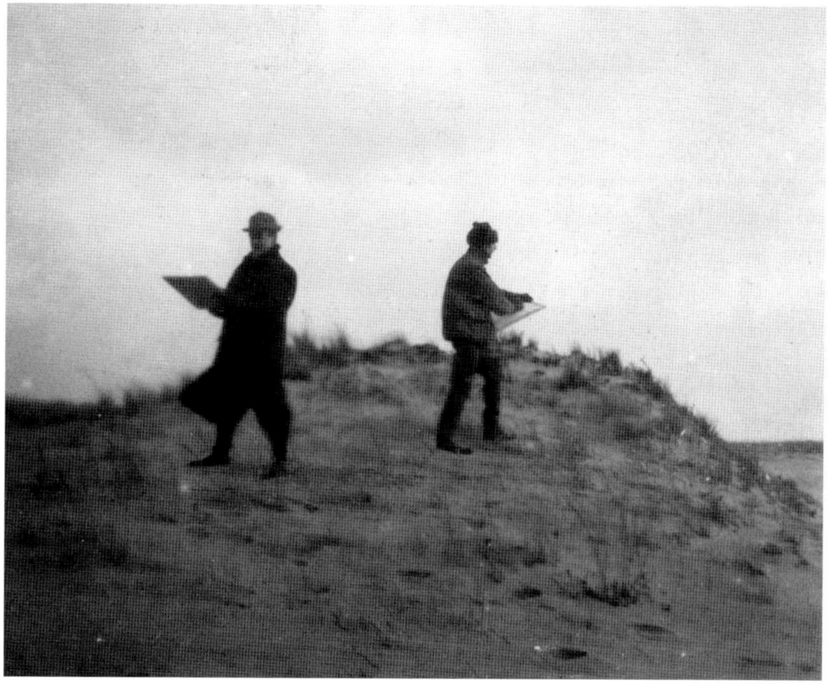

Artists are drawn to the natural beauty of the Vineyard. These two men in the 1930s were sketching the Chappaquiddick landscape from opposite directions.

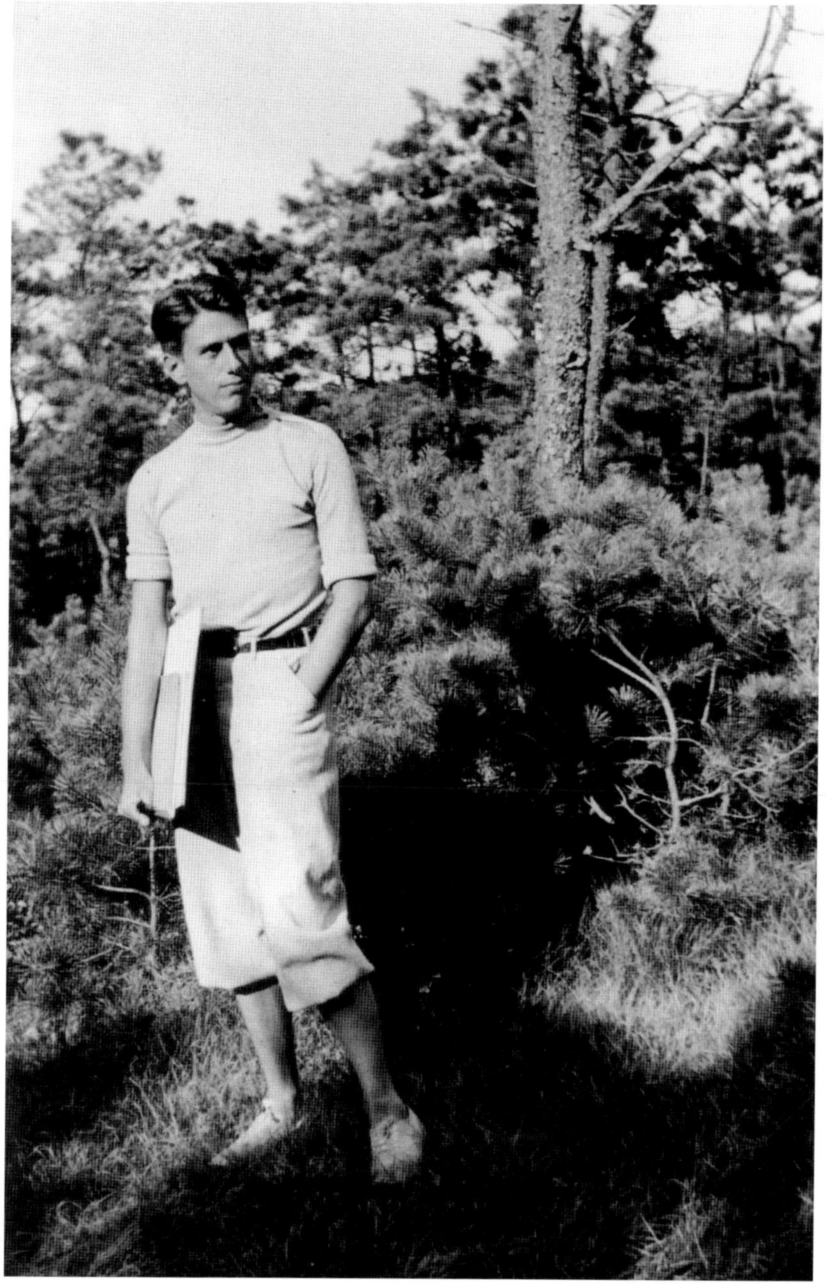

Paul Cadmus was part of a circle of artists, including Edna Reindel, who returned to the island repeatedly in the 1930s. Cadmus visited his friend Thomas Nevin Jernegan Dexter of Edgartown, whom he had met while studying in New York. Cadmus is seen here in front of Albert Jewett's cottage in 1937.

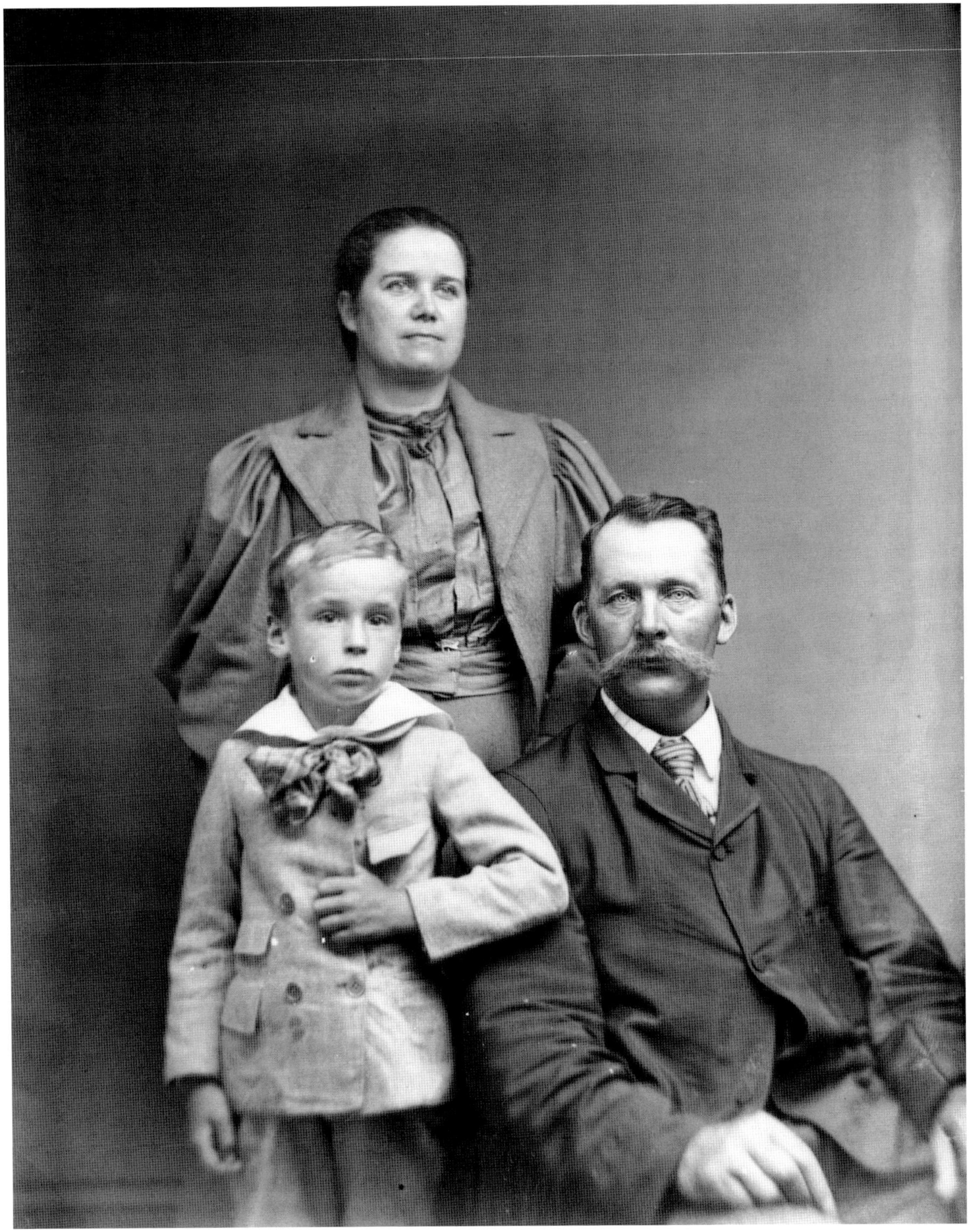

Some families who began as summer residents moved to the island year-round and remained for generations. This was the case for the Blackwell family. Henry Blackwell stopped in Chilmark on a boating trip in 1864 and liked it enough to begin buying land. Soon, he was joined by brothers and sisters. His niece Florence Blackwell married postmaster F. Elliott Mayhew. She later became a founder of the Chilmark Public Library. She is seen here with her husband and their son Walter in 1895.

This photograph has a satisfied message written on the back: "Makonikey Point, Martha's Vineyard, 1913. Supper on the beach. Home by moonlight in the *Lorna*." Makonikey Point straddles the border between Vineyard Haven and West Tisbury.

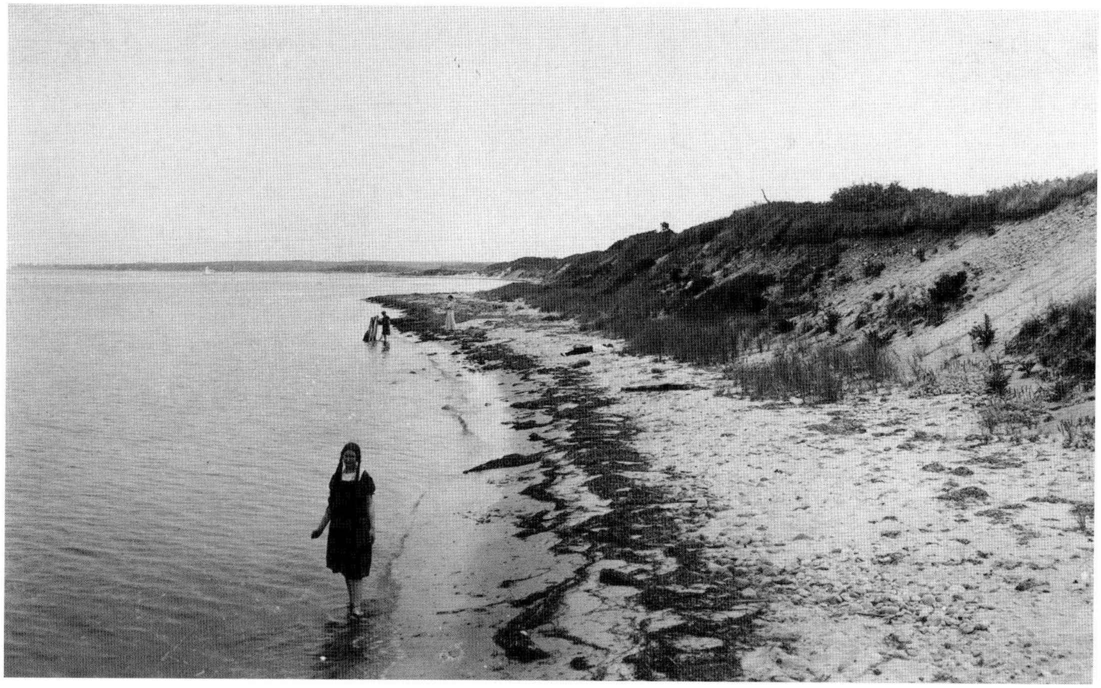

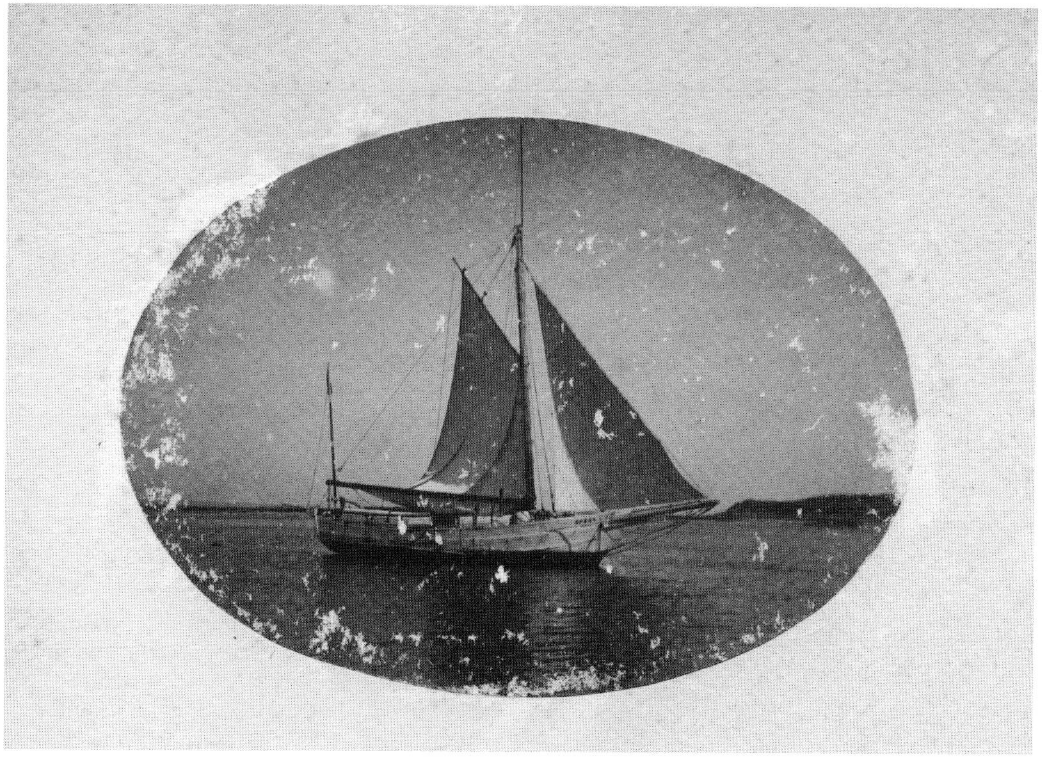

After Joshua Slocum sailed solo around the world in the *Spray* and wrote the best-selling book *Sailing Alone Around the World* about his adventures, he bought a farm in West Tisbury and moved there with his wife. But he was not satisfied for long. After only a year and a half, he left the Vineyard, choosing to spend most of his time sailing on the *Spray*, seen here anchored in Menemsha Creek in June 1903. He disappeared on the boat in November 1909 and was never found.

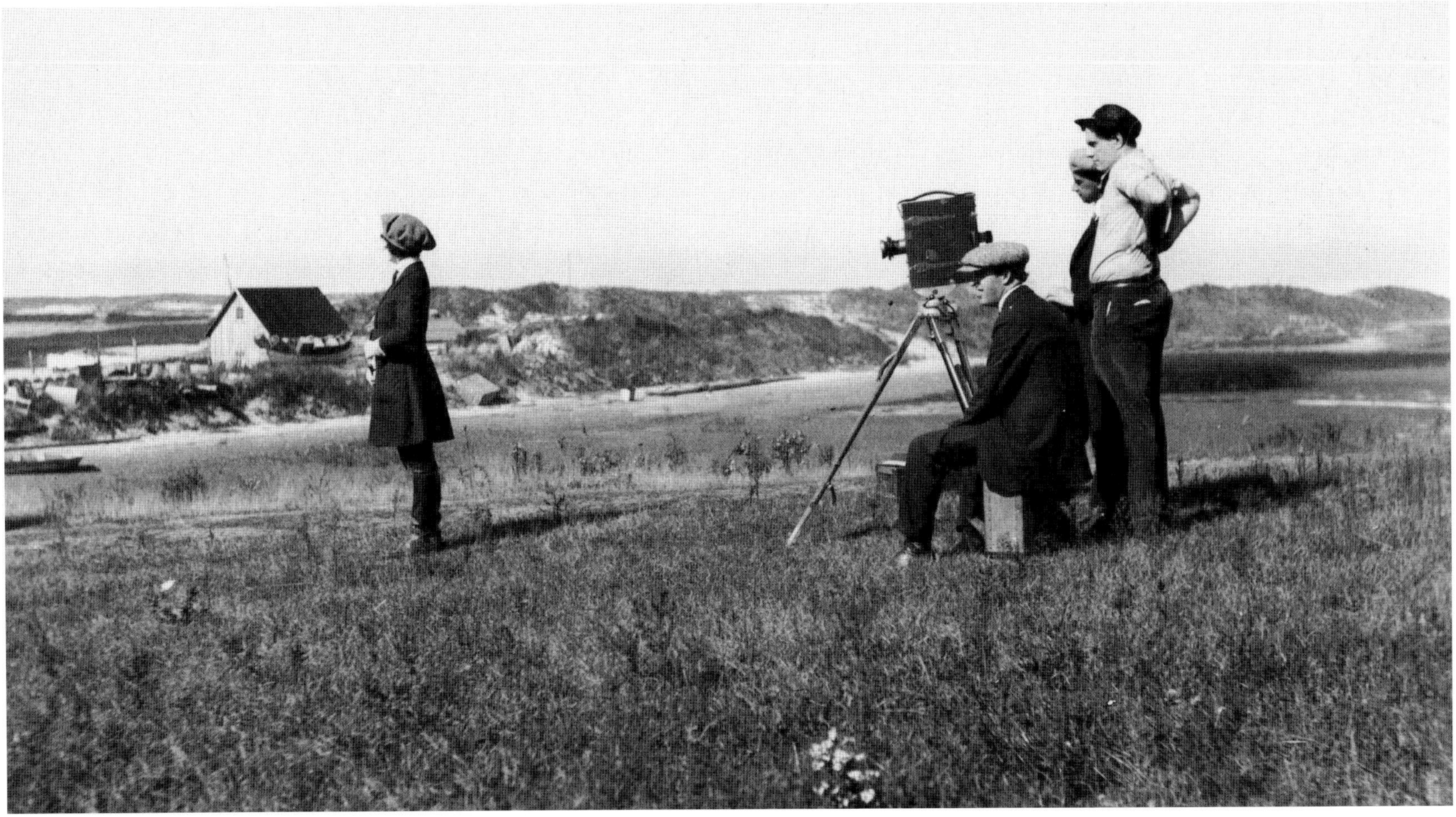

The silent movie *Annabelle Lee*, based on Edgar Alan Poe's poem of the same name, was filmed in Menemsha in 1920. It starred Lorraine Harding and John B. O'Brien and was directed by William J. Scully. *Annabelle Lee* never gained attention comparable to Steven Spielberg's *Jaws*, which was filmed in multiple locations on the island in 1974.

OPPOSITE: September 21, 1938, saw one of the worst hurricanes in New England history hit Martha's Vineyard. It arrived without warning, causing flooding over all the island's coastal areas, knocking down trees, and devastating the small fishing village of Menemsha. The destruction is apparent in this photograph taken shortly after the storm.

FOUR

NATURE AND CLIMATE

The island formed around 5,000 years ago when melting water that had been trapped in the receding ice sheets from the last ice age caused the sea level to rise and surround high ground with water. Before that, ancestors of today's Wampanoag could walk to this land. Tools and other evidence of their activities from 10,000 years ago have been found at several sites on the island.

Much earlier, approximately 23,000 years ago, advancing glaciers had molded the terrain by pushing and folding the clay of the coastal plain ahead of them. When they began their retreat around 18,000 years ago, the glaciers left behind great boulders, sand, gravel, and the multicolored Gay Head Cliffs of Aquinnah.

The natural phenomena that affect all coastal areas are magnified on an island. Bad weather, underwater rock ledges, and currents that cause underwater shoals to shift invisibly are always a hazard to marine traffic. Shipwrecks have been familiar to islanders as long as ships have passed nearby.

Countless storms have buffeted the shoreline, subtly or dramatically eroding natural beaches and cliffs and damaging or destroying manmade buildings, wharves, and roads. Generations of islanders and visitors have worked to both exploit and preserve the Vineyard's natural resources. In the face of storms, climate change, and development, the challenge of balancing the competing needs and wants of people with the need to preserve the natural environment of Martha's Vineyard is one that will never abate.

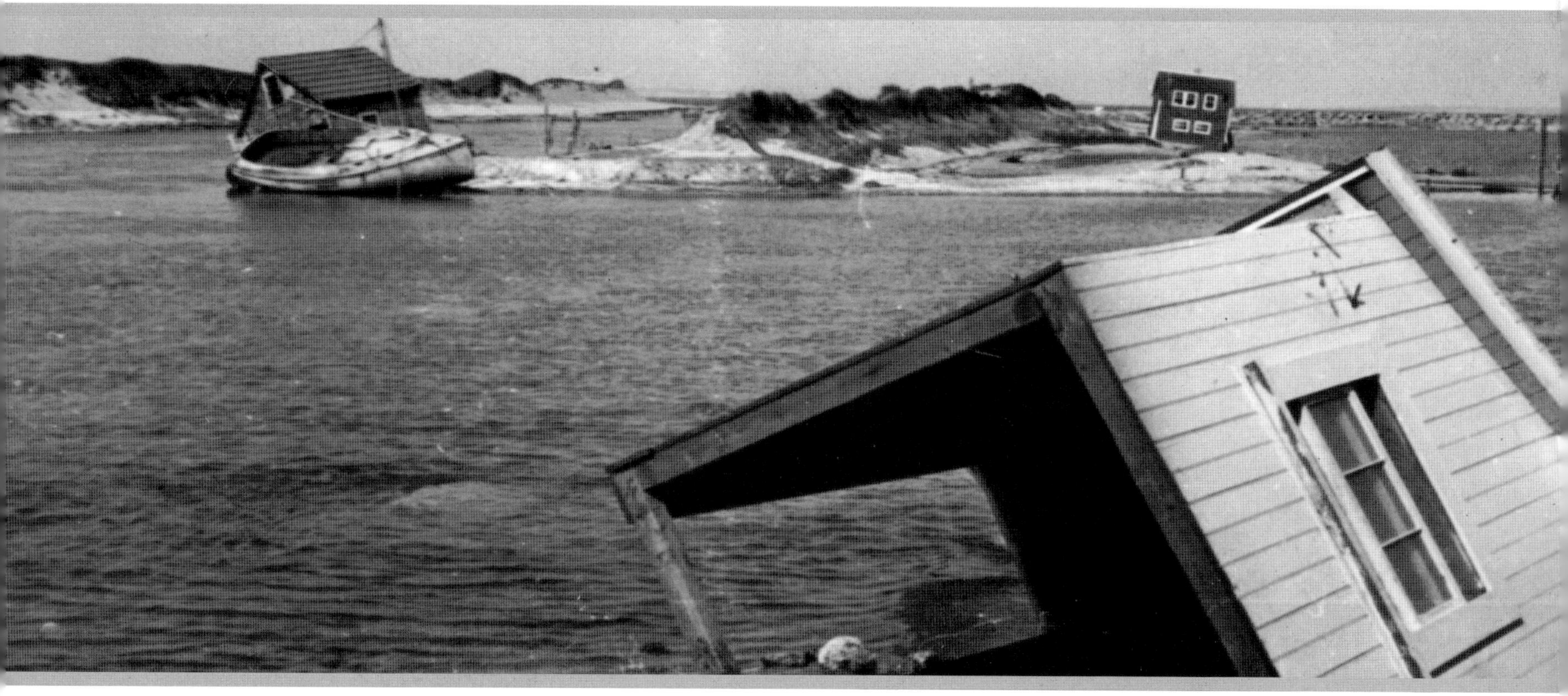

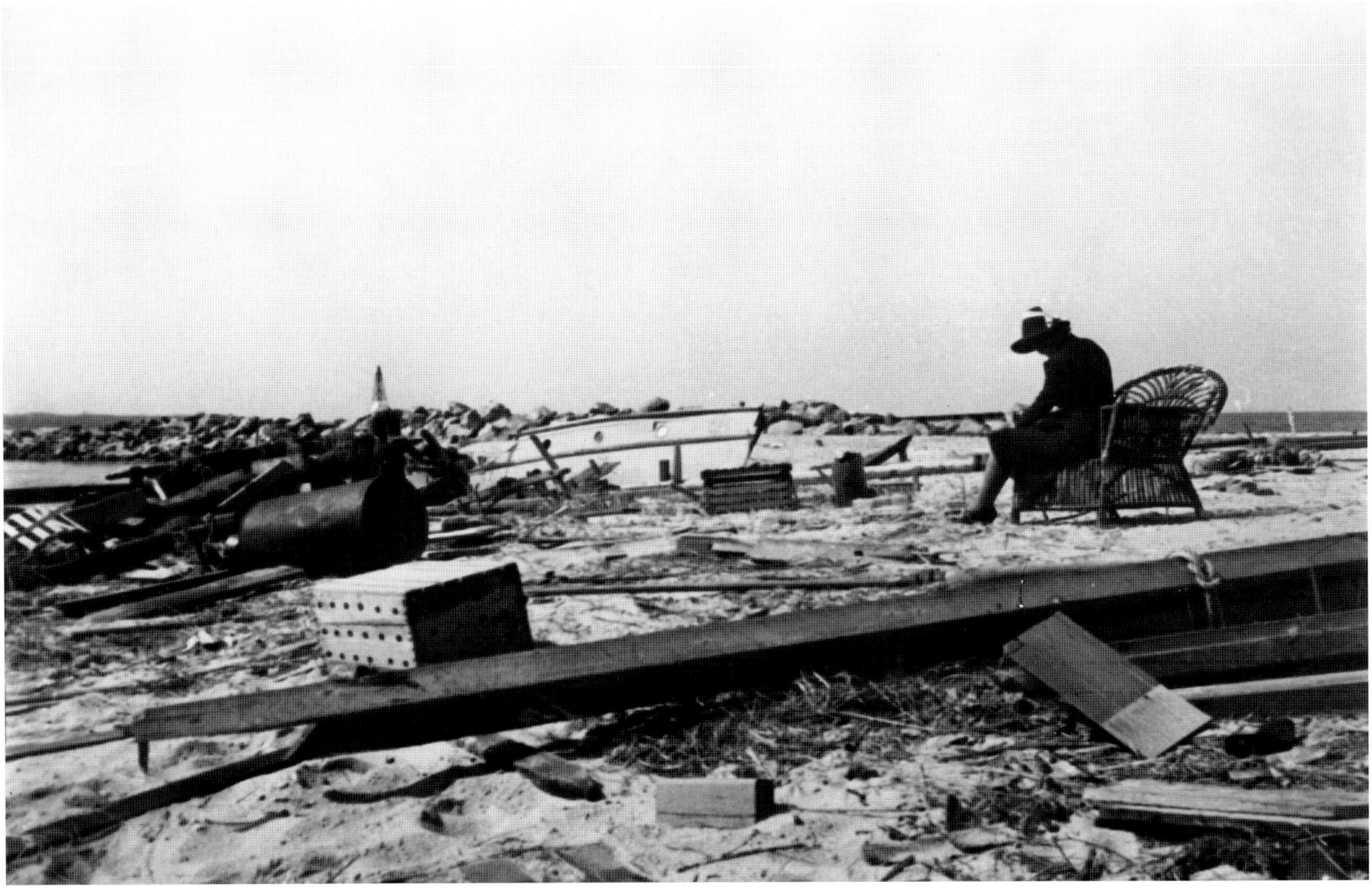

In just two hours, Menemsha went from a prosperous working fishing village to the scene of disaster. It did not take long, however, for the Menemsha fishermen to rebuild and get back to business. The storm affected the rest of the island as well. Buildings were damaged as trees were uprooted and blown into them. The docks and shoreline were flooded. The hurricane of 1938 was remembered as the big one. In this photograph, taken shortly after the storm, an unidentified woman sits amid the debris on the shore in Menemsha.

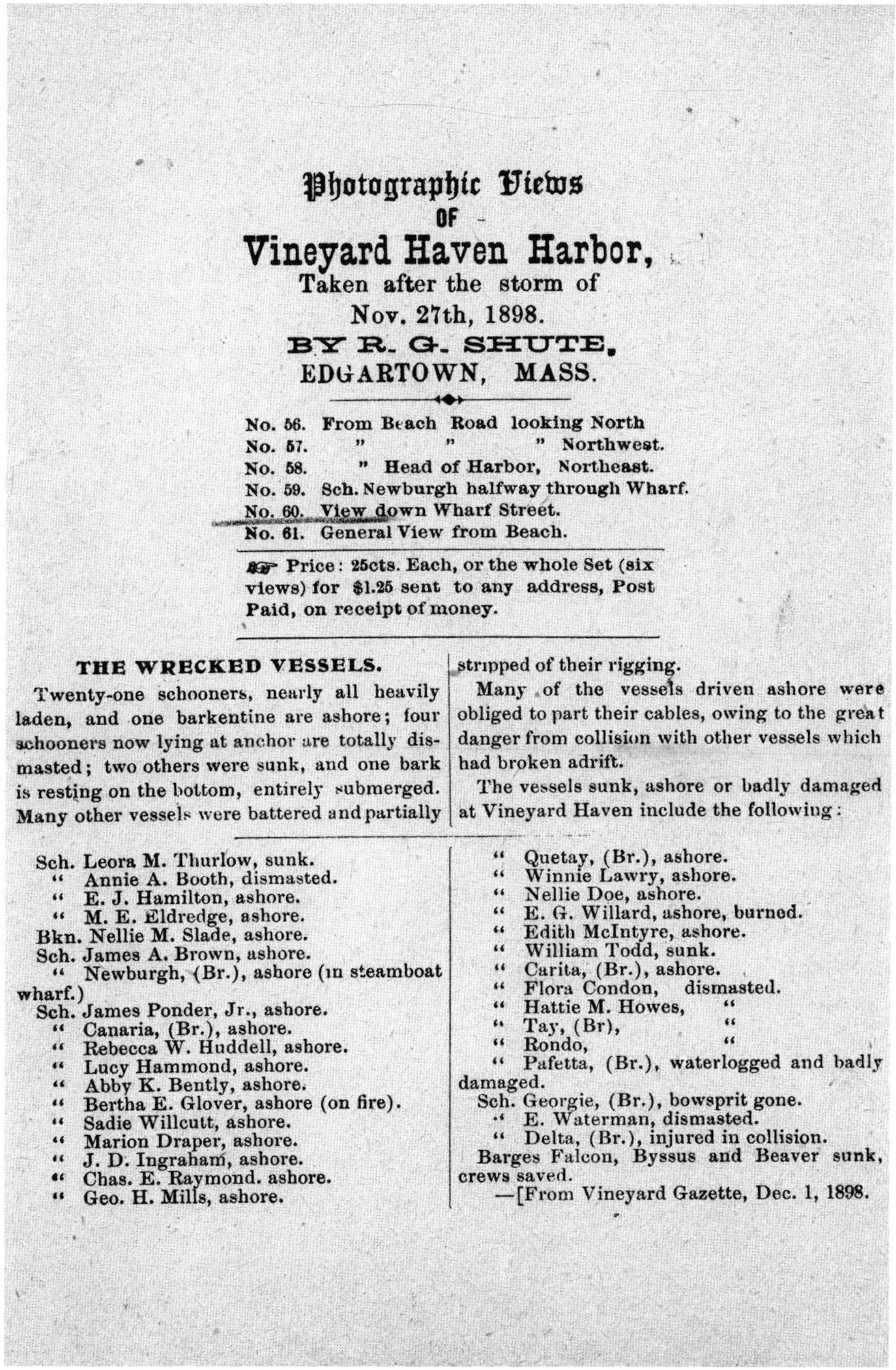

Photographic Views
OF
Vineyard Haven Harbor,
Taken after the storm of
Nov. 27th, 1898.
BY R. G. SHUTE,
EDGARTOWN, MASS.

No. 56. From Beach Road looking North
No. 57. " " " Northwest.
No. 58. " Head of Harbor, Northeast.
No. 59. Sch. Newburgh halfway through Wharf.
No. 60. View down Wharf Street.
No. 61. General View from Beach.

☞ Price: 25cts. Each, or the whole Set (six views) for $1.25 sent to any address, Post Paid, on receipt of money.

THE WRECKED VESSELS.

Twenty-one schooners, nearly all heavily laden, and one barkentine are ashore; four schooners now lying at anchor are totally dismasted; two others were sunk, and one bark is resting on the bottom, entirely submerged. Many other vessels were battered and partially stripped of their rigging.

Many of the vessels driven ashore were obliged to part their cables, owing to the great danger from collision with other vessels which had broken adrift.

The vessels sunk, ashore or badly damaged at Vineyard Haven include the following:

Sch. Leora M. Thurlow, sunk.
" Annie A. Booth, dismasted.
" E. J. Hamilton, ashore.
" M. E. Eldredge, ashore.
Bkn. Nellie M. Slade, ashore.
Sch. James A. Brown, ashore.
" Newburgh, (Br.), ashore (in steamboat wharf.)
Sch. James Ponder, Jr., ashore.
" Canaria, (Br.), ashore.
" Rebecca W. Huddell, ashore.
" Lucy Hammond, ashore.
" Abby K. Bently, ashore.
" Bertha E. Glover, ashore (on fire).
" Sadie Willcutt, ashore.
" Marion Draper, ashore.
" J. D. Ingraham, ashore.
" Chas. E. Raymond. ashore.
" Geo. H. Mills, ashore.
" Quetay, (Br.), ashore.
" Winnie Lawry, ashore.
" Nellie Doe, ashore.
" E. G. Willard, ashore, burned.
" Edith McIntyre, ashore.
" William Todd, sunk.
" Carita, (Br.), ashore.
" Flora Condon, dismasted.
" Hattie M. Howes, "
" Tay, (Br), "
" Rondo, "
" Pafetta, (Br.), waterlogged and badly damaged.
Sch. Georgie, (Br.), bowsprit gone.
" E. Waterman, dismasted.
" Delta, (Br.), injured in collision.
Barges Falcon, Byssus and Beaver sunk, crews saved.
—[From Vineyard Gazette, Dec. 1, 1898.

Of course, there were disastrous storms before the 1938 hurricane. In 1635, William Bradford of Plymouth, just 35 miles away, recorded "a mighty storm of wind and raine as none living in these parts, either English or Indian, ever saw." Two centuries later, the "September Gale" of 1869 did not spare the Vineyard. But the earliest storm to hit Martha's Vineyard to be extensively photographed was the "Portland Gale" of 1898. Lasting a day and two nights, it damaged or destroyed 34 vessels that had taken shelter in Vineyard Haven's harbor. Richard Shute photographed the aftermath and sold a series of six views for $1.25.

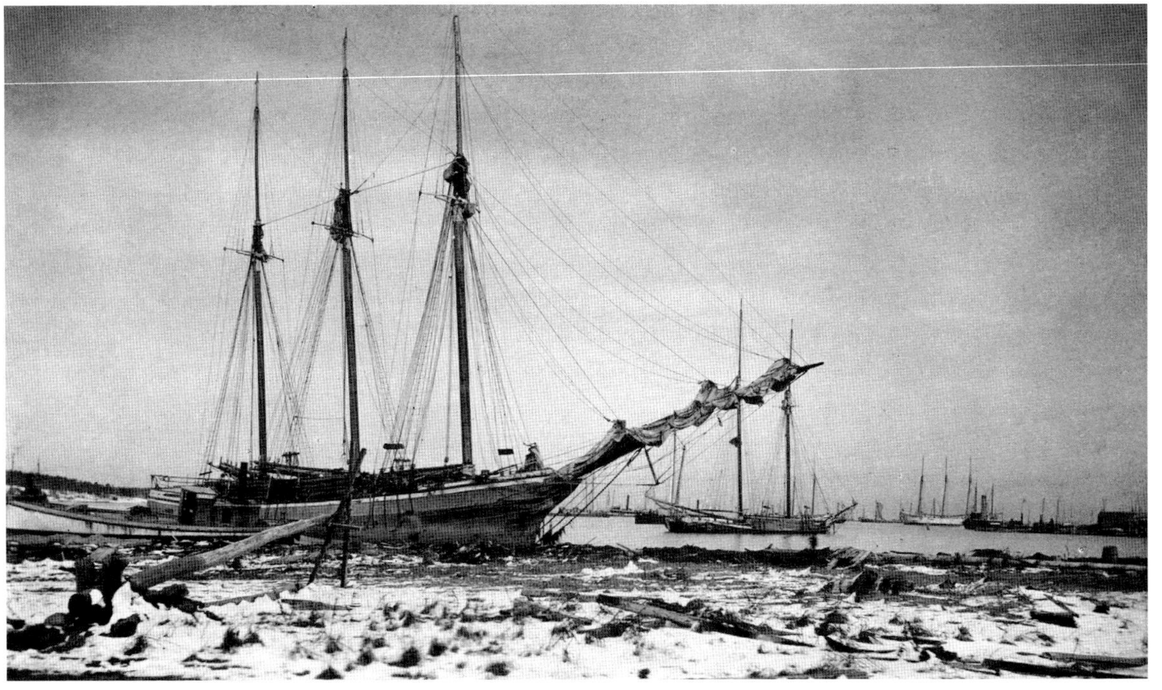

Taken from Beach Road looking northwest, this is photograph No. 58 from Richard Shute's series of views taken after the gale of 1898. It shows a schooner ashore in the foreground. Beyond it are two schooners that appear to have collided into each other, resting on the bottom, with one mast down and the aft portion of one smashed to pieces.

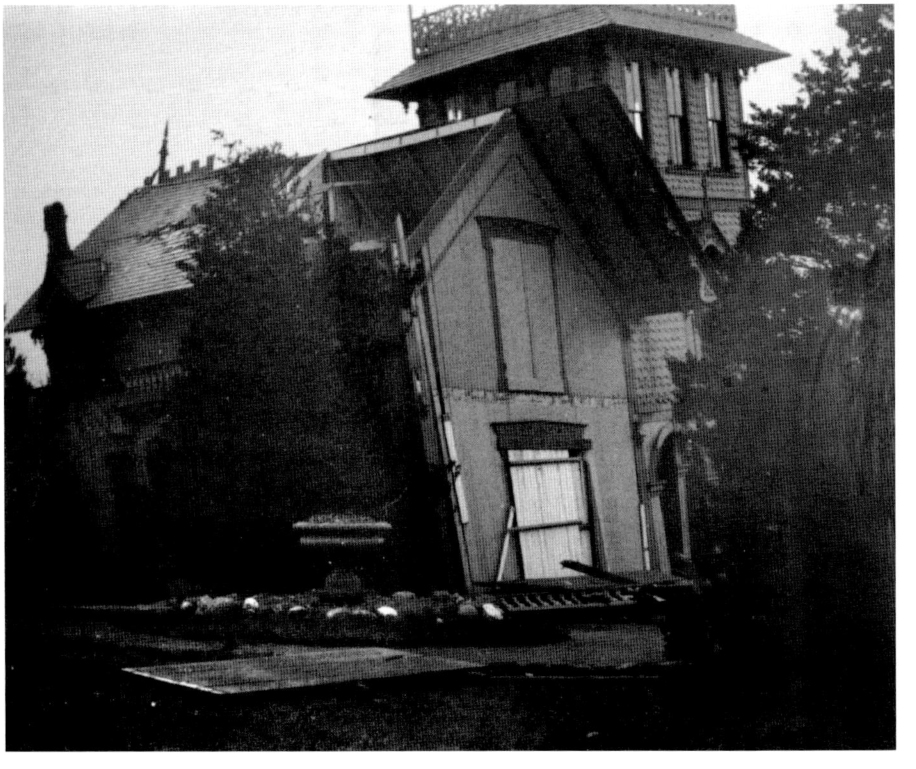

The 1898 gale took its toll on land as well. Charles G. Hine's house on Cedar Neck (now Hines Point) in Vineyard Haven was damaged so badly that it had to be demolished and completely rebuilt. Hine took this photograph when he returned to the island from his home in New Jersey to inspect the damage.

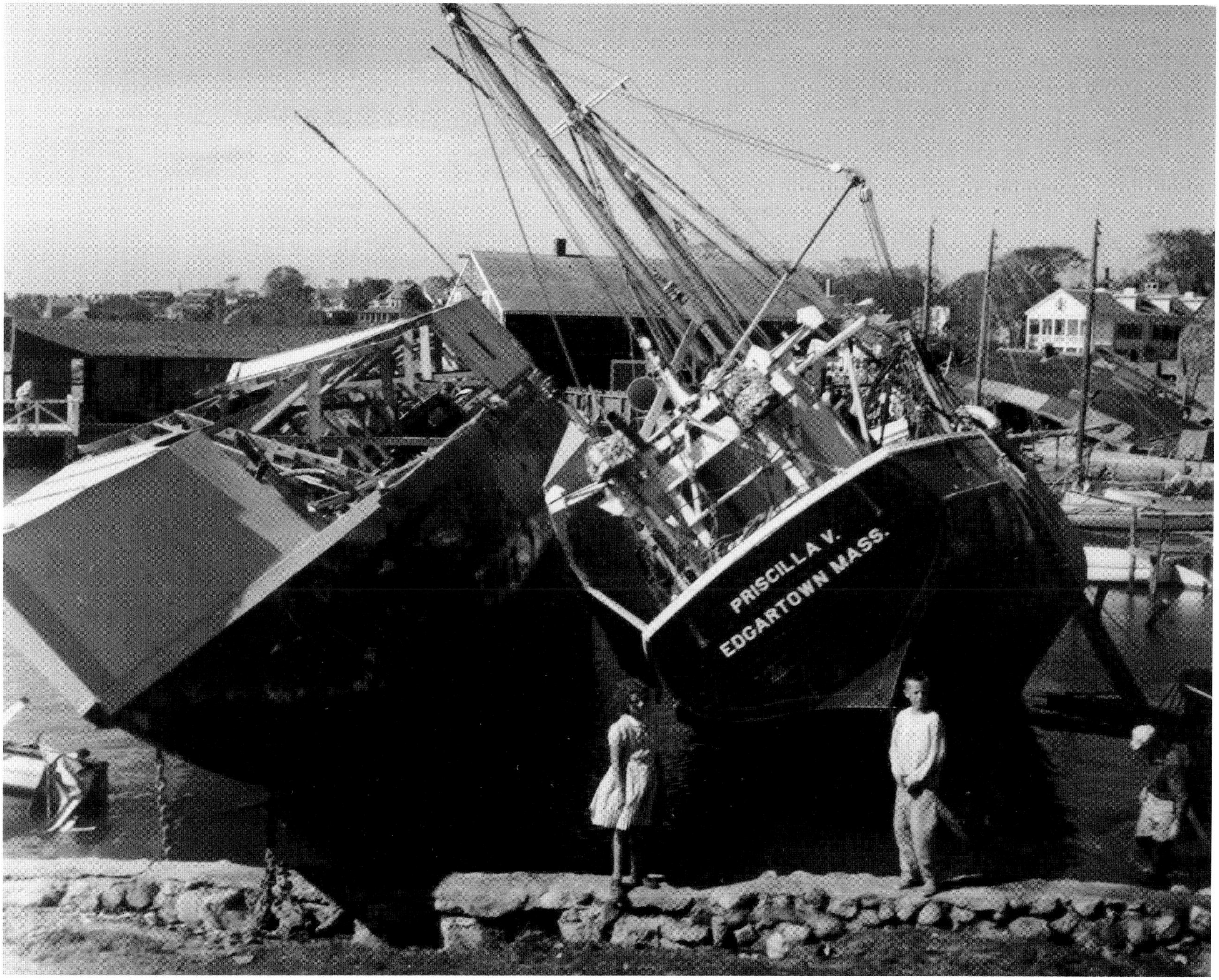

The Great Atlantic Hurricane of 1944 hit the Vineyard on September 14 and caused extensive damage to property in Edgartown and other parts of the island. Boats in the harbor were not spared, with many being dashed onto shore in a way that recalled the Portland Gale 46 years before.

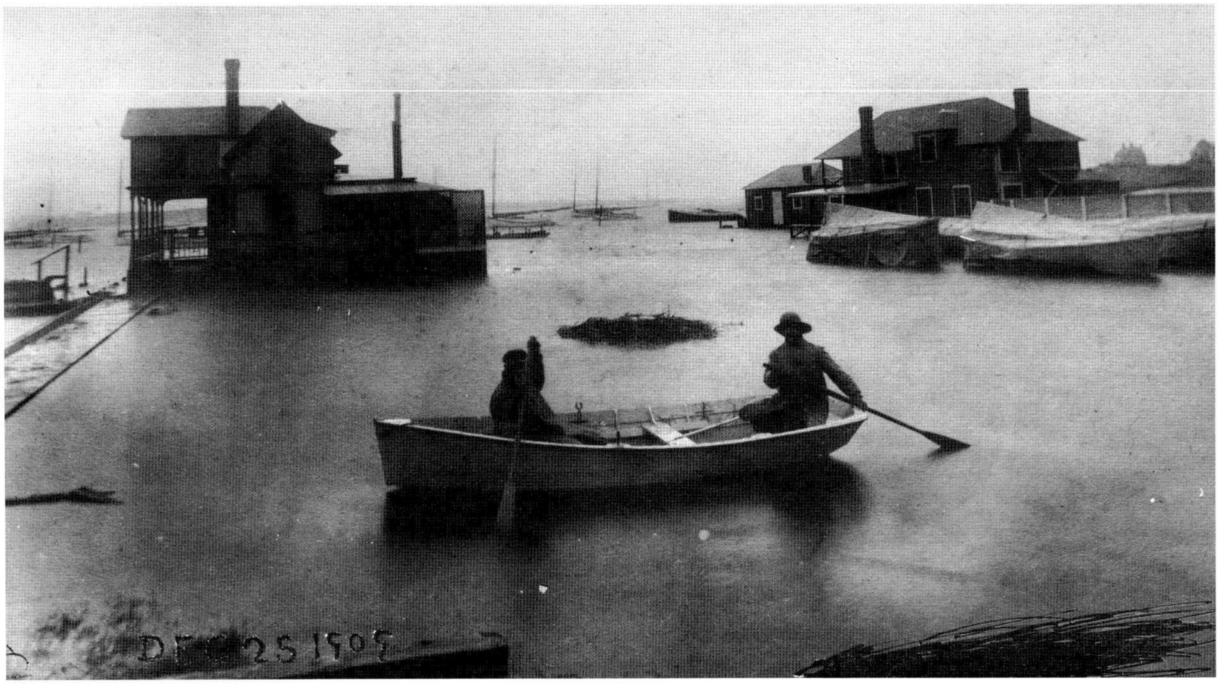

Even when strong winds did not cause damage, flooding from storms was always a risk along the shore. Here, on Christmas Day, 1909, two men take to a rowboat to inspect flood damage to houses on South Water Street in Edgartown. (Photograph by John Bent.)

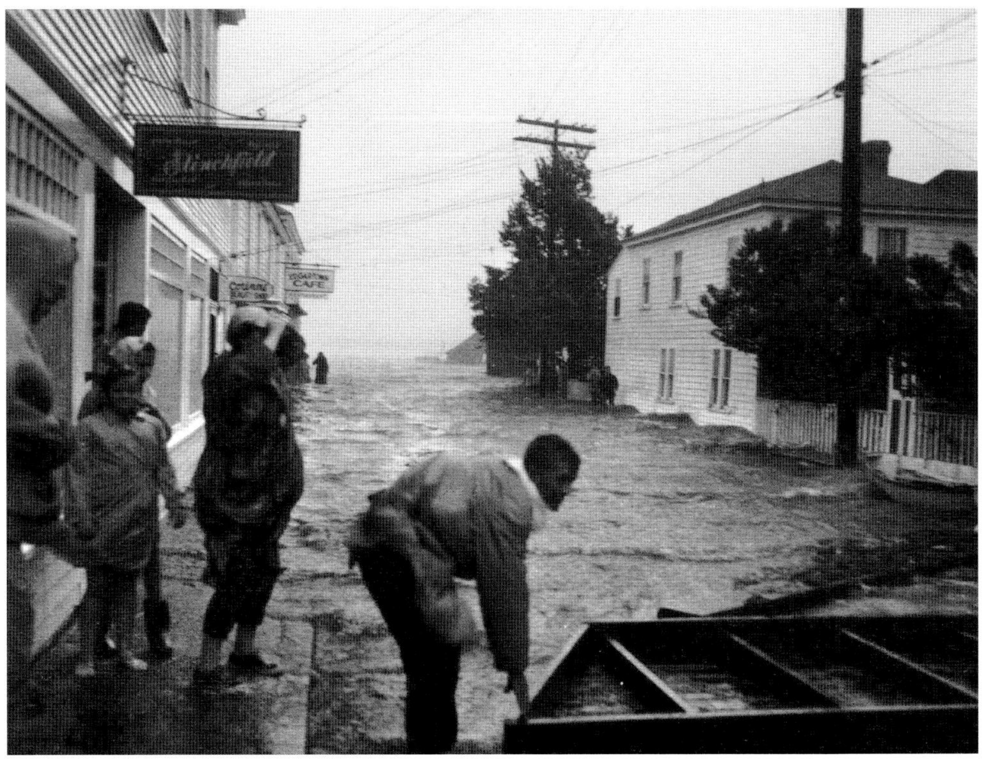

Many still remember the two hurricanes that hit the Vineyard within two weeks in 1954, Hurricane Carol on August 31 and Hurricane Edna on September 11. Carol did the most damage. In Edgartown, flooding extended far up Main Street. Here, people have come out to survey the damage and begin to clear the debris.

The waters around Martha's Vineyard could be dangerous even when the weather was clear. On January 18, 1884, the *City of Columbus* hit Devil's Bridge, a rocky underwater outcropping off Gay Head. A series of bad decisions by the captain and crew resulted in the wreck of the ship and the death of 103 of the 132 people on board.

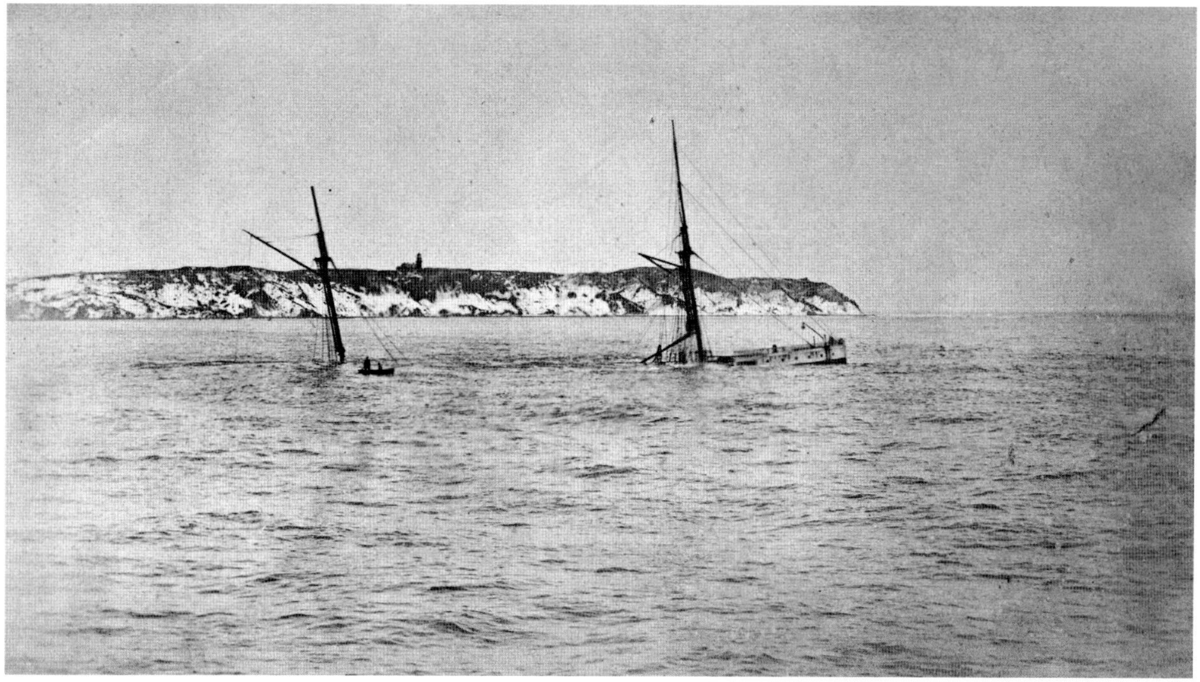

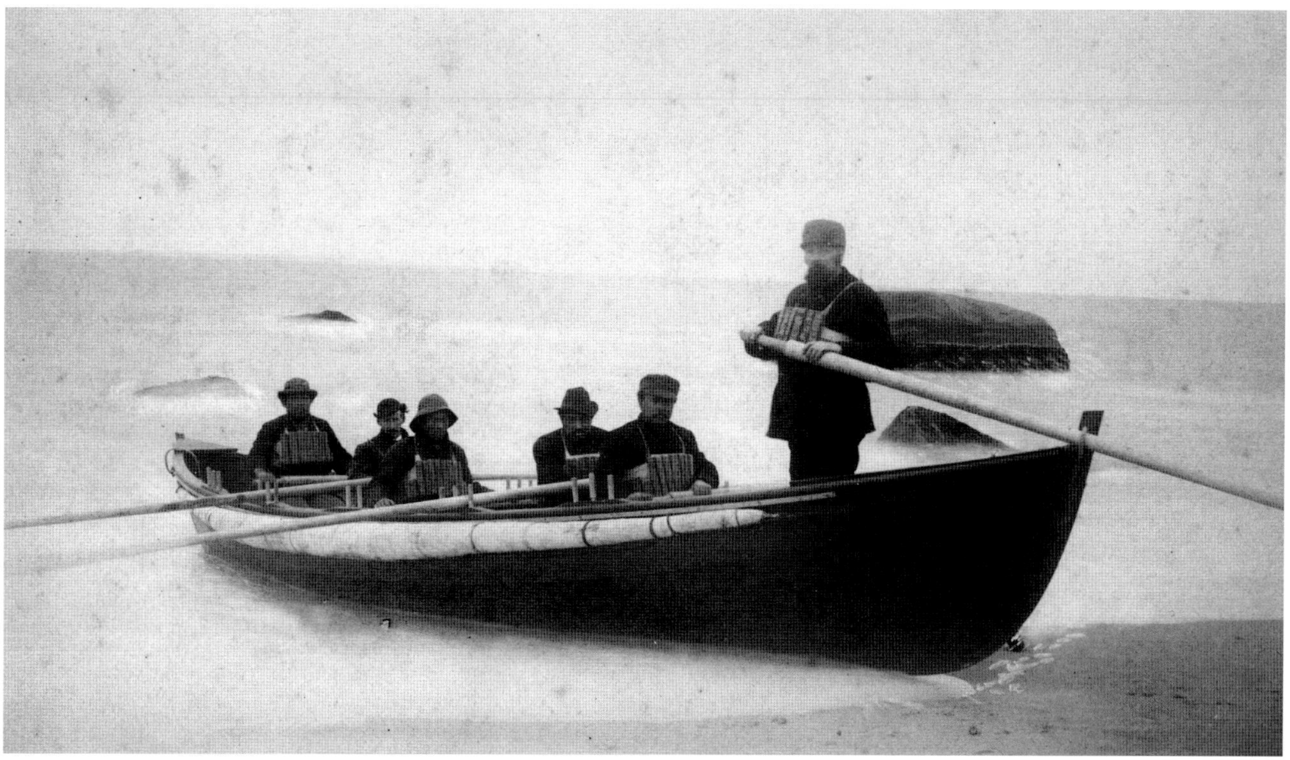

Volunteers risked their lives to save shipwrecked men, women, and children off the coast of Martha's Vineyard. There were lifesaving stations positioned around the island as well as huts where boats and other supplies were stored. The Massachusetts Humane Society awarded medals and cash prizes to rescuers who saved people from wrecked vessels. After the *City of Columbus* wreck, two lifesaving crews from Gay Head, most of the men Wampanoag, braved the high waves and frigid temperatures to save 13 people who had been clinging to the rigging of the ship for hours. The crew seen here was one of them. The men received Carnegie Medals for their bravery. (Photograph by John N. Chamberlain.)

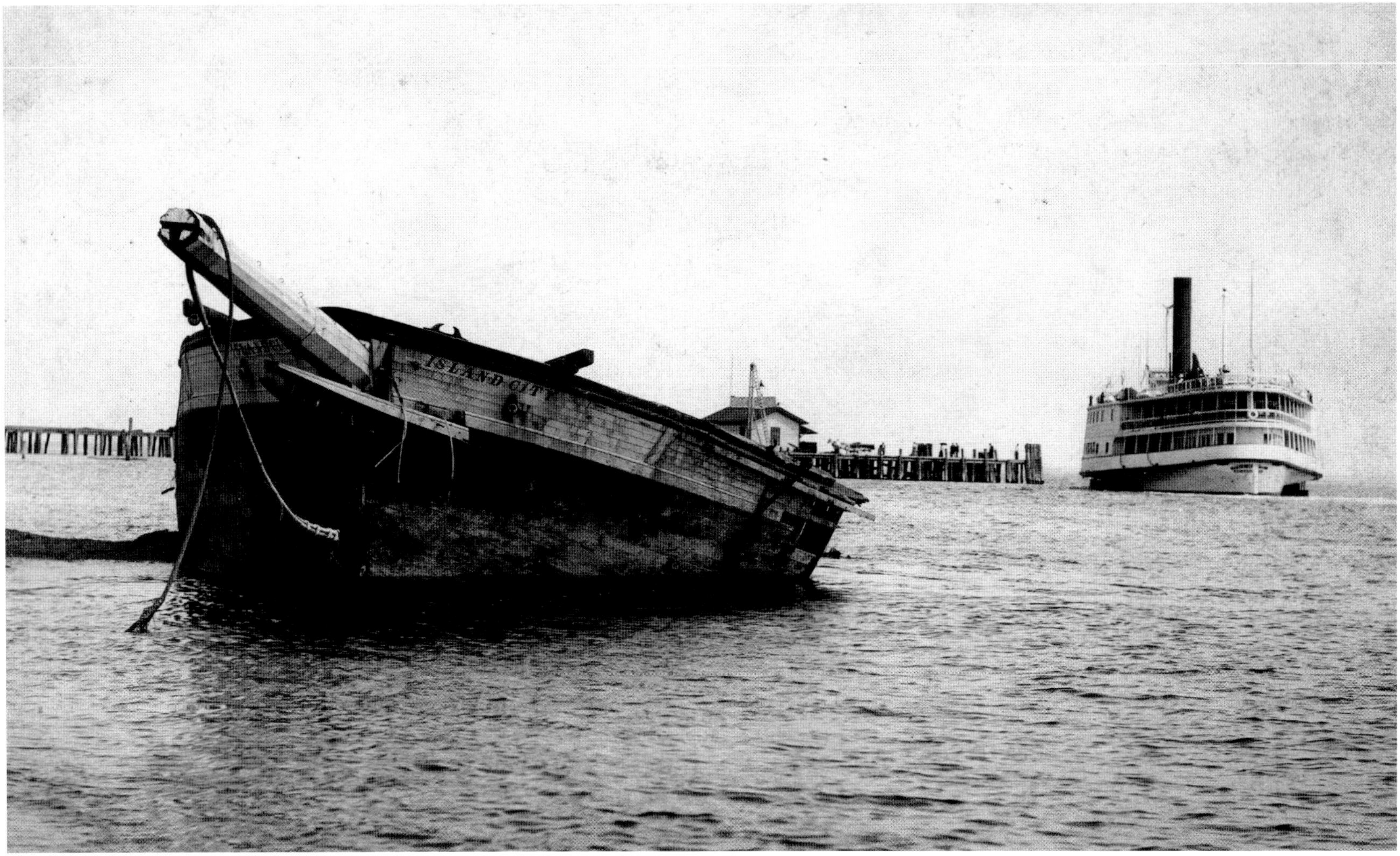

Whether caused by storm, pilot error, or some other mishap, the bones of wrecked ships have been a common enough sight on the shores of Martha's Vineyard. Some appear in photographs year after year, changing shape and shrinking as they are slowly scavenged by souvenir hunters and worn away by tides and more storms. A ferry carrying vacationers to the Highland Wharf in the East Chop section of Oak Bluffs is seen here beyond the remains of a wreck from the gale of 1898. The *Island City*, a coal-carrying schooner en route from New York to Cohasset, Massachusetts, was lost, along with all four hands. (Photograph by John N. Chamberlain.)

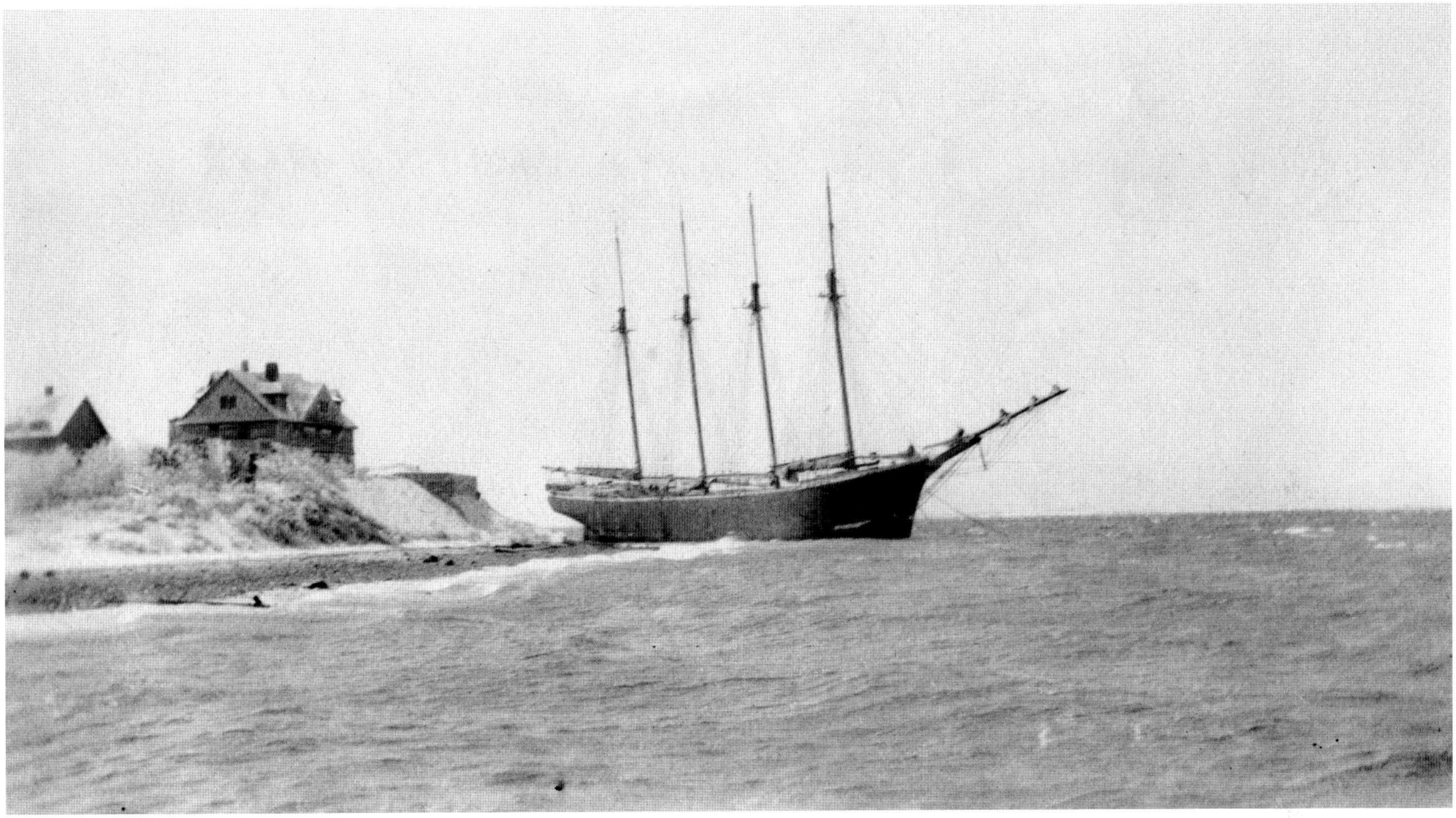

On March 6, 1923, the *Augusta G. Hilton* ran aground off West Chop in a storm. The crew reached safety, but the four-masted schooner remained firmly stuck for six weeks. Newspaper accounts tell of failed attempts to dislodge the vessel, which were distressing to the owner but not to the public. Stranded so close to shore, the *Augusta G. Hilton* became something of a tourist attraction, and people traveled to West Chop to inspect her. When the Scott Wrecking Company was finally able to float her, she was found to have sustained very little damage.

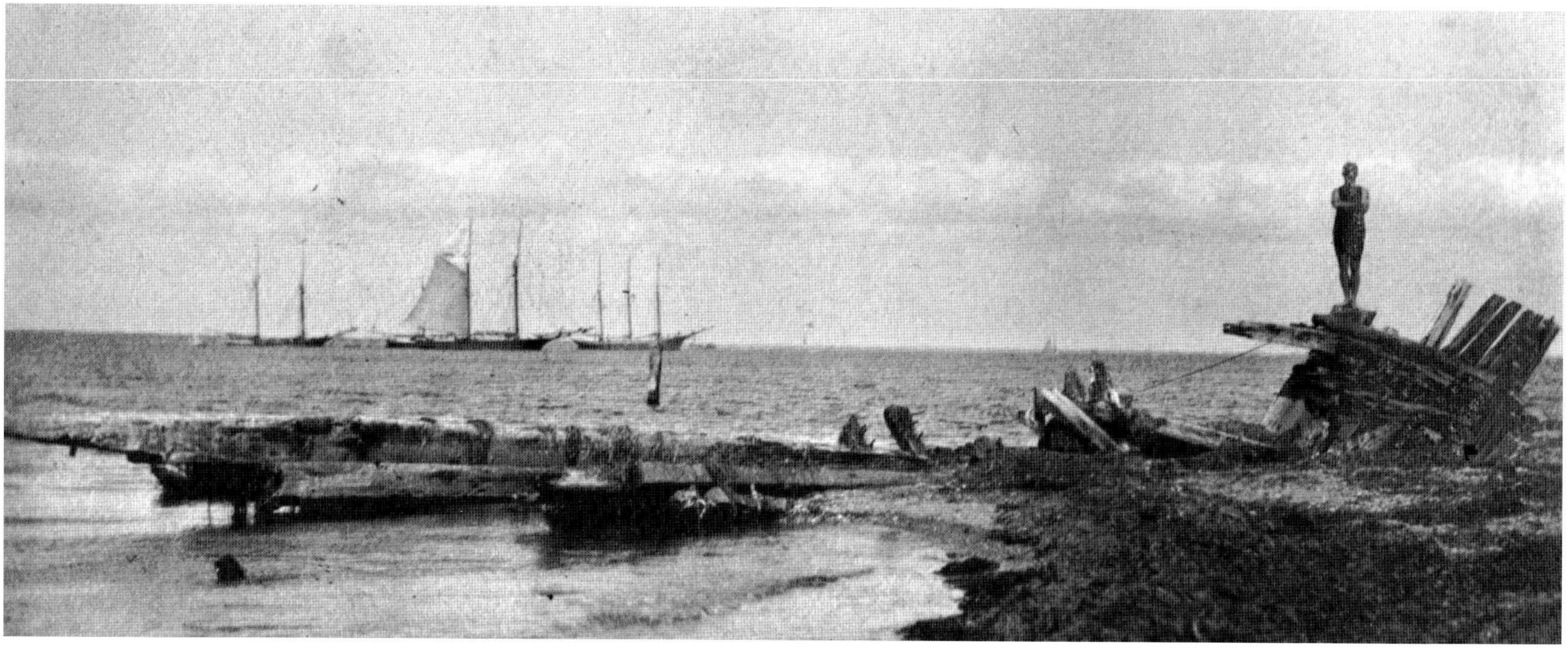

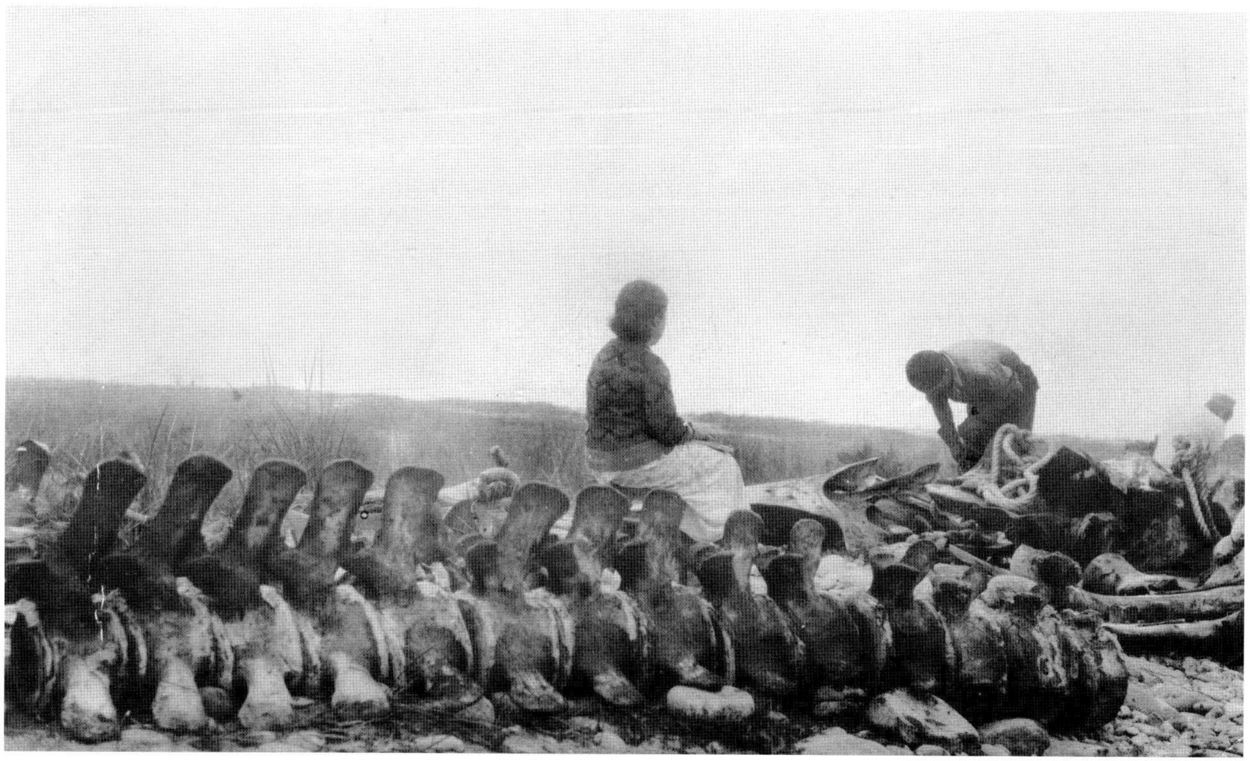

Here, Howes Norris Jr. stands on top of wreckage in Vineyard Haven around 1900.

Sometimes, whales were found beached on the island. They were always valuable and, in Colonial days, the rights to them were even negotiated as part of land sales. This whale was found on Noman's Land in the 1930s, and the course of its butchering was documented in a group of photographs taken by the Wood family.

Year-round residents of Martha's Vineyard have always found that fewer off-island friends and family members want to visit them in the winter. Nevertheless, the ferry from Vineyard Haven to Woods Hole keeps running, connecting islanders to the mainland. This photograph was taken in February 1961.

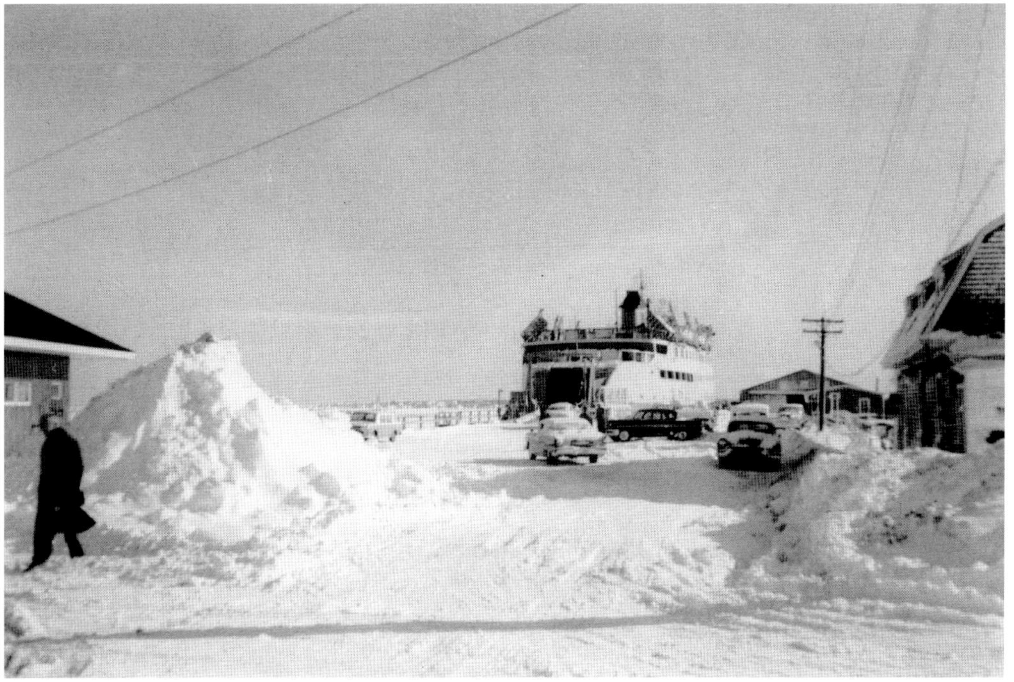

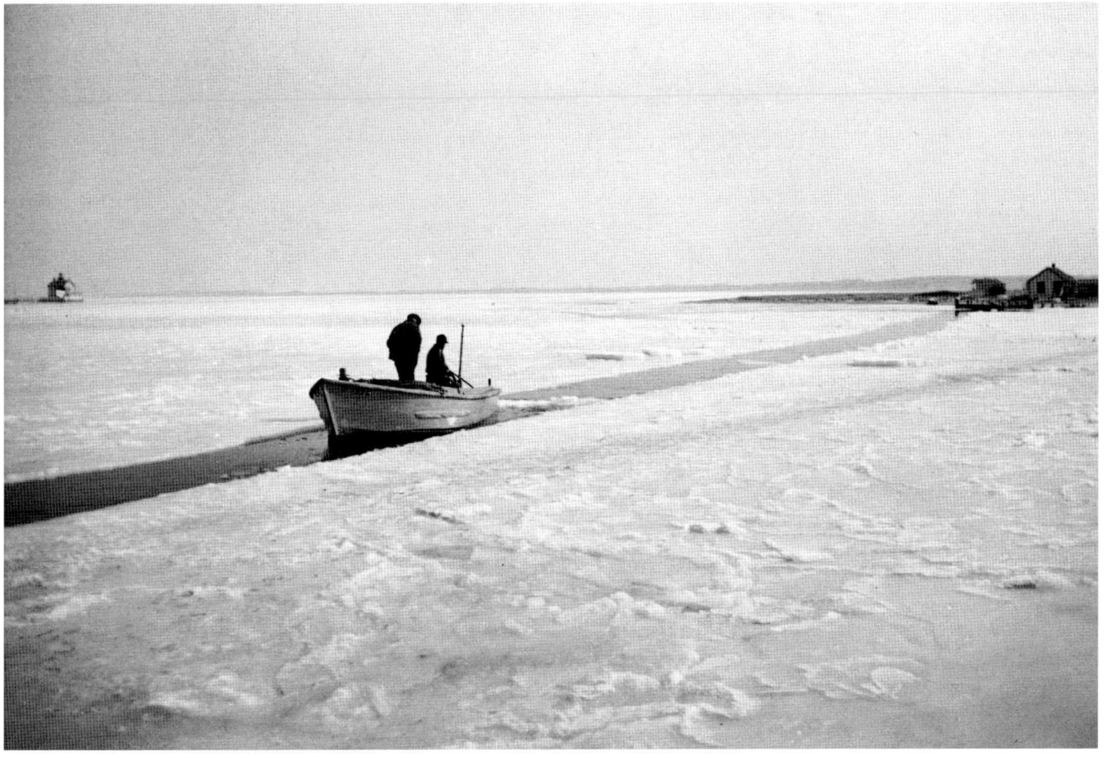

Winters could be harsh, with severe weather isolating some areas. Here, a narrow channel through the iced-over Edgartown Harbor allows a boat to travel from Chappaquiddick to Edgartown. Though this photograph is undated, the old lighthouse can be seen in the background, indicating that it was taken before 1938, most likely during the big freeze of 1934.

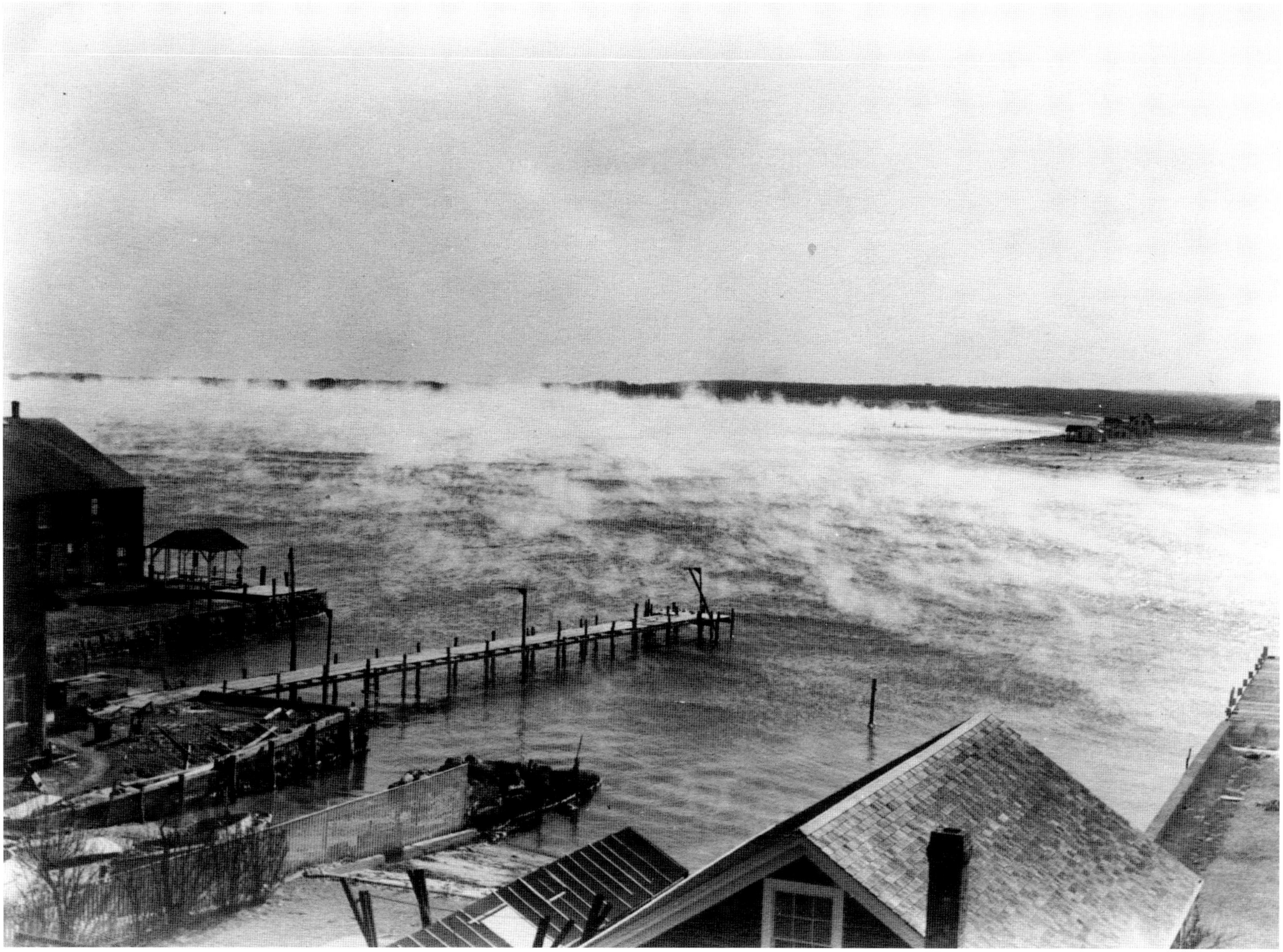

"Sea smoke" occurs when the air is much colder than the water. This 1930s photograph shows Edgartown Harbor from the upper porch of a house on North Water Street, looking toward the Chappaquiddick bathing beach. The absence of boats suggests that it is an off-season shot, perhaps representing the first chill of autumn, the favorite season of many Vineyarders. (Photograph by Clara F. Dinsmore.)

The receding ice sheet from the last ice age left this giant boulder on Indian Hill in West Tisbury. Smaller stones have been cleared away from the field and turned into a stone wall, one of many built long ago that still remain in the fields of up-island towns.

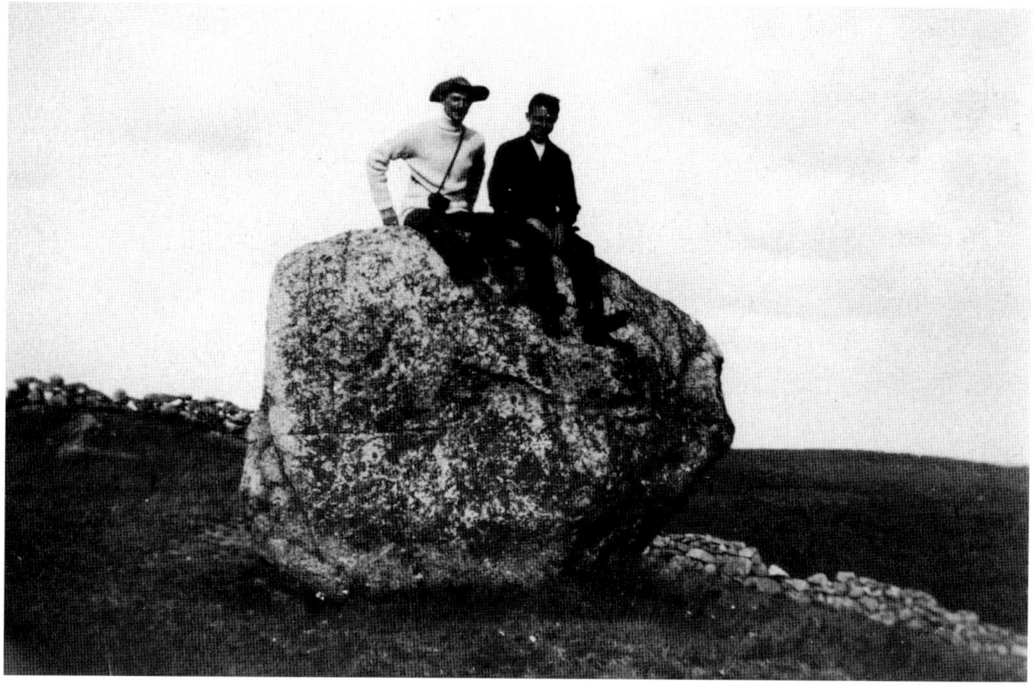

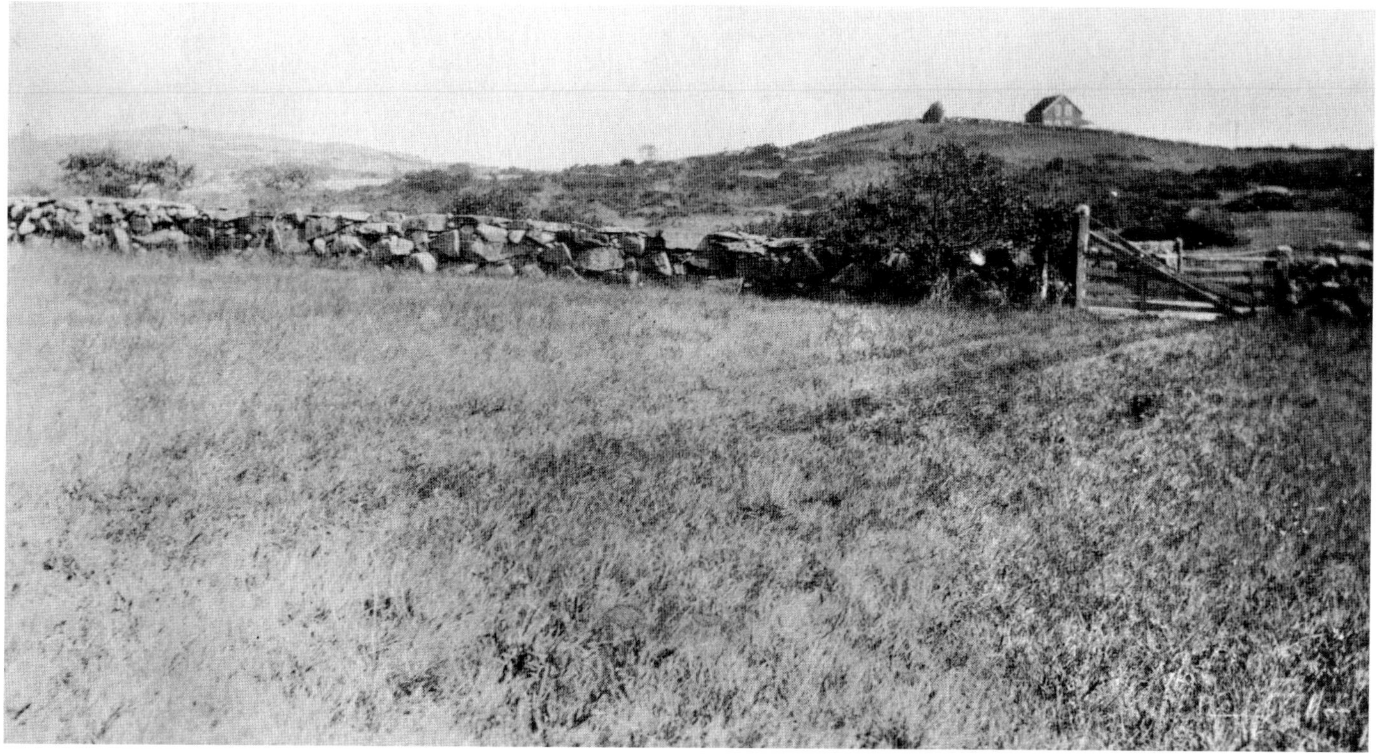

Images from the early 1900s showing land cleared for farming reveal some geological features that are no longer as apparent as they used to be. Here, a stone wall extends in front of a hill (sugarloaf) at Beetlebung Corner in Chilmark.

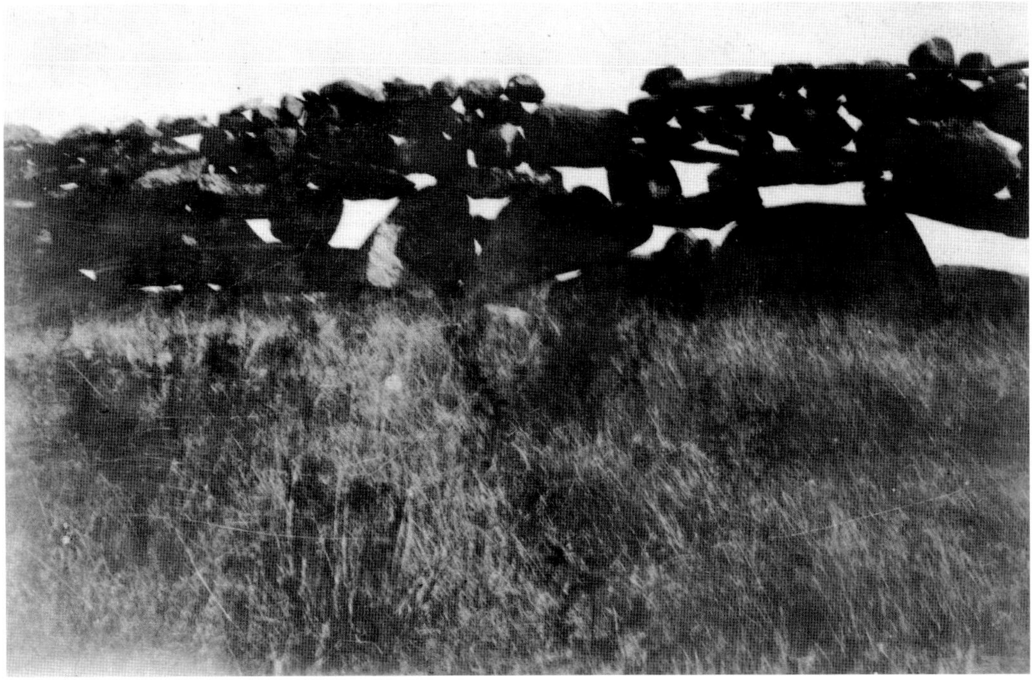

Chilmark is well known for the stone walls that cross its landscape. Functional and beautiful, walls like this one are called "lace walls" because of their narrow depth, of only a single stone, and their many holes. These manmade walls have become the subjects of many artists and photographers over the years.

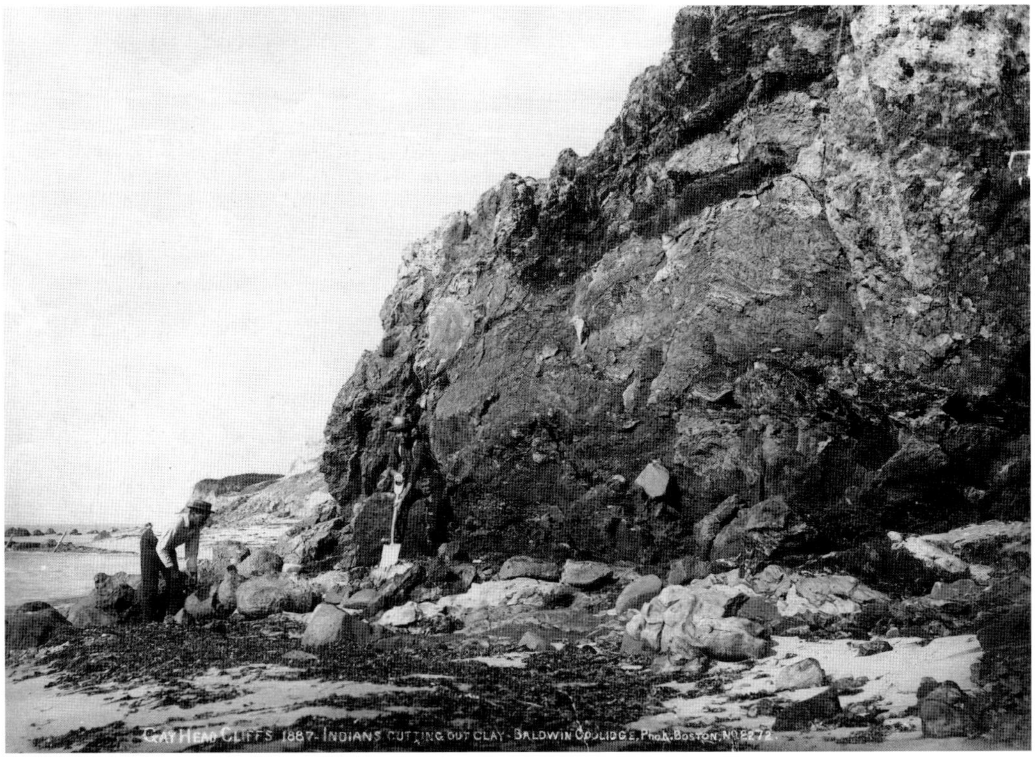

Entitled "Gay Head Cliffs 1887, Indians cutting out clay," this photograph shows two Wampanoag men at work digging the clay that would be turned into colorful pots for sale to visitors. (Photograph by Baldwin Coolidge.)

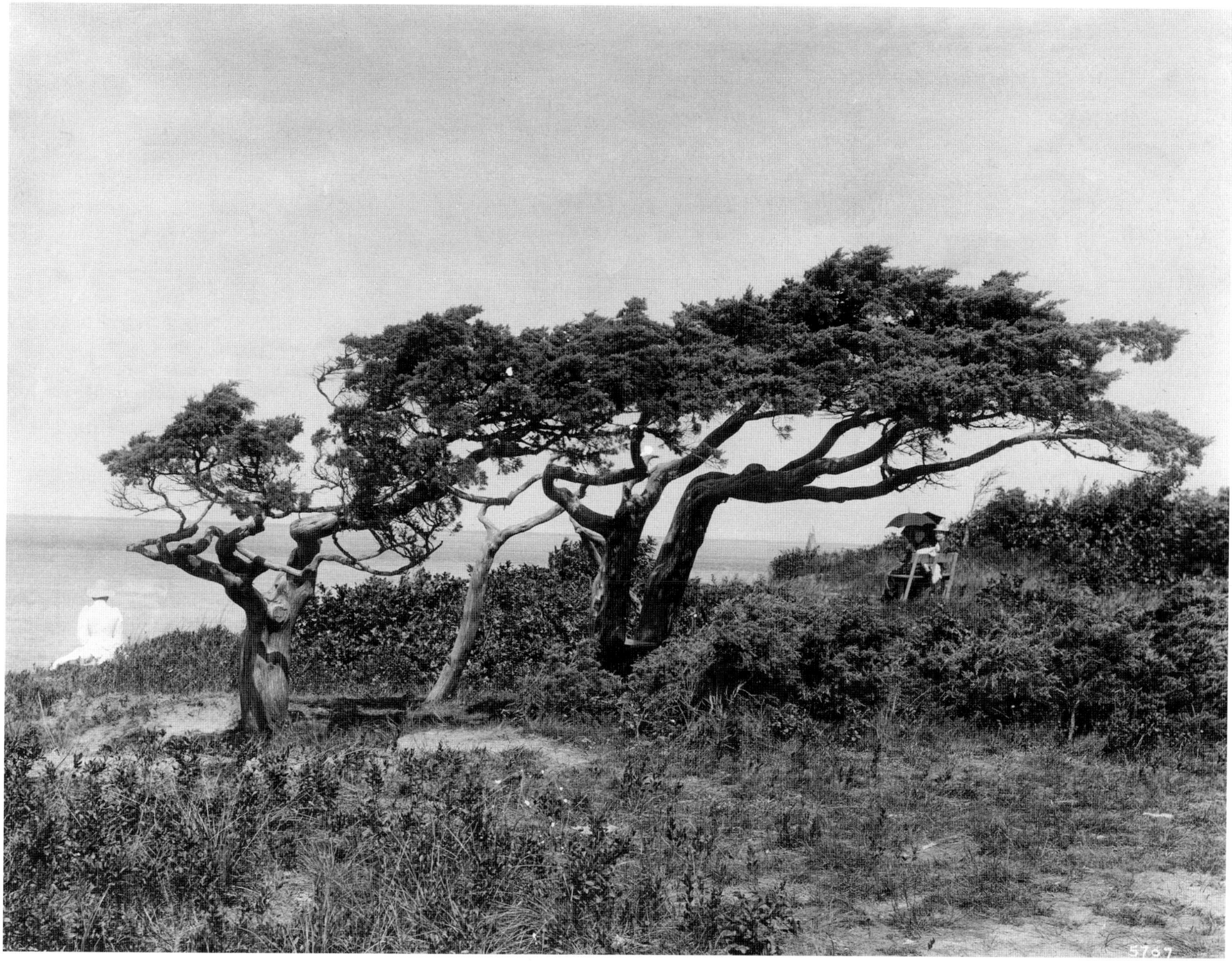

Boston photographer Baldwin Coolidge had a summer studio on Martha's Vineyard. He recorded some of the most memorable images of the Vineyard that remain from the 1800s. Here, a person sitting under an umbrella in West Chop is dwarfed by the cedar trees and the sea beyond. (Photograph by Baldwin Coolidge.)

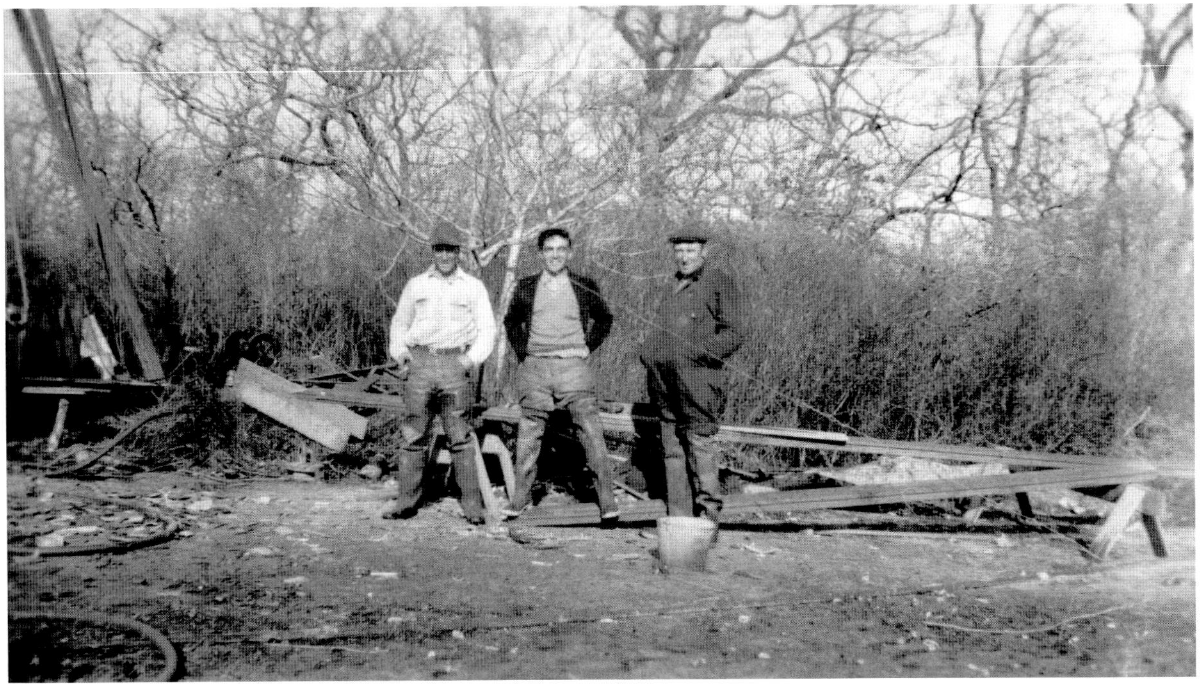

Some of the men who helped build a dam at Edgartown Great Pond in the 1930s are seen here taking a break from the work.

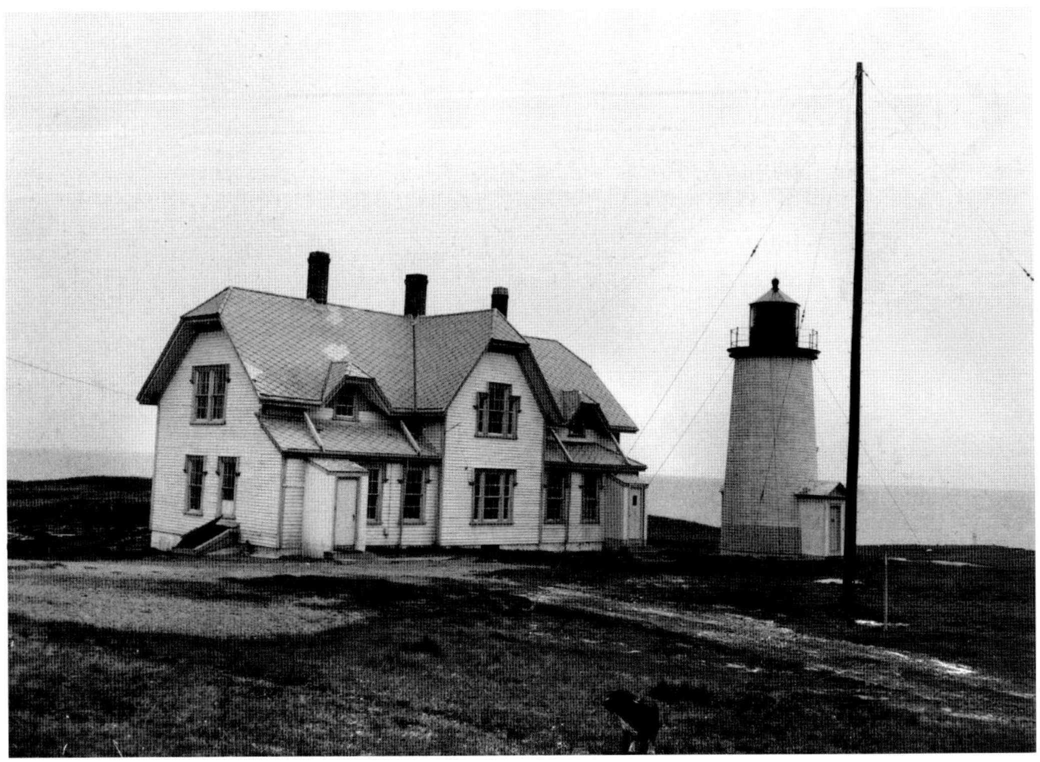

A lighthouse was built at Cape Poge, on the northeastern tip of Chappaquiddick, in 1801. It was replaced in 1884 and again in 1893. Since that date, the wooden lighthouse has been moved four times, most recently in 1987. It is one of only three wooden lighthouses remaining in New England.

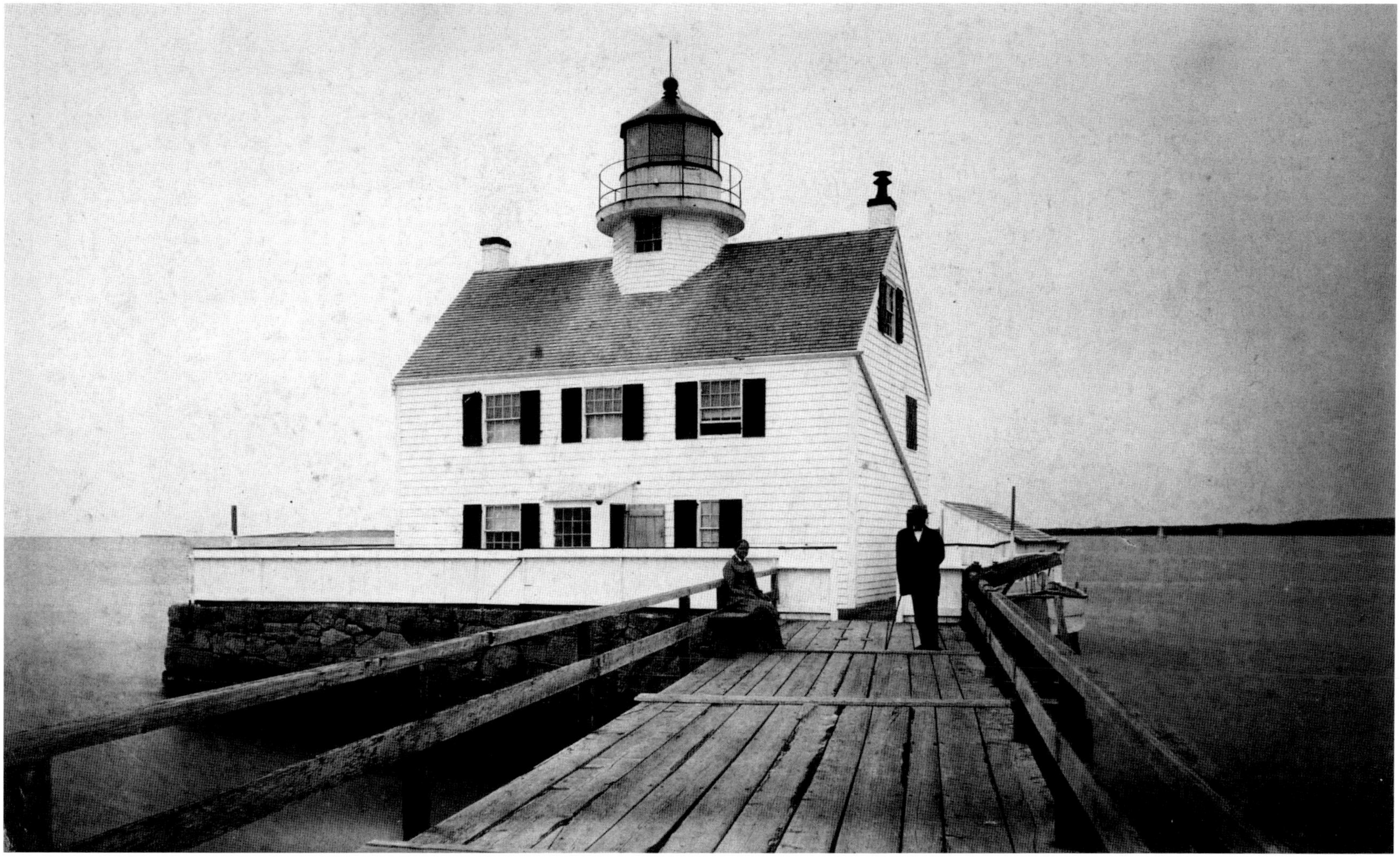

The first Edgartown Light stood out in the harbor. It emerged from the top of the keeper's house, which was connected to land by a wooden walkway. It appears in the background of many old photographs, a reminder of how much has changed. The current lighthouse, a metal tower, replaced this building, which was damaged beyond repair in the hurricane of 1938. The new tower was moved to Edgartown from Ipswich, Massachusetts, in 1939.

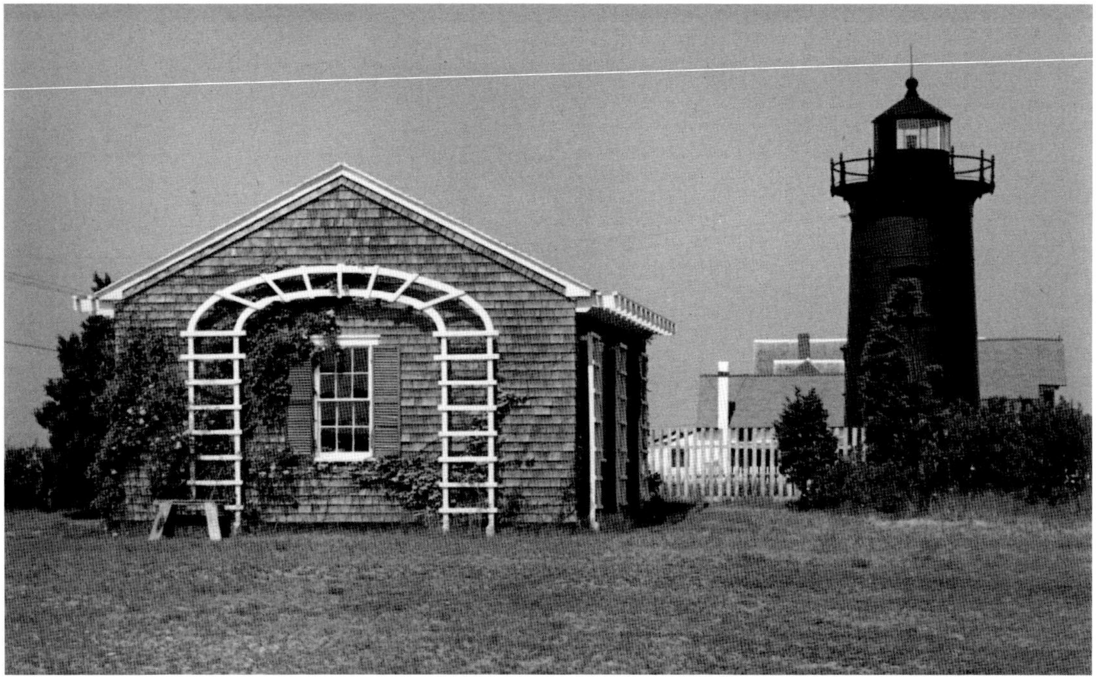

The first East Chop Lighthouse was built in 1869 on Telegraph Hill with private funds raised by Capt. Silas Daggett, a mariner frustrated that the US government was taking too long to build a light on the east side of Vineyard Haven Harbor. In 1878, after that structure burned and was rebuilt, the government finally purchased the property, removed the wooden building, and constructed a cast-iron lighthouse.

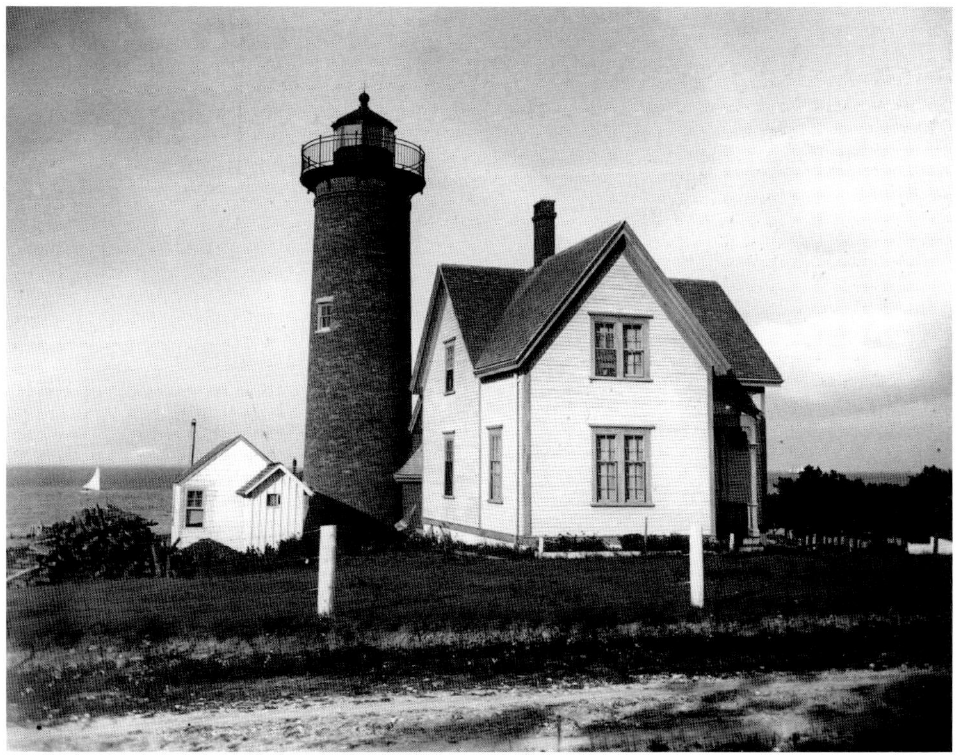

This photograph shows the West Chop Lighthouse between 1892, the year the old lighthouse was replaced with a new brick tower, and 1899, when the tower was painted white. There has been a lighthouse at the western entrance to Vineyard Haven Harbor since 1817.

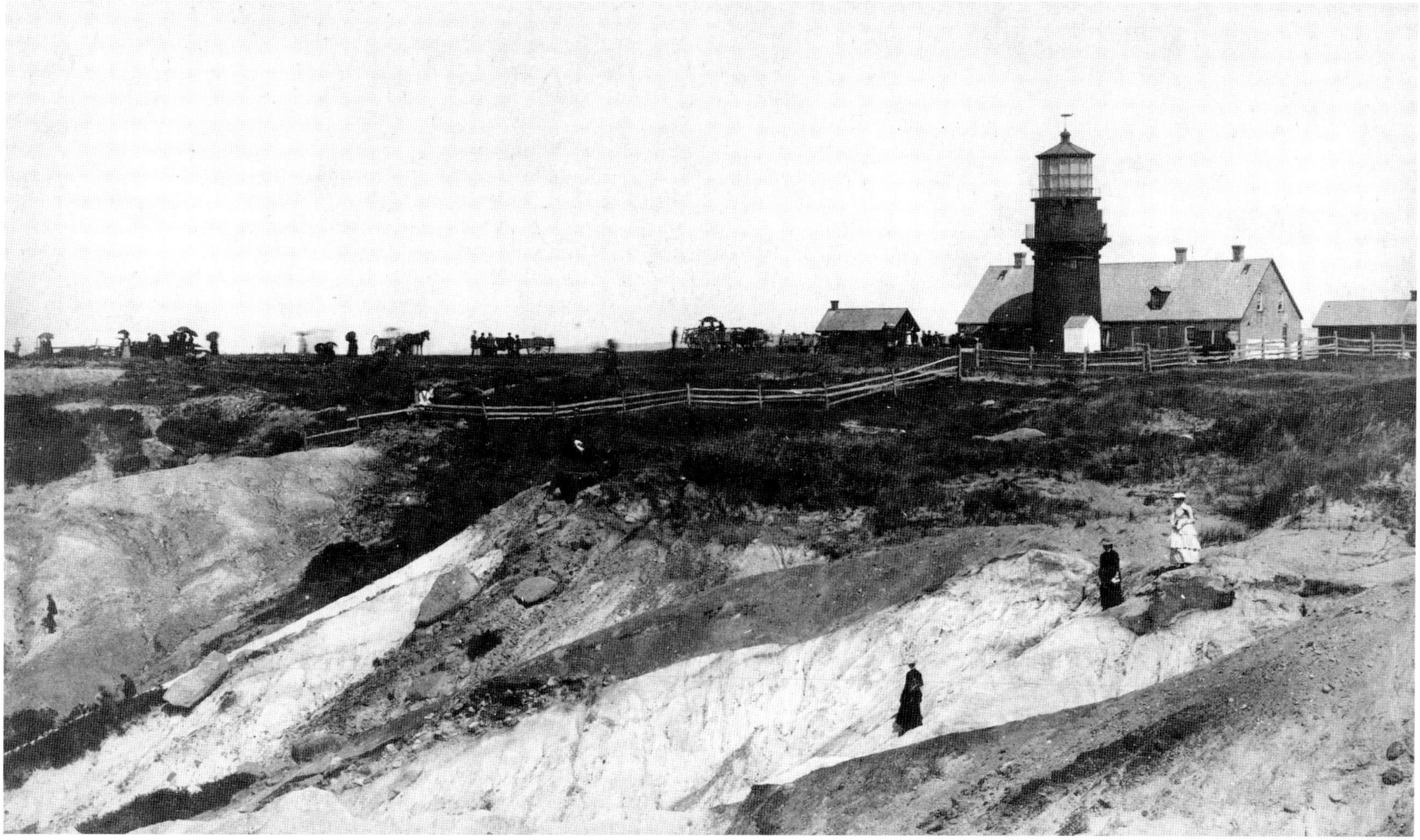

Vineyard Sound between Gay Head and the Elizabeth Islands is narrow and hazardous. It was also part of the busy shipping route down the East Coast of the United States before the Cape Cod Canal was dug in 1911. In 1799, Pres. John Adams approved a contract for construction of the first lighthouse at Gay Head. That lighthouse was moved back from the receding edge of the cliff in 1844. Just 12 years after that, the current lighthouse was built, even farther back. It housed a wondrous first-order Fresnel lens, the largest and brightest available. The spectacular view and colorful cliffs have made this one of the most visited sites on Martha's Vineyard. Over the years since this photograph was taken in the late 1800s, the cliffs have eroded substantially, as a result of both natural and manmade forces. In 2013, the lighthouse stood only 43 feet from the edge of the cliff, prompting a call to move this still-important navigational aid once again before it topples to the beach below. (Photograph by John N. Chamberlain.)